To my special friend & student

Kathy

with fondest

Jeanette   '1996

AVANT-GARDE
BRITISH
PRINTMAKING
1914-1960

7/30   Oiseau de Feu   S W Hayter 55

AVANT-GARDE BRITISH PRINTMAKING 1914-1960

Frances Carey and Antony Griffiths

with a contribution by Stephen Coppel

Published for
The Trustees of the British Museum
by British Museum Publications

The Trustees of the British Museum
acknowledge with gratitude
generous assistance towards the
production of this book from
Austin/Desmond Contemporary Books
Bloomsbury

© 1990 The Trustees of the British Museum

Published by British Museum Publications Ltd
46 Bloomsbury Street, London WC1B 3QQ

British Library Cataloguing in Publication Data
Carey, Frances
    Avant-garde British printmaking, 1914–1960.
    1. British prints. Catalogues, indexes
    I. Title   II. Griffiths, Antony   III. Coppel, Stephen
    IV. British Museum
    769.941

ISBN 0–7141–1646–7

FRONTISPIECE S.W.Hayter (1901–88): *Oiseau de Feu*, 1935 (cat. no. 101)

Designed by James Shurmer

Printed in Great Britain
by BAS Printers, Over Wallop, Hampshire

Contents

Preface

This has not been an easy exhibition to arrange. It forms the fifth in what has become a sequence of exhibitions of modern printmaking organised by the British Museum's Department of Prints and Drawings. Since book illustration does not fall within the scope of the Department's collections (being covered by the Victoria and Albert Museum Library and the British Library), these surveys have concentrated entirely on the separately published single-sheet artist's print. The first of these exhibitions, in 1978, was of late nineteenth-century French lithographs. The second, in 1980, was of American prints from Whistler to the end of the 1970s. In 1984 followed a more ambitious show of German printmaking centred on the age of Expressionism. The fourth, held in 1986, was of Czech prints. In all these exhibitions the process of selection was made relatively easy by the limitations of the Department's collections.

This has certainly not been the case for this exhibition of British prints. A very considerable collection of prints of the first half of the century was amassed by Campbell Dodgson, the former Keeper of this Department, both during his time at the Museum through gifts made through the Contemporary Art Society, and later through his bequest in 1948 of his personal collection of over 5,000 prints, most of which were modern. Over the past ten years a consistent effort has been made to expand the collection into the period after the Second World War, and to add examples of some earlier printmakers who escaped Dodgson's notice – usually because their work was never published and was known at the time only to a small circle of the artist's friends. The result is a collection that is far larger than could possibly be shown, even in a token fashion, in a single exhibition.

A process of severe selection has therefore been necessary, and much has had to be left out. The strategy adopted has been determined by the position that this exhibition holds in the sequence outlined above. The aim of all four was to present to the British public that aspect of French, American, German or Czech printmaking which offered most interest to a modern audience. Inevitably much was omitted, and none of the four offered anything like a comprehensive survey. In the same way, in the present exhibition we hope to offer to a British and an international audience a selection that will arouse maximum interest both at home and abroad.

The next problem was what the exhibition should be titled. *Avant-Garde British Printmaking 1914–1960* was only chosen with considerable misgivings, since not all the items in the exhibition can sensibly be called avant-garde. The title does, however, have the virtue of making it clear that the exhibition does not purport to offer a comprehensive survey, and that the weight of the selection has tended towards the more unusual work, often made by artists who were not primarily printmakers, and away from the mainstream production dominated by specialists in the field.

The exhibition begins with the Vorticists and ends in the late 1950s, before the arrival of the new artists and publishers who transformed the British print world in the 1960s. Within this period there are two major casualties. The most notable is Sickert, who, with his followers such as Sylvia Gosse, has been completely omitted. This is because half his career had already run by 1914, and we think it is impossible to understand his later prints without reference to his earlier ones. Moreover, he is such a major figure that he exceeds the confines of any survey exhibition, and we intend in 1995 to devote an entire exhibition to his work on paper, both prints and drawings. The same is true of the other great British printmaker of this century, Stanley William Hayter. A few of his prints of the 1930s have been included, as they relate so closely to the work of other artists in the exhibition. But all his later, and in many people's view, finest works, made while in America and after his return to Paris in 1950, have been left out. Again, we intend to devote a future monographic exhibition to his work, using the material in the Hayter archive which was purchased by the Museum in 1988. For the rest that has been omitted, the General Bibliography lists many other publications which will supplement this one.

The structure of the catalogue is almost the same as that used in *The Print in Germany 1880–1933*. For all the artists there is a biography that concentrates on those aspects of their career that are most relevant to their printmaking; the bibliography is similarly weighted. The material has been grouped into eleven sections, some of which are looser in association than others, and none of which are mutually exclusive. A short preface to each section gives the immediate background for the prints that follow. The main introduction to the catalogue, by contrast, gives a more general account of the underlying factors that influenced or determined the nature of print production during this period. It therefore describes the way in which publishing and distribution radically changed after 1929, and the problems that the original print has had ever since in finding a market in this country.

At an early stage in the planning of this exhibition, Stephen Coppel of the National Gallery of Australia in Canberra spent some months in London working in the British Museum while preparing his monograph on the British linocut artists. It was clear that he was by far the best-qualified person to write this section of the catalogue, and we were delighted that he accepted our invitation to do so. We are most grateful to him for generously contributing so much new information.

The organisers of any exhibition incur numerous obligations, and this is no exception. We are grateful to our fellow institutions, the Tate Gallery, the Victoria and Albert Museum and the Museum of London, as well as the British Council, and to James Birch, Bartolomeu Dos Santos, Mel and Rhiannon Gooding, James Kirkman, the Henry Moore Foundation, Ken Powell, Mr and Mrs Gordon Samuel and William Turnbull, as well as to others who wish to remain anonymous, for lending us a number of prints which we could not otherwise obtain.

In compiling most previous catalogues for exhibitions in the Department of Prints and Drawings, the chief source of information has been published scholarship. This catalogue, however, has been an exception. Published sources are relatively few. Among them we would single out for their usefulness and quality the various publications of Pat Gilmour, formerly curator of the print collection in the Tate Gallery and more recently at the National Gallery of Australia in Canberra, who has done more than anyone in the last twenty years to analyse the history and practice of printmaking in Britain since the 1930s. Bryan Robertson gave exhibitions in the 1950s at the Whitechapel Art Gallery to many of the post-war artists with whom this catalogue is concerned, and we should like to acknowledge the contributions he made in those exhibitions and their catalogues as well as in his more recent writing on British art of the period. The biennial catalogues of new acquisitions at the Tate Gallery have also proved invaluable, and we have tried to emulate their exemplary standards of cataloguing.

Our first source of unpublished information has had to be the memories of numerous artists and their relatives. Those whom we have approached have been unfailingly helpful, even when they were baffled by our interest in impromptu experiments conducted several decades ago, and we would here express general gratitude to all of them. They are individually mentioned in specific entries. Next we have been helped by many dealers in the field. First among them is Gordon Samuel of the Redfern Gallery. His pioneering exhibitions of modern British prints and the excellently researched catalogues accompanying them were a great stimulus to our own efforts, and since then he has been exceptionally generous in his help, allowing us to draw both on his memory and on the archives of the Redfern Gallery. The Lefèvre Gallery and Gimpel Fils have also allowed us to consult their archives. Other dealers whom we must thank for their help are Adrian Eeles, Austin/Desmond, Peter Black, Christie's, Charles Booth-Clibborn, Gordon Cooke, Robert Douwma, Jane England, Robin Garton, Hilary Gerrish, Nick Lott, Christopher Mendez, Sotheby's and William Weston.

Our researches have also depended on the reminiscences of many of the people involved in printmaking at the time. We warmly thank for their help Denis Bowen, Bartolomeu Dos Santos, Arthur Driver, Robert Erskine, Alistair Grant, Stanley Jones, Katherina Mayer Haunton, Alex Postan, Dudley Snelgrove, Joe Studholme and Stephen Willats. Others are thanked in the main text of this catalogue.

Equally invaluable has been the access we have been given to the resources of the Tate Gallery. We would like to thank Beth Houghton and her staff in the Library, Sarah Fox-Pitt and Adrian Glew in the Archives, and Paul Moorhouse in the Print Department. We are also grateful to the staff of the Victoria and Albert Museum Library and Print Room for their help in our enquiries. In New York, David Kiehl has been as always a mine of information and has continually encouraged us in this project.

Within the British Museum, we owe thanks to many in the Department of Prints and Drawings: above all to Anne Forsdyke for her indefatigable pursuit of the answers to the numerous questions that we put to her, as well as for her reminiscences of many of the artists of the period; to Paul Goldman who also followed up a number of enquiries; to Janice Reading who has dealt with the loans with her normal efficiency; to all the staff of the Student Room for their efforts on our behalf; and to the staff of the Department of Conservation for preparing and mounting the works for exhibition. For the photographs we have been able to depend as usual on Graham Javes and his colleagues John Williams and Kevin Lovelock. At British Museum Publications we have put our editor, Teresa Francis, under excessive pressure, and we thank her for her forbearance and good humour as well as for her expert editing of our text.

Introduction

The period of just under half a century covered in this catalogue saw changes in the field of art that were quite as marked as those in the political and economic arena. The years 1914 to 1960 are often treated as a distinct period by art historians concerned with the history of painting and sculpture. At the beginning stands Vorticism, the first consciously revolutionary movement in British art, reflecting the Futurist and Cubist revolutions on the Continent; at the end comes the new wave of painters of the 1960s. But this is not the case in printmaking history. The year 1914 does not mark the beginning of a period; it is in the middle of one that starts with the etching revival of Seymour Haden and Whistler in the 1860s and ends with the great crash of 1929. The depression of the 1930s affected all artistic activity, but had a far more lasting impact on printmaking than on any other medium. What had been a great industry was completely destroyed; so much so, that in the mid-1950s the efforts of one man – Robert Erskine of the St George's Gallery – were credited with making it possible again to publish prints in Britain.[1] It is only at the very end of the period covered by this exhibition, and beyond it into the 1960s, that a print publishing industry was re-established in this country, with the foundation of the Curwen and Kelpra printing studios, Editions Alecto and later the Petersburg Press.

This introduction must therefore begin by exploring this semi-forgotten background. Since by definition an avant-garde sets itself apart from the mainstream, the focus here will be on the large number of artists who made a prosperous living as specialist printmakers rather than on the artists included in this catalogue – most of whom were primarily painters or sculptors. The range of quality is very wide: some of these specialist printmakers now seem poor artists; others are excellent. But all were part of a system of publishing and collecting that collapsed in the 1930s, and with it went their careers and livelihoods.

The etching revival of the 1860s in Britain was begun, as Sickert used to stress, by amateurs. Seymour Haden, its high priest and the founder of the Society of Painter-Etchers, was a surgeon by profession. But by the turn of the century, a commercial professionalism had taken over the business, and the Scottish trinity of D.Y.Cameron (1865–1945), Muirhead Bone (1876–1953) and James McBey (1883–1959) achieved immense success – indeed almost canonical status – in the field. A number of enthu-

siastic collectors avidly pursued their work, and were serviced by a new breed of professional publishers. A secondary market had also sprung up in auctions, and the constant steady rise in prices served to fortify collectors in their confidence in the sound sense of their hobby. Around this market developed a flourishing literature of collectors' guides, specialist journals, and columns in more general periodicals, written for the most part by a small group of specialist authors. In terms of market share, it seems that this contemporary production was a much bigger business than the market in Old Master prints. Internationally, British prints were widely admired, and were regarded as a source of national pride. A typical article by Gui St Bernard in 1931, after lamenting the British inferiority complex in painting, concluded as if with a truism: 'In one field, however, and a big one at that, no nation can approach our standard. We have finer graphic artists than any other country – and a surprising number of them.'[2] Prints were indeed collected by leading museums in Britain and abroad as well as by private individuals. The major printmakers were celebrities: Cameron, Bone and Frank Short were all knighted. Even the long feud between the Royal Academy and the engravers was finally resolved in 1928, when the laws were changed to provide that 'among the forty Academicians not less than two shall be engravers, and that there shall not be less than two Associate Engravers'.[3]

This world was so utterly different from anything that exists today in Britain that it takes a considerable effort of the historical imagination to reconstruct it. Scholarly investigation has tended to concentrate on individual artists, but rather than pursue this line, it may be more profitable to follow two other threads that run through the period and which offer a key to understanding it. The first of these is the division of the market into distinct areas according to printmaking techniques. The other is the role of the publisher in organising the market.

Since one takes it for granted that a modern printmaker such as Jasper Johns or David Hockney will have made prints in most of the different media, it is a surprise to find that this rarely happened in the first four decades of this century. A printmaker was known as an etcher or a lithographer or a wood-engraver, and seldom thought of trying another technique. The exceptions are few: C. R. W. Nevinson and Paul Nash among the artists in this catalogue, D.Y.Cameron and John Copley among those not. Each technique was contained in its own world, with its own artists, its specialist societies, and, more often than not, its specialist publishers.

Of these worlds by far the most important was that of the intaglio printmakers. This had such a complete dominance that American observers often expressed their surprise. The British annual publication *Fine Prints of the Year* was, for most years of its existence, confined to intaglio prints; it was only in 1935 that this was felt to be so absurd that the policy had to be changed. By contrast, the American annual *Fifty Prints of the Year* was always open to all techniques. Within the field of intaglio, the prime media were always etching and drypoint, both sanctioned by the precedent of Rembrandt and the approval of Seymour Haden. The Society of Painter-Etchers and Engravers founded by Haden in 1880 had been given the prefix of 'Royal' in 1898. Its membership was limited to 50 full members and 150 associates, and work was restricted to monochrome.[4] A similar society existed in Glasgow, the Glasgow Society of Painter-Etchers. One final seal of official approval was the establishment of the Rome Prize for Engraving (i.e. printmaking) in 1920; prizes had long existed for painting and sculpture, and printmaking was now put on a par with these. Needless to say, all the early holders of the scholarship were intaglio artists.

Of the other intaglio processes, aquatint was damned by its historical association with reproductive topographical printmaking, and it was felt to be daring to use it. Mezzotint was equally suspect through its association with portraiture. Stipple was obsolete. Equally obsolete was engraving, and it was only in the 1920s that it was revived by Stanley Anderson, R. S. Austen and Stephen Gooden in a consciously archaising way.

In the years before the First World War, the only medium to compete even remotely with etching was lithography. Activity here was centred on the Senefelder Club, which had been founded in 1908 by Joseph Pennell with the support of F. E. Jackson, A. S. Hartrick and others. It held its first exhibition in 1909, and established a studio and press to further its artists' endeavours.[5] The club had a significant influence, particularly during the First World War, when Jackson seems to have helped persuade the War Office to commission sets of lithographs from a number of artists on 'Britain's Efforts and Ideals'. The lithographs of Nevinson and Nash must certainly be seen in this context. But much of the impetus behind the club disappeared after 1917, when both Pennell and John Copley resigned after a disagreement over whether it should become more commercial in its approach. In 1920 the club held an exhibition at the Leicester Galleries, but in 1921 it moved to the Twenty-One Gallery, where it was to retain its base into the 1930s. Like the Painter-Etchers,

the Senefelder Club offered a lay membership, which entitled the member to one print a year. But the main business of the Twenty-One Gallery was in dealing with landscape etchers of a Palmerish style, and lithography was only a sideline. And virtually none of the other main publishers paid any attention to the technique, even if they occasionally handled the work of individual lithographers. The same was true of the collector: a writer in 1923 commented on 'a lamentable lack of support as yet from the collector'.[6] It was only in the 1930s that the position began to change in a way that could not have been foreseen in the 1920s.

If the challenge of lithography soon faded, a stronger competitor emerged in the form of the wood-engraving.[7] This had been 'revived' in the 1890s in the context of the Private Press illustrated book, first by the Kelmscott Press, and then by Rickett and Shannon's Vale Press. In the early years of the twentieth century it had been taught by Noel Rooke at the Central School, and found a number of practitioners before the war. But it was only after the war in 1920 that Robert Gibbings founded the Society of Wood-Engravers 'to hold exhibitions devoted solely to woodcutting and engraving by the European method'.[8] This found a home first at the Chenil Gallery, and then from 1925 at the newly established Redfern Gallery in Old Bond Street. In 1925 Edward Gordon Craig led a secession of those whose work was less dependent on book illustration into a new English Wood-Engraving Society, which in turn was offered premises at the St George's Gallery in George Street, Hanover Square. When this gallery closed in 1931, the society closed with it, and its members rejoined the Society of Wood-Engravers. It is worth noting that these two galleries-cum-publishers were the only ones which regularly dealt in wood-engravings.

Wood-engraving as a medium was always closely linked with the Private Press book, and almost all its practitioners worked mainly as book illustrators. But there was always a significant production of single-sheet prints as well, which were sold separately (as often were proofs of the book illustrations). Wood-engraving seems always to have had a 'progressive' or 'arts and crafts' as well as an intellectual air about it. It was socially superior, and some leading figures (such as Gwen Raverat) were very well connected indeed. It never had the same wide popular appeal as etching, and was never the subject of any commercial speculation or significant rise in values. As a result, there was always a greater variety of approach than in etching, and often a higher general standard.

One landmark in the appreciation of relief prints was Herbert Furst's *The Modern Woodcut, a Study of the Evolution of the Craft*, which was published in 1924. This is by far the best-informed book on any aspect of printmaking published in Britain in this period, and has sections on

Continental developments as well as those at home. This was made possible by Furst's education in Berlin and London, and his job between 1897 and 1916 as manager of the London branch of Hanfstaengl, the German publishers of Fine Art reproductions.[9] Between 1920 and 1922 he founded and edited the periodical *The Apple*, which included many commissioned woodcuts; these could also be purchased in separately printed editions. In 1920 he also began a series of part-publications entitled *Modern Woodcutters* (see cat. nos 11 and 15 below), and in 1927 he founded *The Woodcut*, an annual which survived for four issues. For Furst there was no distinction between the woodcut and the wood-engraving, nor had this distinction been observed in the minutes of the Society of Wood-Engravers in 1920. Nevertheless, as the 1920s went on, the tendency to neglect woodcut in favour of wood-engraving became increasingly pronounced. When Charles Ginner began making his remarkable prints in 1917, he called them woodcuts, but from the late 1920s, without changing his technique, relabelled them wood-engravings. Why this should have happened is unclear, but part of the answer must lie in the increasing subservience to book illustration and the aesthetic of the illustrated book in England at that period. There is nothing in the British Private Press movement – or publishing in general – to match the vigour of such Continental woodcut productions as Frans Masereel's narratives in pictures which had such an influence abroad at the time.

The hostility to colour on the part of the above societies forced colour printmakers into an utterly different world. A small group which had studied under Frank Morley Fletcher and made colour woodcuts in the Japanese manner founded the Colour Woodcut Society around 1920. Another secession, around 1931, produced a Society of Graver-Printers in Colour, which was more catholic in its admittance of intaglio and relief colour printing, but more exclusive in that the artist now had to be his own printer (unlike the Japanese tradition). The linocut artists of the Grosvenor School (see section 3 below) can also be seen in this context: a charismatic teacher (Claude Flight), a new technique and a group of pupils leading to a new society and a dealer to provide exhibition premises.

Throughout this period there seem to be only two societies which covered a wider range of graphic art. The Society of Graphic Art was founded in 1920 'to uphold and maintain the interests of all those forms of art that do not use colour as a form of expression', and so, although including drawings, excluded anything in colour. It organised an annual exhibition for prints and drawings in the Royal Institute Galleries that lasted from 1921 to 1940, under the presidency of Frank Brangwyn. There was also a Society of Printmakers, which lasted for

one exhibition in 1924 at the St George's Gallery. The latter was perhaps only an *ad hoc* creation like the 1948 Society of London Painter-Printers which only appears on the occasion of another exhibition at the Redfern Gallery, but had no other existence.

The link of these societies and their different techniques with different galleries leads to a consideration of the publishing business. One obvious point is that each gallery sought to establish its own identity as publisher and dealer. The association went beyond that with a technique and a society: it also extended to a style. The best example is the Twenty-One Gallery which specialised in the sub-Palmer style associated with F.L.Griggs and Graham Sutherland. Their other artists not surprisingly included Paul Drury and William Larkins. When Joseph Webb and Leonard Brammer came on the scene in the early 1930s, it was inevitable that the Twenty-One Gallery should publish them too. Arthur Greatorex had a line in flashy drypoints of winsome half-clothed ladies. Almost the only dealer that was catholic in its range was Colnaghi's, which stood unchallenged at the top of the market, its pre-eminence securely founded on its other business as the leading dealer in Old Master prints.

The mid-nineteenth-century print publishing trade had been almost entirely concerned with large or very large reproductive prints made after the favourite Royal Academy paintings of the day. The dominant firms were old-established West End dealers such as Agnew's, Colnaghi's, Lefèvre and Graves, joined by interlopers such as Gambart. The new business in small etchings had nothing to do with this trade, and initially seems to have been handled by a new breed of dealer. Prominent among them were Scots, such as Annan, who was a personal friend of Cameron, and London firms like Obach. But as the new photomechanical reproductive processes killed off the traditional print business, the old firms had to readjust. Graves stuck to producing reproductive mezzotints after eighteenth-century portraits, and went into terminal decline. Agnew's abandoned print publishing altogether in favour of picture dealing. Colnaghi's absorbed Obach in 1911, and proceeded to become the largest of all the print publishers.[10] Lefèvre likewise moved with the times, and began to handle modern etchings. The Fine Art Society, which had been almost the first in the business, commissioning and publishing Whistler's *Venice* set in 1881, remained active with a main line in Brangwyn's prints but also dealing in many other etchers, and especially in dramatic architectural subjects.

The expansion of the etching market after the First World War produced a new crop of dealers, and during the boom years of the 1920s more and more entered the business. By 1929 there were one or more specialists in most of the major cities of Britain: in Glasgow Annan,

Bennett, Connell and Simpson; in Edinburgh Aitken Dott, the Hanover Galleries and Taylor & Brown; in Aberdeen Middleton's; in Liverpool Nicholson and Walker & Co. (the Rembrandt Gallery); in Stockport Highton; in West Kirby (Cheshire) McDonald; in Cambridge Bowes. Some of these also had branches in London. In London the main dealers were (alphabetically) Colnaghi, Deighton, Dickins, Dunthorne, the Fine Art Society, Frost & Reed, Furst, Greatorex, Alex Reid & Lefèvre, Paterson, the Redfern Gallery, the St George's Gallery, Bailey (Sloane Gallery), and the Twenty-One Gallery. More occasional, but significant, publishers were the Beaux-Arts Gallery, the Cotswold Gallery and the Leicester Galleries.

The advertisements of these firms list the artists whom they published. But what exactly were the business relationships between artists and dealers? And what does 'publishing' mean at this period? Nothing has yet been written about this, and only provisional conclusions can be drawn from the evidence that we have pieced together. The most important of these is that artists were not contractually bound to particular dealers, nor were they paid salaries or retainers. The initiative lay with artists; they were not commissioned by publishers to supply prints. In the case of Colnaghi's, the usual practice with established names was to buy editions or part-editions outright from the artist, who would be responsible for the entire costs of production. If the artist was less well known, the prints would be taken on consignment. In such a case Colnaghi's took a 25 per cent commission if the print was sold to a collector; if sold to the trade, a further 25 per cent discount was given, to make a total commission of 50 per cent.

Artists were usually linked to a single firm, but not invariably so.[11] Thus McBey used Colnaghi's exclusively; Cameron worked through Annan in Glasgow, who used Colnaghi as sub-agents in London. Griggs started with the Twenty-One Gallery, and when he moved to Colnaghi in 1921 the matter had to be placed in the hands of lawyers. The upshot was that the Twenty-One Gallery retained all rights to sell the existing plates, but Colnaghi's had exclusive rights on any new ones.[12] The account book of Hester Frood, a pupil of Cameron, shows that she sold prints to many dealers as well as directly to private collectors.[13] The alphabetical list of plates that she maintained sometimes gives in brackets after each plate the name of a publisher; in these cases she had sold the entire edition to one firm. Other plates have no name, and these were the prints she sold individually, whether to collectors or to dealers. Thus on 16 February 1909 she sold 47 impressions each of six different plates to Connell in Glasgow at 10 guineas per plate. By 1912 she was selling whole or part-editions to Dunthorne, and in 1913 to Colnaghi as well. By 1929 the price for an edition of 35 sold to Col-

naghi had gone up to 70 guineas, and an edition of 45 to 90 guineas. For someone who was producing six or more plates a year, this was very good money. But dealing with different agents could produce problems: her correspondence shows that the plate of Large Jan of 1912 was wanted both by Colnaghi and Dunthorne. The solution was to split the edition between the two.

The next stage was for the dealers to sell the prints they had bought. Many, perhaps most, went directly to collectors, at a mark-up of around 100 per cent. Others went to other members of the trade. Thus Colnaghi's employed a member of staff who made two extended tours every year around all the print dealers in Britain (never abroad), taking with him all their new editions.[14] These, if owned by Colnaghi's, were sold outright at a discount of 33 per cent; they were not left on sale or return. If Colnaghi's had taken them on consignment from the artist in the first place, they were passed on with a further allowance to the dealer. The tour was also extended to take in four or five major collectors. It should be noted that all the dealers visited specialised in prints; there was no visiting or selling to framers or other more general traders.

For the more popular printmakers, collectors were clamouring to be allowed to buy all the new plates as they appeared. This sort of collector wanted to put together all the works of an artist, often in different states, without needing to see the image before deciding to buy. In these cases, firms like Colnaghi's maintained subscription lists, which would include both collectors and other dealers. New plates would then be mailed directly with an invoice. With the leading figures, such as Bone, Cameron or McBey, demand was always greater than supply, and new plates could confidently be expected to command a premium in the sale rooms. Some subscribers exploited this by immediately reselling impressions, much to the annoyance of dealers. Since at this time it was still unusual to number the impressions of an edition,[15] it was impossible to trace which client was cheating in this way. Colnaghi's made an attempt to get round this by numbering impressions on the back in invisible ink which could be read under a special light. But a more effective method was to raise the subscription price; the highest ever reached by Colnaghi was 75 guineas in 1930 for McBey's Venetian Night. This should be compared with the normal price for a new print of between 1 and 3 guineas.

The last link in this chain were the collectors, about whom it is most difficult to find very much information. Many seem to have been lawyers, doctors or businessmen – the prosperous middle classes. Names that are mentioned were F. Rinder (who catalogued Cameron), H.N. Harrington (who did the same for Seymour Haden), Warburton (in Liverpool) and Arthur Mitchell (the brewer). Lord Rowallan formed an enormous collection of McBey during the 1920s and 1930s.[16] Another collector was Campbell Dodgson, the Keeper of Prints at the British Museum; he financed his purchases from a private income, and bequeathed his entire collection to the British Museum, thus laying the basis for its excellent holding of these printmakers. Museums both in Britain and abroad were other important collectors; the Keeper of the Department of Prints and Drawings in the Victoria and Albert Museum, Martin Hardie, was himself a distinguished semi-amateur etcher and member of the Royal Society of Painter-Etchers. In 1921, this society formed a Print-Collectors' Club; members were entitled to a presentation plate each year. By 1923, the membership list, having reached its total of 300, was closed. Many of the other print societies had their own clubs, which worked in the same way.

The market was international, and an important part was played by American dealers and collectors. Since London firms never sent agents to sell in America, marketing was done directly to subscribers or indirectly through other American publishers, who bought part-editions. The main firms there (to judge from the advertisements in *Print Collector's Quarterly*) were Frederick Keppel, M. Knoedler, Kennedy & Co., the Weyhe Gallery, the Schwartz Galleries and C. W. Kraushaar in New York; Albert Roullier in Chicago, Charles Sessler in Philadelphia; and Goodspeed in Boston. This trade also worked in the opposite direction. In *Fine Prints of the Year* for 1927, Malcolm Salaman gave a list of American etchers linked with European publishers (who would have bought part-editions from America), and came up with no less than sixteen names. Paris also formed part of this business: the firms were Le Garrec, Lecaplain, Marcel Guiot, Maurice Gobin and Louis Godefroy. In Berlin the main dealer was Amsler & Ruthardt; in Amsterdam E. J. van Wisselingh. One curious consequence of all this was that Harris Brisbane Dick, the New York collector whose bequest founded the Metropolitan Museum's print department, used on occasion to have three impressions of new publications sent to him, one each from a New York, a Scottish and a London dealer, and to compare them before deciding which one to buy.[17]

This market inevitably created its own literature. In the Bibliography is given a list of British books on prints published between 1900 and 1960. Although incomplete, it shows at a glance how, from a slow start, the number of new titles reached two or three a year around 1930, before dropping away to almost nothing in the 1940s and 1950s. The main annual was *Fine Prints of the Year*, which ran from 1923 to 1938 and was edited first by Malcolm Salaman and later by Campbell Dodgson. This carried full-page reproductions of the selected 100 plates, and at the back listed alphabetically all contemporary printmakers, with a list of their new publications, their prices, address and (if they had one) publisher. The leading specialist journal was the *Print Collector's Quarterly*, also edited by Dodgson, which carried as many articles on contemporary prints as it did on earlier periods. But more striking is the number of articles on modern prints in magazines that were not entirely devoted to the subject. Thus the *Bookman's Journal and Print Collector* began in 1919 with a column of notes on old prints, mostly of the eighteenth century. It was only in 1921 that a new column began, written by Salaman, on 'The Modern Adventure in Print Collecting'. Similarly *Artwork*, a general magazine on painting, sculpture and the arts and crafts, published from 1924 to 1931, not merely devoted a considerable number of articles (by Salaman, Dodgson and others) to introducing new printmakers to its readers, but from the summer of 1928 through to the winter of 1930 published a quarterly catalogue of prints. This most useful document lists all the new publications by name of artist, together with the name of the publisher, the size of the edition and the exact date of publication. The most important of the magazines, however, was of course *The Studio*, which from the turn of the century had not only carried articles on printmakers and full-page reproductions of new prints, but also published many 'Special Numbers' on the subject.

Many of the same writers reappear in all these publications. Dodgson was a museum man; so were Martin Hardie and James Laver of the Victoria and Albert Museum. Laver wrote first for the *Bookman's Journal* from 1924 to 1926, and from 1927 to 1928 for *Artwork*. In his memoirs he describes how this happened: 'One day, Martin Hardie showed me a letter he had received from Wilfred Partington, editor of *The Bookman's Journal* . . . Partington wanted someone to write "etching criticism". How old-world that sounds! Who cares nowadays whether etchings are criticised or not – or produced or not?'[18] By far the most prolific writer, however, was Malcolm Salaman, who only gave up the editorship of *Fine Prints of the Year* after 1935 when he reached the age of 80. Reading his criticism today, one is tempted to think that he single-handedly gave printmaking a bad name in the wider world, so uncritical is his approach and dreadful his prose, which certainly infected Laver's.[19] A contemporary protest was entered by Douglas Percy Bliss, who was himself a very accomplished wood-engraver:

The benevolence of professional critics and museum officials is quite Pickwickian. They cannot be jaded. Mere bulk, even, seems to whet their appetite for more. Among artists no topic is more common than the monstrous number of their fellows. 'The more the merrier' might almost be the slogan of the critics. Witness Mr Malcolm Salaman benignly presiding over scores of special numbers of *The Studio* . . . and breathing to one and all, to expert and beginner, 'God bless you all, you very clever people'.[20]

In 1930 Frank L. Emanuel published a book entitled *Etching and Etchers* in which he gave a cynical view of the print market: 'Machinery is ever at work behind the scenes to raise market values artificially in order to obtain high prices from wealthy competitors.' Among these devices he counted such harmless and accepted procedures as limiting the size of editions, promoting an artist by means of an exhibition, and holding a private view. Sharper is his charge against dealers of 'commissioning or inviting some multiple-critic, who will afterwards review the show in the Press, to write a preface to its catalogue'. But, at least by modern standards, the promotion that went on was very restrained. New editions were not hyped in any obvious way; prospectuses were not issued and little except the most generalised advertising took place. Such pushy advertisements as that of the Twenty-One Gallery in the New York journal *Prints* of 1931 for ten plates just published by Joseph Webb, a 'young etcher (he is 23 years old)', whose few plates 'show remarkable imaginative qualities and a mastery of technique seldom attained even by mature artists', are exceptional. Of course more disguised advertising took place in the articles written about new etchers and the prints selected for reproduction in journals, but this is inevitable in any kind of commentary devoted to contemporary art. Dealers certainly supported the prices of their artists in the sale room, but this could only be on a limited scale as most of them were small firms and none had access to the sort of capital that is common today.

On the other hand there was unquestionably a marked speculative approach to collecting on the part of many. This was a subject that was regarded as very embarrassing, and there is little published comment on it apart from the writings of Thomas Simpson, who described himself as a professional designer of golf courses. In 1919 he printed privately *Modern Etchings and their Collectors*, with extensive tables of auction prices designed to show the soundness of the hobby. In June 1922 he returned to the subject in an article, 'Some Modern Etchings and their Values', in the *Bookman's Journal*. In it he reviewed the period from June 1919 to June 1922, and noted three phenomena: 'I The gamble in [Anders] Zorn and Cameron etchings, and consequent collapse in prices; II The general steadiness during this period of etchings by the other modern and contemporary masters; III The three great sales of [J.L.] Forain etchings in France . . .'. This article provoked a storm of correspondence in later issues, not for its content (which was factual), but for its approach. Leading the attack was Harold Wright, the director of Colnaghi's concerned with the modern print business. He

was at pains to stress that auction results were often chancy and arbitrary, and that Simpson's approach was that of the speculator rather than the true collector, who might rather be considered as an investor. Another writer stressed that 'with the economic conditions as they are today, the materialistic factor cannot be ignored, and he who would pretend to do so is a humbug and hypocrite.'

Auction results of the period prove that prices advanced during the 1920s to undreamed-of heights.[21] The lists of new publications in *Artwork* swelled formidably. Many new dealers were tempted into the market, as can be seen from the increase in the number of advertisements in *Print Collector's Quarterly*. The same is true of printmakers. Arthur Driver reports a story of how E. H. Lacey, a Bradford artist, once entered Colnaghi's remarking that he had heard that etchings sold well and asking how they were made. Harold Wright explained, and added that drypoints were easier because they needed only a plate and needle. Lacey returned a few days later with some plates on which he had scratched with his mother's knitting needle; and these were promptly taken on and sold by Colnaghi's. In his introduction to *Etchings of Today*, published by The Studio in 1929, William Gaunt wrote:

Of the immense popularity of etchings at the present time there can be no doubt. In the Studio special number *Modern Etchings, Mezzotints and Drypoints*, published in 1913, Mr Malcolm C. Salaman commented on the fact that for every artist who practised etching in Whistler's day, there were at least fifty when he wrote. From 1913 to 1929 there has been an increase even greater. The etching is to the twentieth century what the topical woodcut was to the seventeenth, or the line engraving to the nineteenth – an art of the people . . . With this popularity it assumes also a speculative value – a condition of things similar to that which prevails on the Stock Exchange. The etchings of a new man of talent are like so many shares. At first low in price, they are sometimes bought in the expectation that they will increase in value, and quite often they appreciate to an extraordinary extent . . . .

But there were already signs of the coming reaction. The last etching column by Laver in *Artwork* was in the autumn of 1928, and in the winter of the following year the new editor, D. S. McColl, himself reviewed Laver's new book, *A History of British and American Etching*:

Mr Laver performs the feat of differentiating and patting on the back the growing throng, distinguishes, for example, Mr Tittle from Mr Tuttle,[22] without appearing too bored or breathless . . . As I turn over the pages I ask myself how many of these pieces I wish to see again, and the answer must be 'not a great many'. Etching is a form of drawing which is apt to deprive draughtsmen of what felicity they possess . . . At a little distance, moreover, hung on a wall, where the cultured novelist so regularly places them, most etchings resolve into mere scratch and inky clot, and few of them bear a near scrutiny . . . From even the best and most skilful of practitioners a drawing is greatly to be preferred, and yet the farcical truth is that the unique drawing fetches a trifle in the market compared with the multiplied plate. Farcical, but explicable; the collector, who makes the running, is a timid animal. His taste is only a small part his own, and to be the lonely possessor of a drawing fills him not with glory but with misgiving; fortified by the band of subscribers to a limited edition he feels secure, not only in his taste but in the prospect of enhanced value for the future. This situation furnishes the dealers with a delightfully manageable market, to which new-comers are charily admitted, while the prints of the recognized are sedulously nursed at auction sales. The connoisseurs of the craft increase the snowball by their labours upon 'states', whether the variations be significant or merely silly. The result, for the present, is a fantastically inflated scale of prices, which brings blushes to the cheek of the etchers who are artists rather than plate-mongers. The snowball will some day melt, for the sun of prosperity becomes too strong. The glut of practitioners, attracted by the success of a few, will choke the sources of profit, and etching find a more reasonable level among the graphic arts.[23]

This was of course almost entirely true. Newcomers were charily admitted: the Twenty-One Gallery is a clear example of a firm that introduced a new name in a house style every year or two. The untypical was as far as possible avoided. The most striking examples of this phenomenon were Sickert and Augustus John. All the critics acknowledged their importance, but few actually bought their plates. Frank Rutter observed: 'And Sickert, of course, is in a class by himself; though, like John, he has been strangely neglected by professional collectors of etchings. One day no doubt they will wake up – but not till prices have soared to the level of their understanding.'[24] Sickert's trouble, of course, was that his prints were entirely unpredictable, in technique, subject-matter and style. It is characteristic that most of his prints were never published; and on the few occasions that he did have prints formally published, he used the Carfax Galleries and the Leicester Galleries, neither of which were usually involved in this business, and had the title and his name engraved on the plate rather than signing them in pencil.

The collapse after 1929 was comprehensive in its effects. It can be traced in all sorts of ways besides auction prices. The quarterly catalogue of new publications in *Artwork*, having reached a peak of two pages in the spring and summer issues of 1929, was reduced to just over half a page in the autumn and winter, and was abandoned completely the following year. Some statistics of print publishing can be compiled from the lists given in *Fine Prints of the Year*. In 1929, at the height of the boom, 523 prints by 112 artists were published by 24 publishers. Four years later, in 1933, the numbers had halved to 200 prints by 61 artists by 13 publishers. In 1938 they had halved again to 83 prints by 30 artists by 9 publishers. Clearly, many artists had stopped printmaking in favour of other occupations that offered a greater chance of making a living. Equally publishers had had to cut back their pur-

chases sharply. Colnaghi's never made a round of the northern dealers after 1928, and never published another modern print after 1939; henceforth its print trade was almost exclusively in Old Masters. Some firms went out of business. Others struggled on at a very reduced level until 1939. By this time they were so enfeebled that they were in no position to withstand the problems presented by the war. Either they turned to other fields, or they went out of business.[25]

After the publishers, the magazines were hit. *Artwork* closed down in the winter of 1931. *Print Collector's Quarterly*, having recorded in 1935 the closure since the crisis of 1931 of the Continental print magazines *Byblis*, *L'Amateur d'Estampes* and *Die Graphischen Künste*, itself ceased publication in October 1936 'owing to the serious decline in the advertisement revenue'. But although this list of effects could be continued indefinitely, it is important to remember that prints were still published, and that there was still a market. The lists in *Fine Prints of the Year* record that in 1934 Gerald Brockhurst's prurient composition titled *Adolescence* was published by Colnaghi's at the high price of 20 guineas. And in the same year, the same firm took on no less than eighteen plates by the obscure Isabel Codrington at the same time – though this was more likely to have been on sale or return than purchase. Even after the Second World War, some residual interest in prints of this period survived. The absolute nadir of interest in them, according to the research of Kenneth Guichard, lay in the 1960s; between 1963 and 1970 not a single work by Muirhead Bone appears in *Art Prices Current*.[26] It was a new generation of collectors in the 1970s who created the current revival of interest.

The depression of the 1930s affected all branches of commerce, and the question now arises why it affected the print business so much more lastingly than any other branch of art dealing. The answer to this must be that it coincided with a marked shift in public taste. Our discussion of the market has concentrated on the top end – the serious collectors who mounted their etchings and stored them in solander boxes. But this level was underpinned by a widespread public acceptance of the medium. The typical prosperous middle-class home of the 1910s and 1920s would be likely to have hung in the hall and minor rooms a line of etchings and drypoints, all surrounded by a sea of white mount and a thin black frame. The new generation of the 1930s preferred large colour reproductions of Old Masters or (more likely) Impressionist paintings.

It was in these years that Van Gogh's *Sunflowers* achieved the popular success that they have never lost. That acute observer of contemporary life Osbert Lancaster, in *Homes Sweet Homes*, first published in 1939, gently ridiculed the 'cultured cottage' inhabited by writers, film stars, barristers, artists and BBC announcers for its 'hand-printed rhyme sheets, clever little woodcuts and expensive reproductions of those ubiquitous sunflowers' (p. 62). The reproductions in question were very likely to have been printed by the Munich firm of Hanfstaengl for which S.W.Hayter worked briefly in Paris in the late 1920s, making copies of the paintings in the Louvre to serve as colour controls for the printers. They were distributed in London through galleries such as Zwemmer's.[27] The manager there was Robert Wellington and it was he who later founded with John Piper the firm Contemporary Lithographs to provide original prints rather than reproductions for this market (cat. no. 122). Claude Flight was another who aimed at this clientele when he noted that his own and his followers' coloured linocuts were particularly suited for the modern interior.[28]

Another important factor was the complete inability of the British etching world to come up with new ideas. Artists and dealers seem simply to have continued to supply the same product and to have waited for better times to come, or (like Graham Sutherland) to have abandoned printmaking entirely. Where new ideas did exist (as, we shall see, in wood-engraving or lithography), they were largely ignored by the trade. A notable exception is the Redfern Gallery, which not only encouraged the linocut artists after 1929, but in the late 1930s supported colour lithography. The most amusing reaction to this blinkered attitude came in a review of the 1932 exhibition of the Royal Society of Painter-Etchers, written by C.G. Holme, editor of *The Studio*, here making a rare foray into print criticism:

The Society is fifty-two years old. Had I been asked to guess its age, from the aspect of the present exhibition at the galleries of the Royal Water Colour Society, I should have said sixty-five ... There is very little in the show that could not have been done thirty-two years ago. There is very little evidence that anyone has noticed the life and new forms which exist in every direction. The experience of seeing the exhibition comes closer to the living death than a week-end at a Bournemouth lodging house ... If the collectors of prints are only to be found among the Society's contemporaries, that is to say those on the wrong side of fifty, it is indeed a poor lookout for the prospects of print selling, so far as the Society is concerned, unless print collectors are like old soldiers who never die ... Has nobody noticed a football match, a greyhound race, a speed record breaking machine or even the tube railway?[29]

Such criticism mattered; henceforth there was very little commentary on new prints in a magazine that had previously been one of their keenest advocates.

The contrast with the situation in America is marked. There the traditional etching market, closely tied as it was to the British market, suffered a severe blow in 1929. But it put up a vigorous resistance in the form of numerous print collectors' societies which were established in American cities and which commissioned annual prints for distribution to members.[30] Many of these societies were linked to museums, and thus provided collectors with a continuing sense of permanence and reassurance. There were also portfolios and series produced by many artists' organisations, and extravaganzas like the print sale at Macy's in New York in 1932, at which 10,000 prints, many by celebrated masters, were sold in two days at a price of not more than 5 dollars each.[31] More particularly, artists turned increasingly towards lithography, and later under the Federal Art Project to screenprinting, with subject-matter taken from the contemporary scene which gives American printmaking of this time a period fascination that still appeals.

Another difference between the American and British printmaking worlds is worth noticing. The New York magazine *Prints* noted the publication of the 1932 edition of *Fifty Prints of the Year*: 'Twenty-nine conservative and twenty-one modern prints were chosen by John Taylor Arms and Max Weber for the seventh annual exhibition of the Fifty Prints of the Year ... The ratio was decided upon as a result of counting the hundreds of entries, the conservatives being in the majority.' This matter-of-fact statement is startling for the British reader. It is not merely that 'modern' prints were almost as numerous as 'conservative' prints, but that the distinction was recognised at all. Nowhere in the British print criticism of the 1920s is there any hint of a distinction between 'modern' and 'conservative'. Everything was conservative. Modernity was, if anything, an attribute of new media – the wood-engraving possibly, or, more obviously, the linocut – never something that distinguished between works in the same technique.

This background helps to explain the odd chronological spread of the prints discussed in this catalogue. After the small group of works produced around the First World War by the Vorticists or others associated with them, there is an almost complete gap through the mid-1920s, occupied only by the wood-engravings of Paul Nash. It is only at the end of the 1920s that a modern thread can again be traced in the linocuts of the Grosvenor School, or more notably in the work of Ben Nicholson, Edward Burra and others. It might be argued that the heavy weight of the success of the British etching tradition discouraged any artists of independent view from attempting printmaking at all. But like all generalisations this can only be partly true. Most notably it neglects the very wide variation in quality to be found within the mainstream intaglio tradition, and the fact that, *pace* Holme, there were a few artists (admittedly the less commercially successful ones) who did indeed treat themes taken from modern life in an interesting way. But pressure of space

53

John Banting 14/00 1932

Published by Contemporary Lithographs Ltd., London 1937 Edition of 75   John Piper

"Sculptural Objects" by Henry Moore R.A. etc. Published by School Prints Ltd., and printed in Great Britain by W.S. Cowell Ltd.

130

140

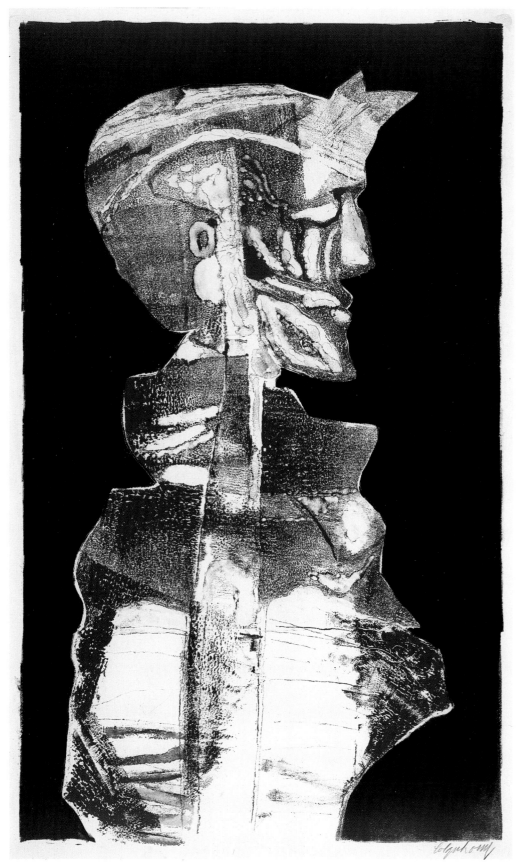

143

4/6 John Minton 1948

162

23/25   Gear '52

223b

has forced the omission of these artists: among them we would count most obviously Sickert and his pupils, and lesser-known figures such as Frederick Dixon. There were also idiosyncratic, often archaising, outsiders such as David Jones or Eric Gill, connected with the world of book illustration, who always had their own groups of admirers.

Nevertheless, the collapse of 1929 does seem historically to have acted as a stimulus to, or at least coincided with, experiments in new types of printmaking by British artists. Even if the etching world did little, a new market for wood-engraving was found with a sideways move from the world of the limited edition private press book into mainstream publishing. The book which was credited with being the watershed in this development was John Farleigh's illustrated edition of George Bernard Shaw's *The Adventures of the Black Girl in her Search for God* in 1932. This sold thousands of copies in numerous editions at half-a-crown each, made Farleigh a celebrity, and paved the way for many other ordinary publishers, as well as magazines such as *Radio Times*, to commission wood-engravings for texts of all kinds. Wood-engraving also found a new niche in the field of design. The important figure here (as so often) was Paul Nash, who found that his interest moved from wood-engraved pictures to wood-engraved designs, and in particular pattern sheets. He had a great influence on a group of students at the Royal College of Art, including Eric Ravilious and Edward Bawden who both emerged as outstanding designers in the 1930s.

One curious experiment (besides those of Gill and Jones) that never got very far was in line-engraving. Edward Wadsworth in 1926 made a series of engraved plates for Bernard Windeler's *Sailing Ships and Barges of the Western Mediterranean and the Adriatic Seas*, and this, with the contemporary French work of Jean-Emile Laboureur, lay behind some interesting engravings made by Bawden in the late 1920s. Bawden was again involved with engraving in 1937, when he made an illustration for an article by Graham Sutherland on 'Graven Images – Line Engraving and the Illustrated Book'. The text proposed that a new mass market for engraving could be reached by transferring impressions on to lithographic plates from which the main edition would be run off.[32]

Many of the most interesting British printmakers of the period escaped the limitations of this country by going to France. The clearest example is Stanley William Hayter, who lived in Paris from 1926 until 1939, as did John Buckland Wright for most of the period and Julian Trevelyan for three years in the early 1930s. John Banting can also be counted among them, for it was in Paris that he must have got the idea for his extraordinary blueprints. With most of these artists, innovation was only felt to be possible within a new technique. Hayter took up the old

art of line-engraving, which he rechristened 'gravure' and equipped with a new 'history'. Trevelyan's most remarkable prints, the 'dream city' group of 1936–7, are indeed etchings, but he handled the medium in a way that would have appalled any member of the Royal Society of Painter-Etchers: he used the wrong ground, drew in a child-like manner, and created most of the design in the inking of the plate and the colouring of the impression after printing.

But the most significant influence on the future of British printmaking in the 1930s and 1940s came from a quite unexpected direction – the poster. It was already a commonplace in the 1920s that Britain, though deficient in great artists, had the finest poster designer in the world in the person of Edward McKnight Kauffer (in fact an American). He made only a few prints (see cat. no. 20), and his designs for posters were drawn onto the stone by expert craftsmen in such firms as the Baynard and Curwen Presses. This art form was sponsored by intelligent patrons like Frank Pick at London Transport and Jack Beddington at Shell, and many of the leading artists of the 1930s, from Paul Nash to Graham Sutherland, were commissioned to provide designs. London Underground ran a poster shop at 55 Broadway, Westminster, where copies could be obtained literally for 'a shilling or two', depending on size. An advertisement for the shop in *The Studio* of April 1933 described its wares as 'Pleasing pictorial posters – pictures to harmonize with your decorations . . . You can change your pictures from time to time to suit your mood – your schemes of decoration, a change of picture makes a new room'.

The cause of poster design was advanced in England in the 1920s and 1930s as a subliminal means of educating public taste, particularly in relation to the more avant-garde styles of composition which people might otherwise shun: 'How many passers-by who profess not to be interested in art discuss the design of a poster without dreaming that they have been lured into the field of art?'[33]

The commissioning of images by serious artists for this purpose prompted Barnett Freedman's question as to why they should not also be given the opportunity 'to produce original works directly on to stones, so that every print might be a genuine picture designed in relation to the medium employed'.[34] Freedman (1901–58) became the great propagandist for the principle that autolithography could be successfully combined with machine production, thereby placing works of art which were original in design and execution within the financial reach of a mass audience. His stand was the result of his unusual combination of an art school training at the Royal College with the skills of a commercial lithographer which he acquired under the tutelage of T. E. Griffits, the chief technician at the Baynard Press. His particular contribution to commercial lithography was to make his original drawings on stone, which were then transferred to grained zinc plates using a transfer paper. As he explained in 1936, collaboration between artists and commercial printers could be fraught with difficulties:

The lithographic printing trade is hedged around with a mass of 'secrets' and private usages, which, combined with stringent trade union rules, make the acquisition of any first-hand information on the subject a little hard to come by . . . The artist must, in fact, become entirely involved in the whole gamut of production, finding out for himself, by experiment and failure, all about paper, ink, the temperature of the printing works, as well as the 'temperament' of the machine minder and the printing works manager.[35]

Freedman, however, found a fellow spirit in Harold Curwen who, in his book on *Processes of Graphic Reproduction*, London 1934, had already criticised contemporary lithography for its loss of vitality because of 'the lack of direct work by the artist'.[36] The Curwen Press became during the second half of the 1930s a notable exponent of autolithographic production, particularly in the field of book illustration, for which the Limited Editions Club of New York was one of its most appreciative clients. Freedman's colour illustrations of 1936 to George Borrow's *Lavengro* were regarded by Oliver Simon, Harold Curwen's partner, as a landmark in this sphere. Curwen played a further role as a propagandist through the influential magazine *Signature, a quadrimestrial of typography and the graphic arts* which it published (at a loss) from 1935 to 1940 and again from 1946 to 1956.

The changing taste for large decorative wall prints, allied with a philanthropic interest in the educative value of art, lay behind a number of schemes initiated during the 1930s for the circulation of prints to schools, industrial and service centres. The British Institute of Adult Education began to tour groups of reproductions from 1933 onwards, and in 1937 Derek Rawnsley, son of one of the founders of the National Trust, started School Prints from Gordon Square in London with the object of hiring to schools sets of reproductions which could be changed every term. As mentioned above, the idea of commissioning original lithographs rather than reproductions for mass distribution lay behind a pioneer series published in 1937–8 by Contemporary Lithographs Ltd, a firm set up by Robert Wellington of the Zwemmer Gallery in Charing Cross Road, with John Piper as technical adviser. The prospectus in 1937 for the first series of ten prints declared the firm's intentions of

producing original works by living artists suitable for the decoration of the school, paying attention to the needs both of the infants or juniors, and of those over eleven years of age in senior or secondary schools . . . Each lithograph has been drawn on the stones by the artist at the works of the Curwen Press. In order that any one subject should not become tiresome by over-repetition, the edition of each picture has been limited to four hundred copies.

The second series in 1938 was more generally aimed at 'households with small incomes' but the purpose was the same, to give the public 'contact with living art', thereby disabusing it of the notion 'that good pictures are exclusively museum objects'. The prints were for sale at the modest price of 31s. 6d. or 25s. each, with a reduction to schools, and, in order to provide a complete service, suitable mounts and frames could be supplied as well at a slightly enhanced cost. Their imagery, however, was by no means avant-garde, with the exception of Paul Nash's *Landscape of the Megaliths* (1st series, cat. no. 124 below) and John Piper's *Abstract Composition* (2nd series, cat. no. 122). Otherwise it was largely conventional and anecdotal, with particular concessions to juvenile taste such as Graham Sutherland's *Sick Duck*.

The first series of Contemporary Lithographs was received with critical acclaim, J. E. Barton in the *Architectural Review* for January 1937 concluding that 'the choice of lithography as a medium has entirely justified itself'. Nonetheless, neither this nor the following series sold to anything like the extent envisaged by Wellington, for reasons which dogged every subsequent attempt to create a market for original prints produced in large editions at low prices. Distribution was the perennial problem. Barnett Freedman wisely counselled artists in 1938: 'Let every man be his own lithographer, but have the business of distribution taken out of his hands',[37] and the problem was as real for publishers as it was for producers. Neither the retailers nor the public for whom the prints were intended possessed the technical knowledge to understand the distinction between reproductive and original work where lithography was involved. If the concept of originality in printmaking was familiar, it was probably associated by them with signed and numbered editions – which these were not. Finally there was the problem that in Britain colour lithography was not associated with original printmaking anyway. In France the battle to establish colour lithography as a serious artistic medium had been fought and largely won in the 1890s; but there had been no parallel movement in this country.

In America the situation differed too, because the graphic arts were supported by public subsidy through the Federal Art Project of the Works Progress Administration from 1935 onwards. The Graphics Division of the FAP actively fostered the growth of lithography, woodcut and silkscreen. Artists submitted sketches beforehand, and after approval the printing was done in workshops where technical advisers were on hand to provide the necessary assistance. Some 200,000 prints were produced in total; these were largely distributed to museums, libraries and educational institutions, while the artists themselves were permitted to retain proofs of their work.[38]

Lithography, in particular, enjoyed a reputation among left-wing American circles as a 'democratic' medium, a view shared in England by the Artists International Association, a co-operative organisation with Communist sympathies, established in 1932. It did not venture into the field of original printmaking until 1939, when a scheme for the publication of 'Everyman Prints', depicting scenes of contemporary life, was devised as a means of providing relief to artists unemployed as a result of the outbreak of war. They were all identical in size (200 × 300 mm) and largely, though not entirely, in monochrome. After the launch in London, further exhibitions were arranged elsewhere; Marks and Spencer was enlisted as a retailer for some provincial towns. Percy Horton, who reviewed the series for *The Studio* in May 1940, analysed the response to the subject-matter of the prints in sociological terms:

Already there are indications that three main classes of people are showing interest in the prints. An entirely new clientele for the artist has been found in working-class people who have shown themselves to be very independent in their judgements. These appear to have a definite preference for works which make a social comment, although a report from the Bristol exhibition on the reactions of visitors indicates that some of them think that the artists have made their commentaries from a far too superior angle. Of the other two classes, what might roughly be called the intelligentsia tended 'to buy names'. Finally there was a considerable uninformed middle-class which bought the safest and least experimental works.

At the outset the scheme benefited both from the imprimatur of Kenneth Clark, then director of the National Gallery, who opened the introductory exhibition, and from a patriotic enthusiasm to support a worthy cause. The initial flurry of interest was, however, not maintained; more prints were sold in the first three weeks than in the following two years and by 1942 the perennial problems of distribution and retailing had ensured that the venture would not be repeated. It was through a varied programme of travelling exhibitions, both during the war and after, that the AIA was best able to demonstrate the view 'that the arts are a necessary part of everyday life, to be maintained in all weathers, and not merely a luxury for the rich in times of leisure'.

This quotation is taken from the 1944 annual report for the Council for the Encouragement of Music and the Arts, founded in 1940, which since 1942 had been under the enlightened chairmanship of Maynard Keynes. In May 1943, in response to a rising demand for travelling exhibitions, Philip James explained in a letter to the artist James Fitton that the Council had decided 'to undertake on a large scale, the production both of colour prints of historical pictures – and also of works by living artists which are being specifically commissioned'.[39] The Council's report for 1944 referred to the continued 'publication of lithographs by contemporary painters for sale to factories, forces centres, youth clubs, British restaurants and other wartime groups. The series now comprises nine lithographs and three collotype reproductions and it is satisfactory to record that, of 42,000 colour reproductions issued so far, more than 35,000 have been disposed of. New subjects will be done by Ruskin Spear, John Piper and H. E. du Plessis. . . .' The CEMA series was not the first of the wartime commissions for contemporary prints, as the National Gallery had already been the publisher for etchings and lithographs commissioned by the Ministry of Information on the recommendation of the War Artists' Advisory Committee. The lithographs among these were a mixture of reproductive and original work, including Barnett Freedman's tour de force, *The 15 Inch Gun Turret, H.M.S. Repulse, August 1941*, a job for which the Admiralty paid him £100 for the 'craftsmanship' and £50 for the drawing.[40]

These wartime initiatives were important because they reached a far wider audience than had hitherto existed for contemporary art, through exhibitions which travelled to every conceivable type of workplace. The commitment was maintained in the immediate post-war period by the Arts Council, as CEMA became in 1945, which began to acquire a collection of its own as well as expanding the exhibition programme in general and opening two galleries in London as a shop window for exhibitions destined for the provinces. Among these, print exhibitions figured quite prominently because of the relative ease and economy of touring graphic material. Twentieth-century topics ranged from *American Silk Screen Prints* in 1946–7 to *The Technique of Modern French Engraving* by John Buckland Wright and *Picasso: 55 Lithographs 1945–47* in 1948; in 1949 followed *Art for All: an Exhibition of Posters and their Originals Produced by London Transport 1908–1949* and *Modern German Prints and Drawings*.[41] Even when it was difficult to obtain original work for exhibition because of import restrictions, the Council rejected the suggestion that reproductions would suffice on the basis of tangible evidence that: 'The public, however, vigorously proclaims its preference for "live" pictures'.[42]

The CEMA print series and the exhibitions referred to above were primarily aimed at an adult audience, but the impulse behind Contemporary Lithographs for children was revived by Brenda Rawnsley, widow of the founder of the pre-war School Prints hire service. In 1945 she enlisted the help of the critic Herbert Read who had published *Education through Art* two years earlier. Read suggested the artists who might be approached to participate in further series of 'auto-lithographs' and chaired the selection committee responsible for choosing four subjects for each term. Twenty-four were printed at the Baynard Press under the supervision of T. E. Griffits; most, but not all, were drawn directly on the stone by the artists concerned, who included Michael Rothenstein, Julian Trevelyan, Edwin LaDell and John Nash, while each lithograph was given its own decorative border because of the shortage of timber for framing. The claim made in the School Prints prospectus that 'the pictures themselves are far from being juvenile in their concept' was not borne out in reality, as the prints had for the most part an entirely conventional narrative content. However, the 3,000 subscribers who materialised for the first two sets encouraged Mrs Rawnsley to commission in 1948 a far more adventurous series from six avant-garde artists of truly international fame. With the aid of plastic plates developed by W. S. Cowell of Ipswich she was able to elicit original lithographs from Braque, Picasso, Léger and Dufy in France and Henry Moore in England (see cat. no. 130), while Matisse, who also agreed to participate, submitted a 'papier déchiré' for reproduction. The set was published in 1949 in an edition of 3,000 at a price of £4, but, despite the boldness of its conception and execution, the European Series, as it was known, proved an expensive failure. Virtually every school refused to subscribe, creating a serious financial problem for School Prints Ltd whose shelves, according to Mrs Rawnsley, remained 'absolutely stuffed with lithographs'.[43] Substantial stocks of both the English and the European series were still intact in the early 1970s when the School Prints premises in Motcomb Street were sold to Patrick Seale.[44]

It was only through public subsidy or commercial commission that any of these mass-produced original print schemes could survive. The Lyons series, consisting of sixteen lithographs commissioned in October 1947 followed by groups of twelve in 1951 and 1955, was a case in point, singled out for particular praise by the Arts Council which circulated an exhibition of the prints: 'This is a collection of the lithographs which this famous catering firm uses to adorn its tea shops and restaurants – and which sells over the counter at a price within the reach of a slender purse. The readiness of a business firm to play its part as a patron of living art affords an example which might well be developed further within industry and commerce'.[45]

The series was conceived as a solution to the shortage of materials for redecoration immediately after the war. The artists were chosen by Jack Beddington who had been responsible for the Shell posters, and the lithography was supervised by Barnett Freedman at Chromoworks Ltd, a firm which by this stage was largely equipped for photomechanical reproduction. About half the artists drew directly on to the unusually large zinc plates used for these lithographs, while the others submitted designs to be redrawn by the professional printers.[46] Freedman was again involved in a similar scheme in the mid-fifties, when Guinness commissioned prints on subjects inspired by the feats commemorated in the *Guinness Book of Records* for their public houses.

Contemporary Lithographs, School Prints and the Lyons series undoubtedly helped to accustom the public to large coloured images but they failed to convince even some of the protagonists of autolithography of the superiority of direct artistic intervention as opposed to careful translation at the hands of lithographic technicians. Photo-mechanisation of the colour lithographic industry during the 1950s destroyed what hope there had been of a successful alliance between artists and commercial printers for mass production of original material. In order to raise the level of appreciation for autographic printmaking, it proved necessary to concentrate on work which was wholly removed from the commercial printing world.

An early endeavour of this nature was the Miller's Press in Lewes, Sussex, run by two redoubtable sisters, Caroline Lucas and Frances Byng Stamper, who had connections among the Bloomsbury Circle which frequented nearby Charleston. Their own taste was strongly Francophile, as evinced by the style of their first publication in 1945, a portfolio of eight lithographs including prints by Vanessa Bell and Duncan Grant. This was apparently produced for a CEMA touring exhibition of lithographs 1792–1945, secured for Miller's by the good offices of A. E. Popham, Keeper of Prints and Drawings at the British Museum. Since colour was eschewed by most of the existing societies for printmakers, the sisters joined forces with the Redfern Gallery in London to form the Society of London Painter-Printers as a vehicle for exhibiting contemporary colour prints in all media. The publishing activities of Miller's from 1945 to 1954 were confined to lithography, to which their patronage introduced, among others, the singular talents of Robert Colquhoun and Robert Mac-Bryde, and the young Eduardo Paolozzi. Although the sisters did acquire their own press in Lewes, they were largely dependent on professional printing firms in London and Paris; the extensive use of transfer paper was the essential prerequisite for their entire operation, as Clive Bell explained in his preface to the first exhibition of the Society of London Painter-Printers in 1948. He expressed a preference for the 'grave richness' of the effects achieved by the French master-printer Louis Ravel as opposed to 'the gaiety and lightness' of the Chiswick Press, a commercial firm in London. Bell, moreover, was fully aware of the limitations of any form of printmaking in which the origination of the design was so far removed from its execution: 'But I will suggest to the painters that, if they wish to obtain the very best results, they, having done their drawings at home on transfer-paper, will be well advised to face for a moment the sound and fury of the shop and make their finishing touches on the stone. That way perfection lies, I am sure.' The artist's isolation from his printer meant that the publisher acted as intermediary, which, in the case of Rex Nan Kivell of the Redfern Gallery, sometimes entailed a cavalier disregard for the artist's intentions.[47]

The Redfern Gallery was virtually the only retail outlet for contemporary prints until the opening of St George's Gallery in 1954, a function it managed to perform without investing any capital in the production of the vast majority of the prints it exhibited. Sometimes the costs were shared: the artist contributed his time and the plate or stone; the printer the paper and his services; and the gallery the retail outlet and the catalogue (if there was one). The sale proceeds would then be split three ways. But more often, the prints were accepted on a sale or return basis, occasionally with negative results on both counts, according to a few aggrieved artists. This precarious arrangement from the artist's point of view explains why so few prints were properly editioned at the time. Even when an edition size was stated, it often represented a notional number of impressions which might be attained if demand warranted the printing of further examples. Apart from the Redfern and the occasional adventitious appearance of prints as an appendage to painting and sculpture exhibitions at other galleries, the artist-printmakers were dependent on organisations like the Arts Council, the Circulation Department of the Victoria and Albert Museum and the British Council for the dissemination of their work at home and abroad. The latter had proved particularly successful in finding customers for School Prints among the museums and educational institutions of Commonwealth countries.

One form of printmaking which avoided the tyranny of distribution was the monotype, which partly for this reason enjoyed a particular vogue among British artists during the 1940s and early 1950s. Its very spontaneity protected it from the obligations imposed by other print techniques; there were no special materials or equipment required, no orthodoxies to be observed and no necessity to find a publisher. It was practised by a broad spectrum of artists, some of whom adopted a carbon transfer process inherited from Paul Klee via Jankel Adler, who used it as a method of drawing, while others made more painterly monotypes from glass or metal plates. As an experimental medium, monotype printing was often incorporated into the more imaginative curricula of the post-war art schools, with Robert Colquhoun, for example, one of its most constant practitioners, lecturing on the subject at the Royal College of Art.

The expansion of art school teaching during the post-war period brought a proliferation of part-time appointments which provided many artists with a staple means of subsistence. It also gave them access to printing facilities and a limited amount of technical advice. Formal instruction in the art schools was heavily weighted towards intaglio methods, particularly at the Slade and the Royal College, where the printmaking department retained its designation as the 'Engraving School' until the early sixties, even though Edwin LaDell who succeeded Robert Austin as head in 1955 was a lithographer. Only the Central School had traditionally accorded any serious place to lithography, while silkscreen printing was not officially recognised as a fine art medium by most of the art schools before the 1960s. Until this time it was purely associated with graphic or textile design, and was to be found, if at all, in those departments. This situation explains the fragmentary nature of much of what has been selected here to represent printmaking in the late 1940s and 1950s. The work in question was the result of individual initiatives, skills hastily acquired at evening classes, by observation of more experienced colleagues and by trial and error on the kitchen table.

Without access to publishing and marketing resources, printmaking in this country was severely inhibited until the advent of St George's Gallery in 1954. This proved to be the forerunner of the emergence of a new type of entrepreneur, uniting the roles of publisher and retailer and even, in one or two instances, printer as well. The gallery's proprietor, Robert Erskine, at a time when 'quite sophisticated clients couldn't bring themselves to take an art-work seriously if other identical examples existed',[48] was imbued with a missionary zeal to educate the public to a proper appreciation of all printmaking techniques as means of artistic expression in their own right, and not as mere echoes of more elevated art forms. Retrospectively, Erskine recalled his objectives as having been to professionalise the production and presentation of the prints he commissioned; to convince customers 'apprehensive of reduplicated art' that 'our product had nothing whatever to do with reproductions'; to introduce new artists who showed 'strong graphic potential' to original printmaking; 'to canalise the artist's print-effort into a form that could be best promoted' and to publicise the activities of British artists in this realm as far afield as possible.[49] It was an ambitious programme which did not remain financially viable for long, but by the time St George's was subsumed within Editions Alecto in 1963, it had undoubtedly helped prints and printmaking to enter the consciousness of some sections of the public in general and of the art world in particular. Erskine had hopes of forming a London counterpart to Hayter's Atelier 17 in Paris, which would also come under Hayter's patronage and occasional supervision and would act as a centre of research to introduce 'the new resources of gravure ... dependent upon experiment rather than upon precept'.[50] This did not come to pass, but Erskine was nonetheless able to coax out of a small number of artists who printed their own work or used the services of C.H.Welch, the professional etching printer, examples of 'brilliant extempore control' of intaglio methods, allied to vividly expressive imagery (see cat. no. 200 below).

The primitive standards of production for artists' lithographs in Britain particularly exercised Erskine and he frequently had recourse to printing houses in Paris. This created problems when the finished editions arrived in Britain, as under the existing regulations they counted as commodities and were liable both to import duty and purchase tax until they were signed and numbered out of a maximum edition of 75. The artists therefore had to go and sign them in bond before they officially entered the country. At a later date Benedict Nightingale described how 'one of the odder responsibilities of Marlborough's prints manager, John Martyn, is to go to a building near Middlesex Hospital, open those packets of lithos his firm has had printed abroad and number his edition in the presence of a customs officer'.[51] Erskine was fully persuaded of the need to open a lithographic workshop in London, divorced from the constraints of trade union regulations, which would only produce original prints. To this end, he approached an aspiring lithographer from the Slade School of Art, Stanley Jones, who after training in Paris for a year returned to England in 1958 to provide the service Erskine required through the Curwen Studio, established in the autumn of that year as a vehicle for Jones's talents.

The division of cost varied according to the nature of the commission, but at no time was St George's Gallery involved in the kind of capital investment which subsequent print publishers had to make. If an artist printed his own work, then the sale proceeds might simply be divided two ways; if an expert printer was involved, 'the printing costs are then prepaid [by the Gallery], print by print. This is not strictly speaking, good business, because a subsequent edition of a different print by the same artist may be better or more popular and thus kill the selling chances of the earlier edition'.[52] In the case of suites of prints, which Erskine found a particularly satisfactory form of publishing from an artistic and a commercial point of view, he would often purchase one plate initially, to show a commitment, then divide the profits after sales.

Different prints were shown every month in the gallery at 7 Cork Street with an annual round-up of the best contemporary British prints of the year from 1957 onwards. Travelling exhibitions were sent all over the world under the auspices of the British Council, and Erskine was assiduous in submitting his artists' work to international competitions such as the biennials in São Paolo and Cincinnati which got under way at the beginning of the 1950s. In terms of educating the public, Erskine reckons that a twenty-five-minute documentary film, *Artists' Proof*, shot in December 1956 in collaboration with the Shell Film Unit, was the most effective thing he produced. Filmed on location were demonstrations of woodcutting, lithography, etching, aquatinting, engraving and silk-screen printing, given by Roland Jarvis, Alistair Grant, Anthony Gross, Merlyn Evans, Anthony Harrison and John Coplans respectively: 'It was obvious to anyone who saw the film that our product had nothing whatever to do with reproductions. The artist demonstrably makes the print himself, using the chosen medium for its own sake, and not merely as a means of recapitulation to gain a wider and more plebeian market'.[53]

A summation of the St George's Gallery's efforts was presented in 1959 as an exhibition at the Whitechapel Art Gallery entitled *The Graven Image*, which, Erskine explained in his introduction, was taking place 'because it is an exhibition of a movement gaining momentum. Ten years ago there would have been very little material to exhibit. In ten years' time there will be infinitely more prints to choose from and ten times as many artists making them'. Both his assessment of the current situation and his prognosis for the next decade were quite correct. A number of artists had already taken heart from St George's Gallery to form, in conjunction with the Zwemmer Gallery, the New Editions Group, which from 1956 until the mid-sixties exhibited a cross-section of the work coming out of artists' studios. Alistair Grant, who was one of the participants, recollects that by the end of the fifties he was deriving a real income from the sale of his prints, sufficient in any case to pay his studio rent. The preface to the 1963 New Editions exhibition paid homage to the notable expansion of printmaking in all media previously acknowledged by Robert Erskine, which rested upon the new initiatives taken by artists who were painters and sculptors in the first instance rather than specialist printmakers. Therein lay the key to the proliferation of publishing ventures of the 1960s and early 1970s: the rise of the art market in general created an ancillary demand for the (cheaper) prints of artists whose reputations were associated with the higher (and more expensive) echelons of artistic endeavour.

The New Editions Group existed to propagate work printed by the artists themselves on their own premises or in art schools. But the significant changes in the print scene in Britain were brought about by the establishment of professional printing studios like the Curwen for lithography in 1958 and Kelpra for screenprinting, which, though it opened in 1957, did not produce its first artist's print until 1961 when Gordon House, the graphic designer, commissioned a series of his own original work. The hand-made, irregularly produced print run off in erratic editions, which had been the hallmark of the 1950s, was rejected in favour of the uniform perfection hitherto associated with the work emanating from Paris and Switzerland. These studios had to find appropriate retail outlets. In the case of Curwen this involved opening a gallery and acting as a publisher in its own right as well as working for others. Editions Alecto was founded as a publishing company in 1962 on the strength of an undergraduate success in selling specially commissioned artists' prints of public schools and Cambridge colleges to alumnae. Within a year it too had opened a gallery, the Print Centre off Kensington Church Street, followed in 1964 by a collection of studios nearby, in Kelso Place, for the actual practice of etching, lithography and screenprinting. Editions Alecto, which acquired Robert Erskine's expertise and stock in 1963, was the direct heir to the ideals of the St George's Gallery. Its directors' intention remained to produce 'original works of art whose price makes them available to a major selection of the community'[54] and through the studio in Kelso Place they were able to realise the kind of collaborative research which Erskine had originally wanted to establish in 1955 under the auspices of Hayter. Editions Alecto, the Curwen Studio and Kelpra between them seized the initiative for the commissioning and production of work on an international scale, by a younger generation of artists who were often exploring print media for the first time.

The initiative, the expertise and many of the artists were to emanate from within Britain during the 1960s and 1970s, but the market lay principally abroad, a factor which remains constant to this day. The British Council did much in the post-war period to raise the profile of British art all over the world, but the American market was the real key to success. A more broadly based educational system in the United States helped to create a large pool of collectors with strong ties to their local universities and museums; the potential there for individual, institutional and corporate patronage far exceeded any comparable prospects in Britain. Printmaking itself in America after the Second World War was largely confined to the Fine Art departments in colleges and universities, of which there were a considerable number, many of them employing former members of Hayter's New York Atelier 17. The galvanising force in America, however, as in Britain, was the surge in demand in the early 1960s for the new styles and imagery introduced in the first place through painting and sculpture, linked to the establishment of professional print workshops capable of assisting in the autographic translation of these features.

Tamarind in New Mexico and Universal Limited Art Editions on Long Island were foremost in this field, but Editions Alecto also worked with American artists, many of whom visited London at the time, while Chris Prater at Kelpra led the Anglo-Saxon world in the production of screenprints. Thomas Hess, writing in January 1972, illustrated the transformation of the American print scene during the preceding decade and a half with a quip from one artist that 'In the 50s when you saw a friend on the Long Island Railroad on an early Wednesday morning, you knew he was going to see his shrink. Nowadays you know he's on his way to work with his lithographer'.[55]

Any chronological division of a subject is somewhat artificial, but c.1960 does have a general validity as a demarcation between 'the whole, vague, Bohemian, badly oganised situation'[56] that was the popular notion of an artist's life in the fifties and the competitive professionalism of every field of artistic endeavour in the sixties. Artists were placed under contract to dealers with a determined eye on the international market, such as Marlborough and Waddingtons, both of whom opened their own print departments, in 1964 and 1967 respectively, for the purposes of publication and retailing. Nevertheless, the issues which Robert Erskine raised in 1959 in his introduction to *The Graven Image* were unresolved ten years later and remain so to this day: 'There are at the moment a number of prejudices lurking which must be dispelled before a wide distribution can be accomplished. Prints are too cheap to satisfy the symbolistic faith of the 'art lover'; they are tainted by association with machinery; they are printed in quantity and they do not have the same characteristics as oil paintings...'.

The market for original prints has never responded favourably in the long run to attempts to democratise the commodity by making it widely available; as high a premium continues to be placed on relative exclusivity as it was in the heyday of the etching market earlier in the century. In the 1960s Curwen were opposed to selling prints in sets even when they were commissioned as a series, since this placed them beyond the reach of the 'quite ordinary people' for whom they hoped to cater.[57] Erskine's conviction that the Vollard concept of a suite of prints was the best way of promoting an artist's work has, however, become a fundamental principle of print publishing, which prefers to rest its hopes on the rock of institutions and wealthy collectors rather than the shifting sands of the interests of 'quite ordinary people'. Screenprinting was the obvious candidate to be the vehicle for the mass production of original material, but eventually it became the victim of its very ease of multiplication in the same way as lithography's reputation had previously suffered. The inherent prejudice against the more highly mechanised techniques of printmaking has led, since the contraction of contemporary print publishing in Britain in the late 1970s and 1980s, to a much greater emphasis on techniques such as etching, aquatint, woodcut and monotype, which have an unequivocally autographic appearance.

Finally, public taste has never been fully educated to a proper appreciation of the difference between original and reproductive work, with customers often paying more for the latter than would be necessary to obtain a respectable example of the former. Clive Bell in 1948 believed that 'the glaring discrepancies between the current reproductions of Van Gogh's more popular pictures and the originals lately seen at the Tate have caused searchings of heart amongst enthusiastic but impecunious picture-lovers'.[58] There was little evidence, though, two decades later of any such heightened awareness. The expansion of the serious print market in the 1960s and 1970s, brought in its wake a flood of material masquerading as original prints through devices such as signing and numbering, but with little or no real claim to this status. Such material found an effective advertising medium in the new colour supplements of newspapers. Recent marketing ventures continue to cause public confusion by offering photomechanical reproductions within a context normally associated with original prints.[59] Hayter's insistence that 'one must distinguish between pure processes of reproduction in which, when successful, the prints are practically as good as the project, and media of original expression in which the print *is* the result, and there is no other *original*, nor could any other medium have given the same expression' is as relevant today as it was more than forty years ago.[60]

Notes

1. Anthony Gross, *Etching, Engraving and Intaglio Printing*, London 1970, p.3.

2. 'The Year's Wood-Engraving', *The Studio* 101 (1931), p.194.

3. Sidney C. Hutchinson, *The History of the Royal Academy 1768–1968*, London 1968, p.167.

4. Sir Francis Newbolt, *The History of the Royal Society of Painter-Etchers & Engravers 1880–1930*, The Print Collectors' Club, London 1930. See also Martin Hardie in *The Studio* 128 (1944), pp.65–74.

5. C. Dodgson and J. Pennell, *The Senefelder Club*, London 1922; see also James Boswell, 'The Senefelder Club', *The Studio* 147 (1954), pp.65–71.

6. *Bookman's Journal and Print Collector*, May 1923, p.50.

7. See Thomas Balston, *English Wood-Engraving 1900–1950*, London 1951 (reprinted from *Image* v, 1950), and the books listed in section 4(d) of the Bibliography.

8. From the minutes of the Society, April 1920, quoted by Sarah Hyde in *Print Quarterly* vi (1989), p.451.

9. A biography of Furst (1874–1945) can be found in *Who was Who* for 1941–50. Between 1935 and 1939 he was editor of *Apollo*.

10. See G. Agnew, *Agnew's 1817–1967*, London 1967, and J. Byam Shaw, *Colnaghi's 1760–1960*, London 1960.

11. William Gaunt, *Etchings of Today*, The Studio, 1929, gives a directory of etchers, most of whom have a publisher listed after their names.

12. See F. A. Comstock, *A Gothic Vision, F. L. Griggs and his Work*, Boston and Oxford 1966, p.19.

13. This book was kindly shown to us by Felicity Owen, to whom we also owe further information on Hester Frood.

14. Our information about Colnaghi's comes from Arthur Driver, who first joined the firm in 1928, and from Katherina Mayer Haunton, the daughter of Gustav Mayer who joined Colnaghi's in 1911 from Obach's. He specialised in the Old Master prints; Harold Wright saw to the modern print business. One of Arthur Driver's first jobs was to make the tour round the North, with the expectation that he would in future take over this aspect of the business.

15. A long correspondence on the subject of whether editions should be numbered was conducted in the pages of the *Bookman's Journal and Print Collector* in November 1923 to March 1924, with contributions by Martin Hardie, Campbell Dodgson and others. It had been normal to limit editions since the end of the nineteenth century, but these limitations were either not marked on the individual impressions, or only in the form 'out of an edition limited to . . .'. The modern fashion of numbering prints in the way '12/30' (meaning number 12 out of an edition of 30) only gradually became the standard during the 1920s. In his letter Dodgson stated that this method of numbering had come to Britain from France.

16. This collection was sold by Phillips at a house sale on 27/28 November 1989.

17. Dick's papers are in the Print Department of the Metropolitan Museum; we owe this information to David Kiehl.

18. James Laver, *Museum Piece*, London 1963, p.109.

19. Salaman's memories can be found in *The Studio* 105 (1933), pp.262ff.

20. 'The Last Ten Years of Wood-Engraving', *Print Collector's Quarterly* xxi (1934), p.257.

21. A useful compilation of prices is given by Kenneth M. Guichard, *British Etchers 1850–1940*, London 1977, pp.11–12. Complete lists of auction results were given in *Print Prices Current*, compiled and published by F. L. Wilder from 1918 to 1939.

22. Tuttle was an American artist who specialised in portrait drypoints of astonishingly low quality.

23. *Artwork*, Winter 1929, pp.v–viii.

24. Frank Rutter, *Art in my Time*, London 1933, p.211.

25. The remaining stock of Twenty-One Gallery etchings by Graham Sutherland was sold at Sotheby's in four sales between 24 March 1970 and 27 April 1971 as the property of the late Mrs A. M. Bernhard-Smith.

26. Guichard, op. cit., p.11.

27. See *Anton Zwemmer, Tributes from Some of his Friends on the Occasion of his 70th Birthday*, privately printed, London 1962.

28. Claude Flight, *Lino-cuts. A Handbook of Linoleum-cut Colour Printing*, London 1927, p.4.

29. C. G. Holme, *The Studio* 103 (1932), pp.249–54. Compare Hayter's story (*About Prints*, p.164) that in the late 1920s he correctly prophesied the end of the fashion: 'My view was based on the proposition that, finding myself bored by these works, if I was bored an enormous number of other people were going to share that boredom sooner or later, and among them some of the purchasers of these works. Whereupon their popularity would cease.'

30. Apart from the Glasgow Society of Painter-Etchers, the only print society outside London that we have been able to trace was one in Sheffield, which was set up in 1930 (*The Studio* 99 (1930), p.293).

31. This was reported in *The Studio* 105 (1933), p.3.

32. *Signature* no. 6 (July 1937), pp.28–34.

33. E. McKnight Kauffer, *The Art of the Poster*, London 1924, p.28.

34. Barnett Freedman, 'Every Man his own Lithographer' in *Art in England*, ed. R.S. Lambert, London 1938, p.107.

35. 'Lithography, a Painter's Excursion' in *Signature* no. 2 (March 1936), p.13.

36. See Pat Gilmour, 'Unsung Heroes, Barnett Freedman', *The Tamarind Papers* vol. 8, nos 1 and 2 (1985), p.18.

37. 'Every Man his own Lithographer', op. cit., p.108.

38. See Jacob Kainen, 'The Graphic Arts Division of the WPA Federal Art Project' in *New Deal Art Projects. An Anthology of Memoirs*, ed. F. O'Connor, Washington DC 1972.

39. *James Fitton*, Dulwich Art Gallery, 1986, p.89.

40. P. Gilmour, 'Unsung Heroes', op. cit., p.22.

41. See *Bibliography of Arts Council Exhibition Catalogues 1942–1980*, 1982.

42. Arts Council Annual Report for 1947–8, p.12.

43. From a taped account of the project made in 1989 (see cat. no. 130).

44. See Mel Gooding, 'School Prints', *Arts Review*, 4 July 1980, p.267.

45. Annual Report 1951–2, p.32.

46. The British Museum owns the first two series complete, presented by Mr L.C. Velluet (1988–11–5–63 to 90).

47. See Pat Gilmour, 'Ceri Richards, his Australian Printer, and Stanley Jones', *The Tamarind Papers* vol. 10, no. 1 (Spring 1987), pp.28–37.

48. Robert Erskine, 'St George's Gallery' in *A Decade of Printmaking*, ed. Charles Spencer, London 1973, p.20.

49. Ibid., p.21.

50. From the preface to the Atelier 17 exhibition catalogue, St George's Gallery, 1955.

51. Benedict Nightingale, 'A License to Print Originals', first printed in *New Society*, 9 February 1967, reprinted in *A Decade of Printmaking*, op. cit., pp.38–41.

52. See Bryan Robertson's preface in *The Graven Image*, Whitechapel Art Gallery, 1959, p.3.

53. *A Decade of Printmaking*, op. cit., p.21.

54. Ibid., p.11.

55. 'Prints: Where History, Style and Money Meet', *Art News*, January 1972, pp.29 and 66.

56. Bryan Robertson, John Russell and Lord Snowdon, *Private View*, London 1965, p.172.

57. Benedict Nightingale, op. cit., p.41.

58. Preface to the 1948 exhibition of *Colour Prints by the Society of London Painter-Printers*, Redfern Gallery.

59. An example, chosen at random, which was reported in the press in June 1990, was the so-called Royal Academicians Collection of signed reproductions issued by the Art Image Company in a limited edition of 250, signed by the artists and selling for up to £600 each.

60. S.W. Hayter, 'The Silk Screen', *Serigraph Quarterly* vol. 1, no. 4 (November 1946).

Technical Glossary

For fuller explanations see Antony Griffiths, *Prints and Printmaking, an Introduction to the History and Techniques*, British Museum Publications, London 1980

Aquatint A variety of etching in which tone is created by fusing grains of rosin to the plate and etching it. The acid bites in pools around each grain; these hold sufficient ink to print a light grainy tone.

Drypoint A process similar to etching except that the line is not bitten into the plate by acid but directly scratched in with a sharp needle.

Engraving A process using a metal plate. Lines are cut into the metal (usually copper) using a v-shaped metal tool called a burin. Since this is pushed in front of the hand, it produces a clean and controlled incision. The plate is inked and printed in the same way as an etching.

Etching The artist draws his design through a waxy ground laid on a metal plate. The lines of exposed metal are then eaten away in an acid bath. After cleaning off the ground, the plate is inked so that the ink lies only in the bitten lines and the surface wiped clean. The plate is printed by laying a sheet of paper over it and running both through a press under considerable pressure.

Linocut An abbreviation for linoleum cut; the same process as woodcut, except that linoleum is used instead of wood.

Lithography A method of printing from stone or zinc. It relies on the fact that grease repels water. The design is drawn on the surface in some greasy medium. This is printed from in the following way: the surface is dampened with water, which only settles on the unmarked areas since it is repelled by the grease in the drawing. The surface is then rolled over with greasy printing ink, which only adheres to the drawing, the water repelling it from the rest of the surface. Finally the ink is transferred to a sheet of paper by running paper and printing surface together through a scraper press.

Mezzotint A metal-plate engraving process. The plate is worked over ('grounded') using a semicircular spiked tool (a 'rocker') so that the entire surface is roughened. In this state, the plate will print a solid black. The lighter parts of the design are then created by scraping and polishing down areas of the plate so that they hold less ink in the printing.

Monotype The two most common processes involve:

(a) printing from any flat surface which has previously been covered in ink (usually a glass or metal plate). The ink normally permits no more than one strong and one weak impression.

(b) using a carbon to transfer a drawn design from one sheet of paper to another.

Screenprint This is a variety of stencil printing. A mesh is attached to a frame and a design is either drawn on it in some impermeable medium or a stencil is attached to it. Ink is forced through the screen onto a sheet of paper with a squeegee.

Soft-ground etching A variety of etching which uses a soft etching ground. By laying a sheet of paper on top of the grounded plate and drawing on the paper, the ground is made to adhere to the underneath of the paper. A precise facsimile of the drawing is thus left in the ground and can be etched into the plate in the usual way.

Woodcut Using a block of soft-grained wood, the artist cuts away the background using knives and gouges, leaving the lines standing in relief. Ink is then rolled over the surface of the block, which is printed under light pressure onto a sheet of paper.

Wood-engraving A variety of woodcut which uses a hard-grained wood, such as boxwood, which is too hard to be cut with a knife. Instead, a v-shaped burin is used to incise lines into the block. When printed (in the same way as a woodcut), the lines stand out as white against a black background.

1 Vorticism, its Friends and Foes

Printmaking was, for the most part, peripheral to the welter of experimentation essayed in the fine and decorative arts by the shifting factions within the London avant-garde between 1910 and 1920. Yet there was a quintessentially 'graphic' quality to much of the work of the period, particularly that of the artists allied with Vorticism. Little distinction was usually made between pen and ink drawings destined for translation via line blocks into printed form and those designs conceived as original prints; Herbert Furst in his study *The Modern Woodcut* (1924) criticised both artists and public for thinking 'in lines and in terms of imitation, i.e. of a design originated by pen or pencil or even by brush, rather than by the material and the cutting tool' (p.107). The critic of *The New Age* who reviewed the exhibition of Wadsworth's woodcuts at the Adelphi Gallery in 1919 made a comparison between the prints and Wyndham Lewis's painting *The Plan of War* (reproduced in *Blast* no. 1, June 1914), Lewis's drawings for *Timon of Athens* (published in folio form by the artist in 1914) and the designs published in *Blast* by artists like Frederick Etchells, Helen Saunders, Jessica Dismorr and Dorothy Shakespear, for whom mechanical processes again rendered traditional printmaking techniques superfluous. Furst rightly concluded that 'modernity in art depends not so much on craftsmanship as such, but as a means of expressing the design and intention of the artist' (p.180).

For several of the artists grouped together in this section, however, autographic printmaking, albeit conducted in a very private manner, was a means of exploring ideas which either could not be pursued in painting because of difficulties created by wartime circumstances or which proved more susceptible of resolution on a small scale. Wadsworth, one artist for whom printmaking became a primary means of expression between 1915 and 1919, felt at the end of that period that he was 'gradually being able to evolve something out of a medium which has never, I think, been used in quite the same way before and which in my opinion is very suitable for an expression of form and structure' (quoted by B. Wadsworth in *Edward Wadsworth, a Painter's Life*, Salisbury 1989, p.77). Although Wadsworth conceded the parallels drawn by contemporaries such as Ezra Pound and Frederick Etchells with Oriental traditions of woodblock printing, the real association lay with the mainstream of avant-garde printmaking in Central Europe before the First World War, and in particular with the work of Kandinsky, the artist who most notably excelled at what Wyndham Lewis termed 'this miniature sculpture, the woodcut' (*Blast*, no. 1 (1914), p.136). Wadsworth's affinity with German printmaking of the period was underlined by the inclusion of

a small group of his early woodcuts in an exhibition of black and white prints entitled *Modern German Art*, held at the Twenty-One Gallery in 1914.

Furst quite rightly made a distinction between the intellectualism of Wadsworth's approach to printmaking and the sensibility apparent in the work of Roger Fry and his Omega associates, but in both cases 'form and structure' superseded narrative content. McKnight Kauffer's design *Flight* was, for this particular critic, the epitome of a modernist aesthetic which was like a 'switchback journey, which is undertaken merely for the sake of sensation and leads to no outside destination' (Furst, p.183). By the early twenties much of the radicalism behind the prints catalogued here had evaporated or been channelled into other fields. Ezra Pound in 1917 seized upon Alvin Langdon Coburn's experimental photographs done with a 'vortoscope' as the abstract medium of the future which 'ought to save a lot of waste experiments on plane compositions such as Lewis's "Plan of War" or the Wadsworth woodcuts' (*The Letters of Ezra Pound 1907–1941*, ed. D.D. Paige, London 1951, p.158). However, it was in graphic design that Cubo-Futurism survived most successfully in Britain during the 1920s, owing to the rapid increase of enlightened patronage in advertising.

Edward Wadsworth

1889–1949

Born in Cleckheaton, West Yorkshire, where his family were prosperous mill-owners. After leaving Fettes College, Edinburgh, in 1906 he was sent to Munich for a year to learn machine drawing and German in preparation for entering the family business. His exposure to that city's lively artistic milieu at this period proved decisive in steering him instead towards a professional career as an artist, and on his return to Cleckheaton he entered the Bradford School of Art. From there he won a scholarship to the Slade in 1909, where he became involved with the leading avant-garde figures of the time: Roger Fry, who was lecturing in the history of art, and, among his fellow-students, C.R.W. Nevinson, David Bomberg and William Roberts. Fry included two of his paintings in the last month of the Post-Impressionist exhibition at the Grafton Galleries in January 1913; Wadsworth subsequently assisted Fry in the restoration of the Mantegna Cartoons at Hampton Court and executed a number of designs for the Omega Workshops. It was here that he encountered Wyndham Lewis, with whom he left Omega in October

1913 and later became a founder member of the Rebel Art Centre. He signed the Vorticist manifesto published in the first issue of *Blast*, June 1914, as well as contributing illustrations and an essay entitled 'Inner Necessity' on Kandinsky's treatise *Über das Geistige in der Kunst*. In 1915 he contributed again to *Blast* and showed in the Vorticist exhibition held in June of that year.

In June 1916 he was posted as a naval intelligence officer to the Aegean, where he was based in Mudros on the island of Lemnos until the summer of 1917 when poor health necessitated his return to England. Thereafter he was engaged in Liverpool and Bristol in supervising the 'dazzle' camouflage applied to allied shipping. This inspired the composition he submitted to the Canadian War Memorials Commission in 1919, *Dazzle-Ships in Drydock at Liverpool*, his first painting since 1915. His first one-man show, consisting largely of prints, was held at the Adelphi Gallery in March 1919 and met with immediate acclaim. A second solo exhibition followed in January 1920 at the Leicester Galleries, and was devoted to thirty-seven ink and watercolour drawings of the Black Country executed during the previous year.

During the early 1920s Wadsworth's style and subject-matter underwent a considerable change, effected in part by an alteration in his material circumstances. His father's death in 1921 provided him with sufficient means, which lasted until the Second World War, to take 'twice yearly trips to Paris, holidays on the Continent of six weeks or more duration, three servants in the house and two Rolls-Royces in the garage, with a chauffeur to tend to them' (B. Wadsworth, p.342). He concentrated on marine subjects and harbours, often inspired by Marseilles and other French ports, which he painted in tempera in preference to his earlier use of oil or graphic techniques. These works became increasingly indebted to many of the pictorial devices of Surrealism, in both the choice and disposition of forms. His last one-man exhibition was at the Mayor Gallery in 1933, during the period when he was briefly allied with the group of abstract artists who formed Unit One. Thereafter his best-known work was the pair of marine still lifes commissioned in 1935 for the First Class Smoking Room of the *Queen Mary*, and a series of paintings executed from 1941 onwards for ICI advertisements.

Wadsworth's first experience of printmaking techniques was at the Knirr School of Art in Munich in 1907, where he studied woodcutting in his spare time. His main printmaking activity was almost entirely confined to the years 1913–21, which saw the execution of approximately fifty different subjects in woodcut, many of them printed in several colour variants on papers of different shades, and four lithographs all dating from 1919–20. His efforts at original printmaking then largely petered out. He did, however, produce two etchings in 1922, and some copper-plate engravings in 1926 which illustrated *Sailing Ships and Barges of the Western Mediterranean and Adriatic Seas*, published by Frederick Etchells and Hugh Macdonald. During the 1930s and 1940s a number of colour lithographs appeared which were reproductive of his

paintings. Wadsworth appears to have been directly involved in their adaptation for lithographic purposes in two instances only: *Imaginary Harbour* (1938), published by Contemporary Lithographs, and *Signals* (1942), published by CEMA (Council for the Encouragement of Music and Arts).

The woodcuts are by far the most important aspect of Wadsworth's work as a printmaker and for the four years from 1915 to early 1919 they serve as the only evidence of his artistic development, since no paintings at all survive from this time. The earliest date for the woodcuts is provided by an impression of *Newcastle* dated 1913, which belonged to Jessica Dismorr and was reproduced in the first issue of *Blast*. Many of the prints are undated but can be ascribed to particular years on grounds of style, subject-matter or evidence contained in letters belonging to Wadsworth's daughter, Barbara von Bethmann-Hollweg. The point of departure for any catalogue of the woodcuts is the list of prints in Wadsworth's exhibition at the Adelphi Gallery in 1919, accompanied by a note written by his fellow Vorticist, Frederick Etchells; this is reprinted below in its entirety. He never published the woodcuts in editions, but simply printed a few impressions as the need arose. They exist, therefore, in tiny numbers, with the exception of a selection of fourteen of the later subjects (1918–21) which were printed at the Morland Press and published by Herbert Furst in an edition of 30 as a bound volume, no. 4 in his series of *Modern Woodcutters*. The blocks themselves, according to a reminiscence of his daughter (B. Wadsworth, p.150), were burnt by Wadsworth in 1926 in the garden of his London house at 74 Addison Road, from which he was preparing to move. The British Museum owns twenty of the woodcuts.

1919 Wadsworth Adelphi Catalogue

Exhibition of Original Woodcuts and Drawings by Edward Wadsworth
March 1919
The Adelphi Gallery
9 Duke Street, Adelphi, London WC2

Woodcuts

1. Mytholmroyd	1 guinea	
2. View of a town	1	,,
3. Harbour of Flushing	1	,,
4. Façade	1	,,
5. Yorkshire Village	2	,,
6. The Port	10s.6d	
7. Rotterdam	10s.6d	
8. Street Singers	1 guinea	
9. Greek Village with Windmills	3	,,
10. Scene for a Fairy Tale	1	,,
11. Riponeli (village in Lemnos)	3	,,
12. The top of the Town	2	,,
13. Interior	3	,,
14. Episode	2	,,

15. Brown Drama	3	,,
16. Kt × B	1	,,
17. Invention	3	,,
18. Disruption	2	,,
19. Landscape	2	,,
20. Railway Embankment	10s.6d	
21. Liverpool shipping 1918	2 guineas	
(Woodcut based on the picture painted for the Canadian War Memorial)		
22. The S.S. 'Jerseymoor'	1 guinea	
23. Drydocked for scaling and painting	2	,,
24. Turret ship in drydock	1	,,
25. Dazzled ship in drydock	1	,,
26. Tugs	10s.6d	
27. Dock Scene	1 guinea	
28. Minesweepers in Port	10s.6d.	
29. The Open Window	1 guinea	
30. Hebden Bridge	10s.6d	
31. Illustration	1 guinea	

'. . . the iron walls of the engine room. Painted white, they rose high into the dusk of the skylight, sloping like a roof: and the whole resembled the interior of a monument, divided by floors of iron grating, with lights flickering in the middle, within the columnar stir of machinery . . .'
'Typhoon' – Joseph Conrad

A note

This exhibition consists of three groups of prints. The first group nos. 1–8, are cuts produced before the war; the second, nos. 9–19, were done while serving with the Navy in the Aegean; and the third, nos. 21–28 are a series carried out whilst the artist was engaged in supervising the camouflaging of ships at Liverpool.

A peculiar interest, I think, is attached to the way in which the artist has allowed his somewhat varied milieux to react upon his invention.

The first series includes several woodcuts derived from North of England landscape and the elementary architecture of Yorkshire industrial villages. Print no. 2 shows an interesting simplification of planes and the closely knitted composition of roofs and chimney stacks seems to me a complete abstract of a modern industrial town; whilst the pyramid of box forms in no. 5 conveys convincingly the bleakness and solidity of a northern hill village. Both these cuts are two-block prints and, in spite of the economy of the means employed, the effect is peculiar in depth and body.

In the Aegean group a great technical advance is shown. In these highly complicated prints the artist has achieved a richness and a fluidity in the use of his medium which gives this series a character wholly personal: they stand, indeed, as a quite new development whilst the varied use of forms, ranging from the brush-script delicacy of no. 10 and the curiously interesting 'scatter' of the shapes in no. 14 to the more rigid and architectural quality of no. 11 (here taken a great deal further than in the earlier examples) shows a new outlook as regards the possibilities of the medium.

The third series is frankly more representational. The camouflaged ship was one of the bright spots of the war and it is not too much to say that it would probably never have developed as it did had it not been for the experiments in abstract design made by a few modern artists during the years immediately prior to 1914. Mr Wadsworth has, with immense vigour, seized upon its possibilities as the central motive in these exuberant presentations of dock life under war conditions. The velvet solemnity of no. 23, which shows a fat and towering hull in a dry dock is achieved with the utmost economy of the use of white on black, the characteristic which differentiates the woodcut from all other methods of engraving. The lace-like girder and 'dazzle' forms of no. 25 and the Korinesque treatment of the barrels in the foreground of no. 27 are extremely happy.

The woodcut is a thing to handle and look at closely.

It does not demand wall space but yet can have the seriousness and dignity of a large painting in an accessible form.

Its intrinsic qualities of surface and texture can be achieved in no other way.

This much neglected medium is again beginning to receive the attention it deserves: it is a good thing.

FREDERICK ETCHELLS

Bibliography

Barbara von Bethmann-Hollweg, the artist's daughter, has published, under her maiden name, a biography of her father, *Edward Wadsworth, a Painter's Life*, Salisbury 1989, which quotes from hitherto unpublished correspondence and includes a checklist of his work at the back. Richard Cork has written most extensively on Wadsworth's woodcuts, which he discusses at some length in the Hayward Gallery exhibition catalogue *Vorticism and its Allies*, Arts Council, 1974; *Vorticism and Abstract Art in the First Machine Age*, London 1976, vol. II, pp. 350–76 and pp. 514–25; 'Edward Wadsworth's Vorticist Woodcuts', *The Print Collectors' Newsletter* XVI, no. 2 (1985), pp. 41–4; and 'Wadsworth and the Woodcut' in *A Genius of Industrial England, Edward Wadsworth 1889–1949*, Bradford 1990. Mark Glazebrook produced an initial attempt at a catalogue raisonné of the prints in *Edward Wadsworth, Paintings, Drawings and Prints*, published to coincide with an exhibition of Wadsworth's work at Colnaghi's in 1974. More prints have now been added to this list, some dates have been altered or confirmed and titles reattributed in the light of material owned by the artist's family. The most recent exhibition of Wadsworth was the retrospective held at Cartwright Hall, Bradford, in 1989–90 and later in 1990 at the Camden Arts Centre, London. This was accompanied by the book of essays which contains Cork's article on 'Wadsworth and the Woodcut'.

The W/C and W/D numbers in the entries refer to Barbara Wadsworth's checklist. The letter after her numbers refers to individual impressions that she notes.

2

1 The Open Window, *c.*1914

Woodcut printed in blue, brown and black on buff coloured paper. 161 × 109 mm

Adelphi Gallery 29; Hayward 290–95; Colnaghi 102; W/D 5f

1980–1–26–87

See colour illustration

There are more surviving impressions of this print than of any other Vorticist woodcut by Wadsworth except cat. no. 7, and there are at least six colour variants. None is dated, but the print has been ascribed to 1914 on stylistic grounds. Moreover, in the 1919 Adelphi catalogue it does not come among the first group described as having been produced before the war, but at the end of the list with two other prints known to have been executed in 1914–15. Richard Cork convincingly relates Wadsworth's treatment of the subject to a composition like Robert Delaunay's painting *Window on the City No. 4* (1910–11), which Wadsworth probably knew in reproduction (*Vorticism and Abstract Art in the First Machine Age*, pp. 355–6).

2 Illustration (Typhoon), 1914/15

Woodcut printed in black on Japan paper. Signed and inscribed by the artist with a quotation from Joseph Conrad's short story *Typhoon* (1st ed. 1902). 280 × 255 mm

Adelphi Gallery 31; Colnaghi 115 (reproduction printed upside down); W/D 18b

1924–2–9–143. Presented by the Contemporary Art Society

Two other examples of this woodcut are dated 1914 and 1915, according to Barbara Wadsworth's list and Richard Cork's Hayward exhibition entry (315), while a third is recorded by Barbara Wadsworth as being printed on orange paper. The British Museum's impression is the only one to bear the quotation, which was printed in the 1919 Adelphi catalogue. Gaudier-Brzeska referred to *Typhoon* in a letter of 1 February 1915 written to Wadsworth from the trenches in Northern France: 'I forgot to tell you that I have never read "Typhoon" so that if you can let me have the book I shall be very glad. It will be interesting to see the woodcut – I have no great faith in illustrations but of course one must see the result first of all.' In the event, Gaudier was well pleased with the composition, which he acknowledged in the middle of February as being 'very representative' of Wadsworth's style and a welcome sight 'after 14 days of nothing but muddy holes' (B. Wadsworth, p. 328).

The subject is taken from Conrad's description of the engine-room of the *Nan Shan*, a steamship plying the China Seas, at the height of a typhoon. The author's vivid account was ideal as the inspiration for a Vorticist composition, the very subject of the story suggesting a whirling vortex. It prompted one of the most striking images not just of Wadsworth's career but of the entire Vorticist movement. and one which can be placed alongside Wyndham Lewis's powerful cover for the second issue of *Blast*, *Before Antwerp*.

3

Wadsworth retained a life-long fascination with the pictorial qualities of naval engineering structures and mechanical details. As late as 1944, in a lecture he gave to the Institution of Civil Engineers on 'The Aesthetic Aspects of Civil Engineering', he described the engine-room hatch in the *Queen Mary* as the most satisfying feature of the ship: 'a purely engineering job consisting of a vertical tunnel from the uppermost deck to the engine-room, white, with black accents of the companion ladders and galleries' (B. Wadsworth, p. 328).

3 Street Singers, 1914

Woodcut printed in grey and black. 144 × 110 mm (image)

Adelphi Gallery 8; Colnaghi 107; W/D 10b

1983–10–1–23

This is the only woodcut before 1920 with a figurative title. The title is inscribed on the verso of another impression of this image.

4 Brown Drama, *c.*1914–15

Woodcut printed in grey, black and mustard. 125 × 69 mm (image)

Adelphi Gallery 15; Hayward 310; W/D 21b

1983-10-1-24

Barbara Wadsworth records four colour variants of this subject, which on stylistic grounds would seem to pre-date Wadsworth's war service in the Aegean.

Brown Drama and five of the woodcuts from the Aegean period were used as illustrations for Ezra Pound's refutation of 'The Death of Vorticism' in *The Little Review*, New York, February–March 1919, pp.45–51.

5 Top of the Town, 1916–17

Woodcut printed in black and grey. 70 × 72 mm (image)

Adelphi Gallery 12; Colnaghi 119 (miscatalogued as 'Kt × B'); Hayward 326; W/D 22b

1983-10-1-25

Cat. nos 5–9 were all drawn when Wadsworth was an intelligence officer at Mudros, and cut and printed after his return to England. In 1917 Wadsworth began a correspondence from Mudros with John Quinn, the New York lawyer and collector who was one of the most important patrons of the Vorticist artists. Referring to the Vorticist exhibition at the Penguin Club, New York, in 1917, Quinn expressed admiration for Wadsworth's woodcuts. Wadsworth in his reply remarked,

You seem to like the woodcuts best. To a certain extent I agree with you: I think they are probably the best in that they are the most complete – that is to say, the means of expression is in a more complete accordance with the thing expressed in there than some of the other things which are perhaps more experimental and less mature. Since I have been out here I have had time to work at some designs in further woodcuts which I hope to cut and print when I return to England. The woodcut, I must say, appeals to me more than any of the other similar mediums (etchings, lithographs, mezzotints, etc.): it leaves nothing at all to accident (B. Wadsworth, p.73).

6 Scene for a Fairy Tale, *c.*1916

Woodcut printed in black. 72 × 61 mm

Adelphi Gallery 10; Colnaghi 126 (as 'Untitled Abstract'); W/D 29b

1983-10-1-26

A second impression of this image in a private collection is inscribed 'Scene from a Fairy Tale/Edward Wadsworth 1916'. The 'brush-script delicacy' which Etchells saw in this composition (see above) was particularly indebted to Kandinsky's woodcut style.

4

5

6

8

7

9

7 Riponelli – A Village in Lemnos, 1917

Woodcut printed in dark grey, light grey and black on cream paper. Signed, dated and inscribed with title in pencil.
101 × 75 mm (image)
Adelphi Gallery 11; Colnaghi 124; W/D 27
1924-2-9-145. Presented by the Contemporary Art Society

Seven colour variants of *Riponelli* on grey, buff and off-white papers belonging to the Anthony d'Offay Gallery were exhibited in the 1989 retrospective. The structure of the image is reminiscent of an earlier woodcut, *Yorkshire Village* (1914), which Richard Cork has compared with the Horta de San Juan landscapes by Picasso or Derain's view of *Cadaqués* (1910). Wadsworth himself clearly perceived the similarity between Picasso's work and the hill villages of Yorkshire, for in a letter of July 1915 to Wyndham Lewis he described Hebden Bridge as 'a most inspiring place – like an early Picasso drawing come true' (B. Wadsworth, p.68).

The vibrant orange and purple used for one of the variants recall Lewis's comments in a letter to Ezra Pound of August 1916: 'I have received a letter from my naval colleague at Mudros, who is surrounded by warships and volcanoes he tells me. Such propinquity, and the seclusion of this island office should in the end produce a furtive woodcut or two, painted in "romantic reds"' (*The Letters of Wyndham Lewis*, ed. W.K.Rose, London 1963, p.84).

The Victoria and Albert Museum's impression of this image is inscribed 'Mudros', which is not the title but, as in the following print, simply signifies where Wadsworth executed his design.

8 Interior, 1917

Woodcut printed in dark grey, light grey and black. Signed in pencil 'Edward Wadsworth Mudros 1917'. 107 × 74 mm (image), 147 × 133 mm (sheet)
Adelphi Gallery 13?; Colnaghi 123; W/D 25
1924-2-9-146. Presented by the Contemporary Art Society

The Victoria and Albert Museum's impression of this print is inscribed 'Lemnos 1917' and 'Interior'.

9 Invention, 1917

Woodcut printed in dark grey, light grey and black. Signed and dated in pencil, and inscribed 'Invention'. 105 × 81 mm (image)
Adelphi Gallery 17; Colnaghi 120; W/D 23b
1924-2-9-147. Presented by the Contemporary Art Society

Another impression of the same subject is dated 1918.

10 Liverpool Shipping, 1918

Woodcut printed in black on Japan paper. Signed, dated and inscribed with title in pencil. 259 × 201 mm (image)
Adelphi Gallery 21; Colnaghi 128; W/D 31
1924-2-9-140. Presented by the Contemporary Art Society

Liverpool Shipping is closely related to, but not based upon, the large painting for the Canadian War Memorials Fund entitled *Dazzle-Ships in Drydock at Liverpool*, which Wadsworth only began early in 1919 after his demobilisation. An enlarged and simplified version of *Liverpool Shipping* was adapted lithographically in 1936 for a London Transport poster advertising the Imperial War Museum.

A marine artist, Norman Wilkinson, was responsible for the invention of dazzle camouflage during the course of 1917; it was officially adopted by the Admiralty in October of that year. Its intention was not to render shipping invisible to the enemy but, as Wilkinson explained in a lecture in 1919, 'to produce an effect (by paint) in such a way that all accepted forms of a ship are broken up by masses of strongly contrasted colour, consequently making it a matter of difficulty for a submarine to decide on the exact course of the vessel to be attacked' (*Camouflage*, Scottish Arts Council exhibition catalogue, 1988; we are indebted to this catalogue for all the information given here on dazzle camouflage). The Dazzle Section consisted of five lieutenants to design the schemes, three modellers to prepare the miniature vessels used for testing, and eleven girls with art school training who painted the ship profiles and plans in a classroom at the Royal Academy in Burlington House. Ten further lieutenants were assigned to act as Dock Officers in the various ports, where they were responsible for supervising the application to the ships of the designs approved in London. Wadsworth served as one of these, starting in Bristol in the spring of 1918 and moving to Liverpool by July of that year. He kept a photographic record of the camouflaged ships which must have assisted him with the woodcuts, comprising eight different subjects printed almost entirely in black on white paper. The only known exceptions are an impression of *Minesweepers in Port* printed on grey paper, and the impression of *Ships beside Warehouses* exhibited at Colnaghi (no.134), printed in blue and black on white paper. The ships themselves were largely painted in a combination of shades of black, white, blue and green.

The aesthetic qualities of dazzle painting captured the imagination of the American poet Amy Lowell (see her poem 'Camouflaged Troop-Ship Boston Harbor' in *The Dial* LXV (16 November 1918), p.403) and a number of artists including Horace Brodzky, as well as the attention of the press. A caption in the *Illustrated London News* of 4 January 1919 described the camouflage as 'suggestive of Futurism and Cubism', while the *Evening Standard* report on the *Camouflage* exhibition held at the Royal Academy in 1919 remarked that: 'the "dazzle" section illustrates amusingly an inversion of some of the principles of Post-Impressionism – how to destroy form instead of emphasising it – and the woodcuts of ships by Mr Edward Wadsworth are by far the best things artistically in the exhibition' (see B. Wadsworth, p.99). Wadsworth's exhibits at the Royal Academy were *Turret Ship in Drydock*, *'S.S. Jerseymoor'*, *Drydocked for Scaling and Painting* and *Liverpool Shipping*.

10

11

11 Dazzled Ship in Drydock, 1918

Woodcut printed in black on Japan paper. Signed, dated and inscribed with title in pencil. 127 × 211 mm (image)

Adelphi Gallery 25; Colnaghi 131; W/D 34a

1924–2–9–142. Presented by the Contemporary Art Society

This particular subject was reprinted as plate 4 in Herbert Furst's *Modern Woodcutters*, no. 4, 1921.

12 Turret Ship in Drydock, 1918

Woodcut printed in black on Japan paper. Signed in pencil 'Edward Wadsworth Liverpool 1918' and inscribed 'Turret Ship in Drydock'. 204 × 137 mm (image)

Adelphi Gallery 24; W/D 38b

1924–2–9–144. Presented by the Contemporary Art Society

This subject does not appear in the Colnaghi catalogue although Mark Glazebrook subsequently included an impression of it in his Catalogue 5, *Modern British Artists*, London 1983.

13 Drydocked for Scaling and Painting, 1918

Woodcut printed in black on Japan paper. Signed, dated and inscribed with title in pencil. 224 × 208 mm (image)

Adelphi Gallery 23; Colnaghi 129; W/D 32

1949–4–11–1023. Bequeathed by Campbell Dodgson

Drydocked for Scaling and Painting was adapted by commercial lithographers in Switzerland for the poster and catalogue cover (printed in blue and black) of an exhibition of British prints at the Kunstsalon Wolfsberg in Zurich in 1923. The exhibition was organised by the Board of Trade and the British Museum and included a short intro-

12

duction by Campbell Dodgson. All the prints were for sale, including three woodcuts by Wadsworth listed as 'Camouflaged ship in drydock for repairing', presumably the present subject, 'Interior' and 'Romantic Village'. A copy of the catalogue and the poster are in the British Museum's collection.

14 Ladle Slag, Old Hill 1, 1919–20

Lithograph printed in black on Japan paper. Signed in the stone and below in pencil. 369 × 500 mm (image)

Colnaghi 147; W/C 4

1949-4-11-2139. Bequeathed by Campbell Dodgson

The Black Country subjects interpreted through drawings, watercolours, woodcuts and lithographs form the largest distinct group within Wadsworth's work as a whole. While travelling between Liverpool and London in 1918, he was sufficiently arrested by the scenery around Birmingham, Wolverhampton, Dudley and Leeds to return on foot in the first half of 1919 in order to sketch his impressions; these were then developed into the highly finished compositions shown at the Leicester Galleries in 1920. The exhibition met with enormous acclaim, one critic describing the studies of Ladle Slag as attaining the level of sublimity to be found in 'the ruins of Karnac at night, the Mountains of the Moon . . .' (B. Wadsworth, p.91), while the *Observer*'s critic P. G. Konody wrote rather more penetratingly about how Wadsworth brought from Vorticism into representational art 'a severe sense of form and rhythm, a logic of organisation, that are not found in the work of artists depending entirely on visual impression. These qualities enable him to distil art of the highest order out of material that to the ordinary painter would be not only unpromising but positively forbidding' (*Edward Wadsworth, The Black Country*, Ovid Press, London 1920, and B. Wadsworth, p.91).

Wadsworth executed two lithographs, *Ladle Slag, Old*

13

14

15

Hill 1 and 2, both purporting to exist in editions of 40, which are closely related to the drawings exhibited in 1920, together with a third subject, *Industrial Landscape* (Sycamore Collection catalogue, Bolton Museum and Art Gallery, 1988, no. 213). The British Museum's print is connected with the watercolour illustrated as plate IX in the selection printed by the Ovid Press in 1920, following the success of the exhibition. The drawing was purchased at the exhibition by Sir Michael Sadler, Vice-Chancellor of Leeds University, and is now in the university's collection. The Victoria and Albert Museum owns two impressions of this image, one printed on cream paper, the other on Japan and dated 1920 and numbered 14/40. One further lithograph belongs with this group, although it is not of a Black Country subject: *Quarry: Cornwall* emerged from a summer holiday Wadsworth took in Newlyn in 1920, returning to London on foot. The Victoria and Albert Museum owns an impression presented by the artist.

15 Blast Furnaces II (Netherton Furnaces), 1919

Woodcut printed in black on a paper hand-coloured orange in the background in watercolour. Signed, dated and inscribed with title in pencil. 138 × 181 mm

Colnaghi 136; W/D 41a

1924-2-9-148. Presented by the Contemporary Art Society

Five Black Country woodcuts are recorded in Barbara Wadsworth's checklist, three of which were reprinted for *Modern Woodcutters* in 1921. This particular image was exhibited at the Leicester Galleries in 1920, and appears above Arnold Bennett's note introducing the Ovid Press publication of Wadsworth's Black Country drawings in 1920 and as plate 6 in *Modern Woodcutters*. An impression of one of the other subjects, *Black Country* (Colnaghi 135), was also printed over an orange background, this time on a coated paper, and there are two further impressions on pink and buff coloured papers. These woodcuts excited particular praise. Herbert Furst in *The Modern Woodcut* (1924) cited them as an example of 'emotional abstraction; the landscape is seen not so much as what it looks like but as what it feels like' (p.174), while Wyndham Lewis also singled them out in his obituary of Wadsworth (reprinted in *Wyndham Lewis on Art*, ed. W.Michel and C.J.Fox, London 1969, p.422).

16

16 Crouching Nude, 1920

Lithograph printed in black. Signed and dated in ink; numbered in pencil 6/20. 402 × 504 mm (sheet)

Colnaghi 150; W/C 8a

1922–8–7–26. Presented by the Contemporary Art Society

Only one other print of this period bears any resemblance to this work, and that is another lithograph, *Vorticist Figure*, by the Leeds artist Jacob Kramer (1892–1962), who was a friend of the Vorticists in London and brother-in-law to William Roberts. Both compositions are strongly indebted to the draughtsmanship of Wyndham Lewis, who executed a series of female nude studies in black chalk in 1919–20. Four of these were reproduced in Lewis's portfolio *Fifteen Drawings*, published by the Ovid Press in 1919, of which *Nude II*, in black chalk and watercolour (Manchester City Art Galleries), is the closest to Wadsworth's figure.

David Bomberg

1890–1957

Born in Birmingham, the fifth child of a Polish immigrant leather-worker. In 1895 the family moved to White-chapel, where Bomberg lived until 1913. In about 1906–7 he was apprenticed to a German immigrant lithographer, Paul Fischer, at Islington. At the same time he was attending Walter Bayes's evening classes for the City and Guilds Institute and drawing in the Victoria and Albert Museum, where he was befriended by the American painter John Singer Sargent. In 1905 he broke his indentures with Fischer in order to become a full-time artist. He enrolled in evening courses on book production and lithography at the Central School of Arts and Crafts and in drawing classes by Sickert at the Westminster School; from 1911 to 1913 he studied at the Slade School of Art. He began to exhibit his work in 1913, culminating with six works in the 'Cubist Room' of the *Camden Town Group and Others* exhibition at Brighton in December of that year. Earlier in 1913 a visit to Paris with Jacob Epstein to choose work for a twentieth-century exhibition at the Whitechapel Art Gallery had brought him into contact with the leading members of the Parisian avant-garde.

By 1914 Bomberg had emerged as an artistic personality of great force, intent upon devising his own interpretation of European Cubo-Futurism. Despite his radical approach, he declined to contribute to *Blast* or to join the Rebel Art Centre, although he joined with Wyndham Lewis and the others in dissociating himself from Marinetti and Nevinson's Futurist manifesto in 1914. His first one-man show was held at the Chenil Gallery, Chelsea, in 1915, to great acclaim from the critic and philosopher T. E. Hulme. In November 1915 Bomberg enlisted in the army, and the following June was sent on active service to France, where he remained until November 1918, latterly working on his commission for the

Canadian War Memorials Fund. The commission for *Sappers at Work: A Canadian Tunnelling Company* marked a watershed in Bomberg's development because he was forced to adopt a more representational idiom. By 1919 he was committed once more to a figurative style and he accordingly rejected an invitation to join the De Stijl group in Holland because he felt its purely formal approach 'could only lead again to the Blank Page'.

His career after the First World War was one of great personal struggle, during which he worked abroad for extended periods in Palestine, Spain and Cyprus. Nevertheless, he developed a boldly expressionistic style of landscape painting and portraiture which has had a considerable influence on a generation of British artists who encountered him and his work during the late forties and fifties.

Bibliography

Richard Cork has been Bomberg's principal proponent since the mid-seventies and his publications are an indispensable guide to all aspects of Bomberg's work. The most significant of these are *Vorticism and Abstract Art in the First Machine Age*, London 1976, vol.I, pp.185–213, vol.II, pp.390–403; *David Bomberg*, New Haven and London 1987 (with a full bibliography); and *David Bomberg*, the catalogue for the exhibition shown in 1988 at the Tate Gallery and Yale.

17 Russian Ballet, 1919

Booklet of eight sheets, containing lithographically printed text and six illustrations in four or five colours, each one signed in the plate with the artist's initials

The text facing the six images is as follows:

Methodic discord startles . . . .
Insistent snatchings drag fancy from/ space,
Fluttering white hands beat-/ compel. Reason concedes.
Impressions crowding collide/ with movement round us –
– the curtain falls – the/ created illusion escapes.
The mind clamped fast/ captures only a fragment, for/
    new illusion.

The plates measure 103 × 98mm; 79 × 53mm; 59 × 118mm; 75 × 159mm; 50 × 67mm; 78 × 68mm respectively

1980–1–26–88 (complete booklet)

Bomberg's first wife, Alice Mayes, has described in an unpublished memoir of 1972 the context in which the *Russian Ballet* lithographs were executed ('The Young Bomberg 1914–22', Tate Gallery Archives; cf. Richard Cork's account in *David Bomberg*, 1987, pp.122–6). The prints were conceived by Bomberg as a distraction from his anxiety about the final verdict of the Canadian War Memorials Committee on his second version of *Sappers at Work*:

But David set himself a task to fill in the waiting time – he did not feel like doing any actual drawings – in the meantime. So he turned out some old sketches which he decided to lithograph, for he had learned the method when serving his

apprenticeship with Paul Fischer. He procured the necessary materials including zinc plates and he got very interested in the work, and in the end he made a small booklet, with appropriate wording, which he called 'Russian Ballet', though it had nothing to do with 'Russian Ballet', except for its strange designs, which were cubist designs. He printed, or rather lithographed, fifty of these booklets, and I helped to cut the covers and sew them on, and then we started a mad escapade, David and I and another artist, which was to go into the stalls of the Alhambra and to offer these booklets for sale!

We had sold five or six of them when Diagilev spotted us and chased us back into the ninepenny gallery, where we belonged, and the money was refunded to those who had bought the booklet, and an attendant explained that it was a mistake. But it was great fun while it lasted, and gave me my one chance of speaking with Diagilev face to face. We put the booklets at Henderson's Bookshop in Charing Cross Road, and sold about ten, then after a lunchtime conversation with Jacob Mendelssohn, Lillian's first husband, Mendelssohn offered to take the whole lot off his hands on a sale or return basis.

The 'old sketches' to which Alice Mayes refers belonged to the period 1913–14; it is possible to chart the progression of the lithographed compositions from a group of these sketches now in the British Museum collection (1988–4–9–221 to 249), to studies more closely connected with the finished prints and a number of trial proofs which have appeared on the market in recent years.

The connection Bomberg ultimately made between the earlier drawings and the Russian Ballet was fortuitous, as Alice Mayes indicates in her account. His interest in this subject was not aroused until 1919 when he attended a performance of *La Boutique Fantasque* starring Lydia Lopokova and Léonide Massine, with sets designed by Derain. He had undoubtedly explored the theme of a dancer in a number of his most important drawings and gouaches of 1913–14, but some of the studies for these finished compositions also show a rather casual association between subject and design: one sheet in the British Museum variously titles related sketches 'Horse and Rider' and 'Mother and Child'. The embryonic *Russian Ballet* designs, however, are rather different from this group. The drawings associated with plate 2 in the booklet, for example, display a formal concern with the tension created by the compression of a tiny figure within a lozenge-shaped compartment at the bottom of the image, while the composition of plate 3 is related to Bomberg's studies for one of his most famous paintings, *The Mud Bath* of 1914 (Tate Gallery). The architectonic structure of all the plates firmly establishes their genesis within the period when Bomberg proclaimed 'I appeal to a Sense of Form . . . I completely abandon Naturalism and Tradition. I am searching for a intenser expression' (from his introduction to his Chenil Gallery exhibition, 1914).

The deep purple used for plate 2 does appear in the early studies, but the striking combination of purple, orange and yellow in which several of the lithographs were

fluttering white hands beat ——
compel.   Reason concedes.

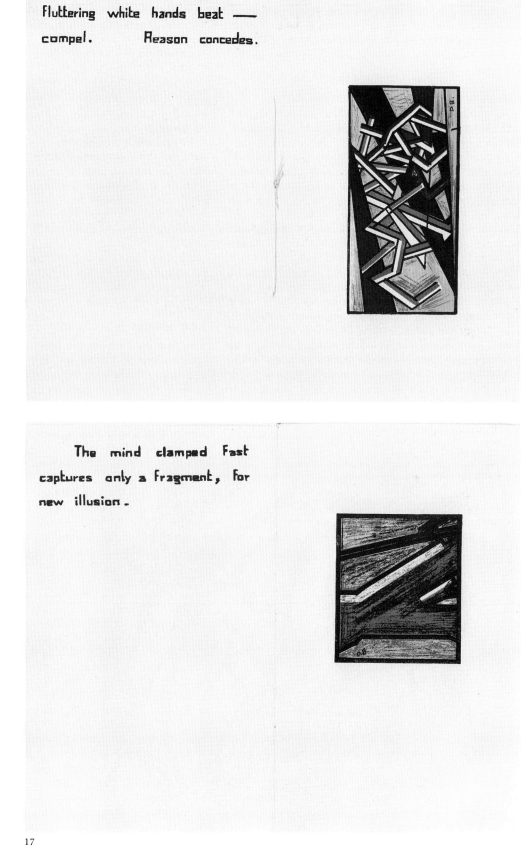

The mind clamped fast
captures only a fragment, for
new illusion.

17

printed may well have been suggested to Bomberg by the costumes and set designs of the Ballets Russes. The entire project, therefore, both prints and text, came to fruition like an Imagist poem, as the result of a chance confluence of ideas.

Henri Gaudier-Brzeska

1891–1915

Born Henri Gaudier near Orléans, the son of a carpenter. He won scholarships to study English and commerce in London in 1906, then at Bristol and Cardiff in 1908–9, followed by a brief period in Nuremberg and Munich. His early artistic interests took the form of architectural, animal and plant studies strongly influenced by Ruskin's precepts. In Paris, where he spent the whole of 1910, his career underwent a dramatic change in direction; he formulated his ambition to be a sculptor, declaring that he was 'finished with Ruskin and the English ... and Christian philosophy' (quoted from H.S.Ede, *Savage Messiah*, p.19) and turned instead to an eclectic array of sources which was to range from classical antiquity to primitive and Oriental art; furthermore, he embarked upon a peculiarly symbiotic relationship with a Polish woman twenty years his senior called Sophie Brzeska, whose surname he henceforth appended to his own.

His development as a sculptor, however, took place in London, where he and Sophie Brzeska settled at the begin-ning of 1911. Despite his considerable poverty and lack of connections, he eventually succeeded in attracting a number of influential mentors, most notably Jacob Epstein and Ezra Pound. By the middle of 1914 he had come to be regarded by Pound and Wyndham Lewis as one of the quintessential exponents of Vorticism, and contributed his own 'manifesto' entitled 'Vortex' to the first issue of *Blast*. Shortly after the outbreak of war, Gaudier joined the French army and was killed in action at Neuville-St-Vaast on 5 June 1915.

Notwithstanding his public role as an uncompromising apologist for Vorticism, Gaudier's cultural eclecticism defied any narrow, prescriptive formulae of expression. In both his sculpture and his drawings he proved a gifted synthesist of the main elements of contemporary modern-ism, rightly including himself among a family of 'moderns' which encompassed Epstein, Brancusi, Archipenko and Modigliani (*Blast* no.1 (June 1914), p.158). Despite his prodigious output as a draughtsman, his attempts at printmaking were limited to the linocut catalogued below and a small number of etchings.

Bibliography

The first book to appear was Ezra Pound's memoir, *Gaudier-Brzeska*, London and New York 1916. H.S.Ede, who began in the late twenties to form one of the finest collections of Gaudier's work, much of which is now dis-played at Kettles Yard in Cambridge, published *A Life of Gaudier-Brzeska*, London 1930, followed by a second edi-tion entitled *Savage Messiah*, London 1931, based on the

18

artist's letters and Sophie Brzeska's diary; this has often been reprinted. Horace Brodzky published his biography in London in 1933. More recent general evaluations of Gaudier's work are to be found in Richard Cork's *Vorticism and Abstract Art in the First Machine Age*, London 1976, vol.I, pp.165–84, and vol.II, pp.428–53; Roger Cole, *Burning to Speak, The Life and Art of Henri Gaudier-Brzeska*, Oxford 1978; and the catalogue for the exhibition at Kettles Yard Gallery, Cambridge, *Henri Gaudier-Brzeska, Sculptor 1891–1915*, 1983.

18 Wrestlers, *c*.1914

Linocut printed in black on off-white paper. Annotated in pen below the image, 'Brodzky imp. 8/50. Wrestlers linocut print cut by Henri Gaudier-Brzeska'. 225 × 279mm

1935–2–26–1. Presented by Horace Brodzky

Brodzky described this and other attempts at printmaking by Gaudier in his book of 1933:

Brzeska saw me at work, cutting designs at my home, and he decided to do some also. Being near Christmas time he cut a version of his 'Wrestlers' to be used as a card. It is reproduced here and is his only effort at cutting. It was printed on my etching-press. At the same time he often brought me his etched plates for printing. The subjects included heads, cats, and a skull. The plates were etched on both sides for economy, and after I had pulled proofs for him he would deface the plate and etch other designs, the same plate being used several times. He also made a dry-point portrait of myself on the spur of the moment. It was done on the back of a discarded plate, which accounts for the many scrapes and corrosion shown in the plate . . . Only two prints were pulled, each of us retaining one (pp.44–5).

An impression of the drypoint, dedicated to Brodzky, was presented to the British Museum by A. W. Brickell in 1935.

The original lino block and a proof impression from it were presented to the Victoria and Albert Museum by Brodzky in 1934. It seems most unlikely that an edition of 50 was ever completed, but in any case the impressions numbered by Brodzky must have been printed posthumously. The sculptural exercise of cutting the lino block presumably appealed to Gaudier, who based his design on a plaster relief of 1914 of the same subject (Museum of Fine Arts, Boston; one of the nine casts of this relief is in the collection of the Tate Gallery). Gaudier-Brzeska's interest in the subject of wrestlers seems to have arisen early in 1913 when he made numerous drawings from life at the London Wrestling Club off Fleet Street.

The print was included in the *First Exhibition of British Linocuts* at the Redfern Gallery in 1929 as one of the more expensive items, at 3 guineas.

Horace Brodzky
1885–1969

Born in Melbourne; his father Maurice, a journalist, left Australia with his family in 1902 after a libel case, taking them first to San Francisco, then New York and finally to London in 1908. Brodzky had begun his artistic studies in Melbourne, and later enrolled at the National Academy of Design in New York and the City and Guilds Art School in Kennington. His first important contact in London was with Sickert in 1908. By the end of 1912 he had held a one-man show of his paintings at his Chelsea studio, become the art director of a weekly journal, *Modern Society*, and made the acquaintance of the sculptor Henri Gaudier-Brzeska. Gaudier, for the brief period of their friendship until his death in 1915, was to be the most influential figure in Brodzky's career; Brodzky was the subject of one of Gaudier's most striking portrait busts of 1913 and the author of a biography of the sculptor, published in 1933. In 1914 Brodzky was included in the Jewish section, chosen by David Bomberg, of the Whitechapel Art Gallery exhibition *Twentieth Century Art, a Review of Modern Movements*. In 1915 he returned to New York, where he remained until 1923, working chiefly as a graphic artist and journalist as well as acting as Clerk of Works to the Vorticist exhibition at the Penguin Club in 1917. From 1923 onwards he settled in London again, where his career flagged until his biography of Gaudier revived his interest in outline drawing. After the Second World War Brodzky published a biography of Jules Pascin, whom he had first met in New York in 1915, and a book on Gaudier-Brzeska's drawings, becoming the art editor of the *Antique and Collector's Guide* in 1948.

Brodzky has been credited as the first serious artist in Britain to produce linocuts, a medium originally popularised for the instruction of children by Franz Cizek in Vienna at the beginning of the century. Brodzky, however, in his book on Gaudier, described his initiation in 1912 in the art of linocutting as a purely accidental occurrence: 'When Frank Harris moved into his King Street offices he had the rooms covered with an unpatterned lino, the scraps of which I soon discovered could be used as a substitute for woodblocks' (Horace Brodzky, *Henri Gaudier-Brzeska*, London 1933, p. 44). He introduced Gaudier to linocutting (see cat. no. 18) after the latter had first encountered Brodzky's work in the form of a woodcut self-portrait printed on the cover of the *Art Chronicle* in 1912. His own linocuts were all executed between 1912 and 1919. Two subjects were included in the *First Exhibition of British Linocuts* at the Redfern Gallery in 1929, the only occasion on which any of them were exhibited until the very end of his life. Apart from the linocuts, he produced a few woodcuts in 1912 and 1921, a group of approximately twenty-four etchings between 1912 and 1930 and a number of posters, magazine covers and book jackets in his capacity as a graphic designer. Some of the linocuts and etchings were reprinted in 1967, with a further edition of fifteen of the linocuts appearing in 1989.

Bibliography

The first book devoted to Brodzky's work was James Laver's *Forty Drawings by Horace Brodzky*, London 1935. Otherwise the only significant publications have been very recent: a biography of the artist by Henry Lew, Melbourne 1987, and the brief catalogue for an exhibition at the Boundary Gallery, London, in October 1989, with an introduction by Frances Spalding and a checklist of works.

19 The Bather, 1914

Linocut. Signed in the block with the artist's monogram.
220 × 204 mm
1924–1–8–5. Presented by the artist

This is the first of a portfolio of nineteen linocuts by Brodzky published by Egmont Arens in New York in 1920. The British Museum's copy is no. 17 from a special edition of 100, printed on Strathmore Alexandra Deckle Edge paper and signed by the artist. A further 200 copies on Royal Antique paper were issued unsigned and numbered from 101 to 300. The majority of the subjects in the portfolio date from 1919, with five exceptions, all dated 1914, prior to Brodzky's return to New York. The list of contents and dates is as follows:

The Bather, 1914	*Tree*, 1914
The Wash Basin, 1919	*Longshoremen*, 1919
Suburban House, 1914	*The Arts Ball*, 1919
Festa, 1919	*Making Up*, 1919
The Expulsion, 1914	*Boxers*, 1919
Dancer, 1919	*Two Figures*, 1919
Portrait, 1919	*Railway Station*, 1919

19

Decoration, 1919	*Bryant Park*, 1919
Builders, 1919	*Dazzle Ships*, 1919
Stonehenge, 1914	

Virtually all the original lino blocks for these prints have survived in the possession of the artist's son, John. Three of the subjects were reprinted during the artist's lifetime, in 1967, while a further ten including *The Bather* were reprinted at the White Gum Press in 1989 in an edition of 25 by the Australian artist Katie Clemson, author with Rosemary Simmons of *The Complete Manual of Relief Printing*, London 1988. These lino blocks are to be presented to the Victoria and Albert Museum.

The earlier subjects of 1914 are distinguished by their dramatic use of the uninked portions of the block to establish the main points of emphasis in the composition. The stark contrast between the black and white areas creates an effect of dissolving forms which is reminiscent of the slightly later wood-engravings by Robert Gibbings, printed between 1918 and 1920.

Edward McKnight Kauffer

1890–1954

Born Edward Kauffer in Montana, USA, he first trained as a scene painter in Evansville, Ohio, and then in 1910 moved to San Francisco to work with a bookseller and art dealer. In 1912 he adopted the middle name of McKnight in deference to the benefactor who encouraged him to pursue his artistic studies in Paris, where he arrived in the autumn of 1913. He moved to England after the outbreak of war in 1914 and within ten years had succeeded in establishing an unassailable reputation as the foremost graphic designer of the post-war era. His first major commission came in 1915 from Frank Pick, the Publicity Manager of the London Undergound Electric Railways, and for the next twenty-five years Kauffer was to be the Underground's chief poster artist. He continued to exhibit as a painter until 1921, acting as secretary to the London Group and participating in the ephemeral Group X, a secessionist body of avant-garde artists including Wyndham Lewis, Edward Wadsworth and William Roberts, which exhibited only once, at the Mansard Gallery in Heal's furniture store in 1920. In 1923 he embarked upon a life-long relationship with Marion Dorn, another American designer who was to achieve particular renown in England.

Kauffer's first retrospective was held in 1925 at the Arts League of Service in Gower Street, the second at the Lund Humphries gallery in Bedford Square in 1935, and a third in 1937 at the Museum of Modern Art in New York. During the thirties his career continued unabated with clients including Shell, the Empire Marketing Board and Lund Humphries, until 1940 when he and Dorn returned permanently to the United States.

McKnight Kauffer was a brilliant assimilator of the successive styles of early twentieth-century modernism: 'By using the methods of the more advanced schools and by putting these before the men in the street in such a way as to catch them off their guard, so that they are lured into liking the poster before they realise that it is just the kind of thing which they loathe in the exhibition gallery . . . he has familiarized a very wide public with the conventions of modern painting . . .' (Anthony Blunt in *The Spectator*, 5 April 1935, quoted by Haworth-Booth). Frank Rutter, in his reminiscences *Art in my Time*, published in 1933, also paid tribute to Kauffer's role as a mediator between modernism and the general public: 'Kauffer has accomplished the miracle of introducing Cubism into the railway-stations and hoardings of England. It is a modified Cubism, without doubt, its ferocity tempered to the shorn culture of the prospective advertiser. But Kauffer has put it over all right . . .' (p.194).

Kauffer's output as an original printmaker was confined to a handful of woodcuts executed in 1916–18, from which further impressions were made in 1922. The British Museum owns three of these woodcuts, all presented by Campbell Dodgson in 1939: *Trees and Houses* (1916), *Rooftops* (1916), *Flight* (1917). A fourth woodcut was *Sunflowers* of 1917. One further image (*Study*, 1918) was included in the Omega Workshops' collection of woodcuts (cat. no. 21).

Bibliography

The indispensable account of this artist's work is by Mark Haworth-Booth, *E. McKnight Kauffer, a Designer and his Public*, London 1979. The same author organised a travelling exhibition of Kauffer's posters of 1915–40 for the Circulation Department of the Victoria and Albert Museum in 1973. A memorial exhibition of the artist's complete work was held at the same museum in 1955. McKnight Kauffer himself wrote on the subject of poster design on several occasions, most notably in his book *The Art of the Poster*, London 1924.

20 Flight, 1917

Woodcut, printed in black on white paper. Signed and dated in pencil. 140 × 230 mm

1939–2–28–3. Presented by Campbell Dodgson

Of all McKnight Kauffer's woodcuts, *Flight* is the one most clearly indebted to Vorticism, which he had certainly encountered after his arrival in London in the autumn of 1915. It remained a 'leitmotif' throughout his career and is unquestionably one of the most successful designs of the twentieth century. The genesis of the composition lay in Kauffer's intense study of the flight pattern of birds during the summer of 1916 when he was staying near Didcot in Berkshire: 'The design *Flight* was not invented in a studio. It came after much observation of birds in flight. The problem seemed to me at any rate a translation into design terms of three factors, namely bird identification, movement and formalization into pattern and line' (quoted by Haworth-Booth, p.23). The subject related both to the interests of the Italian Futurists and to Japanese prints of the nineteenth century, which Kauffer greatly admired. Bevis Hillier first made the formal comparison between *Flight* and a woodcut by Suiseki of 1820 in his *Art Deco of the 20s and 30s*, London 1968, pp.32–3.

Kauffer also produced another version of the design, published in January 1917. It was printed in reverse for advertising purposes with the serrated edges removed

20

from the wings; this achieved its apotheosis in the brilliant poster 'Soaring to Success', commissioned for the launch of the Labour newspaper, the *Daily Herald*, on 31 March 1919. It subsequently appeared on the cover of Ernst Gombrich's *Art and Illusion*, published by Phaidon in 1960.

The Omega Workshops

1913–1920

The Omega Workshops were set up in March 1913 at 33 Fitzroy Square, London W1, by the influential critic and painter Roger Fry, with the express intention of fostering 'almost all kinds of decorative design, more particularly those in which the artist can engage without specialised training in craftsmanship ... actuated by the same idea of substituting wherever possible the directly expressive quality of the artist's handling for the deadness of mechanical reproduction' (Omega prospectus, September 1913).

The dominant figures throughout Omega's existence were Fry himself, Vanessa Bell and Duncan Grant; however, participation in the workshops extended to an eclectic range of artists, fluctuating in accordance with shifts in artistic alliances: Wyndham Lewis staged an explosive departure in October 1913. The production of the workshops, where exhibitions were also held, included textiles, costumes, firescreens, furniture, mural decoration and pottery, with printmaking introduced as an incidental activity in conjunction with book illustration and decoration for cards, menus or stationery. The woodcut was a natural choice of printed medium in view of Omega's founding principles. After taking advice from the Central School of Arts and Crafts and with the assistance of a commercial printer, Richard Madley, Omega issued its first publication in 1915, *Simpson's Choice*, a poem by Arthur Clutton-Brock illustrated with three full-page woodcuts by the Norwegian-born artist Roald Kristian. Two further publications were issued in 1915 and 1917, containing woodcuts by Kristian and Roger Fry: *Men of Europe*, a poem by Pierre-Jean Jouve, translated by Fry, and *Lucretius on Death*, translated by Robert Trevelyan. The series culminated in 1918 with *Original Woodcuts by Various Artists*, catalogued below.

Omega's experiments with woodcut illustrations were emulated by Leonard and Virginia Woolf at the Hogarth Press which they founded in 1917, initially carrying out all the printing themselves. Between 1917 and 1921 they commissioned woodcuts from Dora Carrington, Vanessa Bell and Roger Fry, whose *Twelve Original Woodcuts*, published in 1921, went into a second and third impression in 1922.

Bibliography

The history of the Omega scheme is amply covered by Judith Collins in *The Omega Workshops*, London 1983, and two well-illustrated exhibition catalogues containing full chronologies: *The Omega Workshops 1913–19: Decorative Arts of Bloomsbury*, Crafts Council, 1984, with an essay by Fiona MacCarthy, and *The Omega Workshops: Alliance and Enmity in English Art 1911–1920*, Anthony d'Offay, London 1984.

21 Original Woodcuts by Various Artists, 1918

Volume of twenty-eight pages covered in pink marbled paper, with a woodcut title-page and fourteen individual woodcuts printed in black on the recto of twelve sheets of cream wove paper. Printed for the Omega Workshops Ltd by Richard Madley, London. No. 41 of an edition of 75

1949–4–11–5100 (1–14). Bequeathed by Campbell Dodgson

The contents of the volume are as follows, in order:

Roger Fry (1866–1934): *Still Life*, 180 × 108 mm

Mark Gertler (drawing, cut by Roger Fry): *Harlequinade*, 137 × 140 mm

Vanessa Bell (1879–1961): *Dahlias*, 154 × 109 mm

Duncan Grant (1885–1978): *The Hat Shop*, 185 × 109 mm

Roger Fry: *The Cup*, 154 × 109 mm

Simon Bussy (1870–1954): *Black Cat*, 242 × 127 mm

Roger Fry: *The Stocking*, 184 × 109 mm

Roald Kristian (b.1893; date of death unknown): *Animals*, 71 × 113 and 95 × 147 mm

Vanessa Bell: *Nude*, 185 × 109 mm

Edward Wolfe (1897–1982): *Ballet*, 110 × 185 mm

Duncan Grant: *The Tub*, 110 × 185 mm

Edward McKnight Kauffer: *Study*, 127 × 112 mm

Edward Wolfe: *Group*, 103 × 76 mm

Original Woodcuts by Various Artists was the last communal venture undertaken at the Omega Workshops, which thereafter moved towards voluntary liquidation due to the lack of outside commissions and guaranteed financial support. Of the principal contributors, Fry had had an intermittent interest in woodcuts since 1911 when he encountered Eric Gill, while Vanessa Bell and Duncan Grant were very recent novices who never acquired more than a modicum of skill. Grant recalled: 'We learned to do it ourselves. I think Roger may have helped us at first. I found it very easy, but Nessa had difficulties at first. She kept gouging holes in herself' (quoted by Judith Collins, p.163). Vanessa Bell was indeed far from satisfied with the two blocks she submitted to Fry for the volume: 'I hope you won't think my second block awful ... I daresay it's too incoherent ... However I now send you a print, very bad ones, of each block, so that you can see for yourself' (Collins, p.163). Her woodcut *Nude*, based on a much larger painting of 1917, *The Tub*, was, in the

Duncan Grant: *The Hat Shop*

Vanessa Bell: *Nude*

21

event, particularly admired by Fry, together with Duncan Grant's *The Hat Shop*. Grant's elegant and humorous composition was a reference to his own excursions into hat designs, some of which were made up and sold from the dressmaking department of the Omega Workshops.

Fry, Grant and Bell were deeply indebted to the work of Matisse and Derain in their woodcuts as well as in their painting. But a completely different accent was introduced into the graphic art of the Omega Workshops by Roald Kristian. He had been born Edgar de Bergen in Norway, and appeared in London at the end of 1914 as the husband of the painter Nina Hamnett, whom he had met in Paris. Kristian had a serious interest in woodcutting, reflecting the influence of Kandinsky and the Blaue Reiter artists, as well as the graphic style associated with the Munich magazine *Simplicissimus* in the pre-war period. His woodcuts were exhibited at the Omega Workshops in June 1915, then published as described above in the first two Omega books in the same year, also appearing in *Form* magazine in 1916 and 1917 respectively. By 1918 Kristian had been deported from Britain as an enemy

alien, so the two woodcuts chosen by Fry in 1918 must have come from material he had left behind.

The hallmark of the Omega Workshop products was their amateurism and a preoccupation with surface decoration, usually without regard to basic design. This elicited the fiercest of condemnations from Wyndham Lewis, who referred to 'the curtain and pincushion factory in Fitzroy Square' (*Wyndham Lewis on Art*, ed. W. Michel and C. J. Fox, London 1969, p.66). Not all aspects of the Omega activities benefited from such an approach, yet it did produce a small number of remarkably fresh and lively woodcut compositions which avoided the preciosity of conventional fine book production of the period.

2 The First World War and the 1920s

The Senefelder Club for the Advancement of Artistic Lithography, founded in 1908, had held the first of its annual exhibitions in 1910 at the Goupil Gallery. These continued until October 1913; there was then a break until the fifth exhibition finally opened in November 1915 at a new home in the Leicester Galleries. The motivating force of the club was the American Joseph Pennell, but the solid base of expertise was provided by the Englishmen F.E. Jackson and A.S. Hartrick. It seems to have been Jackson who persuaded the Ministry of Information that lithography provided the perfect medium for recording Britain's *Efforts and Ideals* during the First World War. The *Efforts* came in nine portfolios of six prints by nine artists; the *Ideals* in twelve prints by as many artists – a total of sixty-six prints in all, which were exhibited at the Fine Art Society in July 1917.

This was by far the most ambitious print publication project in either world war, but produced results of only moderate quality. Vastly better were the lithographs that Nevinson and Nash produced as private initiatives. Both showed them at their exhibitions at the Leicester Galleries between 1916 and 1918, and it may well have been that gallery's connection with the Senefelder Club that deflected Nevinson from drypoint, his originally preferred medium, towards lithography, or that led Nash to it in the first place. After the war, the Senefelder Club continued to hold exhibitions, moving in 1923 to the Twenty-One Gallery, but both Nevinson and Nash had already dropped the medium. A few other post-war lithographs by Wadsworth have been included in this exhibition, but it was not until the 1930s that lithography was again used in an interesting way.

The medium that Paul Nash used for his numerous prints in the 1920s was wood-engraving. This medium had an extraordinary vogue at this period, most of the production being intended for the illustration of books and therefore falling outside the scope of this exhibition. Nash did, however, make a number of interesting independent blocks, which have been included here, in which he experimented with abstraction and a variety of decorative effects. But by 1927 he was bidding farewell to such prints, announcing that he was now more interested in woodcut patterns than woodcut pictures. Nevertheless, it was he who a few years later encouraged Edward Burra to make his remarkable experiments in wood-engraving. Another outsider in this area of printmaking was Charles Ginner, whose few wood-engravings handled in a woodcut manner were made irregularly over a long period between 1917 and 1931.

This section concludes with a few examples of intaglio printing. William Roberts seems to have made no prints during his Vorticist period. However, there is a group of six small prints, clearly made at the same time but at an uncertain date, apparently in the mid-1920s; why they were made is still unclear. Quite different in style and a few years later in date are the copper-plate line-engravings made by Edward Bawden. These emerge from contemporary French work, but remained very little known until recent years. They have a sort of precursor in Edward Wadsworth's hand-coloured plates for *Sailing Ships and Barges of the Western Mediterranean*, published in 1926.

Christopher Richard Wynne Nevinson

1889–1946

Born in London; his father was a well-known journalist and war correspondent, his mother a Poor Law campaigner and suffragette. He began studying as an artist at the age of 18, first at St John's Wood School of Art, then at the Slade. In 1912–13 he went to Paris, where he saw the work of the French avant-garde and met many of the leading Italian Futurists. He became the leading figure in English Futurism, and issued with Marinetti the 'Vital English Art' manifesto in June 1914. This set him apart from the Vorticists around Wyndham Lewis.

At the outbreak of war, Nevinson served as a Red Cross ambulance driver, first in Flanders and then attached to the French army. He was invalided out in January 1916 with rheumatic fever. In September that year he held his first solo exhibition of war pictures at the Leicester Galleries, which included a number of drypoints. The success of this led to his appointment as an official war artist and to the commission for the set of *Building Aircraft* for the series of *Britain's Efforts*. He was sent to the Cambrai region in July 1917 (where he flew for the first time); back in England at the end of the year, he worked up his ideas for a second exhibition, held in March 1918.

After the war, he returned to London and to French subject-matter. In 1919 and again in 1920 he visited New York. Through the 1920s, as a well-known press celebrity, he continued to produce a large number of prints, mostly drypoints, but his style grew increasingly conventional. He stated in the preface to the catalogue of an exhibition at the Leicester Galleries in 1919: 'I wish to be thoroughly disassociated from every "new" or "advanced" movement.'

22

Most of Nevinson's prints repeat, in the same direction but with minor changes, the compositions of his paintings. With the exception of two wooducts, all his early prints are drypoints or lithographs. He took up etching for the first time in 1922, but still used drypoint for preference. His first publisher was the Leicester Galleries, but from the early 1920s his work was mainly published by the Lefèvre Gallery, which sometimes worked in collaboration with the Leicester Galleries.

Bibliography

Nevinson's own autobiography, *Paint and Prejudice*, published in 1937 (here quoted from the 1938 American edition), has been aptly characterised as 'endless entertaining talk at a dinner party'. It is very amusing and revealing of his character, but too imprecise to be a reliable guide for the historian. The years until the end of the First World War are covered in Richard Cork, *Vorticism and Abstract Art in the First Machine Age*, London 1976, vol.1, pp.214–38, but no proper study has been made of his later career and no complete catalogue compiled of his prints. The most useful source at present is the catalogue by Elizabeth Knowles of the retrospective exhibition held at Kettles Yard, Cambridge (and elsewhere) in 1988–9. References are given to the illustrated list of prints of the period 1916–20 contained in *Nash and Nevinson in War and Peace*, published by the Leicester Gal-

leries in London in 1977. Another listing of 105 prints is given in Appendix 4 to Kenneth M. Guichard, *British Etchers 1850–1940*, London 1977.

22 A Dawn, 1914, 1916

Drypoint. Signed in pencil. 201 × 150mm
Leicester Galleries 17
1918–2–19–5. Presented by the artist

This must be one of Nevinson's first drypoints, and was shown as no. 33 in the September 1916 exhibition at the Leicester Galleries with the title '1914'. The painting on which it was based was in the same exhibition, as no.46, with the title 'A dawn, 1914'. The 1916 exhibition contained no lithographs; these first appeared at the seventh exhibition of the Senefelder Club at the Leicester Galleries in January 1917, where they were stated to come from an edition of 25 and were priced at $2\frac{1}{2}$ guineas.

In March 1918 Nevinson opened his second exhibition of war paintings at the Leicester Galleries. A few weeks before, a selection of fifteen – all painted between September and November 1917 – was reproduced in the series *British Artists at the Front*, no. 1, published by Country Life, London 1918, with an appreciative introduction by Campbell Dodgson. In his text Dodgson remarked:

I may add that it is his habit since 1916 to repeat some of his compositions in the form of drypoints, which should engage the serious attention of collectors, for he is the pioneer of a new movement in English graphic art. In lithography also, which he first attempted in 1912, he produced in December 1916 some remarkable prints, one of which, *Dawn at Southwark*, must rank among the best of recent lithographs. Some of these war pictures are to be repeated shortly, either on copper or on stone.

Dodgson, who was Keeper of Prints and Drawings at the British Museum, attended the farewell dinner, with Sickert in the chair, held in the Café Royal in 1919 before Nevinson's departure for New York. Before the war, Nevinson and Mark Gertler had studied together in the British Museum Print Room: 'It is impossible to convey the pleasures and enthusiasms we took in the Print Room of the British Museum, in South Kensington, and in the National Gallery' (*Paint and Prejudice*, p.37). It must have been as a result of these links that on 19 February 1918 Nevinson presented to the British Museum no less than twenty-five of his new prints on war subjects: thirteen drypoints, ten lithographs and two woodcuts.

23 Inside Brigade Headquarters, 1917

Drypoint, on simili-Japan paper. Signed and dated in pencil.
354 × 254mm
Leicester Galleries 13
1918–2–19–12. Presented by the artist

The paintings on which most of cat. nos 23–8 were based were made between September and November 1917. The drypoints and lithographs would have been made shortly afterwards, in time for the exhibition in March 1918 in which cat. nos 24–8 were all included. (This drypoint for some reason was omitted, at least from the published catalogue.) The dates given here are taken from the Departmental register of acquisitions, and must be based on information supplied by Nevinson himself.

The painting is reproduced in colour as plate 4 in the *British Artists at the Front* booklet, accompanied by a text probably supplied by Nevinson:

A typical advanced headquarters in a well-built dug-out. Except in cases of special good fortune, work must be done by candle-light, the air is not exhilarating, and you must be careful not to bump your head against the ceiling. A deep dug-out of this kind gives almost perfect shelter, though the sound of any shell bursting near it is curiously loud.

23

24 Survivors at Arras, 1917

Drypoint, on late 18th-century paper. Signed and dated in pencil. 351 × 247 mm

Leicester Galleries 15

1918–2–19–11. Presented by the artist

This print is based on a painting shown as no. 52 in the 1918 exhibition and reproduced as plate 12 of the *British Artists at the Front* booklet. The text reads:

Up to the end of 1916 there were two houses in Arras which had not been hurt by enemy shell or bomb fire. One of them is known to have been Robespierre's birthplace. The other is reputed to have been already the oldest house in the city. If its immunity continues, its seniority will be still more incontestable, for the rest of Arras after the war will have to be built again.

25 'That Cursèd Wood', 1918

Drypoint, on late 18th-century paper. Signed and dated in pencil. 250 × 347 mm

Leicester Galleries 8

1918–2–19–10. Presented by the artist

This was no. 55 in the 1918 Leicester Galleries exhibition. The title is a reference to a poem by Siegfried Sassoon, 'At Carnoy', dated 3 July 1916 and first published in the collection *The Old Huntsman* in 1917. This described the peace of a brigade mustered the evening before an attack, and ends:

Crouched among thistle-tufts I've watched the glow
Of a blurred orange sunset flare and fade;
And I'm content. Tomorrow we must go
To take some cursèd Wood . . . O world God made!

This print was later chosen for reproduction in E.S. Lumsden, *The Art of Etching*, first published in 1924. The text included Nevinson's notes on his technique:

My drypoints are invariably traced on to the surface of a smoked liquid ground: cut through with a ruby point and then the ground cleaned off. After that the ordinary working

24

25

of drypoint: a well-polished plate and a dirty finger of oil and charcoal to study the lines ... I never work on the spot. I can't compose out of doors (p.358).

To this can be added a sentence from his introduction to the 1918 catalogue:

I relied chiefly on memory, a method I learnt as a student in Paris and for which I am ever grateful: nature is far too confusing and anarchic to be merely copied on the spot.

26 The Road from Arras to Bapaume, 1918

Lithograph. Signed and dated in pencil. 472 × 385 mm
Leicester Galleries 37
1918–2–19–22. Presented by the artist

The painting on which this lithograph is based (now in the Imperial War Museum) was reproduced as plate 9 in the *British Artists at the Front* booklet, with this text:

The regular Picardy landscape – straight white road traversing gently rolling chalky cornlands – now waste – like a moon-path over a slowly heaving sea. The trees which once lined the road were sawn through by the Germans when they retreated in the early months of 1917.

Nevinson first learned lithography in 1912: 'While in London I studied lithography under Ernest Jackson at the LCC schools in Southampton Row. Of all the men I have met who deal with the teaching of art, he is the finest and most erudite: a technician and an artist' (*Paint and Prejudice*, p.73). In mid-1917 Jackson had proofed and printed Nevinson's set of lithographs entitled *Building Aircraft*, commissioned by the Ministry of Information as part of the series *The Great War: Britain's Efforts and Ideals* (not in this exhibition).

All Nevinson's lithographs were made on stone, not zinc or transfer paper. 'I got back [to London in 1918] to find that a bomb had fallen on the printing works where my lithographs were kept and my stones were damaged. The reason for the extra ridge on my lithograph of the Arras-Bapaume Road is because I had to put it in to cover the injury done to my original stone' (*Paint and Prejudice*, p.152). This was the second problem that he had had with this composition. Earlier the censor had instructed him to change the flow of traffic from the left to the right side of the road in his painting (M. and S. Harries, *The War Artists*, London 1983, p.44).

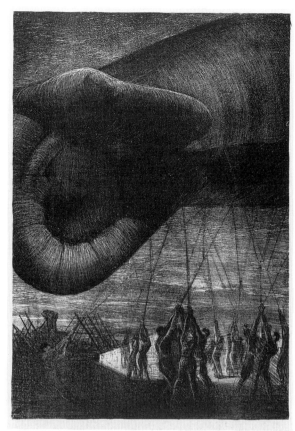

26

27

28

27 Hauling down an Observation Balloon at Night, 1918

Lithograph. Signed and dated in pencil. 515 × 362 mm
Leicester Galleries 32
1918-2-19-25. Presented by the artist

This lithograph, no. 37 in the 1918 Leicester Galleries exhibition, was based on a sketch made in France. Nevinson's hilarious account of being used for target practice by a German plane while suspended under a balloon is in *Paint and Prejudice*, pp. 136-8.

28 Hans and Fritz, 1918

Lithograph. Signed and dated in pencil. 470 × 345 mm
Leicester Galleries 38
1918-2-19-24. Presented by the artist

This remarkable lithograph of German prisoners, which invites comparison with Otto Dix, was shown as no. 40 in the 1918 exhibition. Nevinson painted a similar picture of British soldiers, which ran into trouble with the censor. His furious response has survived: 'I will not paint castrated Lancelots, though I know this is how Tommies are usually represented in illustrated papers etc. – high-souled eunuchs looking mild-eyed, unable to melt butter on their tongues and mentally and physically incapable of killing a German. I refuse to insult the British Army with such sentimental bilge' (quoted by M. and S. Harries, *The War Artists*, London 1983, p.45).

29 Limehouse, 1918

Mezzotint. Signed in pencil. 225 × 150 mm
Leicester Galleries 77
1949-4-11-357. Bequeathed by Campbell Dodgson

Nevinson made three mezzotints of British subjects in 1918 and two of American subjects a year or two later. The three British plates were evidently made at the same time, but it is unclear what led him to take up what was at the time virtually an obsolete medium. The results are probably the finest British mezzotints of this century.

This print is usually wrongly called 'Southwark'. Neither in the 1919 Leicester Galleries exhibition, in which four mezzotints were included, nor in any other exhibition of the 1920s was any mezzotint called 'Southwark'. Moreover, if this were 'Southwark', no impression of the frequently exhibited 'Limehouse' has survived. In an exhibition held at the Manchester City Art Gallery in 1920, this and the following print were priced at 3 guineas each.

29

30

30 From an Office Window, 1918

Mezzotint. Signed in pencil. 253 × 175 mm
Leicester Galleries 76
1980–1–26–97

This print is based on a painting dated 1917 which was purchased by Osbert Sitwell. Sitwell wrote an essay on Nevinson in a small monograph published in 1925 by Benn in the series *Contemporary British Artists*, where the painting is reproduced as plate 8. The accompanying text gives an appreciation of the painting:

The vista through the open window is very three-dimensional, and through the various shafts that are sunk like wells between the high brown buildings, of which only the top windows, flat roofs, and gables are visible to us, float up the unmistakable voices of London ... The angles and curves of pale blue smoke, those cylindrical chimney-pots that turn in the wind with the sound of a ghost in chains and clanking armour, the black shadows and grey lights, the telegraph wires forever intersecting the line of vision and delicately framing in new vistas, even the rather worn tassel of the blind, all proclaim the name of their native city (pp.29–30).

31 Wet Evening, Oxford Street, 1919

Lithograph. Signed and dated in pencil. Edition of 25.
742 × 485 mm
Leicester Galleries 57
1919–4–26–3. Presented by the artist

The painting from which this print was made was no. 35 in the 1920 Manchester exhibition. The lithograph itself was first exhibited in the ninth exhibition of the Senefelder Club, at the Leicester Galleries in January 1919. This was before Nevinson went to New York for the first time, and proves that the title 'Broadway in the Rain' found written on an impression in the Victoria and Albert Museum is inaccurate. The great size of this print – almost that of a poster – sets it apart from the rest of Nevinson's lithographs.

31

32

32 Le Port, 1919

Lithograph. Signed and dated in pencil. Edition of 25.
507 × 388 mm
Leicester Galleries 62
1919–4–26–2. Presented by the artist

Presumably the result of a visit made to France in late
1918 or 1919, before Nevinson's departure for America.
There is very little information about the edition sizes of
Nevinson's prints. He never numbered them, and very few
contemporary exhibition catalogues give any documen-
tation. One of the few that does is that of the Bourgeois
Gallery in New York (1920), from which the information
given here is taken.

33 The Workers, 1919

Lithograph. Signed and dated in pencil. Edition of 50.
515 × 353 mm
Leicester Galleries 59
1980–7–26–31

It is unclear whether the setting for this lithograph is
American or British, but in either case it was certainly
made in Britain after Nevinson's return. It was shown at
the Leicester Galleries in October 1919 (no.50) under the
title given above. In recent literature it has also been called
'Strike Demonstration' and 'Revolution', but there is no
contemporary reference to any such title.

34 Looking down into Wall Street, 1919

Lithograph. Signed in pencil. 487 × 348 mm
Leicester Galleries 55
1980–5–10–22

The sharp viewpoint down between the skyscrapers into
the streets of New York is found in a number of contemporary American works of art. Nevinson later
implausibly claimed that all these were derived from him:
'Since then dozens of painters have copied my technique
in the rendering of modern buildings' (*Paint and Prejudice*,
p.202).

The painting corresponding to this composition and
this lithograph were both shown at the Leicester Galleries
in October 1919 (nos 22 and 51). They are both almost
exactly the same size, but there is a significant difference
in that the smoke in the print, particularly in the right
foreground, is less dense than in the painting (reproduced
in *C. R. W. Nevinson and the Great War*, Maclean Gallery,
London 1980).

35 Looking through Brooklyn Bridge, New York, c.1921

Drypoint. Signed in pencil. 235 × 175 mm
Leicester Galleries 41
1924–2–9–28. Presented by the Contemporary Art Society

The view is through the suspension bridge towards the
skyscrapers of lower Manhattan. The painting of this
composition is dated 1920 in Osbert Sitwell's 1925
monograph (see cat. no. 30 above), where it is plate 23,
and was purchased by Sinclair Lewis. Nevinson later
made a portrait of Lewis, and in *Paint and Prejudice*,
pp.236–8, can be found his reminiscences of Lewis's giant
ego. According to Malcolm Salaman's monograph on
Nevinson in the *Modern Masters of Etching* series (no. 31,
The Studio, London 1932), this is one of a set of ten
drypoints of New York subjects commissioned by the great
New York print dealer and publisher Frederick Keppel,
who gave Nevinson his first New York show in 1919. The
composition and history of this set remain, however,
obscure.

33

34

35

36

36 From a Paris Window, 1922

Drypoint. Signed in pencil. 202 × 152mm

1928-3-10-10. Presented by the Contemporary Art Society

The corresponding painting was reproduced in an article which appeared in the *Sketch* in 1921; the drypoint is dated 1922 in Osbert Sitwell's monograph (pl.34). In the April 1923 issue of *Print Collector's Quarterly*, the Leicester Galleries (who published this print) illustrated it in a full-page advertisement as having been purchased by the Contemporary Art Society. Its price then was 3 guineas.

The years after 1922 mark a turning-point in Nevinson's career, which he identified in his autobiography as 'the beginning of a search for a way out of the aesthetic cul-de-sac which modern art had led me into' (*Paint and Prejudice*, p.208).

Paul Nash

1889–1946

Born in London; his father was a barrister, his mother came from a naval family. At the age of 17 he left school and began to train as an artist, latterly at the Slade School. He began to exhibit before the First World War; this early work was pre-Raphaelite and Symbolist in manner. At the outbreak of war, he enlisted in the army, and after two years of home service was posted as a second-lieutenant to the Ypres salient in February 1917. He returned injured by an accident in June. A successful exhibition in London in July led to his appointment as an official war artist. He returned to Flanders in November, just after the last phase of the battle of Passchendaele. The sketches made during this month were worked up and shown in May 1918 in a second exhibition at the Leicester Galleries.

After the war, Nash's health collapsed, and was to remain poor for the rest of his life. He and his wife settled in a number of places, moving on every few years. During the twenties he took up wood-engraving, but in the thirties, with the exception of a few lithographs, he abandoned printmaking in favour of painting in oils and watercolour in the remarkably individual version of Surrealism that he developed. It is difficult to overestimate his importance to British art at this period. His remarkably wide interests, ranging through all aspects of the fine and many of the applied arts, and his great helpfulness to other artists, made him the central figure in the artistic life of the time.

Bibliography

The standard monograph is by Andrew Causey, *Paul Nash*, Oxford 1980, which includes a catalogue of his paintings, watercolours and drawings. The prints have been catalogued by Alexander Postan in *The Complete Graphic Work of Paul Nash*, London 1973. Nash's auto-

37

biography, *Outline*, left unfinished at his death, was published in 1949 by Faber. A biography by Anthony Bertram, *Paul Nash, The Portrait of an Artist*, was published in 1955, also by Faber.

37 Marching at Night, 1918

Lithograph on brown paper. Signed and dated in pencil. Edition of 25. 515 × 420mm

Postan 2

1918–7–4–3. Presented by the artist

During the first months of 1917 Nash had been a fighting soldier, albeit in a quiet sector of the Front, and so the works shown in the 1917 exhibition at the Goupil Gallery were mostly of quiet scenes behind the lines. The experience of the aftermath of Passchendaele and the opportunity to draw in the front lines made a vast difference to Nash's approach, and this became apparent in the exhibition held in May 1918 at the Leicester Galleries.

Before 1918 Nash had made no prints whatever. The 1918 exhibition, however, contained, along with two paintings and forty-seven drawings, seven lithographs – which were in fact all the prints of First World War subjects that he was ever to make. Although Nash's autobiography breaks off before the First World War, notes for its continuation survive. Among these for the year 1917 is: 'I begin to paint in oils, and to draw on stone. Nevinson helps me with lithography' (*Outline*, p.217). One of the earliest of these lithographs must be *Mine Crater, Hill 60*,

which was shown at the eighth exhibition of the Senefelder Club in February 1918, where it was priced at 2½ guineas. The influence of Nevinson is particularly obvious in the present print, which in its bold handling of chalk and scraper is the finest of the group. This bravura suggests that much of the composition was made directly on the stone. This is supported by the observation that the other lithographs all seem to repeat the composition of watercolours or drawings.

38 Rain, Lake Zillebeke, 1918

Lithograph. Signed and dated in pencil, with the title added in pencil in the lower margin. Numbered 'No. 7/25' at the top right. 255 × 362mm

Postan 7

1918–7–4–4. Presented by the artist

This was included in the 1918 exhibition as no. 47, and is based on no. 37, a chalk drawing titled *Nightfall, Zillebeke District* (Causey no. 200, now in the Imperial War Museum). Like the other six chalk lithographs in the 1918 exhibition, it was published in an edition of 25. In July 1918 Nash presented an impression of all the prints to the British Museum, here following the example of Nevinson.

39 Void of War, 1918

Lithograph on brown paper. Signed and dated in pencil, and numbered 5/12 at the bottom left (and again at the top right, but crossed out). 371 × 444mm

Postan 1

1918–7–4–8. Presented by the artist

This lithograph stands apart from the other six First World War subjects by Nash; they are all chalk, while this is drawn in lithographic wash. Indeed, it is often wrongly taken for a woodcut. The explanation is given by the catalogue (no. 8) which lists it as 'design for poster for exhibition'. (A copy of the actual poster is reproduced in the 1977 Leicester Galleries catalogue *Nash and Nevinson in War and Peace*.) The title of the exhibition was 'Void of War', and the composition of the poster echoes that of the two paintings *Void* and *We are Making a New World* (Causey 226, 227) that were included in it.

Nash's written account of the scenes of Passchendaele was almost as dramatic as his artistic response, and is worth quoting despite its fame:

I have just returned, last night, from a visit to Brigade Headquarters up the line, and I shall not forget it as long as I live. I have seen the most frightful nightmare of a country more conceived by Dante or Poe rather than by nature, unspeakable, utterly indescribable. In the fifteen drawings I have made I may give you some idea of its horror . . . but no pen or drawing can convey this country . . . Sunset and sunrise are blasphemous, they are mockeries to man, only the black rain out of the bruised and swollen clouds all through the bitter black of night is fit atmosphere in such a land. The

39

38

40

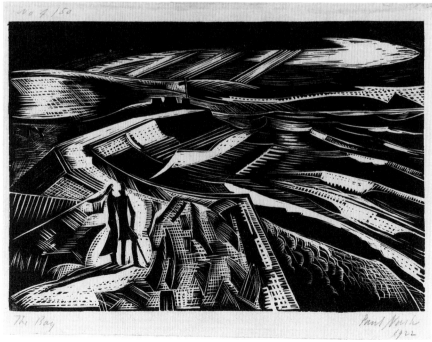

41

42

rain drives on, the stinking mud becomes more evilly yellow, the shell-holes fill up with green-white water, the roads and tracks are covered in inches of slime, the black dying trees ooze and sweat and the shells never cease. They alone plunge overhead tearing away the rotting tree stumps, breaking the plank roads, striking down horses and mules, annihilating, maiming, maddening they plunge into the grave which is this land; one huge grave and cast up on it the poor dead. It is unspeakable, godless, hopeless. I am no longer an artist interested and curious, I am a messenger who will bring back word from the men who are fighting to those who want the war to go on for ever. Feeble, inarticulate, will be my message, but it will have a bitter truth, and may it burn their lousy souls (from a letter to his wife of 13 November 1917, *Outline*, pp.210–11).

40 The Sluice, 1920

Lithograph. The stamp of the Paul Nash Trust appears in the bottom left corner. Edition of 30. 358 × 411 mm

Postan 8

1980–1–26–98

After the war, Nash spent much time in Dymchurch on the Kent coast. Here he was inspired by the long wall built beside the sea to stop Romney Marsh flooding. This is one of a group of three lithographs on this subject; all were made in 1920 and none seems to correspond with a painting or watercolour. The round structure behind the wall is one of the Martello towers built at the beginning of the nineteenth century to prevent a Napoleonic invasion.

41 The Bay, 1922

Wood-engraving. Signed, dated and titled in pencil. Numbered 'No 4/50' at the top left. 120 × 177 mm

Postan 27

1926–3–13–78. Presented by the Contemporary Art Society

The notes for the continuation of Nash's autobiography state that he only took up wood-engraving after the war, and the earliest engravings seem to date from 1919. Most were commissioned as illustrations for books, which brought in badly needed income during the 1920s. These remain some of Nash's best-known prints. There are, however, a small number of independent single-sheet prints, from which the selection here has been made.

42 Dyke by the Road, 1923

Wood-engraving. Signed, dated and titled in pencil. Edition of 50. 123 × 178 mm

Postan 25

1926–3–13–79. Presented by the Contemporary Art Society

Like the previous print, this shows a view of the sea wall at Dymchurch in Kent. The wall served as a metaphor for Nash's own experience in the war: it was the duck-board giving safe passage, while the immensity of the sea and sky reduced humans to puny insignificance.

The dates given by Postan for this and the previous print can be corrected by the autograph dates written on these impressions.

43 Abstract No.1, 1924

Wood-engraving. Edition of 15. 102 × 51 mm

Postan 56

(a) Signed, dated, titled and inscribed 'Proof 2nd block' in pencil

(b) Not signed or annotated. Printed on a decorative paper with a flower pattern

1970–9–19–47 and 48

These two impressions are printed from the same block, but on different papers. Nash seems to have been dissatisfied with the effect of the block, and so tried to vary it by using patterned papers to print on. Similar experiments are found on a number of other wood-engravings of this period. Nash's interest in pattern papers had been stimulated by his friendship with Claude Lovat Fraser in the few years before the latter's death in 1921. It was Fraser who had introduced him to the collection of eighteenth-century end-papers in the Victoria and Albert Museum. Nash was himself later to design a number of pattern papers, four of which are bound into the 1928 Curwen Press *Specimen Book of Pattern Papers*, to which Nash contributed an introduction. He later wrote an essay on the subject (see cat. no. 45 below).

These prints are among Nash's earliest experiments in abstraction. It was not until 1930–31 that he began for a short period to make abstract paintings. The impressions shown here come from a large group of work purchased in September 1970 from the Paul Nash Trust (1970–9–19–21 to 96).

43a

44 Coronilla, 1925

Wood-engraving. Signed, dated, titled and annotated 'Special proof' in pencil. Edition of 25. 116 × 91 mm

Postan 64

1970–9–19–56

The coronilla is a flower. Andrew Causey, however, has discovered that it is also the title of a poem by Harold Monro, first published in 1917, which identifies the flower with a *femme fatale* that lures man into her room at night, drains his energy and kills him (Causey, pp.179–83). The correctness of this association is proven by a second version of this print apparently made in 1930 (Postan 88) in which the centre of the flower is occupied by the small figure of a nude woman. Nash also made a painting dated 1929 which is closely related to the first version of the woodcut (Causey 633). It is interesting that in the twenties Nash's prints and paintings progressed in parallel, rather than the prints following the paintings (or drawings) as they did during the war.

43b

44

45

45 Abstract 2, 1926

Wood-engraving. Signed, dated, titled and numbered 14/25 in pencil. 93 × 76 mm

Postan 76

1970–9–19–66

This print is closely related to another of the same year entitled *Design of Flowers*, of which it seems to be an abstract derivation.

In 1928 an exhibition of almost the entire oeuvre of Nash in wood-engraving was held at the Leicester Galleries, and coincided with the publication of a catalogue of them by John Gould Fletcher in *Print Collector's Quarterly*. All the prints shown here were available for 2 guineas each. The exhibition was not a success, and marked a turning-point in Nash's career: after this he made hardly any more wood-engravings.

In an article entitled 'Woodcut patterns' published in *The Woodcut, an Annual* (edited by Herbert Furst) in 1927, Nash wrote of wood engraving:

. . . there is always the dangerous seduction of skilfulness to be taken into account. Hitherto this has been a temptation mainly for the craftsman. Today it is likely to prove the artist's snare. Because, as an engraver, I fear such a danger invading the art I practise, I have become lately more interested in woodcut patterns than in woodcut pictures. It is always a relief to be rid of the responsibility of representation . . . Wood seems to yield to the evolution of an abstract design or a decorative arabesque as stone excites the sculptor to the creation of pure form. For it is the glyptic character of engraving on wood which is its peculiar charm.

Charles Ginner

1878–1952

Born and educated abroad. His parents intended him to become an engineer, and it was only in 1904 that he began studying as an artist in Paris. He first moved to London at the end of 1909, and in the following year became friendly with Harold Gilman and Spencer Gore. He subsequently became one of the leading figures of the Camden Town Group, established in 1911, remaining particularly close to Gilman. In about 1916 he was called up, and served in the Royal Army Ordnance Corps and then in Intelligence before becoming an official war artist. After the war, he concentrated on painting landscapes and city views in a style that henceforth showed little development.

All Ginner's eleven recorded prints were cut in wood and were made between 1917 and 1931; his notebooks for some reason describe the first eight as woodcuts and the last three as wood-engravings, though there seems to be no technical difference between them. The list of their titles and dates is as follows:

1. *St Jacques, Dieppe*, 1917. Also called 'Dieppe' (cat. no. 46 below)

2. *Flask Walk, Hampstead*, 1919 (listed as lost; no impressions recorded)
3. *A Cornish Cottage*, 1919 (cat. no. 47 below)
4. *The Cathedral*, 1921 (cat. no. 48 below)
5. *A Corner of Porthleven*, 1922. 193 × 140mm. Also called 'Porthleven Roofs'
6. *Somerset Landscape*, 1922. 186 × 139mm. Also called 'Somerset'
7. *Trewall Farm*, 1924. 140 × 190mm
8. *On the Embankment*, 1924. 140 × 191mm
9. *On the West Heath*, 1930. 214 × 264mm. (An impression is in the British Museum)
10. *A Corner of Newlyn*, 1931. 225 × 165mm
11. *Pitt House, Hampstead Heath*, 1931. 265 × 228mm

The notebooks give medium, title and date, followed by a list of all the exhibitions in which a print was included, and a note of the impressions sold (usually at very varying prices) or given as gifts. The measurements given above are derived from identified impressions of the prints. The alternative titles are those found in lists of exhibitions in which Ginner participated. In general, the early prints sold well, but from 1922 onwards sales of new prints were very poor, and most have only one or two sales listed. The last three have notes stating that the edition size was 50, but this was clearly an intended maximum which was never approached.

46

Bibliography

No monograph, nor indeed significant retrospective exhibition, has ever been devoted to Ginner. The most useful source at present is the article by Malcolm Easton, 'Charles Ginner, Viewing and Finding', *Apollo* XCI (1970), pp.204–9. See also various general works, and in particular Wendy Baron's *The Camden Town Group*, London 1979. The four notebooks in which Ginner kept a meticulous record of his entire output have not been published; we have been able to consult a photocopy by courtesy of Christie's Modern Department.

46 St Jacques, Dieppe, 1917

Woodcut, hand-coloured by the artist. Inscribed in pen 'To C.W. Beaumont from Charles Ginner'. 303 × 254mm

1982–6–19–20

The view looks north-west across the town to the sea, with the Gothic tower of the Eglise St Jacques in the background. The topography seems to be fairly distorted; Ginner's sister recalled his saying, 'If I don't like the place where God put the hill, I pick the hill up and put it somewhere else to make a good picture' (quoted in the Tate Gallery catalogue of *Modern British Paintings*, 1964, p.239).

This print was commercially the most successful of Ginner's output. When shown first in the Grey Room of the Goupil Gallery in 1917, five impressions were sold, one of them going to C.R.W. Nevinson for 2 guineas. At later exhibitions up to 1924 he sold another seven impressions. Seven further impressions are listed as gifts, one being presented to McKnight Kauffer. C.W. Beaumont was given his impression in 1917, following the seventh exhibition of the London Group at Heal's. At the 1924 exhibition of the Society of Printmakers at the St George's Gallery this and *The Cathedral* were both priced at 4 guineas. In the same exhibition *A Cornish Cottage* was priced at 2½ guineas.

Cyril William Beaumont (1891–1976) described himself as bookseller, publisher and writer on theatre and dance (see *Who was Who*, vol. VII). He started as a bookseller on the Charing Cross Road, and in 1917 established in his basement the Beaumont Press, a small private press, which continued into the late 1920s. In 1918 he published a collection of poems by John Drinkwater, *Loyalties*, which was the first book to be illustrated by Paul Nash.

47

48

47 A Cornish Cottage, 1919

Woodcut, hand-coloured by the artist. Signed in pen.
192 × 140 mm
1981–6–20–49

Most known impressions of all but the last three of Ginner's woodcuts are coloured by hand, and it was in this form that he exhibited six of them at the 1924 exhibition of the Society of Printmakers at the St George's Gallery. This was scarcely normal procedure in printmaking at that time, but can be understood in terms of Ginner's paintings. These use pure colour in a way most unusual in British art, combining it with a strong emphasis on contour (a style that Ginner called 'neo-realism'). The paint surface is thickly built up with parallel strokes of pigment laid on with a cowhair brush, following the form that is portrayed. This technique is matched in the woodcuts by the variety of different types of hatching used to define different surfaces. These surface patterns were incomplete without colour, which Ginner added after printing.

48 The Cathedral, 1921

Woodcut, hand-coloured by the artist. Signed in pencil.
303 × 257 mm
1982–6–19–19

Ginner's notebooks give no indication of where this cathedral is, and we have so far been unable to identify it.

Only three sales of this print are listed in the notebooks. It was later reproduced on page 159 of *Artwork* for February/April 1925, when it was included in the Arts League of Service's travelling portfolio. The Arts League of Service was founded in 1919, and continued into the 1930s with help from the Carnegie Trust. Its stated policy was 'to represent the various modern movements in art', and it was particularly active in the theatre. In the fine arts, it launched the travelling portfolio scheme in 1921. These selections of 'drawings and watercolours by contemporary artists of repute in the modern movements' at prices from 3 guineas upwards were posted to applicants, who had only to return them within a week and pay the cost of return postage (according to their *Annual* of 1921–2). The scheme does not seem to be mentioned after 1925, and cannot have been a great success.

William Roberts

1895–1980

Born in Hackney, the son of a carpenter. In 1909 he was apprenticed to a commercial art firm, Sir Joseph Causton Ltd; in 1910 a London County Council scholarship enabled him to study at the Slade School for three years. At the Slade his closest friends were David Bomberg, whose work strongly influenced the direction of his own, and Jacob Kramer, whose sister, Sarah, he married.

Roberts joined the Omega Workshops in 1913 after Wyndham Lewis's departure, but by 1914 he had moved within Lewis's orbit, later contributing to both issues of *Blast* and participating in the Vorticist exhibitions of 1915 and 1917 in London and New York respectively. He served as a gunner in the Royal Field Artillery in France from 1916 until April 1918, when he returned to London in order to embark upon a commission from the Canadian War Memorials Fund for a painting of *The First German Gas Attack at Ypres* in 1915.

Roberts, like Bomberg, was forced into a return to a clearly figurative style by the terms of his Canadian commission, which expressly stated that 'Cubist work is inadmissible'. Nevertheless, his studies of wartime subjects (1918–19) received critical acclaim for their 'mordant irony' when his first one-man show opened at the Chenil Gallery in November 1923. By the latter part of the twenties his style of figure drawing had developed the simplified, tubular structure which remained characteristic of his work until the end of his life. From 1925 to 1960 his main income was derived from teaching at the Central School, augmented by the patronage of collectors such as Maynard Keynes. The Wyndham Lewis exhibition at the Tate in 1956 transformed Roberts into an energetic pamphleteer intent upon a refutation of Lewis's mischievous and exaggerated claim to be the sole figure of importance in the Vorticist movement.

Roberts's only attempt at original printmaking was the group of six etchings, two of which are catalogued below, which he executed during the 1920s.

Bibliography

Richard Cork's chapter on 'Roberts and Bomberg the Outsider', in *Vorticism and Abstract Art in the First Machine Age*, London 1976, vol. II, pp.377–403, is the best introduction to Roberts's early work, while his bibliography provides a complete list of Roberts's own writings from 1956–74. There are no major exhibition catalogues, but those for the Tate Gallery's retrospective in 1965 and for another organised by the Maclean Gallery in 1980 contain useful surveys of the artist's work, while the Fitzwilliam Museum in Cambridge put on general exhibition in 1985 with a handlist. We should like to thank John and Sarah Roberts for their help.

49 Self-Portrait, *c.*1925

Etching. Signed in pencil and inscribed 'second state'.
127 × 98 mm
1985-3-30-10

This self-portrait, incorrectly described as 'The Artist's Brother', and a portrait of the artist's son John as a young boy appeared in a Sotheby's sale on 5 December 1984, together with four other etchings by Roberts (lots 364–9). Stylistically the self-portrait is very close to a drawing the artist made of his wife Sarah in 1925 (*William Roberts,*

49

50

an Artist and his Family, National Portrait Gallery, London 1984, no. 26).

Self-Portrait exists in three states, progressing from the lightly flecked surface of the first state to a much denser network of lines and heavier inking in the third. The preparatory drawing for the print, which is now on loan to the Fitzwilliam Museum from King's College, Cambridge, was purchased by Maynard Keynes through the London Artists' Association in 1932. Keynes was a founder and supporter of this organisation from 1925 to 1935, and Roberts first met him there in 1927. (For a discussion of the London Artists' Association see *The Studio* vol. 99 (1930), pp.235–49.)

50 Boozers, c.1925

Etching. Signed in the plate with artist's surname and title and in pencil below with artist's full name. 100 × 100 mm

1985–3–30–11

Apart from the two portraits, *Boozers* is one of the four other known etchings by Roberts, the remaining three subjects being *The Bedroom*, *The Bathers* and *Opera*. The preparatory drawing in pencil for *The Bedroom* still survives in the possession of the artist's family, together with three further finished studies of the same size for etchings which appear not to have been executed: *Tarts, Outclassed* and *To the Lord of Song*. The prints were probably all made at the same time, around 1925 when Roberts joined the staff of the Central School of Art, where he would have had access to etching facilities. Although he was apparently dissatisfied with his results and never repeated the experiment, the etchings in their modest way are among his most successful compositions. The angular, brittle quality of the lines in the anecdotal subjects like *Boozers* was an effective vehicle for the wry humour of these sharply observed episodes of contemporary life.

In both style and content Roberts's etchings betray a marked affinity with the work of the influential French line-engraver J.E. Laboureur (1877–1943), especially with his scenes of American negroes and dockers at Saint-Nazaire and Nantes in 1917–19.

Edward Bawden

1903–1989

The son of a metal-worker in Saffron Walden, he trained at the Cambridge School of Art before going to the Royal College from 1922 to 1925. There he was close friends with Eric Ravilious and Douglas Percy Bliss. Bawden's career was always as a watercolourist and graphic designer. In this field he produced an immense quantity of work in wallpaper, fabrics, ceramics, book covers and end-papers, vignettes, illustrations, posters, and so on. During the war he was employed as a war artist, being evacuated from Dunkirk and rescued after five days at sea when his ship was torpedoed. He taught at the Royal College and the Royal Academy School, becoming an Academician in 1956. In 1981 he presented the contents of his studio to the Cecil Higgins Art Gallery in Bedford.

Unlike his friends Ravilious and Bliss, Bawden does not seem to have made wood-engravings. He did, however, make linocuts throughout his career. These were often transferred to lithographic plates for printing in a process described by Oliver Simon: 'He cut the various separated pieces of linoleum for each colour; transfers were then made from each piece (there might be two or three dozen pieces for a poster) on to lithographic plates for printing' (*Printer and Playground*, London 1956, p.125). Between 1927 and 1929 he also made sixteen engravings, fifteen of which were reprinted in 1988 (see cat. no. 52 below); a few other engravings were made in later years, but only for demonstration or trade work.

Bibliography

Douglas Percy Bliss, *Edward Bawden*, published by the Pendomer Press, Godalming, in 1979, is both a biography and an account of his work written by one of his closest friends. *Edward Bawden, a Retrospective Survey*, with an introduction by Justin Howes, was published by Combined Arts in Bath in 1988, and contains a complete catalogue of the 1981 gift to Bedford.

51 Redcliffe Road, 1927

Engraving. Signed, titled, dated '88' and numbered 13/35 in pencil. 150 × 93 mm

1987–12–12–13

52 The Pagoda, 1927/9

Engraving. Signed, titled, dated '88' and numbered 13/35 in pencil. 168 × 106 mm

1987–12–12–12

In 1927–9 Bawden made a number of line-engravings, having received some training at the Sir John Cass Institute from a professional letter engraver. They were not commissioned or taken up by a publisher, and little attention was paid to them at the time. Six were exhibited at the St George's Gallery in October 1927 in a joint exhibition with Ravilious and Bliss, and in *Artwork* no. 15 (Autumn 1928) Bliss wrote a piece on Bawden which illustrated three of them. This stated:

Recently he has taken up line-engraving for which the clear and intellectual character of his line was manifestly adapted. He employs pure graver-work for his effects, and never relieves the austerity of his style by 'mixing' graver lines with etched or drypointed lines, as so many popular etchers now do. His work is technically akin to that of Laboureur in that he is economical of line, but it is less sweet and witty in style, harder, more caustic at bottom than that of the Frenchman.

The link with the French artist Laboureur (see also cat.

51

52

no. 50) is entirely sound. In a letter to the British Museum dated 4 September 1987, Bawden wrote that he 'became interested in the difficulties of engraving on copper, and fascinated by the engraved designs of J.E. Laboureur, whose work was pleasing because he did not indulge in the tonal elaboration in etching common to the period, that also influenced engraving'. Laboureur's work was very well known in Britain. In *Artwork* for October/December 1925 Campbell Dodgson, whose huge collection of Laboureur was later bequeathed to the British Museum, wrote an article about it, and in 1928 Douglas Cleverdon in Bristol published an edition of Farquhar's *The Beaux' Stratagem* illustrated with seven engravings by Laboureur to accompany other publications illustrated by Eric Gill and David Jones. The advertisement for it in *Artwork*, Spring 1928, states that all the more expensive copies from the luxury editions had been already sold.

Few of Bawden's engravings were printed at the time in significant numbers, and most were sold privately to friends. The plates were rediscovered around 1950 by his son Richard, and since then new impressions have frequently been printed, either by Richard Bawden or by

Thomas Ross & Co (this information was given by the artist in the letter referred to above). A large number of restrikes was made for an exhibition around 1973; these were all numbered out of 40. Another edition of 35 copies, plus 5 artist's proofs, was published in 1988 by Peter Sampson of Merivale Editions, and this was accompanied by an excellent essay by David McKitterick, from which most of the information given here has been taken. The two exhibited plates have been chosen from this edition, of which the British Museum has a complete set. They are excellently printed, and comparison with early impressions reveals no loss of quality whatever. The date '88' on the impressions refers to the date of the printing, not of the engraving.

The first of the two plates shows the house at 58 Redcliffe Road, South Kensington, where Bawden and Ravilious shared lodgings at this time. The other is one of two sardonic scenes set in Kew Gardens. Drawn versions of these were later used as illustrations in Robert Herring's fantasy *Adam and Eve at Kew*, published in 1930, but this text was apparently written around the illustrations rather than vice versa.

3 Claude Flight and the Linocut

The rise of the colour linocut was one of the most remarkable developments in British printmaking between the wars, and no artist was more responsible for this phenomenon than Claude Flight. An artist and teacher of independent mind, Flight attracted many students to his linocut classes at London's Grosvenor School of Modern Art, which had been set up in 1925 at 33 Warwick Square under the progressive direction of the wood-engraver Iain Macnab. In addition to linoblock printing, students here were offered printmaking facilities in lithography and etching as well as tuition in life drawing, painting and composition.

Although Flight only taught at the Grosvenor School for four years, from 1926 until 1930, his technical methods, as well as his style, were taken up by many of his followers from the late 1920s through to the mid-1930s, the period when his influence was at its height. Among the most gifted of his students were the English artists Cyril E. Power and Sybil Andrews, while the Swiss artist Lill Tschudi was one of the most widely exhibited of Flight's foreign pupils in London during the 1930s. A number of his students came from other parts of the world; these included the Australians Dorrit Black, Ethel Spowers and Eveline Syme, each of whom developed her own distinctive use of the linocut medium under Flight's tuition.

Linoleum, which had originally been patented twice, in 1860 and 1863, by its English inventor Frederick Walton, was already being cut to make prints by the early years of this century; the German Expressionists Erich Heckel and Christian Rohlfs were among the earliest artists to experiment with it. In England, Horace Brodzky made several linocuts from 1912 (see cat. no. 19); this Australian expatriate also introduced the technique to his French sculptor friend Henri Gaudier-Brzeska, whose *Wrestlers* of 1914 (cat. no. 18) showed the expressive possibilities of black and white linocutting.

But it was Flight and his disciples who first promoted the colour linocut as the modern medium for a modern age. Much of Flight's thinking in this regard has its origins in the declamatory statements of the Italian Futurists, whose espousal of a new art for a new age had divided the London art world prior to the First World War. Flight was the first post-war artist to recognise the suitability of linoleum for making prints expressive of the speed and dynamism demanded by the Italian Futurists in their pre-war programme. As he declared in his second textbook on the technique, which appeared in 1934:

The lino-cut is different to the other printing mediums, it has no tradition of technique behind it, so that the student can go forward without thinking of what Bewick or Rembrandt did before, he can make his own tradition, and coming at a time like the present when new ideas and ideals are shaping themselves out of apparent chaos, he can do his share in building up a new and more vital art of to-morrow (*The Art and Craft of Lino Cutting and Printing*, London 1934, p.63).

As a twentieth-century print technique, the linocut seemed particularly appropriate to expressing the modernity of metropolitan life, a theme dear to the hearts of Flight and Power. As early as 1912, in a well-publicised interview with the London *Evening News* (4 March 1912), the Italian Futurist leader F.T. Marinetti had declared the way ahead with his bombastic outburst, 'Why, London itself is a Futurist city!', and had openly embraced London's 'brilliant hued motor buses' and the 'totally new idea of motion, of speed' represented by the recently constructed Underground. These ideas later struck a sympathetic chord with the aesthetic aims of Flight and his followers. Their enthusiasm for modernity was sometimes expressed in terms that recalled Marinetti's own pronouncements, best exemplified perhaps by Andrews and Power in their unpublished manifesto-style paper of about 1924, 'Aims of the Art of To-Day': '[O]ur factories and industrial building[s] have a majesty all their own, a titanic, savage, satanic strength, that calls for simplicity and sterness [*sic*] of treatment and cannot be properly represented by prettiness and picturesqueness of handling' (p.15). It is also quite probable that C.R.W. Nevinson, the erstwhile English disciple of Marinetti, later exercised some influence upon Flight and his fellow linocutters in the choice and treatment of their subject-matter in the 1920s.

Nor should the impact of the landmark Paris exhibition of 1925 – *L'Exposition Internationale des Arts Décoratifs et Industriels Modernes* – upon the art of Flight and his followers be overlooked. This monumental survey of contemporary decorative arts and of utilitarian objects showed the extent to which a diluted form of Cubism and Futurism had become a commonplace of modern design. Flight himself recognised the importance of this exhibition, which later gave its name to the style Art Deco, when he wrote in 1926:

The Paris *Exposition des Arts Décoratifs* last summer showed us how universal is the change that is coming over every sort of decorative art. Old and new countries are at one in their attempt to express the spirit of to-day in terms of harmony and simplicity. England alone of the countries represented at the Exhibition was out of sympathy with this collective spirit, but, as the English exhibits were not even representative of the England of to-day, we need not take them into account.

In England the 'movement' has started. We have but to look at a 'modern' poster to realize how universal is its appeal ... [L]ittle bands of 'modern' English painters are valiantly braving the scorn and abuse which always assails anything new in their endeavour to express freely and without restraint, and in terms of their individual experiences, the collective spirit of the times ('The Art of To-day', *Colour 2*, no. 4 new series (April 1926), pp.9 and 14).

The bright decorative colour, broken geometric forms and rhythmic vitality of the Art Deco style were very much absorbed by Flight and his followers in their modern linocuts.

With single-minded determination, Flight sought to change the prevailing view among print connoisseurs and practitioners that the linocut was inferior to the woodcut for making colour prints. From the mid-1890s, a conservative school of English colour woodcut artists, who worked in the laborious Japanese manner of brushing the blocks with a mixture of powdered ink and rice paste, had sprung up under the leadership of Frank Morley Fletcher, the author of the 1916 standard textbook *Wood-block Printing*, which described this method. In 1927, Flight published the first book on colour printing from linoleum, which he had written with the stated purpose of refuting Fletcher's assertion, expressed a few years earlier, that:

the material [linoleum] is not suited for printing a beautiful surface of colour nor for giving the finer qualities of line, and when it is used for colour the result is poor. Linoleum work illustrates very clearly the rule that when the tools and materials of an Art are made easy, the tendency is for design to deteriorate, and for the Art to become base (Frank Morley Fletcher, 'The Woodblock Colour-print. A Democratic Art', *The Original Colour Print Magazine* 1 (1924), pp.4–5.

The Anglo-Japanese woodcut artists, Flight rejoined in his 1927 book (which partly quoted the above statement), were so preoccupied with mastering the difficulties of the technique that their work was out of touch with the spirit of contemporary life.

Contrary to traditional practice in colour relief printing, Flight abandoned the use of the key-block in favour of three to four blocks of similar value. With one block being cut per colour, the composition was progressively built up in terms of superimposed colour and shapes; this method lent itself to designs conceived as simplified, abstracted forms and hence was particularly suited to the expression of modernistic subject-matter. In keeping with his principle that art should serve a democratic purpose, Flight advocated the use of simple materials and tools: ordinary household linoleum was recommended for the blocks, while the ribs of old umbrellas could be readily converted into gouges. No press was required, as printing was always done by using a home-made baren to rub the back of the paper which had been placed over the inked block, while the back of a dessert spoon or the handle of a toothbrush often doubled as a burnisher for printing more detailed work or stronger local colour.

Flight envisioned the contemporary linocut as the means by which modern art could enter the lives of ordi-

nary people as decorations on the walls of their houses or flats. 'Linoleum-cut colour prints could be sold', he argued, 'if only the interest in and the demand for them could be stimulated, at a price which is equivalent to that paid by the average man for his daily beer or his cinema ticket' (*Lino-cuts. A Hand-book of Linoleum-cut Colour Printing*, London 1927, p.4). Populist ideas of this sort, however, never remained more than a utopian dream, for the colour linocuts offered for sale at the exhibitions Flight organised from the late 1920s were usually priced between 2 and 3 guineas each; in 1934, when over $8\frac{1}{2}$ million British families belonged to the working class, with a weekly income of £4 or less, only those from the middle and upper classes could afford to buy these prints.

In an effort to provoke interest in the medium among the widest possible audience, Flight organised numerous colour linocut exhibitions during this period, the best-known being the eight annual British Lino-cut Exhibitions held in London at the Redfern Gallery from 1929 to 1931 and at the Ward Gallery from 1933 to 1937. Under the auspices of the Redfern Gallery, exhibitions of linocuts were also dispatched to the four corners of the globe: to the United States in 1929, where the show toured many cities; to China in May 1931 at the invitation of the Shanghai Art Club; to Australia in December 1932 at the behest of Melbourne's Arts and Crafts Society of Victoria and again to Melbourne five years later; and to Canada in December 1935 at Ottawa's National Gallery of Canada. From the mid-1930s, however, the colour linocut movement was showing signs of losing its momentum and a number of Flight's former pupils were already using the medium to explore different styles or had abandoned it altogether.

Although Flight and his followers professed their faith in a forward-looking art, the linocut group always remained somewhat isolated within British avant-garde printmaking, and perhaps for this reason their prints have been undeservedly overlooked until quite recently. To those artists and critics who viewed modernism as a relentless progression on the high road to abstraction, the aesthetic outlook of Flight and his fellow artists must have seemed insufficiently radical, while the linocutters' insistence upon simple craft-like practices in their printmaking suggested an affinity with the more homely tradition of arts and crafts than with the cool rigour of modernism. Flight and his followers nevertheless produced some of the most arresting images of the inter-war years; by their lively design and decorative colour, these linocuts form a distinctly recognisable group expressive of the vitality and spirit of their era.

Claude Flight

1881–1955

Born in South Kensington, London, the son of a respected mineralogist at the British Museum who was also a Fellow of the Royal Society. In 1912, after stints in various occupations, including seven years as a farmer in Sussex, Flight enrolled at Heatherley's School of Art at the relatively late age of 31. There he met Nevinson – an occasional visitor to the school – through whom Flight is believed to have made contact with the Italian Futurist leader F. T. Marinetti before the outbreak of the First World War.

After three and a half years' service in France as a commissioned captain, Flight resumed his interrupted career with determination. He joined the progressive Seven and Five Society in 1922, where in the company of other London-based artists such as Percy Jowett, Ivon Hitchens and Ben Nicholson he became a regular exhibitor until 1928, when Nicholson's doctrinaire insistence upon abstraction forced him to resign. Many of Flight's linocuts, watercolours and paintings from this period are concerned with the expression of dynamism and movement, and his work was often reproduced and commented upon in the art press and newspapers of the day as representative of the 'ultra-modern' tendency in British art.

Although he made his first prints from lino blocks as early as 1919, it was from the mid-1920s that Flight began his tireless championship of the colour linocut through his teaching, writing and exhibition organising. From 1926 to 1930 he taught the technique of linocutting one afternoon a week at the Grosvenor School of Modern Art; his enthusiasm inspired many of his students to produce their best work in this medium. He also conducted summer classes at his cave in France at the artists' colony of Chantemesle, where, in contrast to the geometrically constructed compositions of his linocuts, many of his impressionistic sketches after nature were made. Flight organised eight annual British Lino-cut Exhibitions in London from 1929 to 1937; he also arranged other shows to tour the British provinces and to travel abroad to the United States, Australia and China during the same period. In 1941 his London studio at Rodmarton Mews (which he shared with his close companion Edith Lawrence, a linocut artist and textile designer) was bombed and all the contents, including his lino blocks and oil paintings, were lost. In 1947, Flight suffered a stroke which forced him to give up printmaking.

Aside from a small group of woodblock prints, Flight concentrated in his printmaking upon the development of the colour lino block; some sixty-four colour linocuts can be attributed to him, all of which were made between 1919 and 1939. A retrospective of his prints, which exhibited thirty-four of his linocuts and eight of his woodcuts and wood-engravings, was held in 1931 at the Albany Gallery in London.

Bibliography

Flight published widely on the technique of colour lino-cutting, and his writings often express his thoughts on modern art and on the democratic role of the linocut. A series of six short articles on the technique originally appeared in the *Arts and Crafts Quarterly* 1, no. 6 (March 1926) and 2, no. 1 (May 1927), a journal which Flight briefly edited from September 1926 to March 1927. These papers served as the basis of Flight's popular and widely used textbook, *Lino-cuts. A Hand-book of Linoleum-cut Colour Printing*, London 1927; rev. ed. 1948, which was illustrated with many of his linocuts. His second handbook, *The Art and Craft of Lino Cutting and Printing*, London 1934, included reproductions of the work of his former pupils at the Grosvenor School as well as black-and-white linocuts made by children. Flight also wrote several interesting articles on his aesthetic convictions, of which 'The Art of To-day', *Colour* 2, no. 4 new series (April 1926), pp.7–9 and 14, and 'Mr. Flight Explains Himself', *The Arts and Crafts* 1, no. 4 new series (July 1928), pp.183–5, are the most important.

The first posthumous exhibition of Flight's work, *A Memorial Exhibition of Oils, Watercolours and Linocuts by Claude Flight 1881–1955 and Edith Lawrence 1890–1973*, with a catalogue with essays by Bernard Denvir and Michael Parkin, Parkin Gallery, London 1973, included many of his linocuts; the Parkin Gallery has subsequently issued several small dealer catalogues of the linocuts of the Grosvenor School.

Flight's contribution to the historical development of the linocut and the influence he wielded upon three Australian artists, Dorrit Black, Ethel Spowers and Eveline Syme, are discussed in Stephen Coppel, 'Claude Flight and his Australian Pupils', *Print Quarterly* 2, no. 4 (December 1985), pp.263–83. An introduction to the British linocut movement is provided by Lora S. Urbanelli in her catalogue to the American travelling exhibition *The Grosvenor School: British Linocuts between the Wars*, Providence, Rhode Island School of Design, Museum of Art, 1988. A catalogue raisonné of Flight's linocuts has been written by Stephen Coppel, for inclusion in his book on Flight and his followers, presently in preparation.

53 Swing-Boats, 1921

Linocut printed from three blocks in cobalt blue, crimson and black on thin tracing paper and pasted to stiff black-brown paper backing. Signed and dated '21 in pencil in image.
216 × 282 mm

1924–2–9–62. Presented by the Contemporary Art Society
See colour illustration

This is one of the earliest linocuts in which Flight successfully incorporates Futurist ideas into his imagery; it thus marks a radical break from the quasi-impressionistic linocuts he had been making since 1919 and which he later claimed were insufficiently inventive with the technique.

As early as 1912, in their first exposure in London at the Sackville Gallery, the Italian Futurists had announced to the public that 'what must be rendered is the *dynamic sensation*, that is to say, the particular rhythm of each object, its inclination, its movement, or, to put it more exactly, its interior force' (U. Boccioni *et al.*, 'The Exhibitors to the Public', in *Exhibition of Works by the Italian Futurist Painters*, London, Sackville Gallery, March 1912, p.12).

It was this search for the dynamic universal rhythms of the world around him that fired Flight's imagination and became enshrined in his artistic credo. As Flight himself explained in 1928:

The subjects which I have taken are such things as buses coming down a street [see cat. no. 54], waves breaking on the shore or carrying a ship on the sea, dancing, or the movement in a crowd, swings [cat. no. 53], or the eddies of the wind and rain: all these have their particular significant rhythm which I have been trying to grasp and place in my colour prints, textiles, sculpture and paintings so as to give the feeling of the universal rhythm in each individual movement ('Mr. Flight Explains Himself', p.184).

In this print, which was reproduced as plate 11 in Flight's 1927 textbook *Lino-cuts*, the regular, pendulum movement of the fairground swing sets in train dynamic lines of force which ripple to the furthest corners of the composition.

The British Museum's impression is unusual in that it is dated. Only the early prints in Flight's oeuvre are inscribed with dates and then only on some of the lower-numbered impressions within the edition; the explanation for this probably lies in the practice of Flight and his followers of printing up the lino blocks as required until the edition was exhausted, so that inscribing an original matrix date on a later impression might well have seemed redundant.

The earliest known exhibition of this print was as no. 37 in Flight's second solo show at the Redfern Gallery (2–28 June 1927); it was also included in the *Exposition de la gravure moderne anglaise*, a huge survey show held at the Musée des Arts Décoratifs in Paris later that year. At a price of 3 guineas each, this print and *Speed* (cat. no. 54 below) proved to be very popular and by 1931 the editions for both had sold out; a second edition, also of 50, was begun for both prints in the late 1920s for the American market; prints from these editions are distinguished by the annotation *USA* beside the edition number.

54 Speed, c.1922

Linocut printed from four blocks in cobalt blue, yellow ochre, vermilion and Prussian blue on buff oriental laid tissue and mounted in reverse on yellow-inked paper backing. Signed in pencil in image, and numbered 8/50 (location obscured by mount). 223 × 286 mm

Victoria and Albert Museum, E.3543–1923 (presented by F. Hoyland Mayor, Esq.)

'HURRAH for motors! HURRAH for speed!' cheered

Marinetti and Nevinson in their inflammatory manifesto *Vital English Art*, a document that incited a storm among the British avant-garde when, in June 1914, it was first published in the London press. Flight, somewhat later, took up the Futurists' challenge to celebrate the dynamism of modern city life. As he observed in 1925:

[T]his speeding up of life in general . . . is one of the interesting and psychologically important features of to-day . . . Traffic problems, transport problems; everybody is on the rush either for work or pleasure . . . The Painter cannot but be influenced by the restlessness of his surroundings . . . (C. Flight, 'Dynamism and the Colour Print', *The Original Colour Print Magazine* 2 (1925), p.56).

Unlike the Italian Futurists, who used the pictorial formula of interpenetrating planes and multiple positioning to convey simultaneity of movement, Flight in this linocut evokes a sensation of speed by the curvilinear distortion of the forms so that the buses appear almost to rush down the street and out of the picture frame. The effect is akin to the shifting movement of a scene on a cinema screen.

This print, which was first shown as no. 65 at the *Third Exhibition of . . . the 'Seven and Five' Society*, Walker's Galleries, London, 20 November–9 December 1922, was later reproduced as the frontispiece to Flight's first linocut handbook and as a detail on the cover of his second. A painting of this composition, in the same direction as the print, was exhibited in London in the mid-1920s and was reproduced as plate XXIII in *The Social Value of Art*, London 1939, a book written by Flight's friend F.R.O'Neill.

Speed and *Paris Omnibus* (cat. no. 55 below) are technically unusual in that the artist printed on the reverse side of the sheet and used the translucency of the fine tissue paper to allow the colours to bleed through to the viewing side. Flight also softened the overall tonality of *Speed* by mounting impressions on a yellow-inked paper backing; he similarly altered the colour key of several of his other prints by affixing them to sheets of dark-toned paper.

Fred Hoyland Mayor, who presented this impression to the Victoria and Albert Museum in 1923, gave Flight his first solo exhibition, in April 1925, at the Mayor Gallery in London.

55 Paris Omnibus, 1923

Linocut printed from four blocks in blue, crimson, viridian and black on oriental laid tissue, washed with yellow-ochre watercolour, and pasted in reverse to stiff black-brown paper backing. Signed and numbered 16/50 in pencil in image. 217 × 280 mm

1928–3–10–14. Presented by the Contemporary Art Society

A variation upon Flight's preoccupation with London buses, this print presents the back view of a departing Paris motorbus as it roars away after depositing two of its passengers; the force of mechanical acceleration is suggested here by the dynamic use of repeated curves. James Laver, an assistant keeper of prints and drawings at the Victoria and Albert Museum, in his review of Flight's

54

55

1927 solo exhibition at the Redfern Gallery (where this example was probably acquired by the Contemporary Art Society), remarked:

Mr. Flight, in his lino-work at least, is a futurist in the strict sense, that is, he is chiefly concerned with expressing the motion of objects, as opposed to those who merely depict objects in motion; and it is with his representations of speed that he is most successful (J. Laver, 'Recent Etching and Engraving', *Artwork* 3, no. 11 (September–November 1927), p.151).

This print is also a good illustration of Flight's method of geometrical construction, whereby the composition was built up according to a system of rhythmic lines and arcs that were tied to the proportions of the frame.

Paris Omnibus was first shown as no. 39, at the listed price of 3 guineas, at the *Fourth Exhibition of . . . the 'Seven and Five' Society*, Wm B. Paterson's Gallery, London, 26 November–22 December 1923. It was reproduced in colour as plate 14 in Flight's 1927 linocut textbook, where the artist noted his procedure of lightly tinting the tissue paper with yellow-ochre watercolour before printing the blocks. A few early impressions of this print, including one at the Achenbach Foundation for Graphic Arts in San Francisco, are dated 1923; the Bibliothèque Nationale, Paris, preserves an editioned example, which is possibly unique in that it was not reversed and backed on coloured paper as appears to have been the case with all other known impressions of this print.

56

56 Street Singers, 1925

Linocut printed from four blocks in yellow ochre, cobalt blue, vermilion and black on thin cream oriental paper. Signed, dated '25 and numbered 1/50 in pencil in image. 312 × 262mm

1926–2–8–1. Presented by the artist

The invasion of sound in a public space is represented in this print by the break-up of form into dynamic abstract patterns; indeed, the voices of the street singers, which are carried by parabolic lines, appear to project beyond the confines of the frame, suggesting a continuation of movement.

Made in 1925, as recorded on the British Museum's impression of this rarely dated print, *Street Singers* and the related painting were first shown at the *Sixth Exhibition of . . . the 'Seven and Five' Society*, Beaux Arts Gallery, London, 6–23 January 1926, as nos 70 and 20 respectively, where they provoked derision in the press on account of their modernity. The price of the print was then 3 guineas.

Street Singers, which was reproduced as plate 13 in Flight's 1927 textbook *Lino-cuts*, was presented by the artist to the British Museum in 1926, not long after the Seven and Five exhibition had ended.

57

57 Women and Washing, c.1925

Linocut printed from five blocks in orange ochre, vermilion, pale blue, ultramarine and light red on oriental laid tissue and pasted to stiff black-brown paper backing. Signed in pencil in image, numbered 6/50 in pencil in image. Signed, titled and annotated '£2.2.0' in pen in bottom margin. 304 × 258 mm

1980-1-26-86

A pair of women struggling to hang out their washing in a high wind is the subject of this print. The motif of billowing sheets is here transformed into a complex rhythm of intersecting arcs, which gives dynamic movement to the composition. Bold colours and rigorous schematisation of form were qualities that best exemplified to Flight the modernist possibilities of linocutting as a twentieth-century print technique.

The only known contemporary reference to this print appears in the catalogue to the Albany Gallery's *Exhibition of Lino-cuts by Claude Flight, R.B.A.*, London 1931, where, as no. 23 under the title 'Washing', it was listed at the price of 3 guineas. Although no dated example of this print has yet come to light, it must belong to the mid-1920s, when Flight was working in a more abstract and geometric manner. A photograph of about 1925, showing Flight pulling a proof of this print, is reproduced on page 8 of the Rhode Island School of Design catalogue.

In 1933, an example of *Women and Washing* was presented by the artist to the Birmingham Museum and Art Gallery, to which he also gave an impression of *Speed* (cat. no. 54). S. C. Kaines Smith, Keeper at the Birmingham Museum and Art Gallery at this time, describes in his book *An Outline of Modern Painting in Europe and America*, London 1932, p.83, a drawing by Flight entitled *Whirligig*, which clearly corresponds to *Women and Washing* in terms of its subject-matter and treatment. It was Kaines Smith who, on the same page of his book, pronounced: 'Claude Flight is the only true futurist that this country has produced'.

Cyril E. Power

1872-1951

Born in Chelsea, London, into a family with a long-standing association with architecture. Power initially trained as an architect with his father's firm, and in 1900 won the Royal Institute of British Architects' Soane Medallion for the design of an art school. For the next twenty years he pursued a promising, if somewhat conventional, career as an architect. In the years prior to the First World War, he also gave lectures on architectural history and design at University College and at Goldsmith's College, and in 1912 he published an ambitious two-volume history of medieval English architecture, which was largely illustrated with his own pen-and-ink sketches.

It appears that the upheavals of the First World War precipitated some sort of turning-point in Power's own life. He had been commissioned into the Royal Flying Corps in 1916, with the responsibility of supervising the repair workshops at Lympne aerodrome near Dover, and it was shortly after moving to Bury St Edmunds following demobilisation that he decided to begin his life afresh as an artist. He took up watercolour painting and began to make the first of some forty architectural drypoints. In 1922, at the age of almost 50, he left his architectural practice and his wife and four children and went to London to pursue his new calling more seriously. He took with him Sybil Andrews, a 24-year-old student whom he had met in Bury St Edmunds and with whom he had exhibited a group of watercolours and pastels the previous year. In London, Power and Andrews both enrolled at Heatherley's School of Art, where Iain Macnab, the enlightened teacher and wood-engraver, was co-principal.

In 1925, Power was invited by Macnab to join his newly established Grosvenor School of Modern Art as one of the two founding lecturers (the other was the critic Frank Rutter), while Andrews obtained the appointment of School Secretary. According to the 1925 prospectus for the school, Power was to give two series of ten lectures on 'The Form and Structure of Buildings, Historical Ornament and Symbolism & Outline of Architectural Styles'. He also conducted twice-weekly afternoon classes on the principles of architectural sketching, with an emphasis on the teaching of 'Simple Perspective for Artists' and the 'Elements of Architectural Ornament & Design'. It was at the Grosvenor School that Power met Claude Flight, upon the latter's appointment to the school's staff in 1926. Flight taught Power how to cut and print from lino blocks, and by 1929 Power was sufficiently accomplished in linocut for his work to be included in the Redfern Gallery's *First Exhibition of British Lino-cuts*.

Power went on to hold a joint exhibition of colour linocuts and monotypes with Sybil Andrews at the Redfern Gallery in January 1933. He made most of his linocuts at a studio at 2 Brook Green, Hammersmith (formerly the Hammersmith School of Art, which had been converted into several artists' studios); he shared this studio with Andrews from 1930 until July 1938, when their working partnership largely came to an end. Andrews re-established herself at Norley Wood near Lymington in the New Forest before eventually moving to British Columbia in 1947; Power returned to live with his family for the remaining years of his life.

Although Power made many architectural drypoints and colour monotypes, it is with the linocut that his achievement as a printmaker indisputably rests. Between 1926 and 1937 he made some forty-five linocuts, many of which are concerned with expressing the dynamism of the modern machine age.

Bibliography

Apart from his substantial architectural history *English Mediaeval Architecture*, 2 vols, London 1912; 2nd ed. in 3 vols, 1923, Power appears to have published no other writing on art. He did, however, outline his ideas on modern art in a long unpublished paper entitled 'Aims of the Art of To-Day', which he wrote with Sybil Andrews in about 1924; a typescript of this paper is held by the artist's family. In the declamatory style of a manifesto, it sets out to steer a path of reasonableness between 'the cult of the crude and ugly' exemplified by the Camden Town School and the 'cult of sugary prettiness' practised by the Royal Academy imitators of high Victorian narrative painting. Emboldened by the conviction that 'art should express and reflect its contemporary period', Power and Andrews give an emphatic declaration of their aesthetic aims: '*We are out to paint what we FEEL rather than what we SEE*'. The paper concludes with a set of definitions, propounded variously by each artist, of the terms 'rhythm', 'counter-rhythm', 'design', 'pattern' and 'distortion'.

An illustrated summary listing of Power's linocuts and a biographical outline of his career are given in the useful catalogue recently issued by the Redfern Gallery, the dealers who exhibited and supported the artist's work during the 1930s: *The Linocuts of Cyril Edward Power 1872–1951*, with an essay by Gordon Samuel and Richard Gault, London 1989. A detailed catalogue of Power's linocuts is being prepared by Stephen Coppel, for inclusion in his monographic study of Claude Flight and his followers.

58 The Tube Staircase, 1929

Linocut printed from three blocks in yellow, cobalt blue and black on thin cream oriental laid paper. Signed in pencil in image. Titled and numbered 6/50 in pencil in image.
444 × 256 mm
Redfern Gallery 13
1932-5-14-43. Presented by the Contemporary Art Society

The bold, architectonic form that so powerfully animates the pictorial space of this print derives from the artist's close study of the staircase that twists for nearly 200 steps at London's Russell Square Tube station. The industrial architecture of London's Underground system appealed to Power's Futurist-inspired belief that art should express contemporary life, and it provided him with the subject-matter for some of his most successful prints.

Preliminary ideas for this print were initially set down in Power's sketchbooks as early as 1926, when he was living and teaching at the Grosvenor School. A quick pencil sketch of a corkscrew staircase first appears on folio 25 in a sketchbook dated 1926 bearing the address '33 Warwick Square' on the flyleaf (preserved among Power's sketchbooks in the possession of the artist's youngest son, Edmund Berry Power). This thumbnail sketch records the basic form of an organic spiral. In the following year the

58

spiral staircase is enlarged and details are given establishing the relationship between light and shade (sketchbook entitled 'Caen Rouen II', 1927, f. 6). At least two working proofs of the linocut have also survived, and these give some indication of the further development of the image on the lino block. An early proof pulled from the key-block in black (exhibited by Martin Sumers Graphics, New York, 1987), shows the areas that will later be gouged away. The verso of a second proof, also pulled in black from the key-block after these unwanted areas had been removed (Coll. Beth and James DeWoody; reproduced in the exhibition catalogue *The Grosvenor School: British Linocuts between the Wars*, with an essay by Lora S. Urbanelli, Providence, Rhode Island School of Design, Museum of Art, 1988, no. 43), reveals evidence of considerable working-over with green and blue chalks and numerous annotations in pencil designating the areas to be printed in colour.

The exceptional appearance of a dated impression from the edition, that numbered 14/50, provides firm evidence for dating *The Tube Staircase* to 1929. It was also in this year that the print was first shown, as no. 33, at the *First Exhibition of British Lino-cuts* (4–27 July 1929), the landmark linocut exhibition organised by Flight at the Redfern Gallery. Priced at 3½ guineas, this print was the second most expensive of the ninety-four linocuts listed in the catalogue, the dearest being Power's *The Escalator* at 4 guineas.

An appreciative notice of *The Tube Staircase* was given by Frank Rutter – Power's colleague at the Grosvenor School, who lectured on modern painters from Cézanne to Picasso – in his warm review of the inaugural linocut exhibition, which appeared in the *Sunday Times* (14 July 1929) under the heading, 'British Linocuts. A New Colour Art for the People':

One of the most original exhibits is Mr. Cyril Power's 'Tube Staircase' (33), a design of great ingenuity embellished by a charming delicacy of colour. It is extremely decorative, and at the same time an illuminating and intimate study of the beauty to be found in an aspect of hyper-modernity.

The uncompromising modernity of this print recalls the industrial subjects depicted by the Vorticist Edward Wadsworth in his woodcuts of about 1914. Moreover, Power's obvious interest in light and shade evokes the decorative patterning found in Wadsworth's 1918 black-and-white woodcuts of dazzle-painted ships. It well may have been Frank Rutter who introduced Power to the prints of Wadsworth, for, in 1919, in his role as director of the Adelphi Gallery in London, Rutter had mounted a retrospective exhibition of Wadsworth's woodcuts and drawings for the gallery's opening show. More concrete evidence of Power's interest in the work of the early English modernists may be adduced from 'Aims of the Art of To-Day' wherein an admiration for Nevinson's art is frankly declared:

[L]ook at Nevinson's 'Mitrailleuse' [presented to the Tate Gallery by the Contemporary Art Society in 1917]. To express the revolting horridness and the noisy incessant vibrating, rattle, he has used ugly sharp, angular and square shapes and drabby crude colour which hurt to look at (p.20).

The British Museum's impression shows the care with which Power controlled the hand-printing of the lino blocks; the blue block, for instance, has been printed with varying pressure in order to obtain a rhythmically graded effect, passing from deep cobalt blue in the central stairwell to light blue in the outer areas of the composition.

59 Lifts, 1930

Linocut printed from three blocks in light cobalt blue, viridian and red on buff oriental laid tissue. Signed, titled and numbered 3/50 in pencil in image. 366 × 232 mm

Redfern Gallery 10

1949-4-11-2051. Bequeathed by Campbell Dodgson

An earlier state of this print was reproduced in line-block as an advertisement for the London elevator firm Hammond Bros & Champness Ltd. Power's design, which had been commissioned by Harold Champness, a partner in the firm and the artist's brother-in-law, appeared in the trade magazine *The Builder* (10 January 1930, p.clxxiv) with the accompanying legend:

We are indebted to the artist for the above impression of Modern Lift Speed after his visit to King William St. House. This building is equipped with five H.&C. High Speed Lifts. May we ask you to consult us on your Lift problems?

When Power came to make the edition of this print in 1930, he further simplified his design by dispensing with the fourth block that had delineated, in dark blue, the cables and the inner rim of the spiral staircase as they appeared in the *Builder* advertisement and in the related linocut trial proofs. A cartouche bearing the artist's signature, which had been cut on the viridian block in the lower right of the composition for the advertisement, was also removed. As a consequence of these alterations, the image appears curiously pared back and unstable; it is almost as if the pair of high-speed lifts accelerate of their own accord, up and down the open lift shaft. The plunging, vertiginous space and the inrush of forms would also appear to owe some debt to Vorticism.

Offered for sale at 2 guineas as no. 31, *Lifts* was one of seven linocuts by Power that were shown for the first time at the Redfern Gallery's exhibition *British Linocuts*

59

60

(23 July–23 August 1930); this show had been organised by Flight as the Second Exhibition of British Lino-cuts.

According to Dr E.R. Roper Power, the artist's eldest son, Power was an acquaintance of Campbell Dodgson, who probably acquired this impression during the early 1930s.

60 Speed Trial, *c.*1932

Linocut printed from three blocks in light cobalt blue, viridian and dark blue on buff oriental laid tissue. Signed, titled and numbered 16 in image. Inscribed in bottom margin lower right 'This is based on Sir Michael [*sic*] Campbell's "Blue Bird" Racing Car'. 196 × 375 mm

Redfern Gallery 31

Collection of Gordon Samuel

Power's fascination with machine-age speed finds its culmination in this print. It is directly inspired by Malcolm Campbell's famous aerodynamic racing machine, *Bluebird*, an enduring symbol of the age of speed in Britain between the wars. On 5 February 1931, *Bluebird* astonished the world when it broke all previous land speed records by reaching 246 miles per hour at Daytona Beach in Florida. Power's homage to *Bluebird* appears to have been made soon after this event. While it is clear that Power was responding to the fervour created by Campbell's recent record-breaking achievement, his image of speed is also in keeping with the spirit of his time. Inter-war Britain was obsessed with breaking speed records for land, water and air, and at different times during the 1930s held world records for all three.

First shown as no. 50 at the Redfern Gallery's annual summer exhibition *Modern Colour Prints* (21 July–20

August 1932), this print was listed for sale at £1 11s. 6d. In 1935, *Speed Trial* was selected for the British Council's touring exhibition *200 Years of British Graphic Art*, which travelled to Bucharest, Vienna and Prague between December 1935 and mid-1936. Campbell Dodgson, who contributed an historical essay to the catalogue for this exhibition of 440 prints and drawings, brought his survey up to date by concluding that, 'in quite recent times the younger artists, including some with a penchant for cubism or futurism, have preferred the linoleum cut for the multiplication of their gay and lively designs' ('Introduction: II. British Engraving' in *Ausstellung von britischen Aquarellen, Zeichnungen und Stichen 1735–1935*, British Council exhibition catalogue, Vienna 1936, p.29).

61 The Exam Room, *c.*1934

Linocut printed from four blocks in yellow, red, viridian and dark blue on buff oriental laid tissue. Signed, titled and numbered 14/60 in pencil in image. Inscribed in pencil in bottom margin lower left 'To Vera Watson/ Aug. 14/ 1949'. 266 × 382 mm

Redfern Gallery 40

1985–10–5–22

The Exam Room was made about 1934, the year in which it was first shown as no. 40 at the Redfern Gallery in a mixed group exhibition entitled *Colour Prints. Also Paintings by R. O. Dunlop, Basil Jonzen, Richard Eurich* (12 July–4 August 1934). Both this print and *The Tube Train* (cat. no. 62), which was also shown for the first time as no. 35 at the 1934 Redfern Gallery exhibition, are concerned with expressing a mood of anxiety or tension

61

within a claustrophobic space; as such, they represent a departure from the themes of speed and movement that characterise Power's prints to this date.

In *The Exam Room*, the candidates nervously twist at their desks, while the invigilators menacingly stand watch or restlessly pace the room to the ticking of the clock on the wall. The distorted, hook-like figures, the upwards-tilted flooring and the staring eyes of the overhead lights convey an overall effect of heightened nervous tension reminiscent more of German Expressionism than of Italian Futurism, the style with which the linocuts of the Grosvenor School are usually associated.

The subject of this print derives from personal experience: Power, who had been elected an Associate Member of the Royal Institute of British Architects in 1902, supplemented his income by acting as an occasional invigilator at the Institute's final design examinations during the late 1920s and 1930s. A quick sketch of the ceiling of the RIBA examination room appears in the artist's sketchbook of 1927, with the annotations 'Optical Illusion/ R.I.B.A./ Ceiling' and 'Conduit St/ Exam Room' (f.16).

Vera Watson, to whom this impression is dedicated, was a family friend and neighbour at New Malden, Surrey; she later went to China to teach midwifery (information from Dr E.R.Roper Power).

62 The Tube Train, *c.*1934

Linocut printed from four blocks in yellow, red, light cobalt blue and dark blue on buff oriental laid tissue. Signed, titled and numbered 2/60 in pencil in image and again in left margin. Annotated in pencil in lower left margin 'Col. Lino £2/2/-'.
310 × 315 mm
Redfern Gallery 41
1985–10–5–21
See colour illustration

An expressionistic distortion similar to that in *The Exam Room* characterises this depiction of mask-faced commuters enduring the monotonous rocking and rattling of the London Underground District Line train on its nightmarish rush-hour run. *The Tube Train* is one of several linocuts of the Underground made by Power. Annotated sketches of the interior of a Tube train are recorded in an undated sketchbook addressed on the flyleaf '22 Buckingham Street Adelphi' (ff.14 and 19); although these sketches are devoid of human figures, they do include such telling visual details as the hanging straps, overhead lamps, sliding doors and the advertisements found within an Underground train compartment.

An experimental proof of this print (now in the Australian National Gallery in Canberra) shows how the artist at one stage contemplated printing the third block in viridian before finally deciding upon the light cobalt blue used in the edition. The existence of such proofs is evidence of the care with which Power selected his colours in order to achieve an effect of heightened tension.

The Tube Train and *The Exam Room* were each offered for sale at 2 guineas by the Redfern Gallery in 1934. The British Museum's impression of *The Tube Train* still bears the original price marked by the dealer in the margin.

Sybil Andrews

born 1898

Born in Bury St Edmunds, Suffolk, where her family had long-established ties. Her education in art began in 1918 when she enrolled in John Hassall's correspondence course during her war work as an oxy-acetylene welder on aircraft in Bristol. Following her return to Bury St Edmunds at the end of the war, Andrews met Cyril Power, with whom she formed a close working partnership till 1938 (see above, under Power).

Andrews was taught colour linocutting by Claude Flight while she was employed between 1925 and 1928 as the School Secretary at the Grosvenor School of Modern Art. Her interest in block-printing had already been stimulated by the example of William Kermode, the Tasmanian expatriate who, in 1922, gave a lecture-demonstration of black-and-white woodblock printing while Andrews was a student at Heatherley's School of Art in London.

Principally known as a linocut artist, Andrews produced her best work during the period when she shared a studio with Power in Hammersmith. Between 1929 and the end of the 1930s, she made some forty-three colour linocuts, many of which are expressive of modernity in their bright colours, bold forms and dynamic movement. While Andrews demonstrated a technical superiority in linocutting, particularly in terms of registration and printing, she developed her ideas under the guidance offered by Power. Working side by side in the same studio, the two artists often shared the same palette, with a preference for similar shades of red, orange, yellow ochre, viridian and dark blue. They also collaborated on a series of posters commissioned by the London Passenger Transport Board from 1929 to 1937; these bold works – advertising sporting fixtures such as the cricket at Lords and the Oval, or the tennis at Wimbledon – were signed under the pseudonym 'Andrew-Power' and largely drew upon the simplified forms of their linocuts.

In 1933, Andrews participated with Power in an exhibition of their colour monotypes and linocuts at the Redfern Gallery; (most of Andrews' monotypes were destroyed by fire in an Ottawa gallery in 1959). Andrews also exhibited with Power in the first three Exhibitions of British Lino-cuts organised by Flight between 1929 and 1931; from 1932 the two artists showed their prints at the annual summer exhibitions at the Redfern Gallery, as well as in touring shows that travelled to China, Australia and Canada during the 1930s.

In 1947, Andrews emigrated to Canada with her

63

64

husband Walter Morgan, whom she had met in the ship-yards near Southampton while doing war work; on the voyage out, the blocks for several of her linocuts melted in the ship's hold. In Canada, Andrews settled at Campbell River, a remote logging township on Vancouver Island, where she eventually resumed her printmaking.

Bibliography

For details of the unpublished paper 'Aims of the Art of To-Day', co-authored by Sybil Andrews and Cyril E. Power in about 1924, see under Power. Andrews has recently published a miscellany of her notes and thoughts on art entitled *Artist's Kitchen*, London *c.*1986, which developed out of her experience of teaching art to a small private class at Campbell River since 1960.

An illustrated catalogue raisonné of Andrews' seventy-four colour linocuts was compiled by Peter White, who also wrote the interesting essay on her prints that accompanies his bilingual exhibition catalogue *Sybil Andrews: Colour Linocuts/Linogravures en couleur*, Glenbow Museum, Calgary, 1982.

63 Concert Hall, 1929

Linocut printed from four blocks in yellow ochre, light blue, dark blue and black on buff oriental laid tissue. Signed and numbered 12/50 in pencil in image. 236 × 280 mm
White 1
Victoria and Albert Museum, Circ. 185–1929

This print, made in 1929, is the first linocut to appear in White's catalogue, although the maturity of its execution and the handling of its subject-matter suggest that earlier essays in linocut must have preceded it. The modernity of *Concert Hall* recalls the construction of vast concert and cinema auditoriums that began in the late 1920s and continued through the 1930s.

The smooth curve of the tiered balcony that sweeps dynamically across the pictorial space of this print invites comparison with Power's architecturally inspired linocuts of this date, notably *The Tube Staircase* (cat. no. 58). Indeed, a quick sketch entitled 'The Theatre', which bears every indication of being a preparatory idea for *Concert Hall*, appears in one of Power's sketchbooks of about 1927 (sketchbook entitled 'Rouen I', f.34). Motifs for several of Andrews' linocuts, such as *Golgotha*, 1931 (White 15) and *Michaelmas*, 1935 (White 33), appear as rough ideas

85

in Power's sketchbooks; moreover, several drawings set down in these sketchbooks are clearly signed with Andrews' initials, including one entitled 'Sadlers Wells, before rebuilding' which appears on folio 38 of the sketchbook referred to above.

The degree to which the two artists collaborated in their printmaking is also recorded on the prints themselves: an experimental proof of Power's *The Merry-Go-Round*, c.1930, numbered E.P.7, bears in the bottom margin the pencil annotation 'Sample printed by S[ybil] A[ndrews]' (reproduced in Sotheby's catalogue *Old Master, Decorative, Nineteenth and Twentieth Century Prints*, London, 1–2 December 1986, lot 693, p.251). It is not without some foundation that the critic for *Apollo*, in his appraisal of the 1933 joint exhibition of work by Andrews and Power (which included *Concert Hall*), was moved to exclaim: 'These prints are so much alike that it is often difficult to distinguish the authors' ('Miss Sybil Andrews and Mr. Cyril E. Power at the Redfern Gallery', *Apollo* 17, no. 98 (February 1933), p.49).

This impression was purchased by the Victoria and Albert Museum from the Redfern Gallery's *First Exhibition of British Lino-cuts* (4–27 July 1929), where, as no. 42, it was one of five linocuts shown by Andrews, each of which was listed at a price of 3 guineas.

64 The New Cable, 1931

Linocut printed from four blocks in light cobalt blue, warm reddish brown, viridian and dark blue on buff oriental laid tissue. Signed, titled and numbered 'Second State 10/60' in pencil in image. Annotated in pencil in bottom margin lower right corner 'Col. Lino £3/3/-' and in bottom margin lower right '$15.00'. 312 × 426 mm

White 17, ii

1985-6-8-14

By the time Andrews completed this print in 1931, she had made some seventeen colour linocuts within three years. This burst of creativity produced some of her best prints. *The New Cable* represents a theme that often recurs in Andrews' work and one that she very much made her own: human figures engaged in heavy, physical toil. Subjects such as men shouldering crates of oranges, hauling ropes, cranking winches or swinging sledgehammers (White 3, 4, 6, 26) allowed Andrews to express the rhythm of repetitive human movement as well as to evoke the dignity of hard, manual work.

This print is the second state of the subject after the removal of the light cobalt blue background which the artist felt made the image too oppressive (White 17). Vestiges of this colour block are visible on the singlet of the large worker on the platform and on the crank of the cable. Examples of the first state (such as that numbered 26/50 in the Art Gallery of New South Wales, Sydney) are usually recorded with the alternative title 'The Giant Cable'.

First shown as no. 37 in Claude Flight's *Third Exhibition of British Lino-cuts* at the Redfern Gallery in 1931, this print was one of six new linocuts sent in by Andrews; it was offered for sale at 3 guineas. An example entitled 'The Giant Cable' was shown in Melbourne in December 1932; another was exhibited in Ottawa in 1935. North American venues account for the contemporary prices in two different currencies noted in the bottom margin of the British Museum's impression.

Lill Tschudi

born 1911

Born in Schwanden, a small textile village south-east of Zurich, in the canton of Glarus, Switzerland. Her father, a businessman, died of Spanish influenza when she was seven; her mother, Ida Tschudi-Schümperlin, was an amateur historian. Educated at local schools and at Lausanne, Tschudi's early interest in the linocut was awakened by the work of the Viennese artist Norbertine Bresslern-Roth, whose lively colour prints of animal subjects she first encountered at a gallery attached to the Antwerp Zoo. An advertisement in the *Studio* magazine prompted Tschudi at the age of 18 to enrol at the Grosvenor School of Modern Art in December 1929. There she received formal instruction in linocutting from Claude Flight, with whom she studied until May 1930, when his teaching appointment at the school ended. Although she was a pupil of Flight for a relatively short period, his teaching and his example made a profound impact upon her subsequent development as an artist.

Between 1931 and 1933, Tschudi continued her art training in Paris, where for two months each year she attended classes offered by the Cubist academician André Lhote as well as classes given by the former Italian Futurist Gino Severini at the Académie Ranson and by Fernand Léger at the Académie Moderne. From 1935 to 1940, she lived in Zurich, eventually returning to Schwanden during the Second World War, where she has since settled permanently.

Although she never took up residence in Britain, Tschudi was a leading exponent of the British linocut movement between the wars. It was in London, rather than in her own country, that she first secured her reputation as a printmaker, becoming a regular and successful exhibitor at the British linocut shows organised by Flight during the 1930s.

Linocut was Tschudi's preferred medium of expression, and between 1930 and 1939 she made some sixty-five linocuts, many of which were first exhibited in London. A significant number of the prints from this decade show her adoption of Futurist ideas of movement and rhythm as interpreted by Flight in his teaching at the Grosvenor School and in his writings. Many of Tschudi's linocuts also exemplify, in their decorative colour, their compelling geometric designs and their insistence on contemporary motifs, the key characteristics of the Art Deco style.

65

65 Fixing the Wires, 1932

Linocut printed from three blocks in black, greyish beige and light cobalt blue on thin off-white oriental paper. Signed in pencil in image and numbered 9/50. Titled in pencil in bottom margin right. 302 × 202 mm

1949–4–11–4600. Bequeathed by Campbell Dodgson

Tschudi had not yet turned 21 when she made this mature colour linocut in March 1932. In the two years since leaving the Grosvenor School she had made twenty-five linocuts; all of which, bar one, were printed in colour from several blocks. Her astonishing technical facility in linocut clearly impressed her former teacher, for Flight chose to reproduce *Fixing the Wires* as a full-colour plate on page 15 of his textbook *The Art and Craft of Lino Cutting and Printing* (London 1934). In addition, single-colour proofs from each of the three blocks used to make this print were illustrated in black and white on the preceding page. Flight, however, mistakenly reversed the order in which they were printed; thus the black proof (fig.7 in Flight's book) should read as the first block, the brown proof (more properly, greyish beige, fig.6) as the second, and the light cobalt blue proof (fig.5) as the third. (The original colour proofs pulled by Tschudi for reproduction in Flight's handbook are now preserved in the Australian National Gallery, to which they were presented by the artist.)

Flight used this print to illustrate his idea that the colour linocut should be conceived as a composition built up from several blocks of almost equal value, and for his didactic exposition of the aesthetic qualities he sought in a successful linocut (see *The Art and Craft of Lino Cutting and Printing*, pp.17 and 52).

It is curious to observe the iconographical affinities of Tschudi's linocut with Nevinson's earlier drypoint of 1918, *Nerves of an Army*, which appeared in a limited edition of 100 for a special issue of J.E. Crawford Flitch's book *The Great War, Fourth Year, Paintings by C.R.W. Nevinson* (London 1918).

Fixing the Wires was first shown in 1932 as no. 1 in the Redfern Gallery's summer show *Modern Colour Prints* (21 July–20 August), a group exhibition of 105 prints in different media, with linocuts representing just over half the exhibits. It was offered for sale at the price of 2 guineas. The Redfern Gallery also selected this print, together with several others by Tschudi, for its series of travelling print exhibitions during the 1930s.

This print was acquired by Campbell Dodgson, Keeper of Prints and Drawings at the British Museum, for his private collection, with a view to its ultimate bequest.

Bibliography

The sole monograph to appear on Tschudi is Hans Neuburg's *Lill Tschudi. Vom figurativen zur abstrakten Expression*, Glarus 1979, which briefly outlines her development from the figurative and modernistic linocuts of the 1930s to the gestural abstraction that dominates her oeuvre from the 1950s. Tschudi's place in twentieth-century Swiss printmaking is discussed and illustrated in Eva Korazija Magnaguagno's illuminating historical survey *Der moderne Holzschnitt in der Schweiz*, Zurich 1987, pp.160–65, 230–31. A complete catalogue of Tschudi's early linocuts from 1930 to 1950 has been compiled by Stephen Coppel as part of his larger study of Claude Flight and his followers, currently in preparation.

66 Ice Hockey, 1933

Linocut printed from three blocks in black, green and greyish
beige on thin off-white oriental laid paper. Signed and
numbered 7/50 in pencil in image. Titled in pencil in bottom
margin centre. 260 × 280 mm

1941–2–8–12. Presented by the Contemporary Art Society

Sporting themes figure prominently in Tschudi's linocuts
of the 1930s. Concerned as she was with expressing the
vital rhythms and movement of everyday life, Tschudi
openly depicted the physical exertions of circus tumblers,
gymnasts, runners and skiers – sporting subjects that
similarly preoccupied many of her fellow linocut artists
who had trained at the Grosvenor School, most notably
Cyril Power and Sybil Andrews.

In this print, ice-hockey players slide and swirl around
a central focal point, their schematic forms joined by the
looping, rhythmic lines of their skates. Tschudi used only
three blocks to make this complex image of dynamic
movement, although her technical assurance with the
linocut enabled her to achieve additional tones by careful
overprinting and allowed her to incorporate the white,
untouched areas of the paper as positive elements in the
composition.

This print was completed in April 1933 in time for the
Fourth Exhibition of British Lino-cuts (17 May–10 June

1933), which was held at the Ward Gallery at 3 Baker
Street, London. Tschudi submitted five new colour linocuts for this show, for which she had been preparing since
the previous September. Two of the prints exhibited – *Start
of the Race*, completed in December 1932, and *Kiosk in
Paris*, February 1933 – were shortly afterwards selected
for reproduction in Flight's textbook of 1934.

It seems that Flight transferred his British Lino-cut
exhibitions to the Ward Gallery following a disagreement
with the Redfern. While the Ward Gallery henceforth provided the venue for Flight's annual linocut shows until
the eighth and final one in 1937, the Redfern Gallery continued to mount colour print exhibitions of its own each
summer, although these were no longer exclusively confined to the linocut. The Ward show of 1933 followed the
style of the three earlier linocut shows organised by Flight,
although as one reviewer for *The Times* (24 May 1933,
p.14) somewhat waspishly observed: 'Exactly what
"British" means in this connexion we are at a loss to say,
and, as a matter of fact, one of the most successful
exhibitors is named Miss Lill Tchudi [*sic*]. Her 'Ice Hockey',
in black, green, grey and white, strikes us as exactly what
the lino-cut ought to be . . .'

Like *Fixing the Wires*, this print remained at its original
price of 2 guineas throughout the course of its subsequent
exposure in England during the 1930s. As Flight declared

66

in the catalogue foreword to the 1933 Ward show: 'The lino-cuts shown here have a decorative quality eminently suitable to the adornment of our small flats; their price at the present time is modest and has been kept low in spite of the considerable amount of mental and bodily labour which the making of each print entails.'

67 Sticking up Posters, 1933

Linocut printed from three blocks in dark blue, brown and viridian on thin off-white oriental laid paper. Signed and numbered 22/50 in pencil in image. Titled 'Plakatankleber' and signed in pencil in bottom margin centre, numbered and annotated 'Handdruck' in pencil in bottom margin right.
302 × 200 mm
1980–1–26–104

Made in August 1933, this print was inspired by the artist's observations of billposters swiftly pasting up poster advertisements outside a Métro station in central Paris.

Like many of Tschudi's impressions that appear to have been annotated by the artist at a later date, this print is titled in German and bears the pencil annotation 'Hand-druck' in the bottom margin, indicating that it was printed by hand. In annotating her work in this way, Tschudi was clearly asserting the primacy of manual printing over press printing, which too often produced prints that looked, as Flight lamented, 'hard and mechanical' (*Lino-cuts*, p.24). The artist chose to make this impression by rubbing very hard on the back of the sheet of paper applied to the inked blocks, thereby achieving solid areas of flat colour. Other impressions from this edition, particularly those that Tschudi printed at a later date on a pliant, white mulberry paper, are found to be more lightly rubbed, with a tacky ink texture being deliberately imparted to the paper surface.

Sticking up Posters was first shown in November 1933 at a Swiss exhibition of the linocuts of Flight, Edith Lawrence and Tschudi at Montreux; the print attracted some local press coverage, being illustrated in the review published by the Geneva paper *La Patrie Suisse* (18 November 1933). For the Ward Gallery's *Fifth Exhibition of British Lino-cuts* in 1934, Tschudi sent in six linocuts, of which four, including this print (no. 43 in the show), had been cut since the previous annual linocut exhibition. A publicity photograph of Flight holding up a framed proof of *Sticking up Posters* was published in the London *Daily Sketch* (29 May 1934), above the caption: 'Lino-cuts, a modern revival of the woodcut, are being exhibited in London by Mr. Claude Flight, an expert in the art, here seen with a pupil's work'.

This print was exhibited later in 1934, at the standard commercial price of 2 guineas, at Liverpool's Walker Art Gallery, and at the Birmingham Museum and Art Gallery in 1939, the exhibition which effectively marked the final flowering of the British linocut movement between the wars.

67

4 Woodcuts and Surrealism

The revival of wood-engraving, which had begun in the last years of the nineteenth century, led to the establishment of the Society of Wood Engravers in 1920. Five years later a secession under Edward Gordon Craig set up a rival group, the English Wood Engraving Society (see Introduction). The titles of both societies – which were in truth separated more by personalities than ideology – firmly linked them to wood-engraving rather than woodcut, which remained neglected in Britain throughout this period. Much of the work exhibited by these two groups was of high quality, and they attracted some of the leading artists of the day, including Paul Nash and, through him, Edward Burra.

The founding father of British wood-engraving was Thomas Bewick, from whom artists learnt to use the graver to build up designs in white line against a black background. The multiple tool, which allowed a number of lines to be engraved in parallel at once, was abhorred. What may seem a small technical detail, however, led to significant consequences: prints were dominated by black, and there were few half-tones.

That this gradually changed was due to a number of artists around Leon Underwood, a dynamic personality who had set up his own school in 1920. One of the pupils, Marion Mitchell, an American, had studied in Paris under Demetrius Galanis, who was well known for his wood-engravings which made considerable use of the multiple engraving tool. Mitchell introduced the art to Underwood and her other colleagues at the school, but it was never formally taught there. The consequence was that their approach was always highly unconventional. Underwood himself published a number of wood-engravings, and Blair Hughes-Stanton and Gertrude Hermes became specialists in this field. During the 1930s, they were regarded as having introduced an entirely new approach to wood-engraving in England: blocks now showed vastly more working, and a very considerable range of textures and half-tones.

Other students only dabbled with the technique, but when in 1931 a group of them came together to form a short-lived society and published a journal, *The Island*, it was wood-engraving that they used for the plates. *The Island* would now be forgotten were it not for the artists associated with it, and the remarkable prints that they made for it. Henry Moore contributed the only wood-engravings that he ever produced; so too did Eileen Agar.

Many of the plates in *The Island* show a precocious awareness of Surrealism, and it is this that links other artists in this section. John Banting was the first, and perhaps the only true Surrealist that this country produced. The blueprints that he made from 1931 onwards

are extraordinary, both in their imagery and in their technique, which had nothing whatever to do with any tradition of printmaking in this country but was instead derived from Man Ray's photograms and Max Ernst's drawings. Almost as unprecedented were the monotype drawings of F.E.McWilliam; their technique also came from the Continent, and in particular from Paul Klee.

At the opposite pole from the Surrealists in the 1930s were the Constructivists. Their leader was Ben Nicholson, a number of whose beautiful linocuts of the late 1920s and early 1930s have been included here. They were printed in tiny numbers, and given to friends rather than sold. Their link was less with traditional printmaking than with the contemporary interest in relief printing for textiles and decorative papers.

Ben Nicholson

1894–1982

Born at Denham, Buckinghamshire, the eldest child in an exceptionally artistic family. His parents, Mabel Pryde and William Nicholson, were both painters, the latter being one of the most influential illustrators and graphic designers of the turn of the century. One brother, Kit, became an architect, and his sister, Nancy, an interior designer. His formal artistic education consisted of just one year at the Slade (1910–11), from which he claimed to have derived the sole benefit of a lasting friendship with Paul Nash. His marriage to another painter, Winifred Dacre, in 1920 seems to have encouraged his interest in landscape, which was allied to a predilection for still-life composition, influenced by his father's work. During the 1920s, Nicholson lived in Cumberland and the Swiss Ticino, one of the places to which he formed an enduring attachment. Another was Cornwall, where, on his first visit in 1928 with his fellow artist Christopher Wood, he discovered the 'primitive' work of the fisherman Alfred Wallis, which had an immediate effect upon his own.

From 1931 until the war, Nicholson lived in the Mall Studios in Hampstead with the sculptor Barbara Hepworth, at the heart of an increasingly cosmopolitan artistic community. During the early thirties his work underwent rapid stylistic development, reflecting his personal contact with Picasso in 1932 and then with the abstract artists in Paris connected with the Association Abstraction-Création. By 1934 he had begun to produce carved and painted reliefs, refining an austere, geometric style which placed him at the centre of the Constructivist movement in London during the latter half of the thirties.

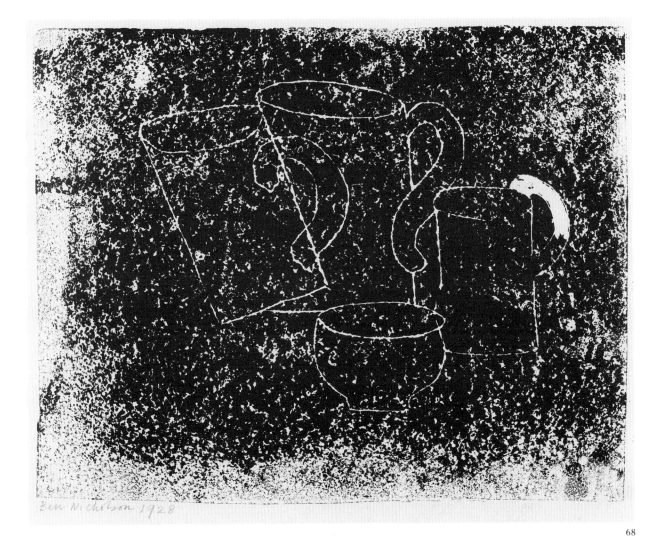

Ben Nicholson 1928

68

From 1939 to 1958 he lived at St Ives in Cornwall, producing a wealth of spare, linear drawings of the landscape and paintings which assimilated his several interests in landscape, still life and abstraction. During the post-war period, architectural subjects became an important component in his work, ranging from Cornwall to Yorkshire, Tuscany, the Aegean and then the Ticino, where he returned to live in 1958 for another thirteen years following his third marriage. During the latter part of his career he concentrated once again on abstract reliefs, introducing a variety of colour and texture which distinguishes them from their predecessors.

The first phase of Nicholson's printmaking, from about 1926 to 1937, was entirely idiosyncratic, arising from the same interest in flat patterns, varied textures and incised surfaces which preoccupied him in his paintings and reliefs. Apart from a single woodcut published in 1934 (cat. no. 75) the prints made at this time were all linocuts produced in tiny numbers for his own private use or for the benefit of a small circle of close friends. In addition to the single-sheet images on paper, he experimented with linoblock printing on fabric, exhibiting a group of these designs at the Lefèvre Gallery in 1933. Subsequently in the late thirties he gave these blocks to his sister Nancy, who ran the Paulk Press; after the war she sold runs of fabric printed with three of his designs at her shop in Motcomb Street, London. Two lithographs, reproductive of his paintings, were printed in 1939, but his direct interest in printmaking lapsed until 1948, when he began a series of drypoints of still lifes and landscape subjects taken from Cornwall (see cat. nos 192–3 below). Etching was ideally suited to his drawing style, and from 1965 to 1968, in collaboration with a Swiss printer, François Lafranca, he completed an extensive series of plates. Finally, 'in the spring of 1968 he declared that this phase was over; and after that he never made any more engravings' (*Ben Nicholson: Etchings Printed by Lafranca*, Kunsthalle Mannheim, 1984, p.35).

69

Bibliography

The most important general publications are the two volumes with introductions by Herbert Read, *Ben Nicholson: Paintings, Reliefs, Drawings*, vol. I, 1911–47, Lund Humphries, London 1948, and vol. II, 1948–56, London 1956; John Russell covers a slightly longer period in his *Ben Nicholson: Drawings, Paintings and Reliefs, 1911–1968*, London 1969. The catalogue for the Tate Gallery retrospective in 1969 provides the most succinct overview of Nicholson's career to that date, while Jeremy Lewison's catalogue for Kettles Yard, Cambridge, in 1983, *Ben Nicholson: the Years of Experiment 1919–39* is excellent on the period in question. There is no comprehensive study of Nicholson's prints apart from the fold-out pamphlet which accompanied the Victoria and Albert Museum's travelling exhibition of 1975, entitled *Ben Nicholson: the Graphic Artist*; Christopher Neve in *Country Life*, 17 July 1975, pp.132–3, wrote an interesting review of this exhibition under the title 'Three Mugs and a Bowl'.

More recently Jeremy Lewison has compiled a catalogue raisonné of the early prints, *c.*1926–39, with an introductory essay, 'The Early Prints of Ben Nicholson', which was published in *Print Quarterly* II (1985), pp.105–24. Nicholson's linocut designs for fabrics are discussed in Lewison's article and in *The Nicholsons: a Story of Four People and their Designs*, York City Art Gallery, 1988. The later etchings are all reproduced in the 1984 Mannheim catalogue referred to above.

Nicholson's personal papers are deposited in the Tate Gallery archive and will be available for consultation at a future date.

The references LH in the catalogue entries are to the Lund Humphries volumes; the Lewison references are to the catalogue of 1985.

70

71

68 Three Mugs and a Bowl, 1928

Linocut printed in black, signed and dated below image in
pencil. 245 × 317 mm

Lewison 2b

1982–10–2–13

Lewison records eight impressions of this image. Nicholson retained this particular example in his own possession until the end of his life. All his linocuts between 1926 and 1930 were still lifes composed of varying arrangements of domestic crockery, objects which often became family heirlooms by virtue of their significance in his own work and that of his father. In a letter of 1952 to Patrick Heron, Nicholson acknowledged his particular debt to his father: '. . . the still life theme stems mainly from Chardin via my father, not only did my father paint innumerable still lives but from as long as I can remember my home was full of the most lovely spotted mugs and striped jugs and glass objects which he'd collected' (Tate Gallery Archive). Of these compositions *Three Mugs and a Bowl* makes the least concession to either decorative content or spatial recession, and epitomises the reasons for Nicholson's attraction to monochromatic linocut printing.

69 Jug with Two Mugs, *c.*1929

Linocut printed in black. Inscribed on verso, 'belonging to
C.S.Reddihough – lino cut – BN Bankshead'. 275 × 331 mm

Lewison 7b

Private collection

One other impression of this subject is recorded by Lewison: it is in H.S.Ede's collection at Kettles Yard, Cambridge. Bankshead was Nicholson's house in Cumberland, where he lived from 1920 to 1931. The composition almost exactly mirrors that of a painting, *Still Life*, dated 1929.

70 Profile, sometimes called 'Head', 1933

Linocut printed in black. Signed along right-hand side in ink,
'BN 1933'. 425 × 331 mm

Lewison 9g

Private collection

Nicholson's removal from Bankshead to Hampstead in 1931 interrrupted his attempts at linocutting until 1933, which proved to be his most productive year in this medium. His relationship with Barbara Hepworth had a decisive impact on his imagery and in 1932–3 Nicholson, for the only time in his career, made the human figure or profile one of the chief subjects of his compositions. A notable series of paintings and drawings recorded a significant visit he made to France with Hepworth in the spring of 1932, when they met Braque, Brancusi and Arp in Paris en route to Provence, and Picasso on their return journey. The most remarkable of these was *St Rémy, Pro-*

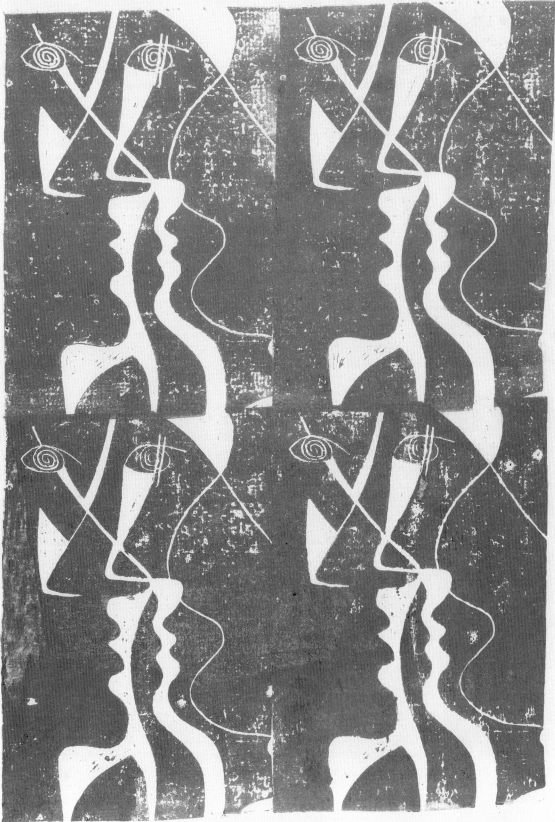

BN 1933

73

74

vence, 1933 (LH 1.53), a rich, dark painting with the lines incised into the surface, which may have been the point of departure for the profile heads he executed in linocut.

The single profile head catalogued here in two different impressions was the most important of all Nicholson's linocuts, of which he pulled at least fourteen impressions. A photograph taken by Barbara Hepworth of Nicholson's studio in 1933 (Lewison, fig. 57) shows three of the impressions pinned to the walls. Lewison describes the considerable variation in inking and registration which exists between the impressions; the one described above, printed on a sheet taken from a spiral bound sketchbook, is presumably an early impression as there is no sign of the split in the block which becomes progressively more apparent in all the others, with the exception of one at Kettles Yard (Lewison 9d).

71 Profile, sometimes called 'Head', 1933

Linocut printed in blue-black. Signed and dated 'Ben Nicholson 1933'. 428 × 385 mm
Lewison 9l
Private collection

Only two impressions of *Profile* were apparently printed in blue-black ink; the other one belongs to the Victoria and Albert Museum (Lewison 9a).

72 Man and Woman, Heads in Profile, 1933

Linocut printed in grey. Inscribed below in ink, 'BN 1933'.
515 × 358 mm
Private collection

This particular linocut printed with four repeats was exhibited as no. 5 in the Victoria and Albert Museum's exhibition of 1975 and is catalogued by Lewison as a variant of an image printed in black in two repeats (10d). The profiles, however, do not correspond with those reproduced by Lewison, and it must therefore be considered as a separate composition. Both prints are related to *Painting*, 1933 (LH 1.50), which depicts similarly overlapping profiles and can be seen in the 1933 studio photograph (Lewison, fig. 57) propped against the lower edge of one of the impressions of *Profile* (cat. nos 70–71).

The repetition of the motif is reminiscent of Nicholson's linocut designs for fabric, which were virtually all executed at the same time. The right-hand side of a design known as *Princess* (Lewison 16), depicting a profile head surmounting a crown, appears, for example, in two repeats printed on paper in the same studio photograph mentioned above. It would be quite impossible to draw a distinction between the fine and decorative art functions of Nicholson's linocuts which, like so much of his work, seemed to respond to the plea Paul Nash had made for the English to consider 'patterns as important as pictures' ('Woodcut Patterns' in H. Furst (ed.), *The Woodcut*, no. 1 (1927), pp.30–38).

75

73 Foxy and Frankie (1), 1933

Linocut printed in black, retouched with oil paint. Signed and dated and inscribed '1'. 159 × 149 mm

Lewison 11.1

Tate Gallery (P.07201)

74 Foxy and Frankie (3), 1933

Linocut printed in black, retouched with oil paint. Signed and dated. 159 × 148 mm

Lewison 11.3

Private collection

Foxy and Frankie is a series of five sequential abstract linocuts to which Nicholson subsequently assigned the names of the two cats he owned in Cornwall during the war. They relate to a small group of paintings he executed in the same year, most notably *Painting (Hibiscus)* (LH 1.64), which reflect the influence of Picasso's experimentation with rectilinear abstraction in the late twenties, as well as the work of Alexander Calder and Paul Klee in the early thirties. In the *Foxy and Frankie* prints, Nicholson not only assimilated certain structural elements from these artists but also the humour inherent in their articulation.

75 5 Circles, 1934

Woodcut printed in black. Signed and dated below in pencil and inscribed '5 Circles woodcut'. 159 × 201 mm

Lewison 14e

1982–10–2–14

Unlike the linocuts, *5 Circles*, the only woodcut Nicholson executed, was printed not by himself but by a professional printer for publication by Anatole Jakovski in a portfolio of twenty-three prints by European artists which appeared in Paris in 1935 (Editions G. Orobitz). The portfolio was intended to act as an *édition de luxe* for a subsequent collection of essays by Jakovski on Marcel Duchamp and the artists from whom the prints were commissioned, but its lack of financial success prevented the publication of the essays. The published album, which can be seen in the Victoria and Albert Museum Library, was printed in an edition of 50, of which the first 20 were available for sale and the remaining 30 were given to the artists and collaborators. An unspecified number of artist's proofs were also made; the British Museum's impression may well be one of these, as it came from the artist's estate, and Nicholson himself, in a letter of 1964 to Carol Hogben at the Victoria and Albert Museum, claimed that he 'never saw a copy of the book & always presumed it was not published' (quoted by Lewison, p.110). A second edition of 300 was later printed from the block and published by the Kestner Gesellschaft in Hanover in 1962.

This particular image is directly related to Nicholson's

contemporary experiments with abstract reliefs, demonstrating the sculptural appeal that the whole process of relief printmaking had for him. His inclusion in the Jakovski album as the only British representative among a galaxy of the Continental avant-garde including Arp, de Chirico, Ernst, Kandinsky, Miró and Picasso, to name but some of the other artists, demonstrates the extent to which he was already perceived on the Continent in 1934 as part of the mainstream of European modernism.

Eileen Agar

born 1899

Daughter of an extremely wealthy Scottish businessman, she spent her early years in Argentina. On her father's retirement she returned to London in 1911, studying first at Leon Underwood's school in Hammersmith in 1920 and then at the Slade in 1921–4. She broke with her parents in 1922, but on her father's death in 1925 was left an annual income of £1000. In 1926, she met the Hungarian writer Joseph Bard, who introduced her to a wider European culture, much of their time before the war being spent abroad. She exhibited on only a few occasions before the 1936 Surrealist exhibition in London, of which she was one of the 'discoveries'. She has continued to paint to the present day, having perhaps the longest artistic career of anyone included in this exhibition.

Almost all of Agar's work consists of paintings, collages and sculptural constructions; she is known not to have made more than a few prints. The earliest were three relief prints published in 1931 in *The Island*, the periodical financed by Agar and edited by Bard (see below). These all belong to the period before her involvement with Surrealism. A fourth print is a small abstract woodcut used for an invitation card. In 1948 she exhibited a lithograph, *Shrimps at Sea*, at the Redfern Gallery.

Bibliography

The main source on Agar's life (which corrects many previous statements) is her autobiography, *A Look at My Life*, which was published in London in 1988. There has not, however, been a large retrospective of her work, and information has to be culled from various dealers' catalogues, especially those of Birch & Conran in London.

76 Two Lovers, 1931

Woodcut, printed on thin Japan paper. Signed and numbered 4/5 in pencil. 122 × 176 mm (dimensions of block)
1986-7-26-28

This print was published on page 13 of the first issue of *The Island* in June 1931, underneath the heading 'The Bird: by Eileen Agar'. Below it were six lines of verse:

. . . I catch the morning from Aurora's hands
Chanticleer hails the freshness of her ray
No haunting past dare stir the peace
The earth is listening with tree-leaf ears
When near the shore the sandals of a child
Touch for a second the blueness of the sea.

For this reason this print has always been titled 'The Bird', although the image has nothing to do with birds. It seems probable that the title refers to the poem rather than to the print, though the placing of the print presup-

77

poses that it in turn has something to do with the poem.

The impressions printed in the magazine itself are on a harsh white paper. Both the signed and numbered prints exhibited here come from a contemporary *tirage à part*. The original wood block for this print is now in the possession of Messrs Birch & Conran in London.

77 Family Trio, 1931

Lineblock, printed on thin Japan paper. Signed and numbered 3/5 in pencil. 167 × 167 mm

1986-7-26-29

Published on page 63 of the September issue of *The Island*. Another impression of this print, illustrated as plate 21a in Agar's autobiography, has been hand-coloured, perhaps through a stencil. The original drawing (in reverse), in pen and black ink, and the printing block are both in the possession of Birch & Conran. The block is in fact metal, and appears to have been made photomechanically from the drawing. It is this block that produces the inky margin seen outside the image in this impression. Agar's third print for *The Island* (a bell, entitled *Vivos Voco* (on page 39 of the September issue) was a linocut.

These two prints show the effect of the two years that Agar had spent in France in 1929-30, and are quite unlike the work in the same issues of *The Island* by the other members of the Underwood school.

In the December issue of *The Island* is a half-tone reproduction of one of Agar's paintings, with a page-long essay by her on 'Religion and the Artistic Imagination' as a contribution to a collection of opinions about this subject by the 'Islanders', Gandhi, Nevinson and others.

Her argument can be crudely abbreviated as follows:

There is no male element left in Europe, for the intellectual and rational conception of life has given way to a more miraculous creative interpretation, and artistic and imaginative life is under the sway of womb-magic . . .
  Russia obviously repudiates Christianity, and the female concept as a form of life . . . this extreme rationalism will give a Jewish character to their outlook . . .
  Only in the child-like emotional veracity of the negro can America find its creative fulfilment, for, excepting the Indian tradition, there is no other cultural background to the present-day amorphous civilisation of America . . .
  Expressed in the symbolism of the Earth, Sun and the Moon, the Holy Trinity of Christianity is realised and surpassed by these three emergent cultures in Russia, Europe and America.

It seems that *Family Trio* symbolically represents these three cultures: the male on the left is the Russian/Jewish element, the female in the centre is the European/female element, while the child to the right is the American/negro. Agar's painting of the same subject and very similar composition was included in the 1988 exhibition at Whitford & Hughes in London titled *The Surrealist Spirit in Britain*, and the connection with Agar's later essay is made in the catalogue entry by Louisa Buck.

Henry Moore

1898-1986

Born into a Yorkshire mining family, and, after service in the army in the First World War, studied at Leeds School of Art. He then won a scholarship to the Royal College of Art from 1921 to 1924, where he specialised in sculpture. He supported himself mainly by teaching until, in the 1930s, he began to win a national reputation for his work. After the Second World War his fame became international.

Moore's first prints were two wood-engravings which were published in *The Island*. He made one other print, an unfinished lithograph titled *Spanish Prisoner*, to raise money for Spanish Republicans imprisoned in France in 1939. He did not resume printmaking until after the war, when he was persuaded to try two new processes: lithographs drawn on plastic plates and printed by W.S.Cowell (cat. no. 130), and collographs for the Ganymed Press (cat. nos 131 and 132). Moore's first large-scale production in lithography was the set of eight illustrations to André Gide's translation of *Prometheus*, printed by Mourlot in Paris in 1950. Apart from a brief trial with etching under the tutelage of Merlyn Evans in 1951, Moore's interest in printmaking once again lapsed until the early 1960s. Thereafter ensued his period of greatest productivity, when he was very dependent upon the services of master printers like Stanley Jones at the Curwen Studio for lithography, and on Jean Frélaut and Alistair Grant for etching.

THE ISLAND

A Wood Engraving : by Henry Moore

Bibliography

A vast amount has been written about Moore and his work. A convenient source is William Packer, *Henry Moore, an Illustrated Biography*, London 1985. The most important work on his prints is the four volumes by Gérard Cramer, Alistair Grant and David Mitchinson entitled *Henry Moore, Catalogue of Graphic Work*, vol. I, 1931–72; vol. II, 1973–5; vol. III, 1976–9; and vol. IV, 1980–84, published in 1973, 1976, 1980 and 1986 respectively. CGM references in the catalogue entries refer to this work. Pat Gilmour wrote an excellent catalogue, *Henry Moore, Graphics in the Making* for the Tate Gallery in 1975, after the presentation of a complete set of Moore's prints to that institution. A selection of the prints is discussed by David Mitchinson in *Henry Moore, Etchings and Lithographs 1949–84*, British Council, 1988. Currently in preparation under the auspices of the Henry Moore Foundation is a book on Moore's printmaking methods.

Copyright in all Moore's work is vested in the Henry Moore Foundation.

78 Figures, Sculptures, 1931

Wood-engraving (p.7 of *The Island* no. 1, 5 June 1931).
128 × 199 mm
CGM 1
The Henry Moore Foundation

This print was made for the first issue of *The Island*. It is there simply captioned as 'a wood-engraving by Henry Moore'; the title given above was chosen in 1966 when the block was reprinted in an edition of 50 plus 10 artist's proofs by Gérard Cramer in Geneva.

Moore had met Leon Underwood at the Royal College of Art, where the latter taught life drawing in the painting school. When Underwood set up his own school of art, Moore often joined in the drawing classes. Underwood was a great admirer of Aztec sculpture, and he must have strengthened Moore's interest in non-European carving. It is therefore not surprising that Moore was one of the 'Islanders' in 1931, and was persuaded to contribute to the illustration of their quarterly. His second wood-engraving (a reclining nude) was published on page 14 of the same issue. That he had little interest in wood-engraving as a medium can be guessed from the fact that he never handled it again, but his prints are some of the most interesting among the remarkable illustrations included in the journal.

Blair Hughes-Stanton

1902–1981

The only son of the very successful landscape painter Sir Herbert Hughes-Stanton. He had little formal education, joining a cadet school ship at the age of 13. As an artist, he trained at the Byam Shaw School. While there, he was greatly influenced by Leon Underwood, and in 1921 moved to Underwood's new school in Hammersmith. When Underwood went to America at the end of 1925, Hughes-Stanton was left in charge. Although he continued to paint and draw, he soon gained a reputation as a printmaker for his wood-engravings. The first to be published were illustrations to T.E.Lawrence's *The Seven Pillars of Wisdom* in 1926; with the proceeds he married Gertrude Hermes in the same year.

Much of Hughes-Stanton's subsequent work was in the form of illustrations for private press books, first with the

Cresset and Golden Cockerel Presses and then, between 1930 and 1933, for the Gregynog Press in Wales. In 1933–6 he briefly set up his own press, the Gemini Press, with the backing of Robert Sainsbury, but by 1935 the Depression had put an end to all commissions for illustrations. He therefore returned to the single-sheet print, and in the next four years made seven large blocks. During the Second World War, he was shot by a guard in a prisoner-of-war camp at Corinth and almost fatally wounded, and although he returned to his art after the war, it was never with the same success.

Between 1928 and 1930 he was closely associated with D. H. Lawrence, and illustrated some of his books. It was partly in response to the philosophy of those novels – and partly to his new affair with Ida Graves – that he created the overtly sexual iconography that marks the prints of this period, in which couples float within womb-like shapes. The prints of the later 1930s, however, reveal a greater concern for formal semi-abstract design that makes them less personal but perhaps more impressive achievements. All three catalogued here belong to this latter group.

Bibliography

The American poet John Gould Fletcher published two articles on Hughes-Stanton's prints in *Print Collector's Quarterly*: the more important one (which also discusses the work of Gertrude Hermes) was in vol. XVI (1929), pp.183–98; the second, which supplements it, is in vol. XXI (1934), pp.353–72. John Lewis also wrote an essay on the wood-engravings, in *Image* 6 (Spring 1951), pp.26–44. A monograph on the life and work of Hughes-Stanton has now been written by his daughter Penelope,

who has kindly allowed us to use it in preparing these entries as well as giving us much other help. It is being published in 1990 by the Private Libraries Association, and contains a checklist both of the books that he illustrated and of the single-sheet prints. There are fifty-nine of these: twenty-five made between 1924 and 1930; four colour prints of 1934–5; the seven large prints of 1935–8; seven further prints in 1950–51; and finally a group of sixteen colour prints made between 1958 and 1961.

79 Creation, 1936

Wood-engraving. Signed, titled, dated and numbered 8/20 in pencil. 205 × 307mm

1990–3–3–10

This is the most abstract composition that Hughes-Stanton ever made, and betrays a conscious determination to move away from the organic shapes that had dominated his earlier prints. He uses an extraordinary variety of methods of laying wood-engraved lines in order to create different textures and a range of grey tones.

80 Figures II, 1937

Wood-engraving. Signed, titled, dated and numbered 13/15 in pencil. 229 × 293mm

1990–3–3–11

Cat. nos 80 and 81 are closely related in both subject-matter and style. Their very similar titles (variations of which are found on different impressions) have often led to their being confused. Both show a man and a woman (identifiable as the artist and Ida Graves) on a scrolled Regency couch which belonged to them both.

79

80

81

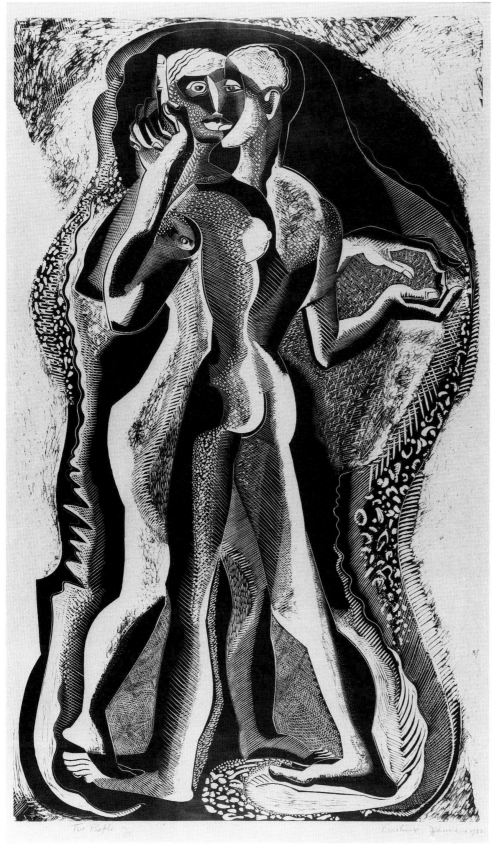

The preparatory drawings for both prints, in pen and black ink and in the same direction and size, have been presented to the British Museum by the artist's widow, Mrs Anne Hughes-Stanton (1990–3–3–61 and 62). They show a wide variety of types of pen work, equivalent to the different types of hatching in the wood-engravings. Hughes-Stanton also made a pair of paintings of exactly the same design; in these the compositions are not only clarified by colour, but the surfaces are again differentiated by the use of various paint textures and finishes.

81 Two Figures (a), 1938

Wood-engraving. Signed, titled and numbered 1/15 in pencil. 230 × 293 mm

1949–4–11–978. Bequeathed by Campbell Dodgson

The composition shows a female nude on a couch, with a seated man placing his arm around her. The guitar was added at a late stage in the design, and replaces a painting seen in the background of the preparatory drawing.

Dodgson's records show that he purchased this print from the Zwemmer Gallery in April 1938 for 2 guineas. The gallery must have taken some impressions on consignment, for the print is listed in *Fine Prints of the Year* for 1938 without the name of any publisher. It was available from the artist himself at Stratford St Mary, near Colchester, for 2 guineas; the edition size is given as 20.

Gertrude Hermes

1901–1983

Born in Kent of German parents; her father was a designer and manufacturer of silk wear. In 1920–21 she studied at the Beckenham School of Art; in 1921–2 she went to Munich for six months, but returned to England to study at the Underwood School in 1922–5. There she took up wood-engraving and sculpture, the two media in which she more or less specialised. She married Blair Hughes-Stanton in 1926; they had two children, born in 1927 and 1928. She moved with him to the Gregynog Press in Wales in 1930, but in 1932 they separated. In 1940 she went to Canada with her children, returning in 1945 to continue her career as a sculptor and printmaker; she also taught relief printmaking, first at the Central School and later at the Royal Academy Schools.

The first important exhibition of her prints was shared with Hughes-Stanton, Agnes Miller Parker and William McCance at the St George's Gallery in 1928. During the 1930s her production was fairly evenly divided between single-sheet prints, of which she made eighteen, and book illustration. After 1945 she began to make colour wood-engravings, and then colour linocuts from the late 1940s.

Bibliography

A retrospective exhibition of Hermes's work from 1924 to 1967, mounted in 1967 at the Whitechapel Art Gallery, was the first one-man show that she ever held. Another was held at the Royal Academy in 1981, but was accompanied only by a small pamphlet. An article on her work and that of Hughes-Stanton was published in *Print Collector's Quarterly* XVI (1929), pp.183–98, by John Gould Fletcher. James Hamilton contributed an essay on her period at Gregynog to the 1988 edition of her *Selborne* illustrations. A catalogue raisonné of Hermes's work is to be published by her daughter Judith Russell and James Hamilton. We would like to thank James Hamilton for his assistance with this entry.

82 Two People, 1933

Wood-engraving. Signed, dated, titled and numbered 12/30 in pencil. 509 × 306 mm

1989–4–11–138

This is one of the largest prints by Hermes. Its exact date is uncertain: another impression in the Tate Gallery (P. 77069) carries the date 1934, but the subject and its treatment clearly relate to the emotional turmoil associated with the earlier collapse of her marriage. The figure on the left is certainly female, but the sex of the one on the right is not determined. The compiler of the Tate Gallery's *Illustrated Catalogue of Acquisitions 1984–6*, 1988, p.377, points out that the womb-like shape which encloses the two figures can be found in many works by Hermes and Hughes-Stanton in the 1930s, and that there seems to be some influence from African sculpture: Leon Underwood was a great enthusiast in this field, and in his *Figures in Wood of West Africa*, London 1947, reproduced African carvings belonging both to Hermes and to Hughes-Stanton.

This print is an excellent example of the variety of wood-cutting techniques practised by the artists associated with the Underwood School, who used a wide range of tools in order to create different textures.

Ceri Richards

1903–1971

Born in Dunvant, a mining village near Swansea, the son of a tin-plate worker. After leaving school in 1919 he was apprenticed to a local electrical engineering firm and attended classes in technical drawing. In 1921 he enrolled as a full-time student at Swansea School of Art, proceeding on a scholarship to the Royal College in London in 1924. For financial reasons he was compelled to start work in 1927 as a commercial artist for the London Press Association, but continued what he regarded as his real development through his musical interests in modern French composers as well as in the visual arts. From 1933 until the war he experimented with collage, relief constructions and sculptural objects, and allied himself briefly with the Objective Abstractionist Group, which included Victor Pasmore and Ivon Hitchens, and with the London Surrealists. Julian Trevelyan described Richards in the mid-thirties as being

obsessed with Picasso, and, as he had then to work in an advertising agency, he spent his lunch hours making photostat copies of reproductions from Picasso books that he could not afford to buy. He also built the most magnificent reliefs out of bits of wood and brass that have stood the test of time as few reliefs do, and which have the same savage grandeur that belong to some African carvings, objects from another world that occasionally deign to show themselves to us poor mortals (*Indigo Days*, pp.55–6).

By 1939 Richards was able to establish a full-time career in the fine arts through teaching first at Chelsea, then at Cardiff School of Art during the war, returning to London in 1945. His work of the post-war period was dominated by themes often drawn from music or poetry, in particular the work of Dylan Thomas and Debussy, which he would explore in an extended series of images, both prints and paintings.

Richards made his first tentative foray into printmaking in 1939 with three linocuts of London costers, followed by a single lithograph dated 1940 of the same subject, all of which he printed himself. The *Rape of the Sabines* provided the theme for a sequence of monotypes in 1947. Lithography was however to prove his most successful print medium. His involvement began in earnest in 1945 with three illustrations to one of Dylan Thomas's poems commissioned for *Poetry London*, then burgeoned from the late forties onwards under the encouragement of the Miller's Press, the Redfern Gallery and the Curwen Studio. Towards the end of his life he also worked with the Kelpra Studio on a number of colour screenprints.

Bibliography

The catalogue for the Tate Gallery's exhibition on Richards in 1981 contains a full chronology and select bibliography. His prints have received quite full attention in three publications: the catalogue raisonné compiled by his friend the Italian poet Roberto Sanesi, *The Graphic Works of Ceri Richards*, Milan 1973; the catalogue by Mel Gooding, *Ceri Richards Graphics*, for the National Museum of Wales, Cardiff 1979, and an article by Pat Gilmour on 'Ceri Richards, his Australian Printer and Stanley Jones' in *The Tamarind Papers*, vol. 10, no. 1 (Spring 1987), pp.28–37.

83 Costerman, 1939

Linocut printed in black on a thin tissue paper. 280 × 220 mm
Sanesi 1
Estate of Ceri Richards

83

84

84 Costerman, 1939

Linocut printed in black. Inscribed in pencil 'A/P Ceri Richards 39'.
268 × 225 mm

Sanesi 2

Museum of London

In the late thirties Richards became involved with one of the most vivacious subjects of his career, the costermongers and their Pearly Kings and Queens, whom he observed at the Bank Holiday fairs on Hampstead Heath. They remained a dominant theme in his reliefs, drawings and prints until 1952. Sanesi records only three impressions of each of the two versions of *Costerman* catalogued here; the third subject of the group was a costerwoman at a coconut shy, printed in three colours, which is described as existing in only one impression. Apart from making numerous informal sketches of the costers, Richards did ask some of them to pose for him; the costerman of the linocuts with one eye sewn up was someone that Richards had encountered in a pub in Hampstead.

The choice of linocut, a simple, relatively crude medium, may well have been suggested to the artist by his subject-matter. He used it for this series alone, creating a group of images which have the quality of popular art, akin to the woodcuts adorning broadsides or traditional ballads.

Edward Burra

1905–1976

Born and brought up in Rye in Sussex, where, with the exception of five years spent at Chelsea Polytechnic and the Royal College of Art, he remained based for the rest of his life. His parents were of independent means, and Burra, who from the age of 14 suffered from rheumatic arthritis, lived with them until their death. He made numerous trips abroad, often to France but also to America and Spain. He developed his idiosyncratic idiom, a mixture of German Neue Sachlichkeit, Mannerism and Surrealism, applied to outline drawings and very large watercolours, early in his career, and this manner never changed significantly in later years.

Burra made only a few prints – the group of woodcuts described here, and three etchings in 1972 (see the Tate Gallery Report for 1972–4, pp.97–8). The woodcuts were made in a group around 1929 at the prompting of Paul Nash, who at that time was living close to Burra (see the 1985 Burra exhibition catalogue, p.145). Six of the prints were exhibited (*hors catalogue*) in the November 1929 exhibition of the Society of Wood Engravers at the Redfern Gallery, and two were again shown in their 1930 exhibition. These, however, seem to be the only occasions on which any of them was exhibited, and only these six prints were ever given a title, or numbered or signed. The blocks then lay forgotten in Burra's house, 2 Springfield Cottages, where five of them were discovered in 1970 by the journalist Barrie Penrose (see his account in the *Observer Magazine* for 25 July 1971). Through him and Alexander Postan the blocks were reprinted and sold by Observer Art in an edition of 45 plus 9 artist's proofs, and then given to the Tate Gallery.

Most of the prints are known in several states. The first just show an outline engraving of a strong contour design (like his drawings of the period) on the block, occasionally elaborated in intermediary states. In the final state part of the background was very crudely hacked away to create some contrast between light and dark. Proofs were taken by Burra himself, by hand using the back of a spoon, usually on a thin Japan paper. The 1929 'edition' of six of the prints, numbered out of 25 (15 in the case of *Mary, Queen of Scots*), was made in the same way. Burra told the Tate compiler in 1972 that this number was purely nominal, and that he only printed a few impressions from each block. This is borne out by the fact that no impression of any of the prints numbered higher than 3 has yet been recorded.

Apart from the 1971 reprints, all the surviving early impressions come from two sources. Those numbered, titled and signed come from the stock of the Redfern Gallery and were left over from the 1929 exhibition. The rest, a group of about thirty-seven unsigned impressions, were discovered and purchased from Burra by Postan in 1970, shortly before Penrose found the blocks. Postan sold most of his impressions to Colnaghi's, whose analysis of the states (as given in their catalogue of British prints of 1975) is quoted in the list below. Since the titled Redfern impressions had not been rediscovered when the 1971 reprints were made, new titles were invented for the prints by Stanley Hardy of the Hamet Gallery. These later titles of course have no validity, but in the absence of any other are used in the list below for the two non-Redfern prints.

The list of Burra's woodcuts given here follows the order of the Tate Report for 1970–72 (pp.89–91). The first eight prints all measure 152 × 101 mm and are on both sides of four blocks; the ninth is on a fifth block measuring 305 × 248 mm. The blocks themselves are end-grain and intended for wood-engraving, but the way in which Burra cut them is more like a woodcut; this term has therefore been used to describe the prints.

1. *Two at a Bar* (cat. no. 85 below). Two states; not titled in 1929
2. *Guitar Player*. One state
3. *Fleet's in*. One state?
4. *Boy with a Jug*. Not titled in 1929
5. *Souvenir*. Two states?
6. *Balcony* (cat. no. 86 below). Two states
7. *Cupbearer*. Two states
8. *Café* (cat. no. 87 below). Three states
9. *Mary, Queen of Scots*. One state?

In addition to the above, there are at least two further woodcuts, the blocks for which were not rediscovered in 1970:

85

10. *Girl with Plant.* 103 × 77 mm. Two states. (Illustrated in Colnaghi's catalogue *British Printmakers 1850–1940*, 1975, no. 94)
11. *Mac's Bar.* 164 × 111 mm. (Illustrated in William Weston's Catalogue 4 of 1980, no. 20)

Bibliography

The standard monograph, *Edward Burra, Complete Catalogue* by Andrew Causey, was published in Oxford in 1985. The same author wrote the catalogue for the exhibition held at the Hayward Gallery in the same year, which also saw the publication by William Chappell of *Well Dearie! The Letters of Edward Burra*. William Chappell was also the editor of *Edward Burra, a Painter Remembered by his Friends*, London 1982. There is no convenient publication on the prints, which were not included in Causey's catalogue of 1985. We would like to thank Alex Postan for help with these entries.

85 Two at a Bar, *c.*1929

Woodcut, on thin Japan paper. Not signed or numbered.
152 × 101 mm
1980–6–28–12

Some confusion has surrounded the circumstances in which the group of woodcuts to which cat. nos 85–7 belong was made. A letter from Paul Nash of February 1928 survives in which he offers to teach Burra how to make a wood-engraving. This provides a *terminus post quem*; the Redfern exhibition of 1929 gives a *terminus ante quem* for six of the prints at least, while an early impression of *Mary, Queen of Scots* carries the date 1930. As for their purpose: when asked by Barrie Penrose whether they were intended as illustrations for a book, Burra is quoted as having replied. 'Are you crazy, dearie? Nobody would have asked me to do a book before the War. As it was, I worked both sides of the blocks because they were pricey to buy. I did them for pleasure, nothing else.' This disproves the assumption of Rex Nan Kivell (quoted in the Tate Gallery Report for 1970–72) that because the prints were brought to him by Robert Gibbings of the Golden

86

87a

87b

Cockerel Press, there must have been some intended publication in mind.

The Colnaghi catalogue records that there were two states of this print. This is the second state, with part of the background cut away, and is known in eight impressions. There was no contemporary edition.

86 Balcony, *c*.1929

Woodcut, on thin Japan paper. Signed, titled and numbered 2/25 in pencil. 152 × 101 mm

1983–5–21–34

This print is known in two states: this is the second, published in 1929. (The first would have been before the background was cut away.) Some impressions of the second state suggest that more of the block had been cut away between the central figure and the man on the left, but this must be caused by differences in printing pressure: the background was so unevenly cut away that much of it caught the ink and printed if extra pressure was applied when hand-printing that area.

This and the following print were included in the 1930 exhibition of the Society of Wood-Engravers at the Redfern Gallery. For some reason, this was priced at $1\frac{1}{2}$ guineas, while *Café* was priced at 1 guinea.

87 Café, *c*.1929

Woodcut. 101 × 152 mm

(a) Second state, on thin wove paper. Not annotated in any way. 1988–1–30–16

(b) Third state, on an irregular sheet of Japan paper. Not annotated in any way. 1985–6–8–19

An impression of the first state, which has only the two figures and the vase at the right, was no. 96 in the 1975 Colnaghi catalogue. The vase at the left and the flowers in the right-hand vase were added in the second state. Only two impressions of the first two states were recorded. In the third state part of the background was cut away, and it was in this form that the woodcut was published in 1929.

When this block was reprinted in 1971, it was given the rather more obvious title 'Clowns'.

John Banting

1902–1972

Born in London, he studied art at evening classes at Westminster School of Art while working as a clerk in Lloyds Bank. In the late 1920s he began to win a reputation as a designer of book covers and for the stage, and was connected with the Bloomsbury circle. In 1930 he visited Paris, where he met Breton and others, after which he became the nearest thing to a Surrealist that Britain ever produced, maintaining contacts through his frequent visits to France. The 'Dragoman' column in the *Daily Express* for 10 November 1931 described Banting as 'one of the hardest-working British artists in Paris who lives Chattertonesquely in a garret', and remarked upon the affinity of his drawings with those of Cocteau. His first one-man exhibition was in 1931; he participated in the 1936 Surrealist exhibition at the New Burlington Galleries, showing two paintings and three watercolours, and a third one-man show was held at the Storran Gallery in 1938. After the war he moved to Ireland and fell into alcoholism and poverty; he was virtually forgotten as an artist until he was 'rediscovered' two years before his death.

Julian Trevelyan remembered Banting in the 1930s as 'a wild creature at this time, dancing in night-clubs all night and creeping home to his mother's little house in Roehampton by the first Underground' (*Indigo Days*, p.67). He appears in many of the memoirs of the period: he and another homosexual, Brian Howard, were very close friends of Nancy Cunard, and he contributed a description of dancing in Harlem to her anthology *Negro* (1934). In 1937 he went to Spain with her as a supporter of the Republican cause. His greatest artistic friendship was with Edward Burra, near whom he lived in Rye and then Hastings from 1961 until his death.

Almost all Banting's prints fall into one of two groups:

1. In the early 1930s he made about twenty linocuts. Only one of these can be regarded as a self-standing work. The rest were used as elements to be cut up and arranged in collages (some thirty or forty of which are known), though five or six of the more complete compositions were occasionally left intact (see cat. no. 91 below). Impressions of two of these survive printed onto cork. Seven of the lino blocks were found by Alexander Postan; six of these (dated 1931–5) were reprinted in 1971 in an edition of 45; he then presented the blocks to the Tate Gallery Archive (7227.1 to 7; see Tate Gallery Report for 1972–4, pp.80–82).

2. From 1931 until the 1950s (if not later) Banting produced a very large number of blueprints using the cyanotype process (see cat. nos 88–90 below). Apart from numerous individual prints, some of which were used in collages, there were two collections: an album of twelve blueprints was made in 1931–2 (see cat. no. 88), and another twenty-three were made for a manuscript album entitled *For Social Service*, of which he stated that he had produced ten copies in 1933 (one is now in the Tate Gallery Archive, 779.5.5). This was published in facsimile in 1946 as *A Blue Book of Conversation*.

Banting also made a solitary etching, *The Spirit of Appeasement*, for the portfolio entitled *Salvo for Russia*, published in 1942.

Bibliography

No monograph or retrospective exhibition has ever been devoted to Banting. His own personal papers, mostly from the 1950s and 1960s, are in the Tate Gallery Archives. An article by Louisa Buck on 'John Banting's Designs for the Hogarth Press' was published in the *Burlington Magazine* CXXVII (1985), pp.91–2. For his life, see *Brian Howard, Portrait of a Failure*, ed. Marie-Jacqueline Lancaster, London 1968 (which contains contributions by Banting), and Anne Chisholm, *Nancy Cunard*, London 1979, *passim*; Banting's own reminiscences of Nancy Cunard are printed in *Nancy Cunard: Brave Poet, Indomitable Rebel*, ed. Hugh Ford, Philadelphia 1968. We are indebted to Alex Postan for much help with these entries.

88 Album of 12 Blueprints, 1931–2

1. *The Secret Visit*

Titled, signed, dated 1931 and numbered 8/100.
236 × 163mm
1983–5–21–32

2. *The Oracle*

Titled, signed, dated 1931 and numbered 8/100.
236 × 161mm
1983–5–21–31

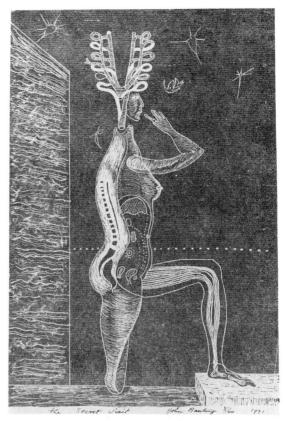

88/1

88/2

88/5

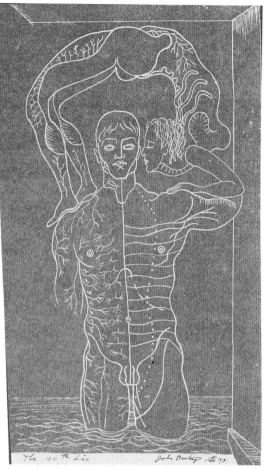

88/3

3. *The 100th Lie*
Titled, signed, dated 1931 and numbered 14/100.
244 × 146 mm
1982-6-19-15

4. *Untitled*
Signed and numbered 4/100. 253 × 200 mm
1983-1-27-9

5. *Untitled*
Signed, dated 1932 and numbered 14/100. 320 × 205 mm
1982-6-19-16

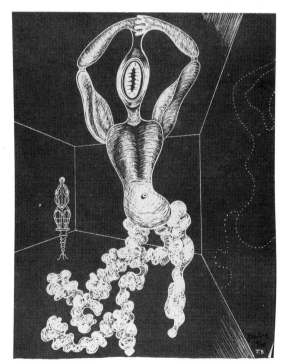

88/4

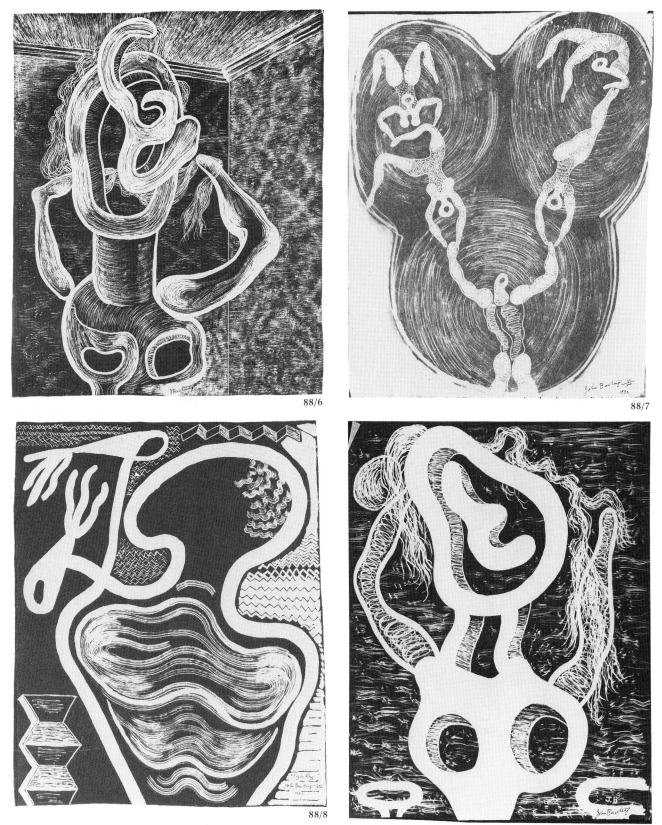

88/6

88/7

88/8

88/11

6. *Untitled*

Signed and numbered 4/100.

256 × 217 mm

1983-1-27-10

7. *Untitled*

Signed, dated 1932 and
numbered 14/100.

255 × 207 mm

1982-6-19-13

8. *'Tiger Rag'*

Signed, titled, dated 1932 and
numbered 14/100.

333 × 280 mm

1982-6-19-12

9. *Untitled*

Signed, dated 1932 and
numbered 8/100.

277 × 385 mm

1983-5-21-33

10. *Untitled*

Signed, dated 1932 and
numbered 14/100.

330 × 273 mm

1982-6-19-11

See colour illustration

11. *Untitled*

Signed, not numbered
(but from set no. 14).

254 × 197 mm

1982-6-19-14

12. *Untitled*

Signed and numbered 14/100.

208 × 315 mm

1982-6-19-10

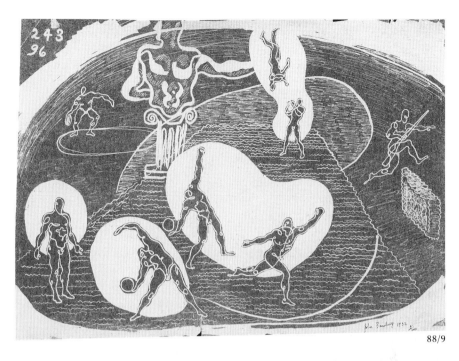

88/9

88/12

The process of making blueprints is familiar in architecture and engineering, but very rarely found in the field of fine art. Among the few other examples that we know is a tempera drawing by the American sculptor David Smith over a blueprint of 1933 (no. 55 in the exhibition of his drawings held at the d'Offay gallery in London in 1986). The process was invented in 1842 by Herschel, and depends on the photo-sensitivity of iron salts which, after exposure and washing, leave a Prussian blue deposit. The artist simply draws on transparent paper, and the design is then printed down onto prepared paper by exposure to light; the image is fixed simply by running water over it. Alexander Postan informs us that Banting never owned his own printing equipment (apart from a simple screw press), and would have had the blueprints made in a local bureau used by architects. (See Jan Denow, *Handbook of Alternative Photographic Processes*, New York 1982 – a reference which we owe to the kindness of Alan Donnithorne.) Since the areas where the light does not come through remain white, the tones of the original drawing are reversed. The drawing can be in any medium: the examples below include both pen and chalk. The British Museum also owns two very large drawings in pen on tracing paper, as well as the blueprints made

89

from them (1982–11–6–14 to 17; not in this exhibition).

It seems likely that Banting got the idea for his blueprints in Paris, from Max Ernst. In around 1918 Man Ray had invented his photogram technique; this involved placing objects or cut-out shapes onto photo-sensitive paper and exposing the whole to light. In 1931, in collaboration with Man Ray, Ernst made nineteen small prints to illustrate the English translation by Kay Boyle of *Mr Knife and Mr Fork*, the first chapter of René Crevel's novel *Babylone*, which was published in Paris in 1931 by the Black Sun Press. These developed the photogram a stage further: instead of using actual objects, Ernst made drawings and frottages on transparent paper, and then exposed them onto sensitised paper (see Robert Rainwater, *Max Ernst, Beyond Surrealism*, New York Public Library, 1986, p.16). Ernst's technique (used by him only in this book) is the same as Banting's, with the difference that Banting substituted the iron salts of a blueprint for the ordinary photographic paper used by Ernst.

The British Museum's set of the *12 Blueprints* is complete, but not uniform: it contains parts of three different sets numbered 4, 8 and 14. The collection also contains the portfolio cover (470 × 310mm) which belonged to set no. 8 (though it does not itself carry a number). The annotations on the prints are in pen and blue ink, and all are irregularly cut and mounted on brown backing sheets (measuring about 450 × 288mm). Banting did not arrange the prints in any order, and that given here follows (for the sake of ease of reference) that given by Messrs Garton & Cooke to the complete set numbered 6 which they described in their catalogue 41 of 1987 (the set had previously been sold by Sotheby's on 2 December 1986,

90

91

Mythology, Auckland City Art Gallery 1980, which gives a full account of Lye's work.) Other quotations evident in the blueprints are from Brancusi's *Endless Column*, while the profile used in *The Oracle* may well have been intended as a portrait of Brian Howard.

89 Untitled Blueprint with Guitar-Face, early 1930s

Unsigned and undated. 315 × 220 mm (maximum dimensions)
1982-6-19-17

This composition is related to the top linocut in the collage cat. no. 91 below. Despite the appearance of being a chalk lithograph, magnification shows that it is indeed a blueprint.

90 Untitled Blueprint with a Forearm and Guitar Strings, early 1930s

Signed on the verso in blue biro. 563 × 381 mm
1987-5-16-55

Like the previous print, this can be dated to the early 1930s. In a letter dated 7 December 1974 in the Tate Gallery files, Julian Trevelyan wrote about the imagery of these works: 'He never spoke to me about their significance, but I know that they were all derived from what he called guitar faces . . . He was mad about jazz, and the idea behind guitar faces was of someone playing himself.'

lot 685, and is now in the possession of Dave and Reba Williams; another set, numbered 11, was sold at Phillips on 13 March 1990). Only four of the prints are titled; three are dated 1931 and eight 1932 (although these dates are omitted on some of the British Museum prints, they are found on other examples). The highest number yet found on any print from this set is 14, and there is every reason to think that very few more than this were ever printed.

The imagery used in the series is very varied, Max Ernst being as important here as he was in the actual method of printing. Banting clearly owed a debt, for example, to Ernst's surreal adaptations of illustrated scientific textbooks. In this respect he shows a marked affinity with the work of the New Zealand artist and film-maker Len Lye (1901–80), who was living in London from 1927 to 1944. Lye's imagery combined Australasian tribal motifs with molecular structures and biological organisms, as well as exploiting the photogram technique at the very beginning of the 1930s to create amorphous, abstract compositions. Banting may have obtained some of the ideas for his own motifs from Lye's first film, *Tusalava*, which concerned 'life-cells, attack and repudiation'. This was shown by the London Film Society in 1929. Later, in 1935, Banting was to provide the art direction for another of Lye's films, *The Birth of a Robot*, which used puppets and models. (We are indebted to Andrew Murray for drawing to our notice the catalogue *Len Lye, A Personal*

91 Collage, Containing Three Linocuts of Guitar Faces, 1935

Signed and dated in pen. 508 × 377 mm (overall size of backing sheet)
1986-7-26-12

The collage has three prints pasted one above the other. The top one is itself a collage of two impressions of the same block, one in blue and one in black, which have been cut down and pasted one on top of the other. The centre and lower prints are also from the same block, and both are printed in black, but the centre one is on a light brown paper while the lower one is from two pieces of dark brown paper assembled together. The collaging together of these impressions is typical, and reveals Banting's interest in shifting colours. This reached its logical conclusion in the rainbow colours he chose for the 1971 reprints. The block for the top print in this collage is in the Tate Gallery (7227.7), but was never reprinted as it was too decayed to withstand the printing pressure.

Another collage, entitled *Tribute to Eddie Condon* (the white American jazz guitarist, 1905–74), sold at Christie's, London, on 14 November 1986, lot 170, bears another impression of the lower print, and is dated 1930. If the date can be believed (which is not certain since Banting only signed and dated many of his works late in his

92

life), the making of the linocuts can be put back at least to 1930; they were then reused in collages through the 1930s. Alex Postan informs us that the signature and date on this collage are certainly late, but thinks that the date is entirely believable.

F. E. McWilliam

born 1909

Born and brought up in Banbridge, Co. Down; his father was a doctor. In 1928 he left Ireland, and studied at the Slade under Henry Tonks and A. H. Gerrard, who turned his thoughts to sculpture. Here he met Henry Moore, who remained a close friend. He moved to France in 1931, intending to settle there, but was forced to return to England the following year after the collapse of the pound. For the next three years he worked on his sculpture in relative isolation in the country, but the 1936 Surrealism exhibition in London had a great impact on him. He moved to Hampstead, near many of the other leading artists of the day, and changed from an organic/abstract manner to one much more akin to Surrealism, though he regarded himself more as a fellow-traveller than a zealot and in 1939 was describing himself in the *London Bulletin* as an independent.

He first exhibited in the Surrealist section of the Artists International Exhibition held in Grosvenor Square in 1937, and held his first one-man show at C. L. T. Mesens's London Gallery in March 1939; this included twenty-one sculptures, many in Hopton Wood stone, and twenty-six 'mono-print drawings'. During the war he served in the Royal Air Force, and afterwards taught sculpture from 1947 until 1968 at the Slade. He has continued to work in London, and has frequently exhibited, first with the Hanover Gallery and more recently with the Waddington and Mayor Galleries. Roland Penrose once described him as 'an inventor of styles', and his work during the post-war years has been marked by an extraordinary variety of types, materials and approaches towards sculpture.

McWilliam seems never to have made prints in any medium other than the monotype. These monotypes are among his most significant drawings; indeed, there is no real dividing line between the monotype and the pure drawing in his work.

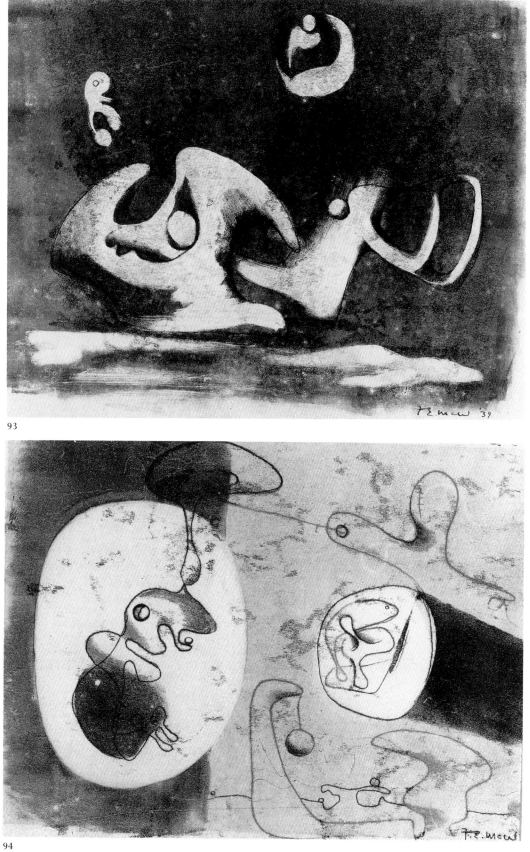

93

94

Bibliography

The only monograph, entitled *McWilliam* and published in London, 1964, has an introduction by Roland Penrose. There have been two large retrospective exhibitions with substantial catalogues: the first by Judy Marle and T.P. Flanagan at the Ulster Museum in 1981, and the second, organised by Mel Gooding, at the Tate Gallery in 1989. All these works concentrate on the sculpture, and have virtually nothing to say about the drawings. The only article on these is by W.J. Strachan, 'The Sculptor and his Drawings, III: F.E. McWilliam', *The Connoisseur* vol. 186 (1974), pp.32–9, which, nonetheless, omits all reference to the monotypes. We would like to thank the artist himself for his help with these entries.

92 Studies for Mandible Sculpture, *c.*1938

Monotype in red and blue-black, printed on an irregularly trimmed thin sheet of paper laid down onto a thick wove backing sheet. Initialled within the composition, bottom left. 440 × 565 mm (maximum dimensions)
1981–10–3–24

The above title was given to this print by the artist in a letter of 25 January 1990 to the British Museum. The shape composed of lower jaw, side of head and ear is the same as that in the sculpture *Mandible* of 1938 (Tate Gallery catalogue 1989, no. 23). The twenty-six 'mono-print drawings' included in the 1939 exhibition at the London Gallery were priced between 3 and 6 guineas each (the complete list is printed in *London Bulletin* no. 11, March 1939). In his letter McWilliam suggests that this print was one of the works titled 'Drawing for sculpture' in that exhibition. Many of them can be seen in the contemporary photographs reproduced in the 1989 Tate catalogue.

In the same letter McWilliam gives the following account of these prints:

When a student at the Slade I shared a studio with the Irish painter John Luke, who was very keen on technique. From him I learnt about mono-printing. I prefer 'transferred ink' to either 'monotype' or 'monoprint' as it is exact and doesn't emphasise printing . . . I simply inked (printer's ink) a sheet of glass and hung a sheet of drawing paper in front, then drew (pencil) on the paper back which picked up a slightly smudged and of course unique image on the other side. Sometimes I drew or wiped the inked surface and then lightly pressed the paper on that – as in the case of *Studies for mandible sculpture*.

The pencil lines that McWilliam refers to are indeed to be seen on the verso of this drawing.

All three prints by McWilliam shown here were included in the 1989 Tate exhibition, although none was listed in the catalogue.

93 Living Rocks, 1939

Monotype, printed in black and green. Initialled and dated in pen. 330 × 420 mm (maximum dimensions)
1989–12–9–17

The title given to this print on acquisition was 'Wandering Rocks', along with the information that it had been included in the 1939 London Gallery exhibition. The catalogue for that exhibition, however, lists no work of this title. McWilliam tells us that he thinks that it was no. 38, 'Living Rocks'.

94 Drawing with Green and Black, after 1938

Monotype. Initialled bottom right in the drawing.
222 × 276 mm
Collection of James Birch

The title is written in McWilliam's hand on the back of the frame, together with the date 1938. But in his letter of 25 January 1990, he states that he now thinks that it was made somewhat later. The drawing was made in three stages: first the blue was transferred; then the green by a combination of pressing and drawing; and finally the black in the same way.

5 Hayter and Associates

The four artists grouped together in this section were all friends who worked abroad (mainly in Paris) for much of the time in the late 1920s and 1930s. The central figure was Stanley William Hayter, the most influential of all twentieth-century British printmakers and a man of very strong character and enormous energy. His early training had been as a scientist, and he saw art, unusually, as a process of discovery in which co-operation was essential. He therefore threw open his studio – known as Atelier 17 – to all interested artists, both in Paris and, during the Second World War, in New York. It was in fact in New York in the 1940s that he both created his own greatest prints and decisively influenced the development of American abstract expressionism by acting as the link between the exiled European Surrealists and the new generation of American artists such as Jackson Pollock. But Hayter's work of this period, as well as that after his return to Paris in 1950, falls outside the scope of this catalogue because it did not really influence British artists.

Hayter himself was greatly influenced by Joseph Hecht (1891–1951), who used the burin to engrave rather charming prints of animals. But Hayter turned the technique to far more serious ends, combining it with an automatic drawing technique derived from Surrealism. Indeed for a number of years he was 'officially' recognised as a Surrealist by Breton.

It says much for Hayter's enthusiasm that he was such a close friend of the other three artists in this section, for the work of all four of them was quite different. John Buckland Wright came to be the closest to Hayter, but as soon as Hayter departed for America he returned to his own more conventional subject-matter of female nudes. Julian Trevelyan was a young Cambridge graduate who had had no professional artistic training whatever when he arrived in Paris in 1931. Hayter therefore adopted something of the role of a mentor towards him, and indeed in his autobiography Trevelyan speaks of being overawed by Hayter, although he always managed to retain a certain stylistic independence from him, even when working at close quarters in Paris. After his return to England, Trevelyan proceeded to produce a group of prints on the theme of 'dream cities' that are completely original in approach.

The last of these artists, Anthony Gross, was a close friend but never a disciple of Hayter's. From his first exhibition in London at the age of 18 in 1924, he had achieved instant success with his dark and brooding plates which embodied all the tricks of inking that the etching revival liked so much. But even before the collapse of the market in 1929, he had begun to reject this style and was working his way towards a new one, seen in full vigour from 1933 onwards. The strongest stylistic influence on him in this period was La Jeune Gravure Contemporaine, a group of contemporary French printmakers. Hayter certainly played no part in this, but must nevertheless have encouraged Gross to keep up with etching when he may have felt tempted to abandon it completely in favour of watercolour or oil painting.

The last curious factor that links these artists is that after the Second World War each of them wrote a treatise on printmaking techniques; these were severally and jointly the most influential British textbooks of the period. So what had begun as a revolution in Paris ended as a new academicism – albeit of an enlightened kind.

Stanley William Hayter

1901–1988

Born in Hackney, from a family of painters that included Sir George Hayter, portrait painter to Queen Victoria. He trained as a chemist at King's College, London, and worked in Iran for an oil company in 1922–5. In 1925 he decided to devote himself entirely to art, and in the following year moved to Paris, where he remained until the outbreak of the Second World War, with only occasional visits back to London. Although he continued to paint and draw, he became known primarily as a printmaker, and in particular as an engraver. In 1927 he opened a printmaking workshop at his studio and this developed into the famous Atelier 17, where many of the major figures of the international avant-garde were to work. The Atelier held a number of group exhibitions in Paris, and Hayter himself showed in London, notably at the 1926 Surrealist exhibition.

In 1939 he returned to England, where he worked briefly in camouflage before leaving for America. He re-established the Atelier in New York in 1940, where it was given a new home at the New School of Social Research. In 1950 he returned to Paris for good, where Atelier 17 was reopened and indeed still survives.

From 1926 until his death Hayter produced a steady flow of prints, totalling over 300 plates. The earliest are somewhat conventional topographical plates, but by 1929 he had begun to be influenced by Surrealism. His experiments during the 1930s can be followed in the works catalogued here. However, these form only the first phase of his career; of even greater significance for the history of the print were his large New York plates and the colour prints he made after the war by various new processes of his invention. Hayter's personal archive of

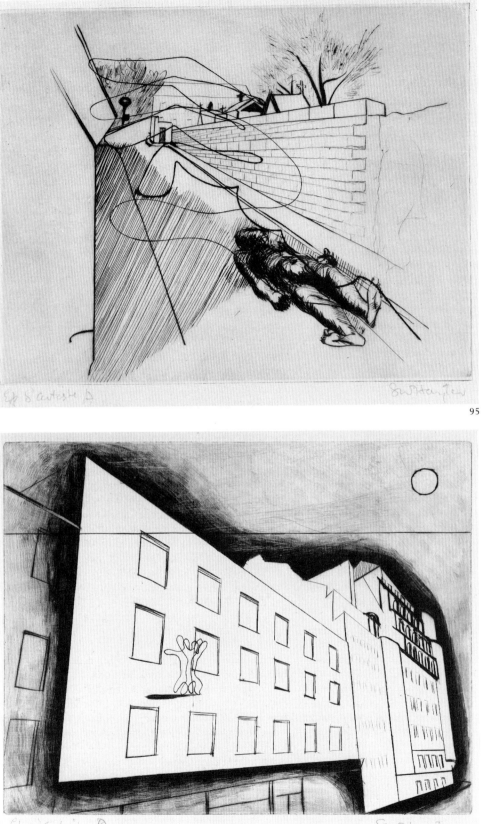

Ép d'artiste A   SWHayter

95

Ép d'artiste A   SWHayter

96

his own prints up to 1960 was purchased by the British Museum in 1988 and 1989.

Bibliography

A catalogue of Hayter's prints is being prepared for publication by his widow, Désirée, in collaboration with Peter Black; we are most grateful to her for enabling us to consult an early draft of the typescript. The best commentator on Hayter's work is Hayter himself, in two books that have been immensely influential. *New Ways of Gravure*, New York 1949, describes Hayter's techniques and his theory of what he called 'gravure'; expanded editions were published in 1966 and 1981, but quotations here are taken from the original edition. *About Prints*, Oxford 1962, is addressed to the intelligent layman and gives a general introduction to the field of modern printmaking.

The most significant modern work is *The Renaissance of Gravure, the Art of S.W. Hayter*, ed. P.M.S. Hacker, Oxford 1988. This incorporates Hacker's catalogue of the retrospective exhibition held at the Ashmolean Museum in 1988, and a number of essays; that by Graham Reynolds, 'Hayter: the Years of Surrealism', is devoted to the period covered in this exhibition.

95 Paysage Urbain: Père Lachaise, 1930

Engraving and drypoint. Signed and annotated 'Epreuve d'artiste A' in pencil. 206 × 268 mm

1974-2-23-4

The set of six plates entitled *Paysages Urbains* was Hayter's first mature work after four years spent in mastering the technique of engraving. They show some of the first superimpositions of outline drawings of figures on actual townscapes (here a corpse against a hand emerging from the cemetery of Père Lachaise) – a drastic recasting of the long-established tradition of topographical intaglio printmaking. It may be significant that he already knew Alexander Calder, who was creating his circus of wire constructions at the time. The series was printed by Raymond Haasen and published in an edition of 50, plus 5 artist's proofs, by Editions Quatre Chemins in Paris in 1930. The British Museum possesses the entire set as artist's proofs. The rich burr comes from the burin lines; drypoint is used for the shading of the foliage of the trees and for the corpse in the foreground.

96 Paysage Urbain: Rue d'Assas, 1930

Engraving with mezzotint. Signed and annotated 'Epreuve d'artiste A' in pencil. 205 × 267 mm

1974-2-23-7

The rue d'Assas runs behind the Jardin du Luxembourg in the VIᵉᵐᵉ. The tone around the building has been added with a mezzotint rocker, but has not been burnished.

97 Nu, 1933

Engraving. Signed, dated, titled and numbered 1/30 in pencil. 200 × 312 mm

1988-4-9-27

Three states are recorded of this print, which is perhaps the closest that Hayter ever gets to showing direct influence from Picasso, whom he knew well. It demonstrates that by this year Hayter had adopted the Surrealist practice of giving rein to the Unconscious, and married it to his use of burin engraving. In 1933 he first exhibited with

97

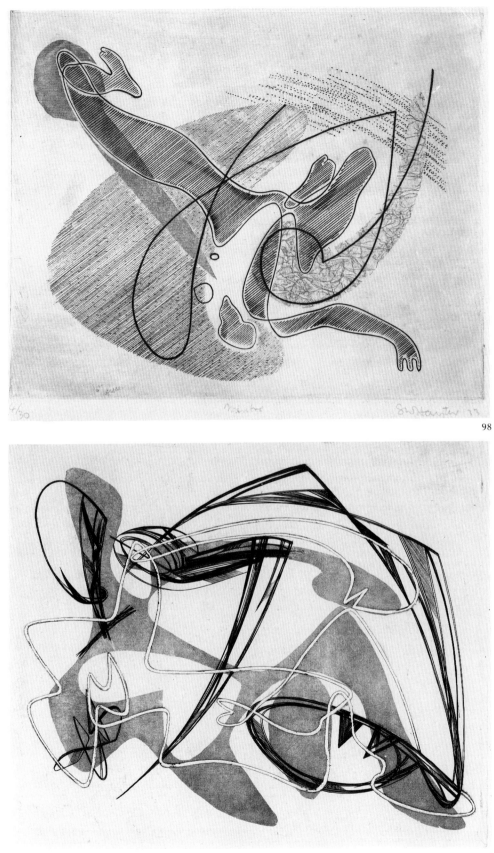

98

99

the Surrealists in Paris, and only left the movement in 1938 after the quarrel between Breton and Eluard.

98 Meurtre, 1933

Engraving with soft-ground and aquatint. Signed, dated, titled and numbered 4/30 in pencil. 233 × 295 mm

1989–6–17–10

The plate was built up in four stages: first engraving, then the soft-ground and aquatint, and finally more engraving. Up to 1932 Hayter's prints rely more or less entirely on engraving, but from 1933 onwards he extended the range of devices to include fabric pressed into soft-ground, and aquatint of various grains. He describes these techniques on page 110 of *New Ways of Gravure*, and on page 217 states: 'About 1933 it started to become clear that the use of the vivid line of the burin for the mechanical production of values in a plate was illogical, and the first impressions of textures on soft ground were made to produce a neutral surface when needed.'

99 Viol de Lucrèce, 1934

Engraving, soft-ground and scorper. Signed, dated and numbered 1/30. 294 × 357 mm

1955–1–8–1. Presented by Douglas Cooper

This was the first plate in which Hayter used his newly discovered technique of engraving a line so deeply into a plate with a scorper (gouging tool) that it no longer held any ink but printed as an embossed white line. As can

be seen very clearly in this print, this creates another level of space in front of the composition. On page 217 of *New Ways of Gravure* Hayter remarks that 'the hollowing of the plate to print white relief was suggested by nineteenth-century Japanese woodcuts, and was first used by us in 1933'. This plate went through four states, the last being dated 29 April on a trial proof in the British Museum. The soft-ground gives an effect very similar to an aquatint grain.

This print was admired by Picasso, who owned an impression. Another owner was Douglas Cooper, who presented his impression to the British Museum in 1955. The copper plate is now in the Museum of Modern Art in New York.

100 Woman in a Net, 1934

Engraving with soft-ground and scorper. Signed, dated, titled and numbered 22/30. 218 × 297 mm

1989–6–17–13

101 Oiseau de Feu, 1935

Engraving, soft-ground, roulette, burnishing and scorper. Signed, dated, titled and numbered 7/30. 209 × 157 mm

1939–7–30–46. Presented by the Contemporary Art Society

This was one of two prints by Hayter presented to the British Museum by the Contemporary Art Society in 1939. They were the first of his prints to enter a public collection, and this was one of the factors cited by Hayter

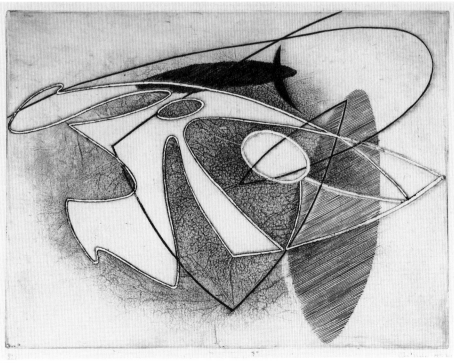

100

as influencing his desire for his archive to come to the British Museum.

There are five states: the first two are engraved, and the third has the soft-ground fabric bitten in. The fourth introduced a new idea: another soft-ground is laid over the plate, and an ordinary metal comb drawn through it. Where the plate is untouched this creates dark bitten lines, but where there is already a soft-ground the new ground counteracts the old lines, creating a white again. In the final state, the deep embossed white areas are added with a scorper.

102 Combat, 1936

Engraving, soft-ground and scorper. Signed, dated, titled and annotated 'Etat X' in pencil. 399 × 497 mm

1973-4-14-5

This is the largest and most ambitious of the plates made by Hayter in the 1930s. Despite the reference to the tenth state, Désirée Hayter has only found eight states of this plate; this is an impression of the last of them.

In *New Ways of Gravure*, page 155, Hayter states that 'the source of the material in all my works is unconscious or automatic. That is to say, an image is made without deliberate intention or direction.' Yet there is abundant evidence for the care with which he planned his plates, and this is a very good example of his approach. In the collection of the Brooklyn Museum in New York are two preparatory drawings for this print. They show how the image originally emerged from a mass of elliptical lines

101

102

103

that had no conscious direction. The design was conjured and refined from these lines in the second drawing.

Once the image had been fixed on paper, its transfer to the copper plate was far from unconscious; it was remarkably precise. But after the first proof had been taken, Hayter proceeded to rework it over and again, building up layers of new design and elaborating the spatial complexity. The Brooklyn Museum has impressions of all eight states, which show how each state gave rise to new ideas which in turn led to further transformations of the image. Hayter describes the development of a later colour plate, *Cinq Personnages* of 1946, in chapter 10 of *New Ways of Gravure*, and makes further remarks on his procedure on page 271.

103 Pâques, 1936

Engraving, soft-ground and scorper. Signed, dated, titled and numbered 1/30 in pencil. 299 × 174 mm

1989-6-17-15

There are four states of this plate, which was finished on 15 April, three days after Easter – whence the title, for the image is in fact of a pregnant woman. A proof of the second state in the British Museum shows that the main outlines were engraved in the first state; the deep scorper work added in the second; the soft-ground in the third; and some extra engraved lines in the fourth. A proof of the final state, also in the British Museum, has noted in the margin the papers on which each impression of the published edition was printed: five different papers were used, and the edition was printed on at least four occasions, on 16 April 1936, 4 May 1936, 5 July 1937 and 4 May 1938.

It appears that despite the stated edition size, only seventeen impressions were in fact printed; this must have been the case for most of Hayter's pre-war prints. Since he lost all his Paris plates during the German

104

occupation (*About Prints*, p.147), he was unable to reprint them after 1939.

This print was no. 133 in the 1936 Surrealism exhibition in London, together with seven other etchings, two paintings and one object.

104 Paysage Anthropophage, 1937

Engraving and soft-ground. Signed, dated, titled and annotated 'Essai' in pencil. 184 × 354mm

1986-7-26-30

This plate is known in four states. Proofs of all three earlier states, two with pencil indications for passages added in the next state, are also in the British Museum; the first two are dated 17 and 18 July 1937. This impression comes from the collection of John Buckland Wright and has in the top left corner a note 'For Buck'.

The plate was commissioned by the famous French publisher and dealer Ambroise Vollard as part of a series to accompany the text (in Spanish and French) of Cervantes' play *Numancia*. Only five plates had been completed when Vollard was killed in a car crash in 1939, and the project was abandoned (see *About Prints*, p.154).

Numancia describes the heroic but unsuccessful defence of the Spanish city against the Roman invaders in 133 BC. This print illustrates a horrific moment in the play, when the starving besieged Numantians decide to eat their Roman prisoners. The choice of such a play for illustration is clearly intended to refer to the Spanish Civil War. The image of course relates also to the work of Salvador Dali, a fellow Surrealist.

Hayter, like almost all artists and intellectuals of the period, was a passionate supporter of the Republicans, and organised the publication of a small portfolio entitled *Solidarité* in April 1938 (a copy is in the British Museum) in order to raise funds for their support. It began with a poem by Eluard, and the other plates were contributed by Picasso, Miró, Tanguy, Masson, Buckland Wright and Hayter's Canadian girl-friend Dalla Husband.

John Buckland Wright

1897–1954

Born in New Zealand, but after the death of his father his mother moved to Switzerland and then to England in 1908. He was educated at Clifton and Rugby, and, after war service, at Oxford, where he read history. He first trained as an architect, and only became an artist in 1924 on inheriting a small income. He was almost entirely self-trained. He moved to the Continent, settling first in Belgium in 1926 and then in Paris in 1929, where he remained until the outbreak of the Second World War. During these years he was closely associated with Hayter and the Atelier 17, and in Hayter's absence often took over its direction. After the war he taught printmaking at Camberwell from 1948 and then, from 1952, at the Slade until his early death.

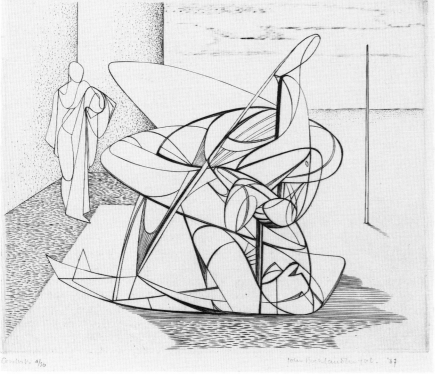

105

Buckland Wright was always known as a print-maker and draughtsman rather than a painter, and throughout the 1930s produced a stream of wood- and copper engravings, most of which were commissioned to illustrate private press books – often of a markedly erotic character – in Belgium and Britain. He did, however, also make a number of single-sheet prints, as well as book plates and Christmas cards. His work is extremely well represented in the British Museum, thanks to a bequest by his widow of an impression of all his prints in her possession.

Bibliography

The most useful source of information is *A Check-List of the Book Illustrations of John Buckland Wright, together with a Personal Memoir* by Anthony Reid, Pinner 1968. There is no published catalogue of the single-sheet prints, but some will be found in an article by R. Gainsborough in *Image* no. 4 (1950), pp.49–62. Buckland Wright himself wrote a standard treatise, *Etching and Engraving, Techniques and the Modern Trend*, The Studio, London 1953, which contains some interesting remarks on contemporary printmaking as well as the best available anthology of reproductions of prints of the early 1950s.

105 Combat, 1937

Engraving. Signed, dated, titled and numbered 4/30 in pencil.
157 × 197mm
1978–1–21–131. Bequeathed by Mrs Mary Buckland Wright

This is one of a small number of prints made by Buckland Wright in the mid- to late 1930s that are closely linked with Hayter's style. In the case of this engraving, the link with Hayter can be seen also in the manner of stippling the background, and in the title, which is the same as that of cat. no. 102. The image here seems to be of a classical wrestling match, and there is no overt reference to Spain. In an exhibition of Buckland Wright's work held at Dulau & Co. in London in 1937, this print was priced at 1½ guineas.

Anthony Gross

1905–1984

Born in Dulwich; his father was a map publisher of Hungarian birth. Educated at Repton, and then at the Slade; he learned etching at the Central School under W.P. Robins. In 1924 he achieved, as a contemporary advertisement in the *Bookman's Journal* put it, 'fame at eighteen', with plates in the Paris Salon and at the Royal Academy, as well as a contract with the publisher W.R. Deighton of the Abbey Gallery. He continued his training in Paris in 1924 under C.A. Waltner at the Ecole des

Beaux-Arts, and in the following year in Madrid. From a base in Paris he spent much time travelling round Europe. By 1928 he had made fifty-three prints, all in an academic manner with plentiful use of drypoint and soupy wiping of the plate.

The collapse of the market for etchings in 1929 seems to have coincided with a change of heart. His paintings became inspired by Van Gogh, and his drawings closer to those of the Montparnasse expressionists. In later years he himself never exhibited his early work, regarding *La Foule* of 1929 as being his first significant etching and the *Sortie d'Usine* series his first real achievement. In the 1930s, besides his etchings, which now showed a strong influence from Dufy, he spent much time on animated films, and it was these that briefly brought him back to London in 1934–6. He returned again at the outbreak of the war, when he worked as an official war artist. From 1948 to 1954 he taught etching at the Central School, and from 1954 to 1976 at the Slade, returning to France during the vacations.

The list of his prints compiled by Graham Reynolds shows that he continued to etch through the 1930s, completing another seventy-five plates before the war. There was then a hiatus, but from 1946 he worked steadily until his death: 226 plates are described before the list breaks off in 1968.

Bibliography

The list of prints is to be found in *The Etchings of Anthony Gross*, with an essay by Graham Reynolds, published on the occasion of an exhibition of his work at the Victoria and Albert Museum in 1968. A large retrospective exhibition was held at the Ashmolean Museum in 1989. The catalogue, *Anthony Gross, Paintings, Drawings, Prints* has a thorough introductory essay by Jane Lee. Much interesting material can be found in Gross's standard treatise, *Etching, Engraving and Intaglio Printing*, Oxford 1970. A volume of essays about Gross is due to be published in 1991, and will include one by Graham Reynolds on the prints.

106 Sortie d'Usine no.1, 1930

Etching, dated in the plate. Signed, titled and numbered 10/40 in pencil. 238 × 305mm
1969–6–14–49

The *Sortie d'Usine* series consists of six plates made in 1930–31. At the time, Gross was living in Paris near the Porte d'Auteuil, on the edge of the poor working-class suburb called the 'Zone'. The life of this area served as the subject for his paintings and drawings, as well as for this set of prints which begs comparison with Hayter's series of *Paysages Urbains*. Despite a few obvious similarities – notably the transparent figures placed in false perspective against the buildings – Gross was never a member of Atelier 17 (although a personal friend of

106

107

108

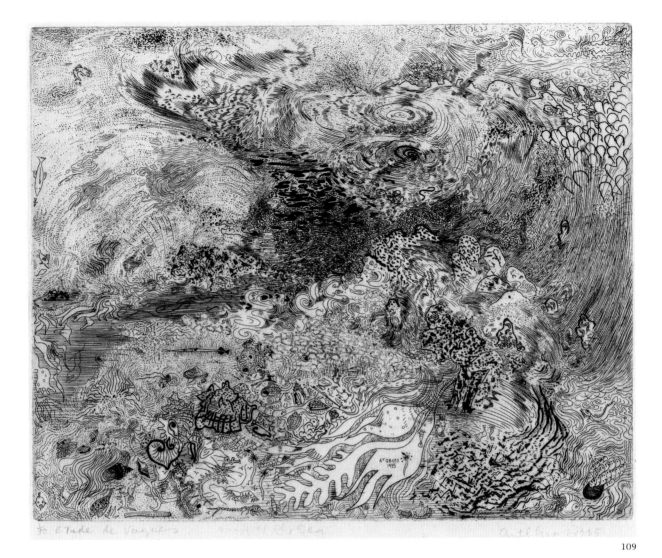

109

Hayter from 1926), and never subscribed to its theories or participated in its researches.

Some, perhaps all, of the *Sortie d'Usine* series was reprinted by Gross in a further edition in 1968.

107 Sortie d'Usine no. 4, 1931

Etching, dated in the plate. Signed, titled and numbered 9/40 in pencil. 316 × 237 mm

1969-3-15-14

108 Kites in Battersea Park, 1934

Etching, dated in the plate. Signed, titled and numbered 15/50 in pencil. 285 × 197 mm

1949-4-11-325. Bequeathed by Campbell Dodgson

As Trevelyan observed: 'Some of the most elaborate plates such as those of Anthony Gross contain an enormous amount of work which has all been drawn into one ground' (*Etching, Modern Methods of Intaglio Printmaking*, London 1963, p.27). This complete reliance on the etched line and absolute mastery of biting different depths is the hallmark of Gross's prints until his last years. Equally characteristic is the humorous and sympathetic observation of everyday life and delight in incident that recalls both his involvement with animated films and the work of the American etcher Peggy Bacon (1895–1987). A note written on the box in the bottom right corner reads 'Kite Factory. AYGros Proprietor'.

109 Etude de Vagues (Study of the Sea), 1935

Etching, dated in the plate. Signed, titled (in French and English), dated, and numbered 1/50 in pencil. 189 × 238 mm

1969-6-14-65

This astonishing tour-de-force is perhaps Gross's greatest print. Like cat. nos 106 and 107, it comes from a group of thirty-five etchings by Gross purchased by the British Museum in two lots in the first half of 1969.

Julian Trevelyan

1910–1988

Son of the poet R.C. Trevelyan and nephew of the historian Sir George Trevelyan; his first wife, the potter Ursula Mommens, is descended from Charles Darwin. Educated at Trinity College, Cambridge, then left for Paris to become an artist. He was based there from the beginning of 1931 until January 1934, while travelling extensively through Europe. His first exhibition was held in January 1932 at the Bloomsbury Gallery, where he showed pictures of Macedonia and Mount Athos. A second, in March 1934, held in conjunction with his future wife, included a mixture of surrealist paintings, reliefs done in cork (described as 'cork dreams') and etchings, together with more straightforward landscape watercolours. In 1935 he joined the English Surrealist Group, and participated the following year in the large London Surrealist exhibition. From the mid-1930s the Trevelyans' home at Durham Wharf on the Thames at Hammersmith became a lively social and artistic centre. They mounted exhibitions (including one of engravings by Hecht in 1938), ran a picture library which hired out contemporary art, and inaugurated a famous annual boat-race party that continued after the war.

Trevelyan's work began to change direction in the late 1930s, after he joined Tom Harrisson's Mass Observation scheme, which took him to the industrial north. This and the influence of John Piper inspired a series of collages composed of 'newspapers, copies of Picture Post, seed catalogues, old bills, coloured papers and other scraps' (*Indigo Days*, p.84). By the end of 1938 he had gone back to painting what he considered 'real things . . . factories, industry, trains, slag-heaps', an interest which survived his war-time experience as a camouflage artist. After the war, he taught etching first at the Chelsea School of Art, and then from 1954 to 1964 at the Royal College of Art, where he greatly influenced a new generation of printmakers, including the young David Hockney.

Trevelyan worked both as painter and etcher. His first prints were made in Paris in 1931, where he enrolled himself in Hayter's atelier. 'He soon had me tied down to the problem of expression in the limited technical medium of etching, which was just what I needed at that moment' (*Indigo Days*, p.26). Some sixteen plates can be associated with the Paris years, four of which were shown at the 1934 exhibition at the Bloomsbury Gallery, priced at 1½ guineas each: their titles were listed as 'Legend from Aesop', 'Legend from Jane Austen's "Love and Friendship"', 'Figure after Piero della Francesca' and 'Nocturnal Encounter'. After his return to London, he made another group of about sixteen 'dream city' plates in 1935–7. For the next two decades he seems to have made few prints apart from Christmas cards, but from the 1950s until his death he exploited the medium with renewed vigour, and by his death had made many hundreds of plates. From about 1966 he was under contract to Waddington's, with

the result that his plates were properly editioned for the first time. Until this point he had only printed a few impressions of his plates as needed, and full edition numbers were very rarely, if ever, reached. In the early 1970s Trevelyan reprinted some of his early plates in editions of around 25 before cancelling the plates, and these later impressions on a stark white paper are sometimes seen. All the impressions catalogued here, however, were printed in the 1930s; most were acquired in a group in May 1987 directly from the artist.

Bibliography

Trevelyan's autobiography, *Indigo Days*, was published in London in 1957 and gives his very amusing and well-written reminiscences of the Parisian and London art worlds of the 1930s. He also wrote a treatise entitled *Etching, Modern Methods of Intaglio Printmaking*, London 1963, which is important for the study of his prints. *Julian Trevelyan, a First Retrospective*, held at the Watermans Arts Centre, Brentford, in 1985, with an essay by Nicholas Usherwood, is the only modern study of his work. Nothing has yet been published specifically about his prints, but the present authors intend to compile a catalogue of the early etchings for publication in *Print Quarterly*. Trevelyan's papers were bequeathed to Trinity College Library, Cambridge; and the Tate Archive received his personal scrapbooks, photo archive, print record book and 340 designs for prints of the period 1953–82. Mary Fedden, his second wife, has given a selection of twenty-eight sketchbooks to the Tate and a further four to the British Museum. We would like to thank her for her help with these entries.

110 'The Beautiful Vale of Usk . . .', 1932

Etching with fabric pressed into soft-ground. No annotations.
174 × 235 mm
1987–5–16–66

The text around the outside reads: 'The beautiful vale of Usk resounded with her woeful cries: "deliver me, oh brother, from these unspeakable torments." Alas poor Sophia . . .'. That in the centre reads: 'Catastrophe' and 'Remember, Sophia, doors have ears'.

The print was made in two stages: first the ectoplasmic figures and centre text were etched. Then a soft etching ground was laid over the plate, into which a fabric was pressed; the white areas in the centre and the text around the outside were then reserved with stopping-out varnish before the plate was rebitten. A few gaps along the bottom margin where the acid failed to bite have been worked over with a roulette.

The quotation is loosely taken from Jane Austen's early satirical novel *Love and Friendship*, which was published for the first time in 1922. It supplied Trevelyan with the text for another etching of this date which he actually titled *Love and Friendship*. Both designs belong to a larger

110

group of similar compositions which he elaborated in a sketchbook marked 'Paris 1932' (Tate Gallery Archive); these vary from rough pencil sketches to finished preparatory studies painted in grey or turquoise gouache with the lettering executed in white. The sketchbook contains a study for *The Beautiful Vale of Usk*; other compositions in it draw their literary inspiration from Maria Edgeworth's *Early Lessons*, though these do not appear to have been turned into prints.

No late impressions of this print are known, but Trevelyan did make a small number of restrikes of *Love and Friendship* for friends after the exhibition at the Watermans Art Centre in 1985.

111 Composition with Floating Shapes, probably 1933

Etching and aquatint. Signed and numbered 2/20.
138 × 244 mm
1987–5–16–72

After the sequence of images described above, Trevelyan appears in 1933 to have explored a series of more precisely defined compositions containing surreal and geometric shapes confined by a brick wall against the background of a night sky. This type of subject is probably to be identified with the two paintings and one etching exhibited at the Bloomsbury Gallery in 1934 as *Nocturnal Encounters*. In the introduction to that exhibition, Trevelyan explained that these images came as 'the result of a good deal of tentative "fishing around" in the subconscious'

and were 'built up more slowly on a theme whose mood only was suggested by some poem'.

The strangely sub-aqueous atmosphere of the print catalogued here belongs to the same family group as those mentioned above. It echoes some of the images from a dream described by the artist early in 1934, which he used as a metaphor for his failing relationship with an elusive American girlfriend.

At this date Trevelyan saw himself as a kind of artistic schizophrenic as a result of the varied influences to which he was exposed in Paris. The more representational work he referred to as his 'Jekylls' and the abstract experiments in oil, etching and cork as his 'Hydes'. 'Neither group is entirely anterior to the other, and I can only explain that the Jekylls respond directly to things seen during the summer, while the Hydes are winter-cogitations on forms that seemed ever-present in the fairyland of the Subconscious' (from the introduction to the 1934 Bloomsbury Gallery catalogue). 'My Jekylls and Hydes still lived in separate compartments where each had only half the necessary nourishment' (*Indigo Days*, p.53).

Mary Fedden has kindly informed us that the zinc plates for this and cat. no. 112 below survive in Trevelyan's studio.

111

112 Usher, probably 1933

Etching, with soft-ground and aquatint. No annotations.
249 × 153 mm
1987–5–16–69

Made in three stages. First the three lines were bitten, some very deeply, others more lightly. Then a fabric was pressed into a new soft etching ground, and stopped out to leave a white margin along the left and right sides. Finally a fine aquatint ground was laid on the plate, but stopped out so that only the margin was bitten. This produced an irregular join between the soft-ground and aquatint areas, which shows white in places. Trevelyan toned down some of the more glaring gaps in this impression by going over them with a pencil. The use of the impressed soft-ground fabric texture, invented by Hayter in 1933, shows that the plate cannot be dated earlier than that year; its sophistication suggests that it is one of the last prints that Trevelyan made in Paris. It may have been made at the same time as the etching *Figure after Piero della Francesca* (1987–5–16–73), for which a preliminary idea exists in the sketchbook dated 'Summer Autumn 1933' (Tate Gallery Archive).

113 The Tenements of Mind, 1936

Etching with plate tone and impressed leaves. Signed, dated and numbered 6/25 in pencil. 202 × 350 mm
1980–10–11–20

This and the following print were made after Trevelyan's return to London from Paris, and were both exhibited (together with three paintings) in the 1936 Surrealism exhibition. In *Indigo Days* he describes their close links with his paintings:

112

113

114

I had now abandoned canvas and oil paint entirely, and was engraving with a knife on wooden panels. I had invented a sort of mythology of cities, of fragile structures carrying here and there a few waif-like inhabitants. *Dream Scaffold, The Tenements of Mind* – such were the titles of some of the panels on which I was now engaged. I think they owed something to early Klee, and probably also in their technique and presentation to certain early works of Ben Nicholson. They expressed a need I felt for something more poetic and mysterious than the brutal hammers of Hélion, and I can well understand Ozenfant's comment when he saw them: 'Ça manque un peu de rosbif'. Looking back at them now, they appear to me quite decorative and valid, but I cannot now identify myself with them; I look at them as if they were the work of some other young man, which is not the way I feel about the earlier work I did in Paris. This, though obviously very immature, is most definitely mine.

Trevelyan expanded on his idea of the city in an essay entitled 'Mythos' which he contributed to *The Painter's Object*, an anthology of essays edited by Myfanwy Evans (the wife of John Piper) and published in London in 1937. In this is reproduced one of his engraved panels.

A zinc plate was used to make this etching. Instead of a normal etching ground, Trevelyan used a stopping-out varnish; this splinters when drawn through and after etching produces the irregular coarse line seen here. (He describes this technique in *Etching*, p.63.) The plate was then wiped very lightly so as to leave swirls of ink lying on the surface, and three leaves were placed on it before printing; the ink lying under them was prevented from coming through by the thickness of the veins, but bled through elsewhere to give a ghostly skeleton effect.

The British Museum owns two impressions of this plate, both printed in the same way with leaves but with inevitable variations. Trevelyan himself kept two other impressions, both printed quite differently with cut-out 'keyholes' and coloured diamonds as in cat. no. 114. One of these impressions, printed in recent years, carries the hand-written title 'The Bat'. There can, however, be no doubt that this is indeed 'The Tenements of Mind', the title under which the Museum purchased it in 1980.

114 Dream Scaffold I, 1936

Etching with reserved shapes and colour patches. Signed, titled and dated in pencil. 198 × 351 mm

1987-5-16-74

This print was etched and printed in exactly the same way as cat. no. 113. But instead of leaves, Trevelyan has cut out six 'key-hole' slips of paper, and used them to prevent areas of the plate from printing. The three diamonds, two orange and one blue, were added by hand to the impression after printing. The number and placing of these areas is more or less constant in the different impressions that we have seen, both of this and of many of the other thirteen plates in the group of 'dream cities' of 1936–7 (another impression is reproduced opposite page 65 of *Indigo Days*). These prints are closely related to a few curious works on slate that Trevelyan made at this time, where he scratched the design into the irregular slab, adding white and coloured patches in gouache just as in the prints.

The British Museum also possesses the cancelled original zinc plate for *Somnambulist I* of 1937, together with a plaster print made from it (1985-6-8-21 and 22). Such plasters were occasionally made by Hayter and his associates. It was an easy way of proofing a plate without needing a press, since the inked plate needed only to be placed on a surface of wet plaster, and taken off when dry. The ink was left on the plaster, which could then itself be further carved and coloured to become a decorative item in its own right. (See Hayter's *New Ways of Gravure*, chapter 9, and Trevelyan's *Etching*, pp.92–3.)

6 1930s Lithographs and the Curwen Group

After the remarkable production of lithographs during and after the First World War, interest seems to have fallen off in the 1920s. Even Nevinson made few more after about 1922. The only bodies that sustained any real concern were the Senefelder Club, which held annual exhibitions at the Twenty-One Gallery (as it continued to do throughout the 1930s), and the Central School, where A.S. Hartrick gave classes to interested students. It was there that James Fitton learnt the process, and as a result exhibited at the Senefelder Club exhibitions from 1925. In the 1930s Fitton, Boswell and Holland (the three James) became the outstanding cartoonists for the *Left Review*, and, although the cartoons in the paper were line-block reproductions of drawings, all three continued to make lithographs; Boswell used the technique as a cheap method of producing hand-outs to be sold at demonstrations and marches. The idea of the cheap and democratic nature of lithography lay behind various projects of the Artists International Association (AIA), the travelling exhibition of 1939 *Britain Today. Cross-Section*, and the series of Everyman Prints (see cat. no. 121) that they published as a relief measure to alleviate unemployment among artists at the beginning of the Second World War.

Meanwhile the abundance and recognised excellence of British poster design was embodied entirely in the medium of lithography. This meant that there were already firms such as the Curwen and Baynard Presses that were expert in the production of colour lithographs. In the 1930s this created opportunities in two directions: the first was in books illustrated with original lithographs made by artists, the second was in the establishment of a number of series, both before and after the war, of large lithographic prints drawn directly by artists. The pioneer project of this kind was the series published by Contemporary Lithographs Ltd, a firm set up by Robert Wellington who ran the Zwemmer Gallery, with the help of John Piper (see cat. nos 122 and 124).

Throughout this period a central role was played by Oliver Simon, a director of the Curwen Press, a printer in both letterpress and lithography and an enthusiastic promoter of the idea that artists should be used to enhance the visual effect of all sorts of printed material, from leaflets to books. To this end he founded and edited *Signature*, a quarterly journal, and enlisted as contributors artists such as Sutherland, Piper, Bawden, Ravilious and many others. It was for these pages that Sutherland's aquatint (cat. no. 125) was commissioned, and here that the development of Piper's ideas from abstraction to Regency revivalism can be clearly followed.

The destruction of the Curwen plant in the Blitz put a (temporary) end both to *Signature* and to Curwen's

ability to produce lithographs. This opened the way for another firm, Cowell's in Ipswich. They made themselves extremely open to artists, and as a result Ravilious used them for his ten *Submarine* prints in 1941, as did the publisher Frederick Muller for five of the seven titles in the series of *New Excursions into English Poetry* (see cat. no. 150). However, it was in the immediate post-war period that Cowell's made their most interesting contribution to lithographic printing techniques, which is discussed in section 7 below.

James Fitton

1899–1982

Born into a working-class family in Oldham, he left school at the age of 14. He studied at Manchester School of Art in the evenings, while earning a living during the day. When his father moved to London to take a senior post with the Amalgamated Engineering Union in 1920, Fitton followed, freelancing as a commercial artist. In 1925 he began evening classes in lithography at the Central School under A.S. Hartrick, where he met his future wife. In 1933, he himself took over the class from Hartrick's successor, Spencer Pryse. From 1930 he was employed by C. Vernon's Advertising Agency, where he remained (though later only in an advisory capacity) for fifty years. In 1933 he was a founder-member of the AIA, and played an active part in its work during the 1930s, most notably in the political cartoons he made for the *Left Review*. He began to exhibit his paintings at the Royal Academy in 1929, and was elected as Associate in 1944 and a full Academician in 1954. He was appointed by the Academy as a Trustee of the British Museum from 1968 to 1975. The only one-man exhibition of his paintings was held by Tooth's in 1933.

Fitton's first lithographs were made in 1925, and his production until 1931 can be followed in the annual exhibitions of the Senefelder Club – some eleven prints in all. There then seems to have been a gap until 1933, when he took over the evening lithography class at the Central School; a letter of recommendation from Hartrick stated that he was 'one of the ablest of the younger artist lithographers in this country' and added that he possessed his own press. The prints of this second group are much more remarkable than his earlier work, which is fairly conventional; the difference is due to his new interest in German political illustration. His last prints of this period belong to 1935 and (like Boswell's) are reworkings of cartoons in the *Left Review*. Curiously, he did not contribute

117

to the AIA's 1939 *Britain Today. Cross-Section* travelling
exhibition, nor to its Everyman series. One large print,
Pantomime, made on commission from CEMA (Council for
the Encouragement of Music and Arts) in 1941, was made
by professional draughtsmen after a painting he had
supplied.

Bibliography

Nothing has been written specifically about Fitton's
prints. The only significant publication on his work is the
catalogue of an exhibition held at the Dulwich College
Gallery in 1986–7, compiled by John Sheeran.

115 May Day, 1928

Colour lithograph, printed in black and red on thin Japan paper.
Signed and titled in pencil, and numbered (in another hand)
1/100. 265 × 250 mm (maximum dimensions)
1929–6–11–41. Presented by Campbell Dodgson

The Senefelder Club had two categories of member, artists
and lay-members. The latter, in return for a guinea
annual subscription, received a presentation print each
year. This was the presentation print for 1928, and would
have been given to Dodgson, who at this time was one
of four honorary members of the Club – the others being
Léonce Bénédite of France, Ugo Ojetti of Italy and E.F.
Strange of the Victoria and Albert Museum.

This curiously theatrical print is vaguely reminiscent
of 1920s films.

115

116

116 Tattooed Man, 1933

Colour lithograph, printed in three colours on thick brown paper. Signed, dated 1934 and numbered 2/12 in pen. 300 × 275 mm (maximum dimensions)
1935-7-19-2. Presented by the artist

This print was exhibited as no. 47 at the *International Exhibition of Lithographs 1914 to 1934*, mounted by the Senefelder Club from 1 to 27 January 1934 at the Fulham Central Library. The fact that the exhibition opened on the first day of the year proves that the date written on the print cannot be strictly correct, and it must have been made at the end of 1933. The title given is that of the 1934 exhibition; in the British Museum's register of acquisitions it is called 'Prize fighter'.

Fitton gave this and the following print to the British Museum in 1935, together with a third lithograph: a portrait of a man smoking, dated 1928, which is almost certainly a portrait of the artist's father.

117 Trapeze Artists, 1934

Colour lithograph, printed in three colours on thick brown paper. Signed, dated and numbered 2/12 in pen. 378 × 515 mm
1935-7-19-3. Presented by the artist

This print is based in reverse on a painting which was exhibited at the 1934 exhibition of the London Group at the New Burlington Galleries (reproduced on page 13 of the catalogue of the Fitton exhibition held in 1983 at Old-ham Art Gallery). The success of the painting led him to make a lithograph of the same composition, which was shown at the London Group exhibition in the following year (see Dulwich catalogue, no. 64). The title is that given in the British Museum acquisitions register. Many of Fitton's paintings and works on paper of the first half of the 1930s are of circus subjects, an aspect of popular life with which he was clearly fascinated.

James Boswell

1906–1971

Born in New Zealand, he moved to London in 1925, where he studied at the Royal College of Art. He first exhibited his paintings in 1927, and pursued a career as an artist until 1932. In that year, he turned to graphic design for a living, and joined the Communist Party. In 1933 he was among the founder members of the AIA. For the rest of the 1930s he combined political activity as cartoonist for the *Left Review* and *Daily Worker* with working as art director for Shell Petroleum. After the war, he worked for *Lilliput* from 1947 until 1950. The following year he returned to the commercial world, becoming editor of the house journal of J. Sainsbury. He also supplied illustrations for many books, and in 1952 took up his painting again.

Boswell studied lithography at the classes of James Fitton, a close friend, at the Central School from 1933 onwards, but he must have had some earlier experience, for he exhibited two prints in the 1930 exhibition of the Senefelder Club at the Twenty-One Gallery. The titles of these, *L'Anglaise avec son Sang-Froid Habituel* and *The Original Elephant and its Inventor*, suggest that they were already in the satirical manner for which he became famous. Twelve of his lithographs were included in the 1939 AIA travelling exhibition *Britain Today. Cross-Section*, and in 1940 he was in a position to present forty lithographs to the Auckland City Art Gallery. He contributed three prints to the AIA Everyman series, and also made a few linocuts. After the war he made one large colour lithograph for the AIA series on the Festival of Britain in 1951, and a number of smaller prints around 1953 when he became (for the first time) a member of the Senefelder Club.

Bibliography

No study has been devoted to Boswell's lithographs. He himself wrote an interesting pamphlet in 1947 entitled *The Artist's Dilemma*, in which he expressed the problem of the post-war role of the artist: during the war there had been a great demand for his work, but times of peace were far less propitious. He also wrote an article in the *Studio* of March 1954 on 'The Senefelder Club'.

A biography will be found on pp. 13–19 of vol. III of the *Dictionary of Labour Biography*, ed. J.M. Bellamy and John Saville, London 1976, and Boswell is discussed in D.D. Egbert, *Social Radicalism and the Arts*, New York 1970. An exhibition was devoted to his work at the Nottingham University Art Gallery in 1976. The catalogue contains a number of essays and reproductions, but the list of the exhibits (which was separately printed) only gives titles, without a note of the medium. We would like to thank Ruth Boswell for her help with these entries.

118 Empire Builders, 1935

Lithograph, in green and maroon. Unsigned. 255 × 205 mm (maximum dimensions)
1983-7-23-23. Presented by Ruth Boswell

The earliest group of Boswell's lithographs are closely related to his cartoons published in *Left Review*, but, so far as we can tell, none of them actually repeats the compositions of those cartoons (which were pen drawings reproduced as line blocks). This raises the question of what these lithographs were intended for. The answer is supplied by a memoir by Arnold Rattenbury which appeared in the small pamphlet accompanying the Boswell exhibition of 1986 at the Manchester City Art Gallery: it was apparently Boswell's custom to make lithographs of his drawings for sale at anti-fascist demonstrations or similar political events. Such prints could be run off overnight by

118

Boswell himself for only the cost of the paper. It must be because these prints were distributed in this way that they never appear on the art market, and have never been considered as part of the history of British printmaking.

119 A Shilling a Day, 1935

Lithograph. Unsigned. 285 × 125 mm (maximum dimensions)
1983-7-23-24. Presented by Ruth Boswell

Another print presumably meant for sale at political events. All the prints in this group, like the drawings for the *Left Review*, are the clearest demonstration of the influence of George Grosz on British art.

120 The Dying Street, 1938

Lithograph on thin Japan paper. Signed, titled and dated in pencil. 385 × 515 mm (maximum dimensions)
1973-2-24-97. Presented by Ruth Boswell

In 1936 Boswell made a set of four large lithographs of North London street markets. These were still in a Grosz-like manner, but less satirical in flavour. In 1938, with this lithograph, he adopted a new style which he continued to use in a number of large-scale prints until the early 1940s. The German influence has gone, and instead of the line of the pen, he uses lithographic chalk to create large, brooding, and indeed threatening, street scenes. These are unlike anything else in British lithography, and show the strong influence of American lithographs of the 1930s. This print was included in the the *Britain Today. Cross-Section* exhibition, where it was priced at 2 guineas; the edition size was stated as 20.

121 Gitte Bisness, 1939

Lithograph. Signed, titled and dated in the plate. Printed in bottom right corner: 'AIA Everyman Prints'. 200 × 300 mm (maximum dimensions)
1940-2-21-8

The series of Everyman Prints published by the AIA comprised fifty-two lithographs, all on the same size sheets of paper. Those in black and white were sold at 1s. each; those in two colours at 1s. 6d. A pamphlet was published to accompany the series:

AIA Everyman Prints are intended for every home . . . Everyman Prints now widen the range from which the visual taste can be gratified, by offering the direct work of living artists at a price so reasonable that the outlay need not involve anxious consideration, and the collecting of prints is now within the possibility of every purse. Everyman Prints are not reproductions. In each case the artist has actually drawn on the metal plate from which are pulled the prints exhibited for sale. The life of a plate is limited; at the first sign of wear the edition will be closed. The Everyman Print owner, therefore, need not fear that his chosen prints will be on every wall; his collection, whether framed or in portfolio, will repre-

119

sent his own selection. Artists drawing for Everyman Prints believe that they will gain as much as the public from the scheme. The sales will show the creative artist the pictorial interests of the public, and the public will realise the contribution the artist can make to the social and cultural life of our times. (See Lynda Morris and Robert Radford, *The Story of the AIA*, Museum of Modern Art, Oxford 1983, pp.56–8.)

The series was devised late in 1939, partly as a response to the sudden unemployment of artists after the declaration of war. Almost all the prints were of everyday scenes, many relating to wartime conditions, and there was little or nothing of political import. The prints were marketed on a wide scale throughout the country from the end of January 1940, and 3,000 were sold in three weeks. The British Museum, in the person of A.M. Hind, acquired twenty-three plates for £1 6s., of which this is one. Although the series was warmly welcomed by critics (for example, Percy Horton in *The Studio* 119 (1940), pp.160–63), by 1942 sales had only reached 5,000, and one of the most ambitious initiatives this century to sell original prints to a mass market had failed.

120

121

John Piper

born 1903

After serving as an articled clerk in his father's firm, he studied art full-time from 1926, first at a private school and then at the Royal College of Art from 1927 to 1929. In the 1930s he won a reputation both for his art and theatrical criticism and for his drawings and paintings. In 1934 he joined the Seven and Five Society, and was soon producing entirely abstract constructions and paintings. In 1936 he began to make collages of landscapes alongside his abstract paintings, and in 1939 abandoned abstraction completely in favour of the romantic topographical watercolours for which he is now best known.

Piper's first prints were a few wood-engravings made as student exercises in about 1923. There was then a break until two lithographs in 1937 (see cat. no. 122). In 1939 he made a set of twelve aquatints of Brighton views (see cat. no. 123) which announced his break with abstraction and a commitment to a historicising approach to British topography. During the war he made a few more aquatints for a projected work on farmyard chapels (as well as a lithograph for the AIA Everyman series); then from 1944 to 1955 his main efforts went into colour lithographic illustrations for six books, the first of which was an anthology of poems on *English, Scottish and Welsh Landscape*, chosen (appropriately) by John Betjeman and Geoffrey Taylor (see also cat. no. 150 below). It was not until 1953 that he began to produce large single-sheet colour lithographs on commission for publishers. The first were made in Paris, then a group in 1958 in Edinburgh (Harley Brothers), and finally from 1961 onwards at the Curwen Studio. He made his first screenprints with the Kelpra Studio in 1967.

Bibliography

The catalogue *John Piper, the Complete Graphic Works*, compiled by Orde Levinson and published in London, 1987, contains entries and illustrations for no less than 368 prints made between 1923 and 1983. For the rest of Piper's work, the best guide is the catalogue of the retrospective exhibition held at the Tate Gallery in 1983, by David Fraser Jenkins; this also contains a bibliography of 583 items. A biography, *John Piper*, by Anthony West, was published in London, 1979.

122 Abstract Composition, 1937

Colour lithograph, printed in six colours. Printed at bottom left: 'Published by Contemporary Lithographs Ltd, London', with added in pencil '1937 Edition of 75'; signed both in the design and in pencil bottom right. 610 × 458 mm

Levinson 7

1980-1-26-3

See colour illustration

The firm Contemporary Lithographs was established by Robert Wellington and John Piper in 1936. Wellington ran the Zwemmer Gallery in Charing Cross Road, whose main business was in selling imported reproductions of modern paintings. One of his customers was Henry Morris, the director of education in Cambridgeshire, who was using these prints to hang in his schools. This gave Wellington the idea of using living British artists to make the prints, and he enlisted Piper as his technical expert. It thus fell to Piper to accompany the chosen artists to the Curwen and Baynard Presses, and help them make drawings on the plates – a task that he remembered as an 'awful sweat' (see R. Berthoud, *Graham Sutherland*, London 1982, pp.76, 84–5). The first series of ten prints was published in January 1937, and was greeted by articles such as that by J.E. Barton, 'Pictures in Schools' in the *Architectural Review* of January 1937, pp.2–4.

The second series followed in March 1938, and was supposed to consist of fifteen prints, but only fourteen were produced. According to a note in *The Studio* of 1938 (vol. 116, p.301), the series was now aimed not at schools but 'at making available to households with small incomes a representative and wide choice of good modern work, and is an important step in creating a link between public and art, which is comparable to that between public and literature and music'. The complete set of twenty-four prints was exhibited at the Leicester Galleries in September 1938.

The prospectus for the first series states that the editions were to be limited to 400. We have found no statement about the second series, but it is quite clear from the advertised price of 25s. each (see *Signature* no. 8, March 1938) that they were also intended to be printed in a large edition. The series however failed to sell, for reasons pointed out in a perceptive review by Jan Gordon in the *Penrose Annual* 41 (1939):

Nevertheless the problem raised by such an experiment as *Contemporary Lithographs* remains chiefly one of price and of distribution … some of the poor response of the normal Briton to art must be found in the almost incredibly low quality of art appreciation shown by the general distributors, that is by most of the shops that specialise in art prints and framing … and yet this is the filter through which *Contemporary Lithographs* must pass before they can reach the public on anything like an effective scale.

Until the late 1970s the remaining stock was available for purchase at the offices of Ganymed Editions in Great Turnstile, London (we owe this information to Mrs Anne Baer).

The edition of 75 referred to in the pencil annotation on this impression has not been explained; it may relate to a later attempt to relaunch unsold copies in the form of a signed and limited edition.

The composition is one of Piper's last and most impressive exercises in abstraction. It is also the only abstract print in the entire series of Contemporary Lithographs. The other print made for it by Piper was completely different: a long 'nursery frieze' in two sections, one a seascape, the other a landscape.

123

123 The Chapel of St George, Kemp Town, 1939

Aquatint (plate 10 of *Brighton Aquatints*). 196 × 276 mm

Levinson 21

1981-6-20-45(10)

The full title of the book in which this print appeared is *Brighton Aquatints, twelve original aquatints of modern Brighton with short descriptions by the artist and an introduction by Lord Alfred Douglas*, and it was published by Duckworth in London. The text was printed by the Curwen Press, and the plates by A. Alexander & Sons Ltd. The book was advertised in *Signature* 13 (January 1940), where the ordinary edition, stated by Levinson to be 200 copies, was priced at 21 shillings; there were also fifty copies hand-coloured by the artist at 6 guineas each.

The route that led Piper in only two years from the ultra-modern *Abstract Composition* of 1937 to these archaising aquatints (complete with introduction by the long-forgotten friend of Oscar Wilde) is perhaps the most remarkable travelled by any artist of the 1930s. The key seems to have been his friendship with John Betjeman (who helped hand-colour the plates), and it was from him that he learnt how to turn nostalgia into something highly original and interesting. Also in *Signature* 13, Piper supplied a lithographic panorama of Cheltenham to accompany an essay on that town by Betjeman. This begins: 'Book illustration can colour a whole town or county', and proceeds to analyse the different phases of architecture in terms of the periods of copper engraving, aquatint and steel engraving used to illustrate it. Piper's own interest in early nineteenth-century illustrated topographical books (which he collected) re-emerged in 1950 when he contributed an article on 'Picturesque Travel Illustrated' to *Signature*, new series 11.

The plate chosen for illustration here has a certain fame for its use of photo-engraved text to shade the wall of the chapel. Piper's text about the church provides the reason for this unusual effect: 'Inside it has been spoiled . . . But outside it is still one of the most charming of the Brighton churches, its stucco and yellow-brick walls having very much the colour and texture of faded newspaper.' The use of actual newsprint (taken from a newspaper article about European politics) in the plate is therefore a visual pun. The idea for it presumably emerged from the collages 'in which he described the terraces of Brighton and the cliffs of Newhaven in torn newspapers and pen and ink' which Julian Trevelyan remembered in his autobiography (*Indigo Days*, p.53). Piper created a similar effect with typographical elements in one of his lithographs printed by the Curwen Studio in 1966, *Swansea Chapel*.

124

Paul Nash

For biography and bibliography, see pp.61–2

124 Landscape of the Megaliths, 1936

Colour lithograph printed in five colours. Signed in the image.
510 × 760 mm

Postan L18

1937-7-31-4. Presented by the Contemporary Art Society

This was one of the first series of prints published by Contemporary Lithographs in January 1937 (see cat. no. 122). This series was intended for schools, and it is notable that Nash makes no attempt to adjust his art down to the presumed level of a juvenile audience. By contrast, Graham Sutherland made a print of *The Sick Duck* and H.S. Williamson one of *Bears at Tea*, both embarrassing excursions into whimsy.

In April 1937 a large exhibition of drawings by Nash was held at the Redfern Gallery. No. 26 was described as the 'drawing for the lithograph published by Contemporary Lithographs Ltd', and was priced at 45 guineas (Causey 905, now in the Albright-Knox Gallery, Buffalo). It is a very highly finished work, and is based on a text Nash had published in *Unit One* in 1934 (pp.79–81):

Last summer I walked in a field near Avebury where two rough monoliths stood up sixteen feet high, miraculously patterned with black and orange lichen, remnants of the avenue of stones which led to the Great Circle. A mile away, a green pyramid casts a giant shadow. In the hedge, at hand, the white trumpet of the convolvulus turns from its spiral stem, following the sun. In my art I would solve such an equation.

The prospectus for Contemporary Lithographs Ltd is categoric that 'each lithograph has been drawn on the stones by the artist at the works of the Curwen Press'. In the case of the present print, comparison with the Buffalo watercolour shows that the design on the black stone is not the same, and this strongly suggests that Nash himself redrew it directly on the stone. Whether the same is true of the four-colour stones is not so clear. Making colour separations from a watercolour is a highly skilled business, and Nash may well have had help from the experts at the Baynard or Curwen Presses. On the other hand, he was proud enough of the colour separations to allow them to be included in a CEMA travelling exhibition in 1943 (recorded by Causey).

Nash's own interest in these problems is demonstrated by an article he published in the *Penrose Annual* 38 for 1936 (pp.33–5) under the title 'Experiments in colour reproduction, with some observations on modern colour prints'. In its attack on the prevailing standards in the colour print and on the apathy of most education authorities, this reads almost like an advertisement for Contemporary Lithographs Ltd. But it is interesting that Nash's remedy in this article is not to have the artist make the lithograph himself, but to raise the standard of the colour printers.

Graham Sutherland

1903–1980

Born in London, he initially intended to become an engineer. From 1921 to 1926 he studied at Goldsmith's College, specialising in etching, a field in which he rapidly achieved immense success. He was given his first show in 1924, when still a student, by the Twenty-One Gallery, and this firm henceforth acted as his publishers. In 1928 they issued a catalogue of his etchings, and their stock list of the following year shows that most of his plates were already priced at between 7 and 12 guineas each. At this time his work stood in the mainstream of the etching revival: the first plates are Whistlerian, then follows from 1925 the strong influence of F.L.Griggs and Samuel Palmer.

The crash of 1929 finished this phase of Sutherland's career, but, unlike almost every other etcher, he had the courage and ability to change course completely. He began to paint for the first time; he also took up industrial design, and began to write essays for such progressive journals of typography and illustration as *Signature*. In 1934 he went for the first time to Pembrokeshire, where the landscape inspired his first original contributions to British art. By the end of the 1930s he was fully established as a painter, with influential patrons and supporters such as Oliver Simon, Kenneth Clark, Colin Anderson and Peter Watson. This laid the foundation for his huge international success after the war, when as well as being known for his landscapes and animal subjects, he found yet another market as a portraitist. A curious aspect of these later years is the intense dislike that Sutherland manifested towards his early etchings.

Felix Man's catalogue of Sutherland's prints lists thirty-three plates up to 1929, and another three (which were never published) in the next three years. There is then a complete break until 1938, when the print catalogued below was published. This was the last intaglio print he made before the 1970s. In 1935, however, he took up colour lithography for the first time, which after the war became his preferred medium in printmaking. Virtually all his lithographs were printed abroad, principally by Fernand Mourlot in Paris.

Bibliography

There is a considerable literature on Sutherland's life and work. Roger Berthoud's well-researched *Graham Sutherland, a Biography*, was published in London in 1982, the

125

same year that a memorial exhibition was held at the Tate Gallery with a catalogue by Ronald Alley. Another survey of his work was published by John Hayes in 1980. The standard catalogue of his prints, *Graham Sutherland, das Graphische Werk 1922–1970*, by Felix H. Man, was published in Munich in 1970. Another catalogue, with different numbering, *Graham Sutherland, Complete Graphic Work*, by Roberto Tassi, was co-published in London and elsewhere in 1978.

125 Clegyr-Boia, 1938

Etching and aquatint. 197 × 146 mm
Man 37; Tassi 33
1990–5–19–15 (bound in *Signature*)

This plate was published in an unsigned and unlimited edition as the frontispiece to *Signature* 9 (July 1938). It does not accompany any article, but was used simply as a plate in its own right. Sutherland was by this time a close friend of Oliver Simon, the director of the Curwen Press and editor of *Signature*, and had in earlier issues written on 'A Trend in English Draughtsmanship' and 'Line Engraving and the Illustrated Book' (see Pat Gilmour, *Artists at Curwen*, Tate Gallery, 1977, pp.80–84). Documents published under no. 60 in the 1982 Tate Gallery exhibition catalogue show that the plate was commissioned by Simon in March 1938 and delivered in May.

There were in fact two versions: the first (which remained unknown to Man, but is illustrated by Tassi) was evidently found unsatisfactory, and replaced by the second version. The obliterated word on the plate is 'herons': the print was initially intended to be called 'Herons Ghyll'.

Clegyr-Boia is an outcrop of rock near St David's, where Sutherland stayed in the summer of 1934 on his first visit to Pembrokeshire (Berthoud, p.78). The print must have been based on a drawing, and clearly marks the distinction from the early etchings both in its technique (aquatint is used for the first time) and in style. All traces of Palmer have been lost, and instead a Surrealist agglomeration of shapes challenges interpretation. Two years before, Sutherland had contributed two paintings to the London International Surrealist exhibition.

Eric Ravilious

1903–1942

Brought up in Eastbourne, where his father ran an antique shop. He attended Eastbourne School of Art, and then the Royal College of Art in London from 1922 to 1925. He was there influenced by the teaching of Paul Nash and by his fellow students Edward Bawden and Douglas Percy Bliss. He first made a reputation as a wood-engraver, and during the 1930s illustrated a number of books. He also made watercolours and worked as an industrial designer, especially for Wedgwood. He became an official war artist in 1940, and was killed two years later in a flying accident off Iceland.

Most attention has always been given to Ravilious's wood-engravings, which are indeed among the most witty and engaging of their period. Apart from the book illustrations, there are many occasional pieces for letter-heads, borders and other commercial purposes, especially for the Curwen Press. He did, however, make a number of lithographs, which are quite as interesting. The first, *Newhaven Harbour* (or 'Homage to Seurat'), was made for Contemporary Lithographs in 1936. Next came the twenty-four illustrations of shop fronts, which were intended for an alphabet of shops but were eventually published by Country Life in an unlimited edition in 1938 under the title *High Street*, with a text by J.M. Richards. The last were the *Submarines* of 1941, catalogued below.

Bibliography

A complete collection of reproductions of the relief prints is given in *The Wood Engravings of Eric Ravilious*, Lion and Unicorn Press, 1972, with an introduction by J.M. Richards. There is an interesting paragraph on the shop prints by John Piper in *Signature* 5 (March 1937). The most important source for his life and work was written by his close friend Helen Binyon: *Eric Ravilious, Memoir of an Artist*, Guildford and London 1983.

126 Different Aspects of Submarines, 1941

Colour lithograph. No annotations. 279 × 318 mm
Private collection

127 Commander of a Submarine Looking through a Periscope, 1941

Colour lithograph. No annotations. 270 × 300 mm
Private collection

128 The Ward Room II, 1941

Colour lithograph. Signed in pencil at the top. 278 × 318 mm
1945–12–8–146. Presented by the Contemporary Art Society
See colour illustration

129 Working Controls when Submerged, 1941

Colour lithograph. Signed in pencil below. 279 × 320 mm
1945–12–8–147. Presented by the Contemporary Art Society

The complete set of submarine lithographs consists of ten plates. There seems to be no intended order, except for the first plate which serves as frontispiece; this shows an underwater scene with the artist's hand, and is often called, though only in modern sources, 'Submarine Dream'.

The other five plates (in no particular order) are:
Diver
Diving Controls I (with 'Revolutions' on notice board on left)
Diving Controls II (two seamen, one behind the other)
The Ward Room I (two sailors asleep at left)
Testing Davis Apparatus in a 30-Foot Tank on HMS Dolphin
No titles appear on the lithographs; those given here are the ones used by the Imperial War Museum, which in turn have been derived from the titles given to the original watercolours which were acquired from the artist.

Ravilious was approached to become an official war artist to the Admiralty at the end of December 1939. His first idea was to do a portfolio of six lithographs on war subjects, notably submarines, and to this end got an estimate on 23 January from the Curwen Press (who had previously printed his *High Street* illustrations) of £36 for the costs of printing an edition of 50. The idea was put to the War Artists Advisory Council on 1 February, but the Committee was unable to decide whether it would meet the costs involved. Ravilious was initially sent on other postings, but in July and August he actually managed, when based at Portsmouth and Gosport, to draw submarine interiors and make a few trips to sea in them. In a letter to the Committee he described the difficult conditions of work:

It is awfully hot below when submarines dive and every compartment small and full of people at work. However, this is

a change from destroyers and I enjoy the state of complete calm after the North Sea – there is no roll or movement at all in submarines, which is one condition in their favour – apart from the peculiar submarine smell, the heat and the noise. There is something jolly good about it, if only I can manage it, a blue gloom with coloured lights and everyone in shirts and braces. People go to sleep in odd positions across tables.

(This and many other documents on the series are quoted from pp.122–6 of Helen Binyon's biography; the rest is derived through the help of Paul Goldman from the original papers which are kept in the Imperial War Museum.)

On 29 October Ravilious was at home working on the watercolours on which the lithographs were to be based, and wrote to Helen Binyon:

The material at Portsmouth was awfully difficult to come by at all, and of course really first rate and worth having a shot at, but the translation at home is slow work. I do feel very keen about it. This morning I heard that the Committee want to make a children's painting book out of these submarine pictures to sell at a shilling, and print 10,000, so that the rising generation will clamour to go into the Navy.

But the Committee soon took fright at the expense involved, and suggested that Ravilious find a publisher to take on the project. This proved to be extremely difficult. On 20 December he wrote to the WAAC:

Neither Curwen, Ripley, Murray or Lane can produce these submarine pictures, for all sorts of reasons, so I've now abandoned the idea of a book, and yesterday went to see the lithographic printers at Ipswich. They will produce the things simply as pictures in a small edition for £100.

In another letter of 22 December to Helen Binyon he elaborated:

I've been so put about with these submarine pictures and even now have not begun work. The fourth publisher has failed – these people won't take a risk and make too many conditions; after endless consultations they back out. So I'm doing the lithographs myself for fun. The bill is heavy but may be worth it in the long run, as the Leicester Galleries may show them. How fine not to have bloody publishers – and no children's book either. Ipswich will print the things, and I start work tomorrow.

This printer was W.S. Cowell, and the reason that Ravilious had turned to them was that the Curwen Press had been bombed.

By 4 January 1941 he was writing:

I work away at these drawings of submarines, and have nearly finished three. It is fairly difficult and wholly absorbing trying to work out the superimpositions of five colours in all sorts of tones and textures and the rest. Lithography ink is beastly stuff, greasy and thick. The printer at Ipswich is very good and willing to make expensive experiments, and as I pay for the job instead of a publisher I rather want to try what experiments I can. The children's book idea is gone for good, and no bad idea either. Submarines aren't suitable for children.

In mid-February he wrote again to the WAAC:

The submarine lithographs should be finished in about a week's time . . . I feel a bit doubtful of some, having made one or two rash technical experiments (with no publisher to consider!).

In another letter to a friend Ravilious again thought that:

they were not as good as they ought to be. It is a pity. Some aren't bad! Perhaps lithography in five colours is too much and the result tends to be a chromo.

In March the prints were shown to the Committee, which recommended that a set be purchased. The Leicester Galleries also expressed interest in exhibiting the set, priced at 2½ guineas a plate. The Committee finally decided to purchase instead the original watercolours for 25 guineas. In fact only nine were purchased at the time, for 22½ guineas, since Ravilious had mislaid one drawing. They were allocated to the National Maritime Museum; at a later point two more drawings were added, including an eleventh composition, a variant of *The Ward Room I*. Most of the lithographs remained with Ravilious himself, and after his premature death were inherited by his family.

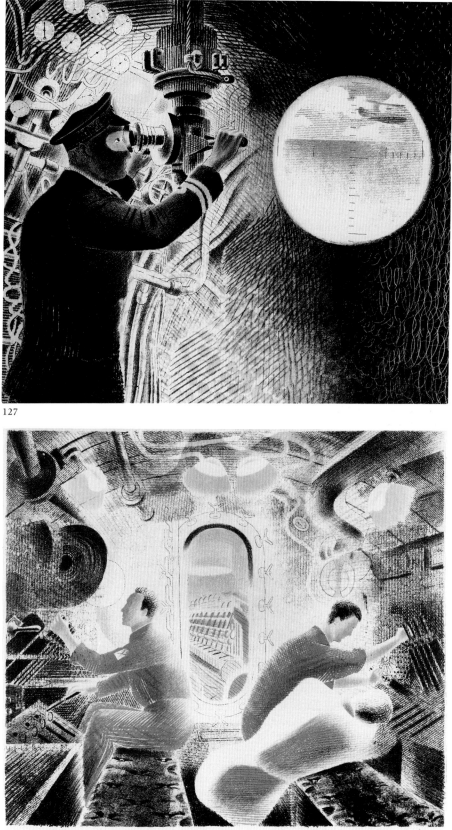

127

129

7 Post-War Lithography and Monotypes

Opportunities for the development of original printmaking remained quite restricted during the second half of the forties, only a few people having access either to presses or to serious expertise, even in the art schools. Stanley Jones subsequently described the lithographic situation in England at this period as one where the whole concept of producing an original print had become 'a lost and amateur occupation' (Pat Gilmour, 'Ceri Richards, his Australian Printer and Stanley Jones', *The Tamarind Papers* vol. 10, no. 1 (Spring 1987), p.28). Philip James of the Arts Council, in an introduction to the second exhibition of the Society of London Painter-Printers at the Redfern Gallery in 1949, emphasised the gulf between the creative relationship that existed between artist and printer in France and the state of affairs in Britain, where

either the trade lithographer, who has all the latest technical advances at his finger tips, is employed under the guidance of an artist who has himself mastered the intricacies of the process, and produces an edition of faultless regularity; or the artist retires to the scullery with the clothes-mangle, and not without a somewhat naïve disregard for technical tricks and proficiency and not without a little adventitious aid from finger tips or any other instrument at hand, rolls off a series of prints with a good deal of hit or miss.

At least two serious attempts at technical innovation were made, however, after the war, both involving Henry Moore, who was a complete novice in the field of lithography at the time. The first case in point was the set of six subjects published as the third series of School Prints in 1949, printed by a process perfected by W.S. Cowell of Ipswich from wartime developments in the manufacture of plastic (see cat.no.130). The second innovation emerged from the collotype process hitherto associated with high-quality facsimile reproduction, which was practised by the Ganymed Press in London from 1949.

One further initiative in the field of lithography was concerned with publishing rather than technical innovation. In 1945 the two sisters Caroline Lucas and Frances Byng Stamper, who had opened the Miller's Gallery in Lewes in 1941, published a portfolio of eight lithographs drawn on transfer paper by Vanessa Bell, Duncan Grant, Caroline Lucas and H.E. du Plessis (a copy belongs to the British Museum, 1985–3–30–12). It was a modest venture but the first of its kind since the outbreak of war; the favourable critical reception accorded to the portfolio fired the two sisters with the ambition to foster a *peintre-graveur* tradition in Britain in emulation of the French example. To this end they formed the Society of London Painter-Printers in 1948, in conjunction with the Redfern Gallery, to promote the exhibition of original colour prints; they also directly commissioned a number of

lithographs from many of the most interesting artists of the day, distributing their designs on transfer paper to a number of different presses in London and Paris.

The most diverse forms of experimentation during the 1940s, however, took place not within any of the conventional printmaking techniques but in relation to the monotype, a form of expression which defies easy classification as print, drawing or painting. It was used sporadically by a number of twentieth-century British artists prior to the Second World War; Sybil Andrews and Cyril Power exhibited a substantial group of monotypes at the Redfern Gallery in January 1933, while F.E. McWilliam's use of the medium has been described above. Their work was printed from glass or metal plates in the manner which Degas, most notably, had previously used to such brilliant effect. The influence of Paul Klee, however, encouraged a completely different type of monotype printing in Britain in the early forties, which was to be used just as extensively as the more traditional method. (The standard account of monotype printing is the catalogue for the exhibition *The Painterly Print*, Metropolitan Museum of Art, New York, 1980, but this excludes the traced method of drawing; for an account of late nineteenth- and early twentieth-century antecedents of this method see Antony Griffiths, 'Monotypes', in *Print Quarterly*, vol. v, no. 1 (March 1988), pp.56–60.)

Klee's stylistic influence on British artists throughout the thirties and forties was considerable, but they owed their consciousness of the specific technique which formed the basis of many of his watercolours and lithographs to Jankel Adler, who conveyed this method to a wide circle of artists, first in Glasgow, then in London during the war. Between 1919 and 1923, in connection with his experiments in transfer lithography, Klee had perfected a technique which used a hand-made 'carbon' paper to create a textured transfer drawing described in Germany as *Durchdruckzeichnung*. Its versatility as a medium was most fully exploited by Robert Colquhoun, but many other artists at the time also attempted it, including Cecil Collins and later some of the St Ives artists, such as John Wells and Wilhelmina Barns-Graham, who had no direct contact with Adler but simply absorbed the prevailing current of interest.

The difficult circumstances under which artists had to work during the war, with severe shortages of all their most basic materials, was another factor conducive to the popularity of monotype methods which required no particular equipment and could be adapted to whatever materials were available. By the end of the forties the interest had gathered such momentum that monotypes were regularly featured in exhibitions in a number of

London commercial galleries, particularly at the Redfern, where they appeared in the London Painter-Printers selections from 1948 until the early fifties as well as in one-man exhibitions. This flurry of activity was by no means confined to artists working in Britain: William Gear in Hanover, immediately after the war, encouraged a German artist, Karl Otto Götz (b.1914) in his exploration of a variety of different monotype effects; Gear continued his own experimentation in Paris (see section 11) and then back in England. Stephen Gilbert (b.1910), another British artist working in Paris in the late forties, also produced monotypes, while Alan Davie in Venice at the end of 1948 claimed to have executed a hundred examples (section 11). In the United States the American Monotype Society was formed in 1941 with a brochure on 'The Why and How of a Monotype' by its secretary, Paul Ashby, which was exclusively concerned with printing from metal or glass plates. By the mid- to late fifties, however, the monotype had been superseded by other methods of printmaking which allowed for the multiplication of images. Colquhoun was a rare example of an artist who continued to use it as a primary means of expression until his death in 1962.

Henry Moore

For biography and bibliography, see pp.98–9

130 Sculptural Objects, 1949

Lithograph printed in black, blue, indigo, red, yellow and orange. Signed and dated in the plate. Printed in the bottom left corner of the sheet: 'Sculptural Objects by Henry Moore. S.P.30. Published by School Prints Ltd, and printed in Great Britain by W.S.Cowell Ltd.' 497 × 860mm (sheet size)

CGM 7

1986–1–25–20

See colour illustration

This lithograph formed part of the 'European' series of School Prints published in 1949. Most of the prints had been commissioned by Mrs Brenda Rawnsley in June 1948 during a week's whirlwind tour of France by chartered plane (see her account of this in the Summer and Autumn 1989 issues of *The Fine Art Trade Guild Journal*. During this visit she secured the participation of Picasso, Léger, Dufy, Braque and Matisse, all of whom agreed to use plastic plates specially developed by W.S.Cowell in Ipswich for a payment of £200. Matisse, due to infirmity, subsequently decided to submit a 'papier déchiré' from which lithographic plates were photographically prepared. As part of the same operation, Moore was invited to execute a lithograph in no more than six colours, 19½ × 30 inches in size, to be published in an edition of 3000. 'With regard to subject matter, we should like to put ourselves entirely in your hands, and only ask you if you would be good enough to do something

suitable for children' (letter from Mrs Rawnsley to Moore, 15 July 1948).

Moore's initial letter of agreement on 6 July indicated his interest in lithography, which was closely allied to his wartime concentration on drawing:

I've only tried my hand at lithography once before – for a poster for the Spanish refugees in 1939, but it wasn't used, the War came and put such things in the background. But lithography is something I've always thought might be suitable to my way of working, and so recently I've said I'll try to do a lithograph for the V&A's lithograph exhibition [to be held to celebrate the 150th anniversary of the invention of lithography], and also I've said I'll do one for Miller's Gallery, Lewes. So by the time I do one for your School Prints I might know a bit more about the technique.

The process in which Moore was to be initiated by this commission was first announced in the *Penrose Annual* of 1949 as a way of improving the quality of large-scale lithographic printing. John Lewis, who was involved in the printing of the 'European' series, provided the following account of the method in *A Handbook of Type and Illustration*, London 1956, p.57:

Instead of drawing on lithographic stones or plates, the artist draws (the reverse way round) on a transparent sheet of plastic grained like a lithographic plate. The advantages are that any opaque material, chalk, pencil, ink etc. may be used, for the sheets of plastic are not transferred but are used in the same way as a photographic positive would be: that is, placed in a printing-down frame against a lithographic machine plate and then exposed to light. By this means an offset printing plate capable of a hundred thousand run can be produced. Also machine plates can be duplicated for the plastic original without any deterioration in quality. Colour separations are made easier, for the artist can superimpose one sheet on another.

On 22 July Mrs Rawnsley despatched to Moore 'two sheets of plastic, two chalking pencils, and a pot of ink for you to doodle with so as to give you some idea of the possibilities and texture of this new plastic material'. This produced two trial sheets of sketches which were proofed by Cowell's and subsequently used for a presentation folder for the Press, but never published (CGM 6 and 8). On 10 September Moore wrote to her: 'I am working on a batch of drawings one of which will be selected as the model for a School Prints lithograph', and suggested that she bring the full-size plastic plates for the print on 21 September. According to a taped account of the whole project made by Mrs Rawnsley in 1989, Moore was apprehensive about using colour in lithography, and asked to see what the French artists had done first, so that 'he could get his colours bright enough to compete with them'. By the end of February 1949, all the material for *Sculptural Objects* had been forwarded to Cowell's, consisting of six separations (presented by School Prints Ltd to the Tate Archives in 1971), a colour chart, one small plastic plate with the artist's signature, one small sketch and one full-size signed sketch to show what the final lithograph should look like. Moore went in person to Ipswich on 10

March to supervise the colour proofing, and the completed series was unveiled to the public at a special exhibition at the firm's temporary premises at 39 Eaton Square on 28 April.

The detailed evidence of Moore's involvement at every stage of the process was particularly important to Mrs Rawnsley in the 1960s, when for marketing purposes she was anxious to establish the autolithographic nature of the European series. Moore signed a statement on 1 June 1966 certifying that he 'drew six individual colour plates on plastic material for the lithograph *Sculptural Objects*', but Mrs Rawnsley failed to convince the cataloguers of Picasso and Braque's graphic work, largely because of the inherent prejudice against any print issued in such a large unsigned edition. Later, in 1970, when the *Observer Magazine* agreed to do an article on the 1948 French trip to promote the sale of the European series, splitting the profits with School Prints, Moore declined to sign a limited number of impressions of his lithograph in order to give them a spurious scarcity value (the article appeared in May 1971 and was published simultaneously in the colour magazine of *Die Zeit*).

Despite its humble status within the hierarchies of print connoisseurship, *Sculptural Objects* is an extraordinarily successful image. The British Council, for whom Moore was to be a major artistic export after the war, purchased a number of copies for distribution abroad, and the success of the collaboration prompted School Prints to commission four more lithographs printed on 'Plastocowell' and published in signed and limited editions in 1950 and 1951 (CGM 14, 15, 12 and 13, published in this order). School Prints had exhausted its stock of the first two by July 1951, but the second two were less successful, and Mrs

Rawnsley told Moore in December 1951 that she had sold less than half the editions of 50. *Sculptural Objects* itself sold only very slowly; the impression shown here was purchased from the remaining stock in 1986.

Undaunted by the commercial failure of the the European series, Mrs Rawnsley was in 1952 promoting a new scheme for small-scale replicas of sculptures, starting with Moore. The launch was to take the form of a cocktail party with 'twelve models made from jelly moulds' (letter to Moore, 27 May 1952). Moore, however, refused to be enticed into a project which, unlike the School Prints, was entirely reproductive in intention and process.

We would like to acknowledge the generosity of Andrew Jones in making available to us the correspondence about the European series which is now in his possession, and of Dave and Reba Williams in supplying a copy of Mrs Rawnsley's tape recording.

131 Figures in Settings and Sculptural Ideas, *c*.1949–50

Collograph. Trial proof before the addition of the colour plates in grey and sepia. Signed in pencil. 261 × 369 mm
CGM 11
1985–5–4–27. Presented by Mr and Mrs Bernhard Baer

Shortly after the execution of his lithograph for School Prints, Moore experimented with the related technique of 'collograph' printing at the Ganymed Press; this was founded in London in 1949 with the benefit of some of the equipment and expertise salvaged from the ruins of its Berlin namesake, formerly one of the leading firms of collotype printers in Europe. Ganymed had previously

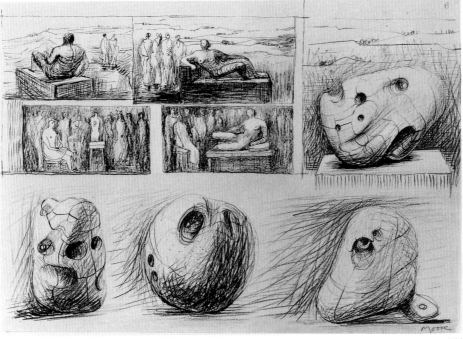

131

printed a collotype fascimile of Moore's famous Shelter drawing of 1941, *Pink and Green Sleepers* (Tate Gallery), and he was clearly intrigued by the possibility of recreating the textural effects of his 'wax-resist' method of water-colour drawing. A letter from Ganymed Press to Peter Gregory of Lund Humphries on 15 November 1949 elucidates the procedure as follows:

We are sending to Bedford Square [the Lund Humphries office] a roll containing a number of sheets of Kodatrace and a small bottle of ox-gall and a bottle of non-waterproof black ink. Will you send this material on to Henry Moore and ask him to draw freely upon any area up to 30″ × 30″. If he likes to do more than one, say a half dozen attempts, we will transfer his drawings to collotype plates and provide proofs. From this experiment I think we should learn a great deal. Apply the wash by means of a brush, or alternatively, he can draw with black pen and ink in the ordinary way. If he does pen and ink, he may not necessarily need the ox-gall added, but the only purpose is to overcome the grease on the surface of the paper and cause the ink to flow. Finally, of course, draw on the matt side. He might care to sign the drawings as a mark of authenticity.

The technique described here therefore involved drawing in separation on plastic sheets, as in the 'Plastocowell' process, but with the difference that the image in this case was transferred photographically to a glass plate covered with light-sensitive gelatine, which hardens in proportion to the transmitted light. The printing method then used was that of a collotype (i.e. directly from the gelatine which holds ink in proportion to its hardness), not a lithograph.

The first experiments from which emerged the rare proof catalogued here were completed by the beginning of 1950, and the original drawings on Kodatrace returned to the artist. But it was not until 15 August 1951 that Gregory recorded that 'two of the prints can be almost proceeded with straightaway, and I have sent Henry Moore away today after a good lunch with another supply of transparent paper and with the determination to get on with his part of the work. I think it will be all through in a fortnight.' In the event, three subjects were published in editions of 75. The prospectus advertising them in 1951 listed them as *Figures in Settings* at 12 guineas (CGM 5), *Woman Holding Cat* at 10 guineas (CGM 10), and *Standing Figures* at 10 guineas (CGM 9); a fourth subject was mentioned as being in preparation.

The term 'collograph' was invented by Bernhard Baer, the manager of the Ganymed printing works from 1950, in order to distinguish these autographic prints from the conventional reproductive collotype process. In a letter of 6 September 1951 to Gregory, Baer asked that the word 'plates' should be substituted for 'negatives' in the sentence referring to the destruction of the originals: 'I feel it would be preferable not to draw attention to the fact that photography is involved in the production.' Copies of each of the published collographs were sold to Curt Valentin of the Buchholz Gallery in New York, which had been handling Moore's drawings since the early 1940s.

132

Since the editions sold very slowly, the fourth projected print was never published, and the process never used again. Much later in the 1970s, Moore did however draw on his experience with the Ganymed collographs and the 'Plastocowell' process to develop a new variety of lithograph known as diazo lithographs. These were also drawn on translucent plastic film, but not in separation, and transferred to the plates by exposure to ultra-violet light.

In 1985 Mr and Mrs Baer presented this and a number of other collographs by Moore to the British Museum, including three proofs of *Two Standing Figures with Studies on the Left* (CGM 17, where it is quite wrongly described as a lithograph printed by W. S. Cowell). Bernhard Baer (1905–83) met his wife Ann Sidgwick through Ganymed. In 1960, when the collotype business was failing, the Baers formed a separate company, Ganymed Editions, to publish original prints. They began with the *Leda Suite* of lithographs by Sidney Nolan in 1961, and until 1979, when the firm was taken over by the Medici Society, they published a distinguished range of work, including that of Arthur Boyd and Brett Whiteley, Kokoschka, Ben Nicholson and Moore (his *Stonehenge Portfolio* of 1973). (An account of the firm is given in *Ganymed, Printing, Publishing, Design*, the catalogue of an exhibition held at the Victoria and Albert Museum in 1981; the Ganymed archive was presented by Mrs Baer to the V&A, where can be found copies of the letters quoted here.)

132 Three Female Figures, *c.*1950

Collograph, printed in black, blue-grey and yellow. Signed in
pencil. 505 × 381 mm

CGM 16

1985-5-4-26. Presented by Mr and Mrs Bernhard Baer

This is a unique proof of an unpublished collograph,
which is closely related to Moore's drawings of the late
1940s. The Cramer-Grant-Mitchinson catalogue mistakenly describes it as a lithograph printed by W. S. Cowell
Ltd.

Jankel Adler

1895–1949

Born in the Jewish ghetto of Łódź in Poland, the son of
a shopkeeper, he 'had a life which might well serve as
the epitome of all that Central Europe has been through,
physically and spiritually, since 1914' (Philip Hendy in
Britain Today no. 187 (November 1951), p.27). He first
moved to Germany in 1913 and studied from 1916
onwards at the School of Applied Arts in Barmen (now
Wupperthal). After the First World War he moved
between Germany and Poland, maintaining contact with
many of the radical groups of the period. In 1921–2 he
settled in Düsseldorf, where he formed a close friendship
with Otto Dix, who painted his portrait in 1926. Dix's style
had some impact on Adler's own work, but a more important influence was that of Paul Klee after his appointment
to the Düsseldorf Academy of Arts in 1931, where Adler
had the adjacent studio. After the Nazi *coup d'état* in 1933
Adler went to Paris, which brought him into contact with
Picasso, the other decisive influence upon his development. He lived in Poland again between 1935 and 1937
and then returned briefly to Paris, where he worked at
Hayter's Atelier 17: in 1948 Hayter was to contribute an
introduction to a book of reproductions of Adler's paintings published in London and Paris by Nicholson and
Watson.

In 1940 Adler joined the Polish Army of the West and
was evacuated from Dunkirk to Britain, where he was
stationed near Glasgow with the Polish artillery. Demobbed on health grounds in 1941, he resumed his artistic career, first in Glasgow and then from 1943 onwards
in London. In both places he quickly established himself
in progressive artistic circles, acting as mediator between
the Continental avant-garde and many younger artists
who had little or no experience outside Britain. His work
was exhibited throughout the 1940s, principally at the
Redfern, Lefèvre and Gimpel Fils galleries. The painter
Michael Ayrton dismissed him in 1946 as 'a good decorative painter without being a very interesting artist. This
is first-rate professionalism in the French sense and makes
me long for the amateurishness of Blake' (from a review
in the *Spectator* of an Adler exhibition at Lefèvre in March
1946). Adler's 'French professionalism' coupled with the

powerful emotive content of his work was, however, of
crucial importance to British art in the 1940s, and the
review in *The Times* of the posthumous exhibition at the
Lefèvre Gallery in October 1950 seems a fairer assessment
of his achievement: 'His art was based on that of Picasso
and Adler made no very radical changes in the idiom he
borrowed, but he used it with complete freedom and as
an appropriate expression of his own quite individual
imagination; his people are never Picasso's and their
expressions are very different even when their bodies are
constructed in much the same way.'

Adler executed a small number of etchings in the
1920s, one of which, *Woman with Cat*, has been reprinted
in a modern edition. Three more etchings, possibly in
unique impressions, survive from the 1940s. Two colour
lithographs (see below) were included in the 1948 Redfern exhibition of the Society of London Painter-Printers.
His principal contribution to printmaking in Britain was
the introduction of Klee's method of transfer drawing, creating a type of traced monotype, discussed in the introduction to this section.

Bibliography

A memorial exhibition was held by the Arts Council in
1951, accompanied by a small pamphlet with an introduction by Michael Middleton. The major modern study
is the 256-page catalogue with parallel texts in German,
English and Polish of an exhibition held in 1985–6 at
the Kunsthalle, Düsseldorf, the Tel Aviv Museum and the

133

Sztuki Museum in Łódź. This concentrates almost entirely on Adler's paintings. The most recent exhibition of his work was of watercolours and drawings from sketchbooks of the 1940s, held at the gallery of Michael Hasenclever in Munich in 1988.

133 Abstract Head, *c.*1944

Transfer drawing. Signed in the drawing. 322 × 250 mm

1990–6–23–22

This is a straightforward example of the technique that Adler learnt in the early 1930s from his direct contact with Klee and his general observation of Klee's work. The technique itself arose out of Klee's pedagogical and practical interests, which have been excellently summarised by Jim Jordan in an essay for the exhibition catalogue *The Graphic Legacy of Paul Klee*, Bard College, New York, 1983:

One of Klee's purposes with the transfer technique was to preserve in transparent layers the sequence of events through which the image had been constructed. In this technique, a preparatory drawing was traced onto another sheet, intended usually for further reworking as a print or watercolour. An intermediate sheet which Klee had coated on the underside with an oil paint or ink was used as 'carbon' paper. The artist traced over the original with a sharp stylus and the contours were offset in oil paint (or lithographic transfer ink) onto the paper below. The contours of the copy however were enriched by a soft fuzziness of the line inherent in the tracing process, and by tones and blobs, offset accidentally by the pressure of the hand ... The transfer technique harnessed a variety of technical experiments in the service of a specific idea. The elements of art were to be autonomous, equivalent; and when they were used in a work together, they were to be co-ordinated rather than mingled or mixed (pp.92–3, 100).

The peculiar texture of the line produced by the transfer method has often led to the work of Adler and his followers in this medium being wrongly described as lithographs. Adler also used the technique in conjunction with watercolour, frequently making a prolonged sequence of images. A sketchbook inscribed 'Wales 1944' (pages of which are reproduced in the 1988 Hasenclever catalogue) is full of these drawings, and another series was made in 1944 to illustrate *An Artist Seen from One of Many Possible Angles: Jankel Adler*, by Stefan Themerson, London 1948.

134 Landscape, 1948

Lithograph printed in black, plum red and yellow. Signed in the composition. 253 × 406 mm

1986–6–21–21

Landscape was exhibited in 1948 at the Redfern Gallery in the first exhibition of the Society of London Painter-Printers, together with another lithograph, *Girl*, both priced at 4 guineas. They both later appeared at the same price in 1954 in the Arts Council catalogue of Miller's Press lithographs.

Benjamin Creme

born 1922

Born in Glasgow, he left school at 16 in order to paint, attending life classes at Glasgow School of Art. In 1940 his work attracted the attention of Jankel Adler; during the following two years he was one of the small group of young artists (which included the poet W.S. Graham) who studied with Adler during his brief stay in Glasgow, attracted by what Creme described as his 'synthesis of Klee's poetry and wit with the tough formal qualities of Picasso'. At the same time Creme became involved in poetry circles through the Parton Press in Glasgow, for which he illustrated W.S.Graham's volume *Cage without Grievance* in 1942, together with Robert Frame, another member of the Adler circle.

In 1946 Creme moved to London and set up a studio in Battersea. His contact with Adler introduced him to the community of artists which included Colquhoun, MacBryde, Minton, Vaughan and Clough, with whom he remained closely associated throughout the 1940s. The year 1950 marked a watershed in his stylistic development, when a visit to France confirmed his desire for emancipation from the figurative influence of Adler and Picasso. His work thereafter in the 1950s became increasingly involved with landscape and abstraction.

Creme's only prints were four lithographs exhibited at the Redfern Gallery in 1949, and the group of monotypes of which two are discussed below.

Bibliography

Creme held a one-man show at the Redfern Gallery in 1955. The information given in the present catalogue is either supplied directly by the artist or taken from the catalogues accompanying two exhibitions of his work at England & Co, London: *Benjamin Creme, Paintings from the*

135

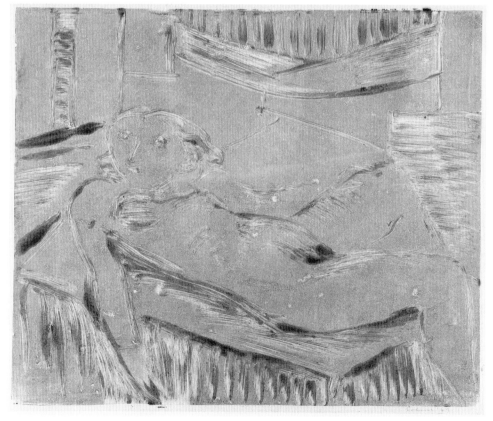

136

1940s and 1950s (1985) and *Creme, Landscapes 1940–60* (1988). We would like to thank the artist for his help.

135 Couple, 1949

Colour monotype. Signed both in the image and in the margin and dated in pencil. Inscribed on the back in pencil by the artist 'Benjamin Creme, 23 Glebe Place Chelsea' and 'Young couple 6 guineas'. 428 × 344 mm

1986-1-25-15

The British Museum owns one example by Creme (*Portrait of a Boy*, 1986-1-25-17), dated 1946, of the type of traced monotype, or transfer drawing, which was practised by virtually all the artists who came within Adler's sphere of influence. Creme did not begin to make monotypes from metal or glass plates (such as the two catalogued here) until the end of the decade. The summer of 1949 was his period of most intense activity, when he also invented his own process of 'polytype' printing using a hard wax surface on some of the plates, which permitted him to take a greater number of impressions. The work was carried out in exceptionally hot weather, and Creme incorporated the textures accidentally created by the rapid drying of the inks into his monotypes. This print and two other monotypes, *Woman* (4 guineas) and *Head of an Actor* (5 guineas), were exhibited at the Redfern Gallery in 1951.

136 Reclining Nude, 1949

Monotype. Signed and dated in pencil. 340 × 414 mm

1986-1-25-16

Robert Colquhoun

1914–1962

Born in Kilmarnock, he studied at the Glasgow School of Art in 1933–7. Much of 1937–9 was spent travelling on the Continent. After being invalided out of the Army in 1941, he and his inseparable companion Robert MacBryde moved to London, where they found a patron in Peter Watson, the collector and publisher of *Horizon*, who paid for their first studio in Bedford Gardens. In 1943 Colquhoun met Jankel Adler, who had moved into an adjacent studio. He encouraged Colquhoun to move away from neo-Romantic landscapes towards figure compositions. In 1942 Colquhoun had his first exhibition in London at the Lefèvre Gallery, where he continued to show regularly until 1951. From 1947 to 1948 the 'two Roberts' lived in Lewes in Sussex, where they were offered a house by their new patrons, the sisters of Miller's Press. By this point Colquhoun had been recognised as one of the leading British painters of the day. During the 1950s, however, his career declined precipitously due to per-

sistent alcoholism. An exhibition after a visit to Italy in 1949 was a failure, and he was dropped by Lefèvre after the early death of Duncan Macdonald, one of the directors. He and MacBryde settled in Dunmow, Essex, at a cottage lent them by Ruthven Todd, the poet and Blake scholar, which they shared with another poet, George Barker, until 1954. They then returned to London again, but only to move between a succession of boarding houses.

During this period one of their few sources of income was the commission for the costume and scenery designs for Massine's ballet *Donald of the Burthens* at Covent Garden in 1951 and for *King Lear* at Stratford in 1953. By the mid-1950s Colquhoun's painting had fallen off, although Bryan Robertson tried to arrest the decline by giving him a retrospective at the Whitechapel Art Gallery in 1958, for which he managed to complete eleven new paintings. This only provided a short respite, and he died at the age of 46 in the midst of preparations for an exhibition of monotypes at the Museum Street Galleries near the British Museum.

Colquhoun was a prolific printmaker. He was taught the technique of offset or transfer drawing by Adler in London, and used it for many of his drawings throughout the rest of his career. By 1946 he was also making monotypes from glass plates, or sometimes marble or lithographic stones; most of these belong to the 1940s, while another large group was made in the last four years of his life. He took up lithography in Lewes, and made a number of single-sheet prints for Miller's using transfer paper, as well as the lithographs commissioned for *Poems of Sleep and Death*, London 1947, one of the 'New Excursion into English Poetry' series published by Frederick Muller. Towards the end of his life, in 1960, he made a group of lithographs at the Curwen Studio with Stanley Jones. He seems never to have made an etching or a woodcut.

Bibliography

The catalogue of the retrospective exhibition held at the Whitechapel Art Gallery in 1958 has a short preface and a biographical note by Bryan Robertson, but does not purport to be more than an introduction to Colquhoun's work. There is a chapter on the work of the 'two Roberts' in Malcolm Yorke, *The Spirit of Place, Nine Neo-Romantic Artists and Their Times*, London 1988, and they were included in the 1989 exhibition held at Edinburgh on *Scottish Art since 1900* (also shown at the Barbican Art Gallery in London in 1990). An exhibition in 1981 at the City of Edinburgh Museums and Art Galleries had an essay by Andrew Brown. We are grateful for help from Roger Bristow, the author of a biography of Colquhoun which is due to be published by the Carcanet Press in 1991.

137 Nine Prints of Vegetation, *c.*1945

Traced monotypes. Each is signed in pencil, and is on a sheet of similar size, approx. 242 × 306 mm
1987–6–20–19 to 27

Three of these prints have titles traced as part of the monotype drawing: two are called *Tree Covered with Ivy*, the third *Gorse Bush*. All but one of them are horizontal compositions. The date of the series is uncertain, but its genesis can most probably be related to a biographical note in the Whitechapel exhibition catalogue under 1945: 'Frequent visits to Denis Worth-Miller and Richard Chopping at Wivenhoe, Essex. Colquhoun spent much time on the river and exploring the district. Later, a series of offset drawings was made based on boats, people and landscape details.' The subject-matter and its treatment can be compared with Colquhoun's landscape paintings of 1943–5. At this time John Minton, who had moved in with Colquhoun and MacBryde in 1943, was producing his own intense studies of vegetation within the pastoral compositions he drew in pen and ink. Colquhoun's interest was undoubtedly prompted by the work of Graham Sutherland, whose 'Welsh Sketchbook' of 1939–41, reproduced in *Horizon* in April 1942, pp.225–35, aroused widespread admiration for its dynamic interpretation of plant and other organic forms. Peter Watson, moreover, acquired two of Sutherland's most important landscape paintings in 1939–40, *Entrance to Lane* and *Gorse on Sea Wall*, which Colquhoun would therefore have known at first hand. This series was never exhibited, which probably explains the absence of any date.

The group was acquired by the British Museum at auction from the estate of Lady Anderson, the widow of Sir Colin Anderson who after Peter Watson was the most important of Colquhoun's patrons as well as being a collector of Sutherland's work. They met during the war, when they were neighbours in Bedford Gardens, and the close connection lasted until at least 1947. Anderson was a director of the Orient Line, and one of the most prominent figures in British artistic patronage of the middle decades of this century. He not only collected the work of many artists and served as chairman of the Trustees of the Tate Gallery, but used his business position to commission fittings for new liners from the leading British designers of the day: see Veronica Sekules, 'The Shipowner as Art Patron, Sir Colin Anderson and the Orient Line 1930–60', *Journal of the Decorative Arts Society* 10 (1986), pp.22–33. His collection of art nouveau is in the Sainsbury Centre of the University of East Anglia.

138 Woman Leaning on a Stove, 1946

Monotype. Signed and dated in pen. 510 × 390 mm
1987–5–16–50

At the end of 1946 Colquhoun spent eight weeks in Ireland, making while he was there and after his return a series of black and white monotypes of Irish peasants. They were exhibited at the Lefèvre Gallery in January 1947, and a similar group of paintings was shown there at the end of the same year. Wyndham Lewis reviewed these monotypes as follows:

Robert Colquhoun is generally recognised as one of the best – perhaps the best – of the young artists. That opinion I cordially endorse. Perhaps I should have said Colquhoun and MacBryde, for they work together, their work is almost identical, and they can be regarded almost as one artistic organism. Usually we say 'Colquhoun' when we speak of it. The latest monotypes of Colquhoun are very fine. They are flat black, white and grey slabs of people: or heads set on elongated slabs, which may be aprons or whatever else very simple women wear. The fact that they are all women dispenses the artist from indicating nether limbs, and assists him in achieving a maximum simplicity of statement.

With this simplification of statement *below* the face, the face should probably conform – as is the case with Rouault – to two or three marked types. Colquhoun uses a kind of Assyrian head which seems to qualify as one of these. But in the case of the Irish peasants the face becomes more varied, and even anecdotal. It is unlikely, however, that Colquhoun will continue for sixty years doing the same thing, as Rouault has: so it is unnecessary to work out details of that sort, as otherwise would be the case (*Wyndham Lewis on Art*, ed. W. Michel and C.J. Fox, London 1969, pp.398, 400).

The mood and composition of this monotype are typical of the monumental figure style developed by Colquhoun between 1944 and 1946, which provided the basis for the considerable critical esteem in which he was to be held during the latter part of the 1940s. The example catalogued here was exhibited in the Whitechapel retrospective as no. 205, when it belonged to the poet Patric Dickinson. Since completing this catalogue, the British Museum has acquired another traced monotype of 1945, *Toy Vendor and the Woman*, which was no.101 in the same exhibition (reproduced as plate 10 in the catalogue), when it was lent by Sir Colin Anderson.

139 Actors Rehearsing, *c.*1947

Traced monotype. Signed within the image and inscribed in pencil in the top left margin 'XVI Actors rehearsing'.
615 × 460 mm
1990–5–19–8

The composition of this traced monotype is very close to that of a 1946 monotype printed from glass which was reproduced on the front cover of the 1958 Whitechapel exhibition catalogue; its title was *Women Talking*, and the owner Frances Byng Stamper. That monotype preceded the group of Irish subjects described above, but is precisely similar in style and execution. *Actors Rehearsing* was probably made slightly later, when Colquhoun was working on a number of paintings for an exhibition at the Lefèvre Gallery in October 1947 which introduced 'a new histrionic element, of dancers, conjurors and other performers' (*Wyndham Lewis on Art*, p.401).

137

138

139

140 Mother and Son, 1948

Monotype printed in colours. Signed and dated in pen.
510 × 388 mm
1990-3-3-30
See colour illustration

The hieratic grandeur and the technique of this work are closely related to another monotype, also dated 1948, called *The Gardener*, in the British Council collection. It appears to correspond in size to a monotype called *Mother and Son* which was for sale at £26 5s. as no. 65 in a Lefèvre Gallery exhibition in May 1949, in which the work of Colquhoun was shown with that of MacBryde and Winifred Nicholson. *The Gardener* was shown as no. 129 at the end of 1948 in the first exhibition of colour prints by the Society of London Painter-Printers, priced at 30 guineas. The carefully defined areas of colour in both compositions have sometimes been mistakenly associated with a relief printing technique, but it seems likely that Colquhoun used stencils in conjunction with the monotype process to achieve this particular effect.

141 Woman and Cat, 1948

Lithograph printed in red, mauve and black. Signed in pen.
381 × 266 mm
1986-6-21-25

This was one of the lithographs that Colquhoun produced for Miller's while living in Lewes. It was shown in the 1948 exhibition of the London Painter-Printers, where it was priced at 3 guineas. The composition is the same as that of *Woman with Leaping Cat* (1945), one of his major pictures, which was purchased by the Tate Gallery in 1954 (and is reproduced in colour in the Whitechapel catalogue). The fact that it is in the same direction confirms that he used transfer paper.

The subject was one drawn from Adler's repertory of images, although Colquhoun invested his figures with a greater sense of drama. Wyndham Lewis described the woman in another treatment of this theme in 1946 (Arts Council collection) as being painted by the artist 'with a fierce and famished cat shooting over her shoulder ... thrusting out a nerveless hand in one of the purposeless gestures invariable with this existentialist humanity of his' (*Wyndham Lewis on Art*, p.400).

142 Four Prints of Monstrous Figures, 1955

Traced monotypes, from a set of five.

a. *Figure Holding Papers with Leg on Stone*
Signed in tracing. 500 × 365 mm
1983-6-25-28

b. *Figure with Outstretched Arms*
Signed in tracing. 500 × 360 mm
1983-6-25-30

141

c. *Dwarf and Tall Figure*
Signed in tracing. 547 × 390 mm
1983-6-25-31

d. *Three Standing Figures*
Signed in pencil and dated 1955. 475 × 353 mm
1983-6-25-32

The colour in the background was added to two of these prints after the traced drawing had been completed, in a second operation.

One general characteristic of Colquhoun's prints is the fact that many seem to have been made – and sold – in series, and his output was linked with specific exhibitions or commissions. This group turned up in a sale at Christie's in 1983 (22 April, lot 693), but has unfortunately no earlier provenance, nor does it seem to have been exhibited. We have therefore so far failed to identify the strange subjects of these prints.

142a

142b

142c

142d

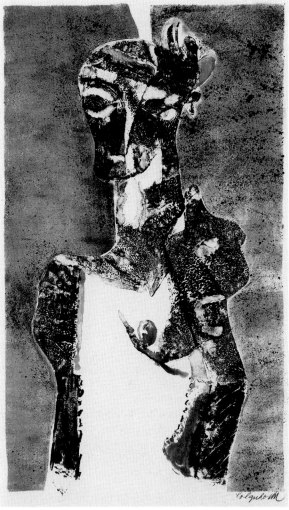

144

143 Half-Length Figure in Profile in Red and Black, *c.*1960–62

Monotype. Signed in pencil. 695 × 420mm

1986–1–25–26

See colour illustration

Although neither this nor the following monotype carries a date, they both belong to the final years of Colquhoun's career and relate closely to illustrated examples of his last monotypes. They completely belie the traditional view that Colquhoun's work suffered a steep decline in his last decade. After his 1958 retrospective he concentrated on monotypes, and although his health was severely impaired, he was still capable of considerable bursts of energy when confronted with the deadline of an exhibition. His death from heart failure came at 5.30 on the morning of 20 September 1962, after working all night in an attempt to finish the new material he had promised to the Museum Street Galleries (which had provided him with a studio) for an exhibition opening a fortnight later.

144 Half-Length Figure in Black, Grey and Yellow, *c.*1960–62

Monotype. Signed in pencil. 656 × 395mm

1990–5–19–9

The forty titles given in the catalogue of the 1962 Museum Street Galleries exhibition are too unspecific to allow cat. nos 143 and 144 to be identified with any degree of certainty. But they do include titles such as *Figure in Yellow and Black* (no. 1) and *Black and Red* (no. 15) which may correspond with them. Another title, *Nigerian* (no. 29), suggests that the resemblance between the work catalogued here and African sculpture is not a coincidence, particularly in view of Colquhoun's proximity to the British Museum's ethnographic collections at the time.

Robert MacBryde

1913–1966

Born in Ayrshire, he left school at the age of 14 for a five-year apprenticeship in an engineering firm. With his savings he went to Glasgow School of Art in 1932, where he met Colquhoun the following year. From this time onwards the 'two Roberts' were inseparable, and when Colquhoun was awarded a travelling scholarship in 1937, the money was found for MacBryde to accompany him. MacBryde's biography henceforth is almost indistinguishable from Colquhoun's. He was the more extrovert of the two, protected Colquhoun, tackled dealers and carried out the bulk of the domestic chores.

MacBryde's subjects were largely still lifes, strongly influenced by Braque. Michael Ayrton, reviewing the joint exhibition of Colquhoun, MacBryde and Minton at the Lefèvre Gallery in November 1944, described MacBryde as painting 'with all the charm that Colquhoun had discarded' (*The Spectator*, 3 November 1944). Later, in March 1947, a furious row erupted between the two Roberts and Ayrton over the latter's dismissive remark in an article on 'Some Young Contemporary Painters' in *Orion* the previous autumn that MacBryde's paintings, while being 'sensitive and elegant in their paint textures . . . do not add much, as yet, to British painting' (vol. III (1946), p.87). In the ensuing correspondence (now in the Tate Gallery Archive), both artists took issue with Ayrton's attempt (as they saw it) to isolate English art from Continental or Scottish influences, in a manner reminiscent of more recent critical controversies. More specifically, they stressed the importance of MacBryde's works, as well as Colquhoun's, for Minton's development. MacBryde described a Minton painting recently acquired by Ayrton as 'an early Colquhoun "curlicue" landscape, a small G.Suth "gorse on the sea wall", some Adler ("poor cook" remember) and could it be that it is held together by some of my "technical tricks"?' In other correspondence of the

145

145 Clown, 1950

Lithograph printed in black, yellow and purple. Signed and numbered 10/30 in pencil. 530 × 395 mm

1986–10–4–35

This lithograph was first exhibited at the Redfern Gallery in December 1950, as no. 30, priced at 6 guineas, from which its date can be deduced. According to an undated list of Miller's publications in the Redfern archives, this print was published by them. The texture of the black key drawing shows that it is certainly a transfer lithograph, while the speckled application of colour recalls the example of lithographs by Toulouse-Lautrec. The subject was one which MacBryde also portrayed in a number of paintings of the time.

John Kashdan

born 1917

Born in London of a Russian father and English mother, he attended the Royal Academy Schools from 1936 to 1939. In the early 1940s he was living in Cambridge, where he became acquainted with Henry Moore, the dealer and collector Gustav Kahnweiler, and the émigré German artist Richard Ziegler, all of whom were to be important influences upon him. His first one-man exhibition was held at the Redfern Gallery in 1945, and was instrumental in introducing him to Jankel Adler, who in turn introduced him to the coterie of artists living in Bedford Gardens, Notting Hill Gate. In 1946 he moved to Devon to set up an art department at the Royal Naval College, Dartmouth, but continued to exhibit in London and America until 1950, when he made a conscious decision to withdraw from public exhibitions. Thereafter he pursued his own work privately, otherwise concentrating on a teaching career at the Guildford School of Art.

Kashdan is primarily a painter, for whom monotype has assumed a particular importance since the early 1940s. Ziegler showed him Klee's method of transfer drawing, which he was using in Cambridge to produce editions of images with duplicator paper. Kashdan's own observation of the textural effects that Moore was achieving in his Shelter drawings with a combination of wax crayon, chalk and watercolour, inspired him to apply a similar technique to the colouring of his monotypes. Adler was another influence, as was Kashdan's contact in the late 1940s with the group of artists in London who were experimenting with the medium.

Kashdan exhibited his monotypes throughout the second half of the 1940s, most notably in an exhibition devoted exclusively to monotypes which went to the Museum of Modern Art in New York, the Art Institute of Chicago and the Philadelphia Art Alliance in 1946–8. From the mid-forties he also experimented with etching on acetate and a primitive form of screenprinting.

1950s to Walter MacElroy, MacBryde reverted to the vexed question of his own identity as an artist, although he there admitted to diffidence about ever discussing his own vision. In general he deferred to Colquhoun's superior talent, and never enjoyed the same success. He had only a single one-man show at the Lefèvre Gallery in 1943, otherwise sharing exhibitions with Colquhoun and other artists, and his work is still much more rarely seen.

After Colquhoun's premature death from heart disease, MacBryde ended up in Dublin, where he was killed by a car when drunk.

MacBryde made at least eleven lithographs, the first being for Miller's in 1948. He also produced many monotypes, a number of which can be found listed in contemporary exhibition catalogues. They are, however, rarely to be seen on the market, and there is none in the British Museum's collection.

Bibliography

No exhibition devoted purely to MacBryde's work has been mounted since his death. The bibliography for his work, therefore, is at present the same as that for Colquhoun.

Bibliography

An article on Kashdan by Harold Osborne was published in *Focus One*, 1946. The only other published source of information is the short catalogue accompanying an exhibition of his monotypes and paintings 1940–55, held at England & Co., Westbourne Grove, London, in October 1989. We are grateful to the artist for his help with the entries.

146 Actors, 1949

Monotype. Signed and dated bottom left in pencil.
395 × 505 mm
1989–12–9–14

Kashdan produced many of his monotypes while he was teaching at the Naval College in Dartmouth between 1946 and 1951. They were made on a glass plate and printed on paper using the pressure either of a hand or a roller. He also on occasion drew through the back of the paper onto an inked sheet of glass.

In its imagery and style, Kashdan's work of this period shared many features with that of the Adler circle, while yet preserving a distinctive vocabulary of its own which drew on literary and musical themes as well as the pervasive influence of Picasso. This monotype refers, the artist thinks, to his interest in dramatic improvisation as a vehicle for teaching in art schools, nurtured in part by his contact with the Group Theatre during the war.

The two monotypes catalogued here form part of a larger group of Kashdan's work acquired by the British Museum in 1989. It includes three other monotypes of 1945, 1946 and 1947, a drypoint of 1945 and two screenprints of 1946.

147 The Insect Woman I, 1954

Monotype worked over in watercolour. Signed and dated in crayon. 535 × 410 mm
1989–12–9–15

The textural quality of this print recalls Kashdan's earlier interest in Henry Moore's wartime drawing technique, but the extraordinary figure itself is derived from the imagery of Kafka's *Metamorphosis*. Kashdan discovered Kafka's work around the beginning of the war, giving the title *Portrait of Kafka* to another monotype of 1945 in the British Museum (1989–12–9–8). Kafka's work came to the attention of many artists at the same time, for, as Peter Watson told John Craxton in 1941, Kafka was 'completely satisfactory to read during this War' (quoted from Michael Shelden, *Friends of Promise*, London 1989, p.80). Adler shared the same interest: his *Metamorphosis* of 1944 was exhibited at the Lefèvre Gallery in March 1946, and the two gouache *Studies for Kafka's Work* and a drawing, *Portrait of Kafka*, were shown at Gimpel Fils in October 1950.

An uncoloured version of this print also exists; both are closely related to Kashdan's other monotypes of the same date depicting costermongers.

146

147

John Minton

1917–1957

His father was a wealthy solicitor and the family was connected to the famous china firm. He studied at St John's Wood School of Art from 1935 to 1938, where he became a close friend of Michael Ayrton, with whom he went to Paris in 1939. At this stage he was much affected by the theatrical style of the group of Parisian neo-Romantics which included Eugene Berman (1899–1972), Christian Bérard (1902–49) and Pavel Tchelitchew (1898–1957). After he was posted to North Wales with the Pioneer Corps in 1942, he began to appreciate the landscape through Sutherland's eyes, and declared himself to Ayrton as 'happier finally in the English tradition' (Tate Gallery Archives, Ayrton 811). In 1943 he underwent one of his periodic emotional crises, which was triggered by the problems of his homosexuality and his rejection of what he saw as Ayrton's inordinately possessive yet uncomprehending relationship with him. He was discharged from the Army in the same year on the grounds of homosexuality, and promptly moved in with Colquhoun and MacBryde until 1946, who together with Adler were to influence the direction taken by his work.

From 1946 to 1952 he shared a house with another member of the same circle of artists, Keith Vaughan, and taught in succession between 1946 and 1956 at Camberwell, the Central School and the Royal College. Minton gained a considerable reputation during the 1940s as a painter (with seven one-man shows at the Lefèvre Gallery), designer and illustrator, as well as attracting atten-

tion for his hectic personal life. His private income enabled him to travel extensively to Corsica, Spain, Morocco and Jamaica, but his work became increasingly decorative, lacking the intensity that he had originally admired in both Palmer and Sutherland. His sense of personal inadequacy and alienation increased through the 1950s, and he eventually died at the beginning of 1957 of an overdose of barbiturates.

Minton was scarcely involved with original print-making, with the exception of the two prints catalogued below and a few attempts at transfer monotypes (two examples are known, one in the Cecil Higgins Art Gallery, Bedford, the other in the Victoria and Albert Museum). He also taught an evening class in lithography at the Working Men's College during the 1950s. His main graphic achievement was as a black and white illustrator, supplying pen and ink line drawings which, in reproduction, helped to establish the high standard of illustration associated with the publications bought by the literate public in the late 1940s and early 1950s.

Bibliography

A memorial exhibition was staged by the Arts Council in 1958; the brief 18-page catalogue has a memoir by Michael Middleton. A chapter of Malcolm Yorke's *The Spirit of Place, Nine Neo-Romantic Artists and Their Times*, London 1988, is devoted to him, and a biography by Frances Spalding is due to be published in January 1991 by John Curtis. We should like to thank Frances Spalding for her assistance with these entries.

148

148 Thames-side, 1948

Lithograph printed in three colours (plum red, yellow and blue). Signed and dated in pen at the top right. 352 × 480mm

1983-6-25-25

At the top left of the margin can be seen 'red' and 'yellow' printed in those colours; these are marks to distinguish the different stones or plates.

This lithograph was included, under the above title, as no. 31 in the 1948 exhibition of the Society of Painter-Printers at the Redfern Gallery, and priced at 6 guineas. The composition is a reworking (with numerous variations) of Minton's painting of 1946, *Rotherhithe to Wapping*, now in Southampton City Art Gallery, which was exhibited in December of that year at the Lefèvre Gallery as one of a group of dockland views. The lithograph is in the same direction as the painting, which confirms the use of transfer paper, already apparent from the surface quality of the print.

As early as 1941 Minton, wandering through the devastated reaches of London's docklands, had been excited by the visual possibilities of the landscape. His earliest treatments of the subject concentrated on the atmospheric properties of bomb-damaged buildings. When he returned in 1945-6, the structural elements and patterns of the dockland scenery became of greater interest to him.

149 Quayside and Lighthouse, 1948

Linocut printed in three colours (yellow, blue and red), on thin tissue paper. Signed, dated and numbered 4/6 in pencil at bottom left. 203 × 310mm

1983-6-25-26
See colour illustration

The title given here is taken from the Lefèvre Gallery exhibition catalogue of Minton's new paintings and drawings in February 1949, where it was included as no. 68 and priced at £3; the lithograph *Thames-side* was the only other print in this exhibition. The subject is the little port of Propriano in Corsica, which Minton illustrated in his notable collaboration with the writer Alan Ross, *Time was Away, A Notebook in Corsica*, which was commissioned and published by John Lehmann, London 1948.

Ross and Minton made their journey to gather material in the late summer of 1947. Minton's pen and ink drawing of Propriano is reproduced on page 59 of the book, and shows a similar view to that in the linocut, with timber stacked up in the foreground. Ross described the town in the following terms:

The coast is lined with strips of very white sand . . . and at the extreme point a white lighthouse rises above the rocks in an assertion of purity. The same mauve tents of hills shut in the bay with overbearing closeness – huge faces so close their breath burns over the festering little port at their feet, breaking its will and hammering in its insignificance. The shore road is littered with cafés perched over rickety jetties,

hotels with stairways slopped over with vegetable ends rotting amongst discarded cigarettes, dirty children sitting abjectly on pavements, hubs of wheels thrown over geranium bushes, and piled along the beach by miniature rail-tracks, thick grey pencils of timber (p.58).

Linocut was an unusual technique to use in 1948, but Minton achieved with it a remarkably interesting image, in which the oppressive hills described by Ross are more successfully evoked than in the book illustration.

John Craxton

born 1922

Born in London; his father was Harold Craxton, professor of the pianoforte at the Royal College of Music 1919-60, and his sister the oboist Janet Craxton. He attended life-drawing classes in Paris in 1939, and continued his drawing instruction at the Westminster and Central Schools of Art at the beginning of the war. The patronage of Peter Watson was a vital factor in his career as for so many other talented figures of the time; it was Watson who paid for a studio in St John's Wood which Craxton shared in 1942-5 with Lucian Freud, and who gave him the entrée to the literary and artistic world associated with *Horizon*, the monthly magazine edited by Cyril Connolly which appeared for a decade from January 1940 (see Michael Shelden, *Friends of Promise, Cyril Connolly and the World of Horizon*, London 1989). In *Horizon* Craxton read Geoffrey Grigson's essay on Samuel Palmer, 'The Politics of an Artist', November 1941, with its reproductions of the pen and ink drawings in the Ashmolean Museum. These had a decisive effect upon his own work, and a few months later, in March 1942, *Horizon* reproduced his drawings in the same medium, *Poet in Landscape* and *Dreamer in Landscape* (Tate Gallery), which were the direct result of Palmer's inspiration.

Craxton was also deeply struck by Graham Sutherland's paintings *Entrance to a Lane* and *Gorse on a Sea Wall*, as well as an impression of Picasso's etching *Minotauromachia*, all in Watson's collection. Sutherland in turn admired Craxton's *Poet in Landscape*, and the two of them, accompanied by Watson, went on a sketching tour to Pembrokeshire in 1943:

There were cloudless days and the land was reduced to basic elements of life; rocks, fig trees, gorse, the nearness of sea on all sides, a brilliantly clear light. Everything was stripped away – all the verbiage that is – to the essential sources of existence. Sitting and talking there one day with Peter Watson, I was told that the landscape was like Greece, and this was possibly the crystallisation of my desire to travel to Greece (quoted in the Tate Gallery Biennial Report, 1982-4, p.135).

Craxton's first visit to Greece took place in 1946, and much of his time thereafter was spent around the Mediterranean. From 1952 he lived on the Continent, and since

1960 has lived in Crete, absenting himself only during the regime of the Greek 'Colonels' in 1970–76 and making occasional return visits to London.

His only attempts at printmaking have been one etching done at the Central School in 1940 (an impression is in the British Museum), the 1944 series of lithographs catalogued below, and two further lithographs exhibited at the Redfern Gallery in December 1954. He also made a small number of monotypes in the early 1940s, inspired partly by his purchase from Ruthven Todd in 1942 of William Blake's colour print *Satan Exulting over Eve* (*c*.1795); one of these monotypes, dated 1943, is in the British Museum (1987–10–3–34).

Bibliography

Geoffrey Grigson wrote an article on Craxton in *Horizon* in 1948. A retrospective exhibition was held at the Whitechapel Art Gallery in 1967, and a chapter about him is included in Malcolm Yorke, *The Spirit of Place, Nine Neo-Romantic Artists and Their Times*, London 1988. We would like to thank John Craxton himself for his help.

150 Three Lithographs, 1944

a. *Trees with Human Heads*
Lithograph in black and yellow. 146 × 212 mm
1987–10–3–63

b. *Landscape with Bridge over Stream*
Lithograph in green, pale green and black. 146 × 209 mm (irregularly trimmed)
1987–10–3–65

c. *Pembrokeshire Estuary*
Lithograph in four colours
(1) Printed in black only. With pencil annotations. 140 × 207 mm
1987–10–3–66
(2) Buff, yellow and pale blue plates only. 159 × 217 mm
1987–10–3–67
(3) Proof with all four plates. 159 × 219 mm
1987–10–3–68
Presented by the artist, as part of a group of seventeen working proofs of illustrations for *The Poet's Eye*.

These three lithographs are proofs of plates 9, 14 and 15 respectively in *Visionary Poems and Passages, or The Poet's Eye. Chosen by Geoffrey Grigson with Original Lithographs by John Craxton*, London (Frederick Muller Ltd) 1944. The book was one of seven anthologies of verse published as a series under the title 'New Excursions into English Poetry'; the general editors were W. J. Turner and Sheila Shannon. The blurb explained:

This series is something of an experiment and demands original work from both the anthologer and the artist, who have worked in collaboration, though there has been no attempt

150a

150b

150c

to give literal and pictorial illustrations of the actual poems ... Each artist has been chosen because he also is in sympathy with his subject and has a visual interpretation of his own to add to the literary interpretation of the poets ... The title of this book serves a double purpose for it describes the work of the artist as well as the anthologer's selection of poetry.

The first three volumes appeared in 1944, the other two being *English, Scottish and Welsh Landscape*, selected by John Betjeman and Geoffrey Taylor and illustrated by John Piper; and *Sea Poems*, chosen by Myfanwy Piper and illustrated by Mona Moore. Four further volumes appeared between 1945 and 1947, illustrated by Michael Ayrton, William Scott, Edward Bawden and Robert Colquhoun.

Although the standard of illustration of these volumes is exceptionally high, that by Craxton is perhaps the finest. He was commissioned to make the lithographs in 1943 and the preliminary drawings and transfers to zinc plates were made in Wales (according to information given to us by Craxton when he presented these proofs). The colour plates were added in Ipswich in 1944, when he worked at the printers W. S. Cowell, staying with the wife of Blair Hughes-Stanton. The finished prints are very sophisticated in technique: in some of the plates he overprinted in white to create a chiaroscuro effect which he had admired in a number of sixteenth-century Italian woodcuts in his possession. It was an effect that he reproduced a little later in both drawings and oil paintings, for example *Estuary of Old Boats*, a drawing dated 7 April 1945 (sold at Sotheby's on 20 July 1988, lot 273), or *Dark Landscape*, a painting of 1945 now in the Tate Gallery (this landscape is the same as that in cat. no. 150b, and was based on the mill at Alderholt in Dorset, according to an account given by Craxton to the Tate Gallery).

Craxton's use of chiaroscuro was an inspired complement to the mood that Grigson wished to create by his choice of poetry. Grigson was working on his biography *Samuel Palmer, The Visionary Years* (1947) at the time of this anthology, while Craxton drew upon the poetic and visual imagery he had derived from Blake and Palmer. The lone figure of the shepherd/poet/dreamer which became the leitmotif of Craxton's early work and appears again in some of the plates for *The Poet's Eye*, is a projection of the artist, who saw himself as trying to 'safeguard a world of private mystery' (Tate Gallery, *Illustrated Catalogue of Acquisitions 1982–4*, p.132). The anthropomorphised 'moon trees' were inspired by 'the strange pollarded trees of St John's Wood that rose up behind the garden walls gesticulating at the sky'. These trees also appear in a watercolour in the British Museum dated 2 May 1942. They are clearly indebted to Sutherland's own metamorphosis of the elements of landscape at a time when Craxton was associating with artists and writers who were interested in Surrealism.

Keith Vaughan

1912–1977

Educated at Christ's Hospital, but never attended art school. He worked from 1931 in the advertising agency Lintas, leaving in the summer of 1939 in order to paint. He registered as a conscientious objector in 1940 after serving with the St John's Ambulance Brigade, and was posted for the rest of the war to the Pioneer Corps, serving also as an interpreter for German prisoners of war. During short leave breaks in London, he contributed reviews to *Horizon* and *Penguin New Writing*, revealing himself as an accomplished writer. In 1941 the War Artists Advisory Committee purchased twelve of his sketches, which were shown in the National Gallery. In 1942 he was introduced by Peter Watson to Graham Sutherland, whose work had already influenced Vaughan's and continued to do so until the late 1940s when the latter found his own voice in figurative composition.

After being demobbed in 1946, Vaughan became a full-time painter with the encouragement of friends like Minton and John Lehmann, the editor of *Penguin New Writing*. His drawings had already been exhibited at the Lefèvre Gallery in May 1944, and this gallery continued to show his work during the 1940s. He followed Minton as a teacher of illustration at Camberwell and then the Central School in 1948, later moving to the Slade in the 1950s. Despite the considerable success of his career (including being made a CBE), he, like Minton, felt increasingly out of tune with the prevailing artistic climate in the 1960s and 1970s, revealing his depression in the journals which he had kept intermittently since 1939. In the face of terminal cancer, he took his own life in 1977, recording the details of the suicide in an obsessive manner reminiscent of an earlier artistic suicide and diarist, Benjamin Robert Haydon (1786–1846).

Vaughan's first prints (apart from a few immature linocuts made in 1928–30) were the large monotypes made in 1948, three of which are catalogued below. Between 1949 and 1956 he made at least nine colour lithographs, mostly published by the Redfern Gallery.

Bibliography

There has been no large-scale retrospective exhibition of Vaughan's work since that held at the Whitechapel Art Gallery in 1962, with a catalogue containing a long biographical section and an introduction by David Thompson. Another good catalogue is that for the exhibition *Images of Man* held at the Geffrye Museum and in Birmingham in 1981. The most important documentary source is his own journals in sixty-two notebooks, about a quarter of which have been published in extracts by Alan Ross, editor of the *London Magazine* (which published many of Vaughan's writings). *Journals and Drawings 1939–1965*, selected by Vaughan himself, was published in 1966. An edition extended to 1977 followed in 1989,

151

with a memoir by Ross. These journals are remarkable (and highly intelligent and self-conscious) pieces of writing, and reveal as much about Vaughan's attitude to life and his homosexuality as about his art. Malcolm Yorke includes a chapter on Vaughan in his *The Spirit of Place, Nine Neo-Romantic Artists and Their Times*, London 1988, and is the author of a biography due to be published by Constable in September 1990. We must also thank John Ball for his help with the entries.

151 Foreshore with Figures by a Boat, 1948

Monotype. Signed and dated in pencil. 382 × 479mm
1987–11–7–15

All the three monotypes by Vaughan catalogued here are dated 1948, as is a fourth also in the British Museum's collection (*Figure Leaning on a Garden Wall*, 1987–4–11–5) which has had to be left out through lack of space. According to information kindly supplied by John Ball, there are records of eighteen or nineteen monotypes by Vaughan,

all of which were made in 1948. Six of them were exhibited at the Lefèvre Gallery in December 1948, priced at 18 guineas each (nos 59–64). The British Museum's subject here can be identified on the basis of size with nos 59 or 60, which bear the same title in the catalogue. Four of Vaughan's monotypes were exhibited again at the Redfern Gallery in December 1949, and finally three, which had been left out of the Whitechapel retrospective, were shown at the Matthiesen Gallery in 1962. There seems to be no documentary evidence of how Vaughan came to be attracted to the medium, but it is hardly surprising that he was, given the fact that so many of his contemporaries were also making monotypes.

In 1948 Vaughan had visited the Ile de Ré and La Rochelle, which inspired the shore scenes of that date. The following year he visited Finisterre, which he used as the title of a lithograph closely resembling the composition of the monotype catalogued here.

152

152 Figure with Extended Arms, 1948

Monotype. Signed and dated in pen. 452 × 347mm

1987-11-7-16

The title given here is that with which the print was acquired from the artist's estate. This and the previous monotype are text-book examples of the range of effects that the process allows. Vaughan has worked the ink with his fingers, with a pointed instrument, wiped it with a rag, and puckered it with dabs from some soft material.

153 Figure, 1948

Monotype worked over with pink enamel. Unsigned, but inscribed in the corner of the backing sheet in the artist's hand 'Figure – monotype & enamel 1948'. 375 × 273mm

1987-4-11-6

This monotype is rather different from the others, in that the sheet of glass was not uniformly covered with ink from which the design was worked. Instead, it was irregularly brushed with ink into which the composition was scratched. The design was later worked up with colour to help define the forms, which would otherwise be very imprecise.

Prunella Clough

born 1919

Born in London, the niece of the designer Eileen Gray. She studied at the Chelsea School of Art in 1938–9, then worked as a mapping and engineering draughtsman during the war. She maintained her contact with artistic circles, forging close links with Colquhoun, MacBryde and Vaughan among others, but her career as a painter did not properly begin until 1946. Her earliest subject-matter was drawn from the beaches and fishing ports of East Anglia; during the 1950s she concentrated upon the urban industrial landscape, becoming increasingly involved with abstraction after 1960. She has taught for varying periods at the Chelsea and Wimbledon Schools of Art.

Clough has made prints throughout her career. In 1948 she acquired her own lithographic press with a 16-inch bed, and with this made a number of small plates which were shown by the Redfern Gallery in 1948–52. In the mid-1950s she also gained access to an etching press, on which she printed plates which have hardly ever been shown in public, but were sold directly to friends and collectors. In 1961–2 she made a group of about twenty 'monoprints' from lino, which were exhibited at the Matthiesen Gallery in about 1962, four of which are in the British Museum. During the 1970s and 1980s she has also worked on screenprints, woodcuts and some very large monotypes.

Bibliography

Although there have been numerous small shows at various dealers' premises, there has only been one large retrospective exhibition of her work. This was held at the Whitechapel Art Gallery in 1960; the catalogue has an introduction by Michael Middleton. There is also a chapter on her in Malcolm Yorke, *The Spirit of Place, Nine Neo-Romantic Artists and Their Times*, London 1988. (Although she was a friend of many artists of the late 1940s, it is impossible to describe her own work as neo-Romantic.)

The only published source of information about her prints is the entries by Liz Knowles on fifteen prints in the Tate Gallery *Illustrated Catalogue of Acquisitions 1982–4*, pp.377–81. We also owe thanks to the artist herself and to Ken Powell for help with these entries.

154 Eel-Net, 1948

Lithograph printed in blue, buff and brown. Signed in pen bottom left. 407 × 280mm

1980-6-28-13

The Whitechapel retrospective contained only one print – a woodcut of 1946 entitled *Zoolite*. With that exception, this seems to be Clough's first print, and was included by the Redfern Gallery in the 1948 exhibition of the Society

154

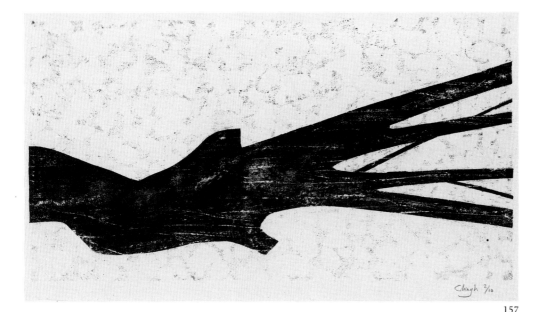

157

of London Painter-Printers (price 4 guineas). Unlike most of the other colour lithographs in that show, which were printed in Paris or at the Chiswick Press, this was printed by Clough herself. It may well have been drawn on transfer paper, since Clough has told us that her methods were varied and that she both drew directly on the stone and used transfer paper.

This print is in Clough's early manner, still in a post-impressionist idiom and with a restrained use of earthy colours typical of her paintings of this period. The subject is drawn from the East Anglian fishing ports, especially Lowestoft, that she was visiting at this time.

155 Geological Landscape, 1949

Lithograph printed in yellow-ochre and black. Signed in pencil. 150 × 201 mm

1986–11–8–3

Under what must be the misprinted title 'Geographical Landscape', this print was shown at the Redfern Gallery in 1949. The Tate catalogue records (apropos another impression in its collection) that it was printed by Clough in her studio from two stones. The Tate has a few other small lithographs of this period, of which only five to ten trial proofs were ever printed in each case, despite their being shown at the Redfern Gallery. The close trimming to the plate edge was done by the artist herself.

156 Fisherman with Scales, 1950

Monotype. Signed in pencil. 455 × 325 mm (maximum dimensions)

1985–2–23–3

This subject derives from Clough's visits to Lowestoft and shows her interest, lasting from about 1950 to 1954, in

155

figures set in their working surroundings – whether fishermen, lorry drivers or factory hands. This monotype was made on a glass plate. A similar painting entitled *Fisherman with Scales, Lowestoft Harbour*, made in 1951, was sold at Christie's on 8 June 1990, lot 275 (illustrated in the catalogue). Another monotype of this subject, in a private collection, dates from the mid-fifties.

157 Sea-Wrack, 1952

Lithograph. Signed and numbered 2/10 in pencil. 192 × 367 mm

1986–6–21–24

This was first exhibited under this title at the Redfern Gallery in 1952, priced 3 guineas. Another impression in a private collection has an old label on the back with the alternative title 'Reed on shore' typed by the artist. Sea-wrack is a coarse variety of seaweed.

156

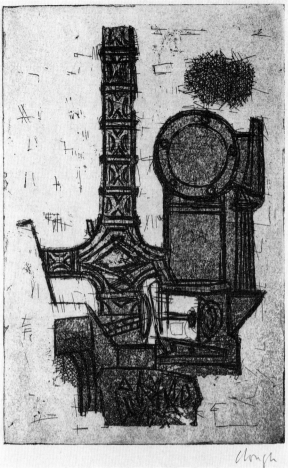

158

158 Gasworks, 1954

Etching and aquatint. Signed in pencil. 150 × 100 mm
1986–11–8–2

This belongs to a group of etchings made in 1954–5 at
the Chelsea School of Art, where Clough was then teaching. Etching was a new medium for her, and all the plates
were on a small scale with simple subjects. None was
printed in an edition, and they have never been included
in one of her exhibitions. The Whitechapel retrospective
included as no. 46 a painting of the mid-1950s with the
title *Chemical Works*, which includes some of the elements
of this composition.

Clough explained her particular attitude to the choice
of subject-matter in *Picture Post* in 1949 (quoted by
Malcolm Yorke, p.293):

Anything that the eye or the mind's eye sees with intensity
and excitement will do for a start; a gasometer is as good
as a garden, probably better; one paints what one knows . . .
Whatever the theme, it is the nature and structure of an
object – that and seeing it as if it were strange and unfamiliar,
which is my chief concern.

Michael Rothenstein

born 1908

Son of Sir William Rothenstein, the painter, and brother
of Sir John, the former director of the Tate Gallery. Studied
at the Central School in 1924–7, but his career was then
interrupted by illness, from which he only recovered
around 1940. In that year he settled in Essex, where the
landscape and agricultural life provided his principal
subject-matter throughout the 1940s and 1950s. He was
then commissioned by the Pilgrim Trust to work for the
Recording Britain scheme, and during the 1940s worked
more as a draughtsman than as a painter. He took up
printmaking in 1948, his first print being a lithograph
for Miller's. In 1949–50 he made a group of monotypes
(from which come the two items below); then followed
a stream of woodcuts, linocuts and aquatints through the
1950s. In 1960 he worked briefly for the first time with
Hayter in Paris, an episode which he later credited with
altering his life. It certainly revolutionised his approach
to printmaking, which henceforth became his main field
of artistic expression. What Hayter was to engraving and
intaglio printmaking, Rothenstein became to relief printmaking, as evidenced by his three books on the subject.
His constant employment of new techniques and imagery
continues to the present day.

Bibliography

Rothenstein's three books on printmaking techniques are
Linocuts and Woodcuts, London 1962; *Frontiers of Printmaking: New Aspects of Relief Printing*, London 1966; and
Relief Printing, London 1970. A retrospective exhibition
was held in 1989 at the Art Galleries in Stoke-on-Trent
and Bradford; the catalogue has an introduction by Mel
Gooding. An exhibition of his prints of the 1950s and
1960s was held in 1987 at the Redfern Gallery. Tessa
Sidey of Birmingham City Art Gallery is preparing an
exhibition with the artist for the end of 1990, called 'Print
in Process', and, in the longer term, a catalogue raisonné
of his prints.

159 Horse and Cart with Two Figures, c.1948/9

Monotype, printed in red, mauve and black. Signed in pencil.
395 × 568 mm
1989–7–22–30

This composition may be related to a group of monotypes
shown by Rothenstein in February 1949 in a joint exhibition with Humphrey Spender at the Redfern Gallery (nos
88, 89 and 104). The subject of all three monotypes was
sugar-beet workers, and they were priced at 9, 17 and
20 guineas respectively.

159

160

160 Guard and Lamp, 1950

Monotype, printed in black and grey. Signed in pencil at top; titled and dated on the verso. 570 × 393 mm

1989–7–22–29

This has been printed in two pulls, with the black over the grey. The preparatory drawing in pen and ink, on the page of a sketchbook, is also in the collection of the British Museum (1989–7–22–32(9)). This forms part of a group of twenty-seven sketches and notes from this period acquired in 1989. One of these sheets contains a list of four paintings and twelve monotypes, perhaps prepared for an exhibition. Fifteen drawings or monotypes were shown at the Redfern Gallery in February 1951, although none can be identified with this or with cat. no. 159.

In the preface to an exhibition entitled *Signals* held at the Redfern Gallery in 1989, the artist explained the significance of the subject for him:

I remember waiting at stations with the red and green eyes of signal lights at night spelling a different message. Some were set under deep, shovel-shaped cowls, though the red suddenly turning to green held no greeting. The signal gantries spanned the rail-tracks, spidery constructions drawing a lattice of angled lines cutting black silhouettes against the half-tone space of sky – dramatic monuments of a vanishing technology. By contrast the old-fashioned post signals, with lamps and coloured arms, could look both funny and human as the flags moved up or down. The winking signal lights, however, and the machine sculpture that upheld them, could be both sad and exciting.

8 St Ives and Corsham

The presence of Nicholson, Hepworth and Gabo during the war firmly established St Ives's credentials as a centre for avant-garde artistic activity; this position was consolidated throughout the forties and fifties by a fluctuating population of painters, sculptors, writers and critics whose contact with artistic circles elsewhere, in London and even New York, helped to sustain the vitality of the community. Some of its members, like Peter Lanyon and Bryan Wynter, were firmly entrenched there; others, like Terry Frost, were more peripatetic in response to the exigencies of paid employment, while the majority were occasional visitors: Minton, Colquhoun, MacBryde, Adrian Heath, Victor Pasmore, William Scott and Robert Adams, to name but a few.

Printmaking was a casual activity for the artists working in St Ives at the end of the forties, virtually none of whom was properly trained in any of the graphic media. They picked up what instruction they could from the few professionals in the vicinity, such as the etcher Bouverie Hoyton at the Penzance School of Art and Guido Morris the letterpress printer, or from their colleagues with marginally greater experience, such as the American Warren Mackenzie, who brought a knowledge of silkscreen printing to St Ives; otherwise they relied mainly upon their own powers of invention. Monotype printing was an immediately attractive medium since it required no special equipment; linocutting had similar advantages, and even silkscreen printing could be carried out quite inexpensively on a domestic scale.

The prints were seldom executed with a view to a commercial outlet, as such opportunities were largely restricted to intermittent appearances in local exhibitions at Downing's Bookshop, the Castle Inn and the shop of the furniture maker Robin Nance, or in the Redfern Gallery exhibitions in London. However, in the early fifties there were two more consistent attempts to stimulate a market for prints. The first was an exhibition called *Prints for under £1*, held during December 1951 at Robin Nance's shop. Bernard Leach, who was himself an etcher as well as the doyen of craft pottery in Britain, explained the *raison d'être* of the exhibition in a review in the *St Ives Times* for 30 November 1951:

Today the artist is having to face the steady loss of private patronage. Public patronage is very slowly coming to his aid but meanwhile here is a small effort by a few local artists to meet the problem. Before the war limited editions of handmade prints of etchings, engravings, wood-blocks etc. sold for anything from five to twenty guineas. They were made for the 'collector' and had an aura of Bond Street and hushed voices about them quite out of keeping with the realities of the present moment. Dealers kept up prices artificially and

helped to persuade the artist that it was necessary and wise to do so. But the bottom fell out of this market. Reproductive processes now being used in St Ives are for the purpose of increasing quantity and lowering costs, and if artists will take the trouble to use these methods with responsibility and pleasure in them it is now obviously to their own advantage as well as that of the ordinary public.

Peter Lanyon, one of the contributors to *Prints for under £1*, hoped it would be the starting point for a proper portfolio, according to a letter he wrote to Patrick Heron in 1951 in which he also referred scornfully to the Penwith Society's attempt to organise a print scheme of its own.

Neither scheme materialised, but the screenprints shown in *Prints for under £1*, which were the most unusual feature of the exhibition, did arouse further interest among the artistic community. The sculptor Denis Mitchell (b. 1911), who had lived in St Ives since 1930, set up screenprinting facilities in his own studio in the early fifties with a view to producing prints and items for domestic use, like table-mats. Leach, in the review quoted above, had praised the silkscreen process for its economy and range of expressive technique, making it an ideal vehicle for the dissemination of new artistic ideas which 'have to be lived with and slowly assimilated, or rejected, by most people, but if it is very expensive, few can undertake the risk'. Mitchell, under the trade name 'Porthia Prints', hoped to impress upon the public the functional as well as the decorative role of abstract design, and obtained a London outlet in the form of an exhibition at Heal's furniture store in 1955. The market did not, however, respond and the enterprise was as short-lived as the print scheme proposed by Lanyon, in complete contrast to the market for craft pottery, which the Leach studio had successfully stimulated, selling through stores like Heal's and Liberty's; by the late fifties the ten or twelve potters employed in the business were turning out 22,000 pieces a year to meet the demand.

Lithography was a medium which tended to require more costly machinery and professional expertise than the other printmaking techniques. It was at the Bath Academy of Art, situated from 1946 onwards in Corsham Court, Wiltshire, that many of the St Ives artists had their first opportunity to work with this process. The principal, Clifford Ellis (1907–85), whose main interest lay in educating future art teachers, devised one of the most imaginative syllabuses of the day, in which he invited a galaxy of promising artists, writers, musicians and art historians to participate; William Scott, the senior painting master from 1946 to 1956, remarked: 'One could as well talk about a West Country Movement as a St Ives School, for it was at Corsham Court where we all met' (Tom Cross,

Painting the Warmth of the Sun, Penzance and Guildford 1984, p.137). Ellis was a lithographer who exhibited at the Redfern Gallery; however, the principal teacher of the subject from 1950 was Henry Cliffe (1919–83), who gave a great deal of technical advice to his colleagues, although Terry Frost claims to have felt somewhat unwelcome in the lithography studio (see Tate Gallery, *Illustrated Catalogue of Acquisitions 1982–4*, p.396). An exhibition at Dartington Hall in Devon in 1955 brought together the lithographs of Corsham students and staff, including examples by Howard Hodgkin, a recent graduate of the Bath Academy of Art who returned to teach there in 1956, William Scott and Kenneth Armitage. (The history of Corsham as an art school has been chronicled in a recent catalogue: *Corsham: A Celebration of the Bath Academy of Art 1946–1972*, published by the Michael Parkin Gallery, London, in 1989.)

A different phase of printmaking began in the latter half of the fifties when Robert Erskine of the St George's Gallery introduced artists such as Terry Frost to professional lithographic printers in London and Edinburgh. Stanley Jones, at Erskine's suggestion, went down to St Ives in January 1958 immediately after his return from Paris in order to open a temporary lithographic workshop. This was done in premises just off Fore Street, using equipment Jones brought with him; for the next nine months local artists were encouraged to experiment with the medium, while Jones proofed their work on stone and plate. Peter Lanyon, Bryan Wynter, Patrick Heron and Barbara Hepworth were among those who took advantage of the facilities. Only a few of the prints were properly editioned, but subsequently several of the St Ives artists were prompted by this experience to collaborate with Jones at the Curwen Studio in London, and the character of their printmaking changed. (We are grateful to Stanley Jones for information on the St Ives project in 1958.)

Peter Lanyon

1918–1964

From a cultivated and prosperous background, he was the only one of the leading St Ives artists who was a native of the town. He studied drawing at the Penzance School of Art in 1936–7; then, on the advice of the writer Adrian Stokes, briefly attended the Euston Road School in 1938, where he was taught by William Coldstream and Victor Pasmore. The following year he was introduced to Nicholson, Hepworth and Naum Gabo, who had just moved to St Ives upon the outbreak of war. Throughout most of the ensuing decade the influence of Nicholson and Gabo on his work was paramount; the example of Gabo, who occupied the studio attached to the Lanyon family home, immediately prompted Lanyon to abandon landscape painting for abstract constructions. From 1940 to 1945 he served in the Royal Air Force but was barred from flying on medical grounds; his ambition in this respect was eventually realised in 1959 when he took up gliding, the cause, five years later, of his premature accidental death. In 1945 he returned to St Ives, shortly afterwards moving into Little Park Owles, the house previously occupied by Adrian Stokes. At this stage he remained very close to Gabo; however, by 1949, the year of his first one-man show at the Lefèvre Gallery, he had returned to the landscape of southern Cornwall and a distinctive style of his own emerged. He taught life drawing at Corsham during the fifties and helped to run a summer art school at St Peter's Loft in St Ives from 1955 to 1960. His reputation as a dominant figure in British art was by then established both at home and abroad. In March 1951 the German painter K.O. Götz included Lanyon in the fifth issue of his magazine *Meta*, devoted to young British artists. Between 1957 and 1964 he was given four one-man shows at the Catherine Viviano Gallery in New York. The resulting contact with American artists, particularly Franz Kline, Robert Motherwell and Mark Rothko, brought about a further change in his style, towards an expansive, open form of abstract composition quite different from the linear abstraction of his early years or the 'Tachisme' of many of his contemporaries.

Lanyon never undertook printmaking in a consistent way, but, like so many of his fellow artists in the late forties and fifties, explored it on a purely *ad hoc* basis. He nevertheless attempted a wide variety of techniques, from monotypes to linocut, slate reliefs, silkscreen, lithography and etching. The selection catalogued here covers almost the full range of his production, with the exception of the slate cuts and lithographs.

Bibliography

The main exhibition catalogues devoted to Lanyon's work are those produced by the Tate Gallery in 1968 with an introduction by Alan Bowness, and by the Whitworth Art Gallery, Manchester, in 1978, written by Andrew Causey; another concentrating exclusively on his drawings and prints was published by the City Museum of Stoke-on-Trent in 1981. Lanyon's son Andrew is publishing a book on his father's work, *Peter Lanyon 1918–1964*, at the end of 1990. Two general publications on St Ives artists are *Painting the Warmth of the Sun: St Ives Artists 1939–1975* by Tom Cross, Penzance and Guildford 1984, published in association with Television South West, and the Tate Gallery's exhibition catalogue of 1985, *St Ives 1939–1964: Twenty Five Years of Painting, Sculpture and Pottery*. We would like to thank Mrs Sheila Lanyon for her assistance with these entries; the items with 1985 registration numbers were purchased directly from her in that year.

161 Abstract Composition, 1946

Traced monotype printed in green with additional work in pen and ink. Signed and dated in pencil. 302 × 257 mm

1985–7–13–36

This composition is a good example of what the artist referred to as his 'Gaboids', done in the year in which Gabo left St Ives for America. Lanyon made a small number of monotypes using either the transfer method of drawing through a carbon or printing from a glass or metal plate. *Portreath*, 1949 (Stoke-on-Trent catalogue no. 42) and *Horse*, 1952 (Stoke-on-Trent no. 52) were two of the latter type; another, of mine chimneys at Levant, *c*.1950, in the British Museum (1985–7–13–39), is a traced design worked over with pencil and crayon. Monotype was listed on the prospectus for the St Peter's Loft art school which Lanyon ran a few years later with Terry Frost and John Wells, alongside 'drawing, painting, engraving, etching, lino, modelling and pottery'. Since the late thirties the monotype had been recommended by enlightened art educators because of the scope it provided for students to learn from chance effects as opposed to the inveterate pursuit of a carefully contrived result (see William Johnstone, *Child Art to Man Art*, London 1941).

161

162 Church Town, 1948

Recto: screenprint printed in brown, green and black with grey gouache added around the edge of the image. 278 × 239 mm

Verso: abstract(?) composition printed in brown, green and turquoise. Signed, dated, titled and numbered 3/7 in biro; inscribed 'silk screen £5'

1989–6–17–277

See colour illustration

This and possibly one other subject by Lanyon inscribed 'Figure of houses, gelatine bichromate print 1947' were among the first artist's screenprints made in Britain. Stencilling as a variety of screenprinting had been briefly used by the Curwen Press for book illustration in the early thirties, when it was the subject of an essay by Paul Nash in the Curwen Press *Miscellany* of 1931. By the latter half of the forties it was established as a commercial medium in Britain for the production of posters, show cards, wallpapers and textiles, but as an artistic medium it had only been exploited in America, where the term 'serigraphy' was coined in the early forties to distinguish between the autographic and the purely reproductive uses of the process. A leading protagonist of silkscreen printing in Britain during the forties was F. W. Mackenzie, who taught at the London County Council School of Photo-Engraving and contributed articles on the technical aspects of the subject to journals like the *Serigraph Quarterly* (published in New York), the *British and Colonial Printer* and the *Penrose Annual* (see vols 43 and 44, 1949 and 1950). Mackenzie's interest was immediately engaged by the 'creative' experiments with silkscreen printing by American artists and

he was instrumental in bringing to England an exhibition of screenprints circulated in Europe by the United States Information Service in 1949–50; in an article for the *Serigraph Quarterly* in 1949 (vol. IV, nos 2 and 3, p.3) he wrote, 'Screen process has aroused a lot of interest in art schools here, and I hope to keep them in the rather purer atmosphere of Serigraphy and away from the mechanical aspects of the process.'

The reasons for Lanyon's initial attempts at screenprinting are unknown, but *Church Town* was executed by the simplest possible method of attaching hand-cut stencils to the underside of a gauze screen, the stencils thereby masking out the areas to which the artist did not wish colour to be applied; the masked area in this case was subsequently covered with grey gouache.

The inscription 'gelatine bichromate print' on *Figures of Houses* of the previous year is a reference to the method of making photographic stencils, which had been used for photogravure and collotype printing as well as for commercial silkscreen printing. Lanyon's father was a photographer and the materials were therefore readily to hand.

Church Town does not appear to have been exhibited during the artist's lifetime, but an impression numbered 1/7 was included in a posthumous exhibition of his gouaches and drawings at the Bear Lane Gallery in Oxford in 1969; the same impression was sold at Sotheby's on 11 December 1989, lot 340. In common with the rest of the edition it had remained with the artist's widow, Sheila Lanyon, until recently.

163 The Returned Seaman, 1949

Linocut hand-coloured in brown, blue, light green and yellow-green. Signed, dated and titled in black ink. 532 × 736 mm

Tate Gallery (P. 07741)

One other impression of this image, with different colouring, belongs to the artist's estate. The original piece of studio flooring used for the print is still in the possession of Sheila Lanyon. A lithograph was made from the linocut in 1973 at the Curwen Studio for publication as part of the *Penwith Portfolio*, in an edition of 90. Lanyon made one other large linocut in 1949, *The Cornish Miner*, and five much smaller blocks called *St Just*, which he printed together in two different combinations of three and four; he subsequently made use of some of their elements when preparing his painting *St Just* in 1952–3 (see Whitworth Art Gallery catalogue, 1978, nos 42–4 and Stoke-on-Trent catalogue, 1981, no. 45). None of these prints was included in Lanyon's first London exhibition at the Lefèvre Gallery in October 1949, which did, however, include a 'slate print' titled *Island Horse*, priced at 6 guineas. Two other slate prints are known, one of boats and another of an abstract composition. In 1950 Lanyon began a tall, columnar linocut of a naked man printed alongside the text of a poem which concluded with the verse 'My boat takes me/to the island and I/in my journey ride/again/my ancestral horse' (see Stoke-on-Trent no. 44). Another early linocut was printed in 1951, a horizontal image which is comparable in size to *The Returned Seaman* (Stoke-on-Trent no. 51).

164 Underground, 1951

Screenprint printed in blue, brown, red, black and white on a dark olive coloured background. Signed and numbered 2/8 in pencil. 210 × 197 mm (central image), 278 × 284 mm (sheet)

1985-2-23-4

Lanyon made a further attempt at screenprinting in 1951 under the tutelage of the American potter Warren Mackenzie (b. 1924), who came to St Ives in 1949 with his wife Alix to spend the next three years working as apprentices to Bernard Leach. The Mackenzies had already practised a certain amount of screenprinting in America (the British Museum owns an impression of one of Warren Mackenzie's screenprints from 1946: 1987-11-7-28), so Lanyon clearly hoped to benefit from their greater experience, although it was not, as Mackenzie believed, his first stab at the medium. In 1986 Mackenzie presented the Tate Gallery with his impressions of Lanyon's two

163

164

screenprints made in 1951, *Underground* and *In the Trees*, together with the screenprints he and his wife had produced at the same time (two of these by Warren Mackenzie are also in the British Museum: 1987–11–7–26 and 27, the gift of Dave and Reba Williams), providing a detailed account of the circumstances of their execution: 'All of these prints were made at St. Ives as the result of Peter Lanyon asking me to teach him to silk screen. He was looking for a process that did not need the elaborate presses etc of etching and lithography. I knew silk screening from school and my army work and we set up a studio in the space above what was then the Leach Pottery' (Tate Gallery, *Illustrated Catalogue of Acquisitions 1984–6*, p.410). 'Peter had some trouble thinking in the additive process of screen printing and . . . after piling on color with several stencils he took turpentine and washed it off the surface of the paper. That produced the transparent stain which is the background of the print. Then he added several opaque stencils over the transparency and produced one of the best prints we did. He only printed a few (5 or 6) and I'm not sure what happened to the rest' (letter dated 2 December 1985 in the Tate Gallery Archive). 'After discovering this wash-off technique he used it in his second print "In the Trees" . . . As far as the subjects were concerned Peter's titles came after the work was completed and were simply what it suggested to him' (Tate Gallery, op. cit., pp.403 and 404).

Underground and *In the Trees* were both included in *Prints for under £1* at Robin Nance's furniture shop, The Wharf, in St Ives, with a poster designed by Alix Mackenzie. Apart from the screenprints contributed by Lanyon and the Mackenzies, Patrick Hayman (1915–88) contributed two linocuts (Tate Gallery, op. cit., pp.376–7)

and John Wells (b. 1907) an etching (Tate Gallery, op. cit., p.470). The exhibition, according to Warren Mackenzie, was sent elsewhere but 'nothing sold . . . in spite of Lanyon's reputation and the beauty of his very experimental prints' (letter dated February 1987 addressed to Dave Williams and now in the British Museum Department of Prints and Drawings).

Impressions of the two Lanyon screenprints were for sale at Gimpel Fils in March 1952 at 5 guineas each and at the Redfern Gallery in November 1952 for 8 guineas. In addition to the impressions of *Underground* owned by the British Museum and the Tate Gallery, a third belongs to the Victoria and Albert Museum.

165 In the Trees, 1951

Screenprint printed in dark green, white and black on bright green coloured background. On recto signed, dated and numbered 2/8 in pencil; on verso signed and titled in biro. 205 × 201 mm (central image), 254 × 238 mm (sheet)

1990–1–27–5

According to Mackenzie, Lanyon again with this image 'printed and then washed off the first screen or two then overprinted with at least three and possibly four screens. There is a dark green, white then black in this order' (Tate Gallery, op. cit., p.404). Its composition is quite close to that of a monotype of 1950 by Bryan Wynter, *Path through a Wood* (exhibited at the Redfern Gallery, January–February 1990, no. 29).

After 1951 Lanyon made a few other sporadic attempts at screenprinting. In 1952 he combined it with relief printing to make *Landscape of Stone Leaves*, in an edition of 20, according to the numbered and dated impressions belonging to the artist's family; one of these is inscribed by the artist on the back 'silkscreen, lino and slate print'. A later screenprint with the same title but a different image was made about 1958 in an edition of only 5, with additional painting in gouache. Lanyon also contributed a design for a table-mat, one of the set of six by different St Ives artists which were screenprinted on linen and exhibited at Heal's in 1955 (see cat. no. 169).

166 Beast, 1959

Drypoint. Signed and numbered 2/24 in pencil. 250 × 177 mm

1980–7–26–28

This impression, purchased from Sheila Lanyon, was pulled from the second state of the plate, which was reworked in three different states altogether. An impression of the final state is hand-coloured with ink and gouache (see Stoke-on-Trent catalogue, no. 79) while the dating of the image is based on a pencil inscription on another impression. (The Stoke-on-Trent catalogue refers to four states, but the differences between the first two reproduced are in the inking rather than in the working of the plate.) The plate was posthumously reprinted in a second edition of 25, signed by Sheila Lanyon.

165

166

Lanyon appears to have made his first attempts at etching around 1950, according to John Wells, who has described how 'several of us, including Denis Mitchell and Peter Lanyon had instruction in etching and engraving at the Penzance Art School with the Principal at that time, E. Bouverie Hoyton, a Rome scholar and very fine etcher and engraver' (Tate Gallery, op. cit., p.471). Two undated etchings by Lanyon almost certainly belong to this period; although they were tentatively ascribed to 1955 in the Stoke-on-Trent catalogue (see nos 77 and 78), they are similar in scale, composition and execution to three tiny subjects printed by John Wells at the Penzance School of Art which are now in the Tate Gallery's collection. In both cases, the work reflected Gabo's influence, a further extension, perhaps, of the *sgraffito* technique of incising lines on a wax- or gouache-covered surface which Lanyon used principally between 1946 and 1949. He had, of course, the further example of Nicholson's few attempts at drypoint etching in 1948 (see cat. nos 192–3 below) and in 1950 Nicholson wrote to Lanyon suggesting that as a mark of mutual esteem they should swap engravings, 'a magical medium beside the heavy drypoint' (included in archive section of Tate Gallery *St Ives* exhibition, 1985). Etching and engraving were included in the prospectus for the St Peter's Loft school, as mentioned above, and it may have been there that Lanyon printed *Beast*.

The image, which emerged more clearly after the first reworking of the plate, contains a male and female figure on either side which are both distinct from one another yet bound together by the lines of the composition. Lanyon had used this device before quite openly in *Two Figures Assisi* (1948), a crayon and watercolour drawing (Stoke-on-Trent no. 35), and the linocut *The Returned Seaman* (cat. no. 163). He saw the human form as immanent in the landscape, whose elements embodied for him either male or female identities (see 'Peter Lanyon: *Offshore* in Progress' in *Artscribe* no. 34 (March 1982), pp.58–61). Haydn Griffiths in the Stoke-on-Trent catalogue also makes a convincing association between *Beast* (particularly in its final state) and the work of Kenneth Armitage, whom Lanyon knew at Corsham.

Terry Frost

born 1915

Born in Leamington Spa, he left school at the age of 14 in order to earn a living in various industrial and commercial firms. He was captured in Crete in 1941, and only began drawing and painting in a German camp with the encouragement of a fellow prisoner, Adrian Heath. After the war, determined to become an artist, he moved to St Ives at Heath's suggestion and studied at a private school of painting there in 1946–7. He then obtained a grant to study at Camberwell School of Art in 1947–50. From 1950 to 1954 he remained based in St Ives, occupying a studio next door to Ben Nicholson's and working as an assistant to Barbara Hepworth, while also doing various part-time teaching jobs in Corsham and London; his first one-man show was at the Leicester Galleries in 1952, and in the same year he participated in Adrian Heath's exhibitions of new abstract work at his studio in Fitzroy Street. In 1954 he moved to Leeds for two years as a Gregory Fellow in painting at the university, later teaching at the Leeds School of Art. He returned to St Ives in 1957, but moved to Banbury in 1963 in order to teach first at Coventry and then at Reading University. He moved his studio to Newlyn in Cornwall in 1974, and has lived there since his retirement from Reading in 1981.

Frost turned to abstract painting in 1949 under the influence of Victor Pasmore, who was teaching at Camberwell, and his work has continued to be abstract in form, though greatly influenced by the landscape of his immediate surroundings, particularly that of St Ives and its environs. Frost's prints have reflected his paintings, and have been made whenever he has had printing facilities easily accessible for use. The selection shown here covers the main periods of his activity in this medium until 1960. The only omissions are examples of the woodcuts he made as a prisoner of war and the few linocuts he made in 1952–4. Since 1960 he has worked principally with lithography and silkscreen, but his most recent publication is a suite of eleven etchings accompanying the poems of Federico Garcia Lorca, published by Austin/Desmond Contemporary Books in 1989.

Bibliography

There have been a number of small exhibitions, but no large retrospective. The best source is perhaps the section devoted to his work in the catalogue of the 1985 *St Ives*

167

168

exhibition at the Tate Gallery. Valuable remarks about his prints are contained in the Tate Gallery *Illustrated Catalogue of Acquisitions 1982–4*, pp.396–8. The most recent catalogues from private gallery exhibitions are *Terry Frost Works on Paper 1947–72*, Austin/Desmond, 1989; *Terry Frost*, Belgrave Gallery, 1989; and *Terry Frost Paintings 1984–89*, Mayor Gallery, 1990. We are also indebted to Terry Frost himself, from whom the group of works 1985–10–5–28 to 39 was purchased directly in 1985, for assistance with the entries.

167 Standing Nude Seen from Behind, One Leg Raised, *c.*1948

Colour monotype. Signed in pencil. 331 × 205 mm

1989–6–17–263

This is one of a number of monotypes made by Frost while a student at Camberwell, before he turned to abstraction in 1949. They fall into two principal groups of subject-matter: female nudes (including the Camberwell model, Miss Humphries; see Austin/Desmond catalogue, no. 2), and swans (Redfern Gallery, *Monotypes*, January–February 1990, nos 12–14); harbour scenes from St Ives appeared in slightly later monotypes.

Frost's interest in monotypes arose at the same time as the general surge of enthusiasm for the medium discussed in the previous section. In his case he may have been further encouraged by the monotypes of another of the St Ives artists, Sven Berlin (b. 1911), for whom he had a particular respect. Monotype printing had been recommended by William Johnstone, Principal of Camberwell School of Art from 1938 to 1947, as a useful learning experience for students, based on his earlier experimentation with the medium (see cat. no. 161).

168 Abstract Based on the Golden Section, 1951

Colour monotype. 250 × 388 mm (sheet)

1985–10–5–33

This abstract was made in 1951, and was based on a painting of the same period using the Golden Section. Frost's first abstract painting, *Madrigal* (see Mayor Gallery catalogue, no. 3), was submitted in 1949 as his summer composition for Camberwell. The painting, the monotype catalogued here and another similar one recently shown at the Redfern Gallery (*Monotypes* exhibition, 1990, no. 15) reflected Victor Pasmore's preoccupation with the application of geometric principles to abstract composition. In 1948 Pasmore was consulting books like *The Geometry of Art and Life* (1946) by Matila Ghika, explaining simple procedures for obtaining golden sections and repeated polygonal patterns, and even receiving practical tuition in the implementation of these procedures, according to his colleague William Johnstone (see W. Johnstone, *Points in Time*, London 1980, p.206). Terry Frost briefly

availed himself of the structural framework this formal discipline imposed, then in St Ives found his own distinctive vocabulary and syntax of shapes.

169 First Silkscreen, 1953

Screenprint in black, grey and red. 238 × 195 mm

1985–10–5–29

This print was made in St Ives in the studio of Denis Mitchell, who worked with Frost as an assistant to Barbara Hepworth. Frost also contributed a silkscreen design to the set of six table-mats produced by Porthia Prints in 1955, which Mitchell organised with Stanley Dorfman. The other artists involved were Peter Lanyon, Robert Adams, Barbara Hepworth, Roger Hilton and Mitchell himself, and their payment simply amounted to two dozen mats each (five of the mats and designs for all six were shown in the Redfern Gallery's *Design* exhibition in 1986, nos 97a–110). The mats were available either as sets or individually, as Dorfman reported to Heal's (see correspondence dated 1 February 1955, in Heal's archives) that some customers bought only one or two, perhaps regarding them more as *objets d'art* than as regular table linen. The novelty of using screenprinting for a form of applied design which could be treated as a work of art in its own right, had already been tried in the late forties by Zika and Lida Ascher, Czech textile designers working in Britain. They commissioned designs for headscarves from the leading British and Continental artists of the day;

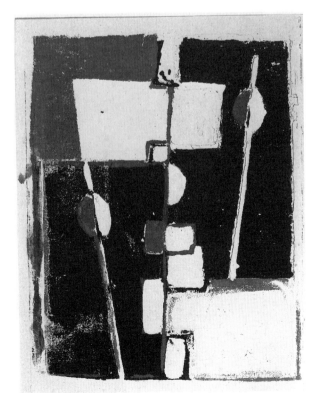

169

these were printed in limited editions and displayed in frames like pictures from 1947 onwards, when a collection of them was exhibited at the Lefèvre Gallery in London to great acclaim (see the exhibition catalogue *Ascher · Fabric · Art · Fashion*, Victoria and Albert Museum, 1987).

170 Ridge, Yorkshire, 1956

Drypoint. Signed and dated, and annotated 'Leeds' in pencil.
177 × 249 mm

1985-10-5-36

This print was made while Frost was living in Leeds. The view is taken from Woodhouse Ridge overlooking Meanwood Valley, from where Frost used to survey the city. The composition of this drypoint is almost identical, in reverse, to a painting entitled *Ridge Painting, Leeds*, which was illustrated as no. 10 in the catalogue of the 1989

Frost exhibition at the Belgrave Gallery. Another painting on the same theme is in the British Council collection.

171 Bow Movement, 1956

Drypoint. Signed and dated, and annotated 'A/P' in pencil; titled on the verso. 130 × 333 mm

1985-10-5-34

According to a pencil note on the back, this print was made in St Ives in the summer of 1956. The image is clearly based on the boats moored in the harbour there, a subject whose possibilities Frost had explored since the early fifties. He described in 1954 the sensations he had tried to capture in an earlier treatment of the theme, *Blue Movement* (1953):

I had spent a number of evenings looking out over the harbour at St Ives in Cornwall. Although I had been observing a multiplicity of movement during those evenings, they all

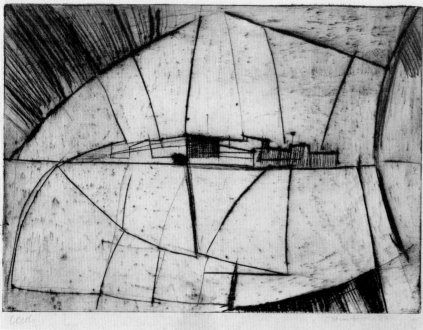

170

171

172

173

evoked a common emotion or mood – a state of delight in front of nature. On one particular blue twilit evening I was watching what I can only describe as a synthesis of movement and counter-movement. That is to say the rise and fall of the boats, the space drawing of the mastheads, the opposing movements of the incoming sea and outblowing off-shore wind – all this plus the predominant feel of blue in the evening and the static brown of the foreshore, generated an emotional state which was to find expression in the painting *Blue Movement.*

In this painting I was trying to give expression to my total experience of that particular evening. I was not portraying the boats, the sand, the horizon or any other subject-matter, but concentrating on the emotion engendered by what I saw. The subject-matter is in fact the sensation evoked by the movements and the colour in the harbour. What I have painted is an arrangement of form and colour which evokes for me a similar feeling.

The process of painting this picture was not as swift and decisive as my description might imply. Its first form was that of a pencil drawing, then a monotone, then one, two and three-colour lino-cuts, a small painting of similar proportions and finally the *Blue Movement* itself. These progressive stages helped me to clarify my ideas, to adjust the various forms

to a state of dynamic equilibrium, and to arrive at a final proportion for the canvas (Lawrence Alloway, *Nine Abstract Artists*, London 1954, pp.23–4).

172 Verticals and Sun, 1957

Lithograph printed in blue and black. Signed and dated in pencil. 520 × 407 mm

1985–10–5–28

Frost made his first lithographs at Corsham in about 1952, although he had previously studied some lithography at Camberwell. He made more in Leeds in 1956–7, printing them himself from zinc plates at the College of Art. These are known in many impressions showing slight variations, and none was ever printed in a regular edition. Frost remarks that these prints were spoiled by the poor quality of the paper he used, and that it was not until he worked in Edinburgh in 1957 that a professional printer pointed out to him the importance of using the right paper.

The hexagonal shape in both the black and blue plates

is found in many works of this period. According to a note in the catalogue of the 1982 Frost exhibition at the Rufford Craft Centre, Notts., this series 'resulted from a vivid experience when he was out walking with Sir Herbert Read on a winter's day near Sir Herbert's north Yorkshire home, and saw the sun setting behind a wood. This hexagonal image dominated his imagination for so long that he came to refer to it as "my shape".' Other versions of this shape are to be found in a painting, *Orange and Black, Leeds* (Mayor Gallery no. 12), sketchbooks in the British Museum (1985–10–5–50) and the Tate Gallery Archives, a lithograph of 1956, *Orange and Brown Sun* (BM 1985–10–5–13) and an aquatint of 1957 (BM 1985–10–5–13).

173 Composition in Red and Black, 1957

Lithograph printed in two colours. Signed and dated in pencil. Annotated in bottom margin 'Printer's Proof'. 405 × 540 mm

1985–10–5–39

This was one of the first prints commissioned from Frost by a publisher, the St George's Gallery, and was issued in an edition of 25. It was printed for Robert Erskine by John Watson, a professionally trained printer who taught lithography at the Central School of Arts and Crafts, and exhibited at the St George's Gallery in July 1957, priced at 5 guineas. The other lithograph commissioned from Frost by the St George's Gallery in 1957, *Red and Grey Spiral* (the British Museum has another, related subject printed in brown and black: *Brown Figure*, 1958 (1985–10–5–30), also published by the St George's Gallery), was printed by Johnston Douglas of Harley Bros in Edinburgh, a commercial firm normally engaged in printing material like whisky labels. The firm nevertheless took to working with artists with great success. John Piper recalled that 'the manager and chief operative was a man who appeared to enjoy his work enormously, and took it very seriously and had some fine results. But within a couple of years the firm had gone bankrupt, and this excellent fellow had disappeared without trace overnight' (Orde Levinson, *John Piper, the Complete Graphic Works*, London 1987, p.11).

Composition in Red and Black was another manifestation of Frost's interest in the movement of boats, related to paintings like *Yellow Verticals* of 1954 (Mayor Gallery no. 8) and *Untitled Composition*, c.1956–7 (Austin/Desmond no. 29). It was exhibited as no. 370 in the Fifth International Biennial of Contemporary Colour Lithography at the Cincinnati Museum in 1958.

Bryan Wynter

1915–1975

Born in London, he trained in Zurich with a view to joining the management of his family's laundry business. He escaped to study at the Slade School of Art in 1938–40, where he met Patrick Heron who became a close friend. During the war Wynter was a conscientious objector. He moved to St Ives in 1945, settling nearby in the village of Zennor, and remained in Cornwall for almost all the rest of his life. From 1951 to 1956 he taught at Corsham. His earliest works during the 1940s were mainly small watercolours or gouaches on paper which have a strong neo-Romantic vein, often dominated by predatory birds menacing the landscape and human habitation. In 1956 his work underwent a radical change, partly in response to the American exhibition at the Tate Gallery; his compositions became wholly abstract on a much larger scale than he had hitherto attempted. Patrick Heron in 1956 wrote of the new direction in Wynter's painting, 'It is as though Wynter were looking into a system of hanging semi-transparent bead curtains, ranged one behind the other' (see Hayward Gallery exhibition catalogue, 1976, p.3), while the artist himself described it thus: 'About 1956 I was trying to create a kind of visual flux, a surface on which the eye found it difficult to rest so that, if it was not rebuffed, it would be compelled to push deeper and come to terms with the forces underlying the painting' ('Notes on my painting', Hayward Gallery, 1976, p.6). The abstract paintings of the latter part of the fifties and early sixties won him considerable acclaim, and the Waddington Galleries in London became his principal exhibitor after 1959. In 1960 he branched out further to make his first kinetic mobiles, known as 'Imoos' (Images Moving Out Onto Space).

Wynter made quite a number of prints early in his career, largely monotypes which he exhibited at the Redfern Gallery. He returned to printmaking in the form of lithography in 1956–8, in association with the St George's Gallery. One of these lithographs, *Phalanx* of 1958, was used for the cover of the Whitechapel Art Gallery's exhibition *The Graven Image* in 1959.

Bibliography

A retrospective exhibition was organised by the Arts Council at the Hayward Gallery in 1976, with a short catalogue and introduction by Patrick Heron. Another, smaller retrospective was held in 1988 at the University of Essex's art centre, accompanied by a leaflet. The Tate Gallery's 1985 *St Ives* exhibition is once again the most useful recent publication, together with the book by Tom Cross, *Painting the Warmth of the Sun*, Penzance and Guildford 1984. An exhibition of Bryan Wynter's work is due to take place at the Orion Gallery in Newlyn, Cornwall, in the latter part of 1991. We would like to thank the artist's widow, Monica Wynter, for her assistance.

174

174 Backyard, Skidden Cottage, *c.*1948/9

Lithograph. 221 × 298 mm

1985-10-5-26

In 1948 Wynter was represented by a colour lithograph, *Landscape with Xerophyte*, in the London Painter-Printers exhibition at the Redfern Gallery, which was commissioned by the Miller's Press. However, the subject catalogued here, taken from a group of cottages in St Ives, was printed on Wynter's own table-top press in the remote moorland dwelling where he settled after the war. His brother has provided the following reminiscence of this period in Wynter's life:

As soon as the war ended Bryan went down to Cornwall and rented Carn, a primitive, wet, granite-built miner's cottage on Zennor Moor 800 feet above the sea and accessible only by a rock and peat-bog track from the coast road. At Carn in his thirtieth year he found release to work as he wanted, though very short of cash, and for some years he turned out small paintings and drawings of the raw high land of rocks, gulls, villages and sea. These brought him recognition through exhibitions at the Redfern Gallery. His body of friends grew (picked, someone said, for their eccentricity). Patrick Heron, his nearest neighbour, Edward Walton, and the poet W.S. Graham were among the closest. He also befriended wild animals, climbed the great Cornish cliffs, skin-dived, drank in St. Ives pubs and mooched around the moors, coming to know their communities of wildlife as an appreciative observer without wishing to take a scientific interest in them. He teased the animals and ate the plants. In his head he carried a library of appalling stories, some of them true, most just possible: they were used to make points in discussion, which he enjoyed. He would talk about inventions, people, jazz, poetry, about underwater, about discoveries on walks, but he rarely, though glad to show his work, talked about the processes through which his paintings came into being. Looking back I think he preserved a deliberate silence on them, perhaps in order to prevent his verbal processes from swamping them. He didn't talk much about art at all. (Memoir by the artist's brother, Eric Wynter, 1984, accompanying an exhibition of Bryan Wynter's paintings at the Prema Project, Uley, Gloucs.)

175 Still Life with Pipes(?), *c.*1948

Monotype over transfer drawing printed in brown, yellow and blue. 195 × 241 mm

1985-10-5-27

The pencil drawing for the traced monotype is on the verso. This corresponds to the brown lines on the recto; the other ochre and lemon-yellow lines are not on the back, nor are the dark blue horizontal lines. The black washes must have been added directly onto the printed image. Wynter submitted a succession of monotypes to the Redfern Gallery exhibitions in 1948, 1949, 1950 and 1951. He also explored other varieties of textural effects using frottage and decalcomania. The subject of this monotype may be related to that of a work called *Still Life with Pipes* in the catalogue of his exhibition of oils and watercolours at the Redfern Gallery in May–June 1948.

175

176

177

176 Georgia, 1953

Monotype printed in green, brown and reddish-brown with
added gouache. Signed and dated in gouache, 542 × 378mm

1985–10–5–45

Georgia is a place near Nancledra, between St Ives and
Lands End. Wynter has largely used the monotype impression here as a basis for a more elaborate and highly
wrought composition; however, he has left a substantial
area of the monotype untouched, thereby displaying the
contrast in textures which was the principal attraction
of the medium for him.

177 The Raven, 1956

Monotype. Signed and dated in pencil. 420 × 360mm

1985–10–5–24

Wynter was extremely fond of animals, and the subject
of this monotype is a tame raven which first made its

appearance in 1955. Birds remained persistent images in
his work right up to the point at which he fully embraced
abstraction.

William Scott

1913–1989

Born in Scotland; his family moved to Northern Ireland
when he was eleven. He studied at the Belfast School of
Art in 1928–31, and then at the Royal Academy Schools
in 1931–5. From 1937 to 1939 he and his wife, Mary
Lucas, lived most of the time in France, especially in Pont-
Aven, where they opened a summer painting school. During the war, from 1942 to 1946, Scott served in the Royal
Engineers. He had moved to Somerset in 1941 and begun
teaching at the Bath Academy of Art, where he became
senior painting master in 1946. In 1956 he gave up
teaching to concentrate on his own work. His paintings

178

were always primarily based on still-life compositions; they became progressively more abstract through the 1950s, partly reflecting his contact with the work of American artists. In parallel with the paintings, Scott also produced a notable series of large finished drawings as works in their own right.

Scott learned the technique of lithography in the Ordnance section of the Royal Engineers at Ruabon in North Wales, where he was posted at Kenneth Clark's suggestion to make better use of his skills as a draughtsman; there he encountered Henry Cliffe, who was later to teach lithography at Corsham. Scott's first prints were the twelve illustrations for the anthology *Soldiers' Verse*, selected by Patric Dickinson, printed at W.S.Cowell's in Ipswich and published by Frederick Muller in 1945. While at Corsham he made a few more works in this medium between 1948 and 1955, most of which were exhibited at the Redfern Gallery. He also contributed one print, *The Bird Cage*, to the first series of Lyons lithographs in 1947, and *Busbies* to the Royal College Coronation series of 1953. During the 1960s he made more lithographs with Curwen, and turned his attention to screenprinting (with Kelpra) and etching.

Bibliography

William Scott: Paintings, with an introduction by Alan Bowness, was published by Lund Humphries, London, in 1964. There are also two significant exhibition catalogues: one for the Tate Gallery in 1972, the other by Ronald Alley and T.P.Flanagan for a retrospective which toured Belfast, Dublin and Edinburgh in 1986. Nothing has been published on Scott's prints, apart from a leaflet accompanying an exhibition at the Curwen Gallery in 1989, covering his output from 1962 to 1988.

178 Cornish Harbour, 1951

Lithograph printed in black, grey and yellow. 333 × 412 mm
Tate Gallery (P. 01071)

This is a proof for the edition of 60, which were printed in four colours, of which one was exhibited by the Redfern Gallery in December 1951 (no. 281) at the price of 4 guineas. It was certainly made at the lithography studio at Corsham, and shows the harbour at Mousehole in Cornwall. At this time, when Scott was living at Hallatrow in Somerset, he spent his summers in Cornwall where he knew well the other artists living there. The print is closely related to a group of harbour compositions, in particular to a painting of the same title and date in the British Council's collection. Scott saw this work as a logical development from an earlier painting of 1939 done at Port Manech near Pont-Aven which he described as 'one of the first pictures in which my concern was with large empty spaces' (quoted from a lecture of 1959 in Adrian Lewis, 'British Avant-Garde Painting I, 1945–56', *Artscribe* no. 34 (March 1982), p.27). The year 1951 marked

an important phase in Scott's reductivist approach to the ostensible content of his pictures. Another harbour composition of 1950–51 includes drying fish-nets as well as tethered boats and jetty walls; then, by a process of elimination, he arrived in 1952 at an almost completely abstract study with only the most minimal reference to the jetty wall extending across the harbour. The construction of these pictures, including the subject catalogued here, paralleled a similar process in the division of space for his table-top still lifes of the same period.

Kenneth Armitage

born 1916

Born in Leeds, he studied at the Leeds College of Art in 1934–7 and then at the Slade School in 1937–9. After service in the Army, he was appointed head of the new sculpture department at the Bath Academy of Art at Corsham, a position he held from 1946 to 1956. From 1953 to 1955 he was Gregory Fellow at Leeds University. Following an exhibition of his sculpture at the British Pavilion of the 1958 Venice Biennale (with work by Scott and Hayter), he became recognised internationally as one of the leading British sculptors. This success enabled him to stop teaching, and he has since worked in London.

Armitage has been only an occasional printmaker. Apart from a few lithographs made in the 1950s at Corsham, he etched a number of plates between 1975 and 1977, mostly on the subject of the oaks of Richmond Park.

Bibliography

Retrospective surveys of Armitage's work, with catalogues, have been mounted at the Whitechapel Art Gallery in 1959 (based on the 1958 Venice Biennale) and by the Arts Council in 1972–3. A small monograph by Roland Penrose was published in 1960 by the Bodensee-Verlag in Amriswil (Switzerland).

179 People Going for a Walk, 1952

Lithograph printed in black, yellow, pink and blue. Initialled in pencil. 370 × 460 mm (maximum dimensions)
1986-1-25-24

According to a letter from the artist dated 26 March 1985 in the files of the British Museum's Department of Prints and Drawings, this lithograph was made and printed in the lithography studio at Corsham, which was under the direction of Henry Cliffe. Armitage remarks, 'I don't know as yet what the edition was, and the "publishing" of prints had not yet happened in those early days after the War'. It was first shown by the Redfern Gallery in November 1952 under the title 'A family going for a walk', and priced at 5 guineas. In the same exhibition was another lithograph, *Standing Figures* (an impression of which is

179

also in the British Museum, 1980–6–28–14). These seem to have been Armitage's first and only lithographs, and none appears in any other Redfern exhibition. This print was later shown at the Third International Biennial of Contemporary Color Lithography in Cincinnati in 1954, and at the exhibition *Corsham Lithographs and other Prints* at Dartington Hall in 1955.

The print is based on Armitage's 1951 sculpture, 29 inches high, of the same title, made in bronze and published in an edition of six (reproduced as plate IV in the 1959 Whitechapel exhibition catalogue); there was also a study in gouache of the same composition. The three main figures are on a single plane behind, while the smaller child stands forward at right angles. The figures are leaning slightly into the wind, like those in another group of the same year titled *People in a Wind*, and in *Friends Walking* (1952). In 1960 Armitage claimed that his interest in structure was first excited by Brunel's suspension bridge at Clifton:

It made me curious. I became, for the first time, interested in structure. Most of us spend our day vertically on our feet and at night we rest horizontally. We live in a world of verticals and horizontals. These are the directions we see all the time in our houses and cities and towns as we walk about. Although it is mainly for movement, it is also for this reason that I like sometimes to make my figures, my sculptures, on a slant, so that they run across this rather rigid pattern (*Kenneth Armitage*, Arnolfini Gallery, Bristol, 1965; quotation from the BBC film on Armitage in the series *The Artist Speaks*, 1960).

9 Post-War Abstraction

Post-war abstraction in Britain was seen by its protagonists as the revival of an international modernism which for much of the forties 'had disappeared under the foliage and chiaroscuro of the romantics' (Lawrence Alloway, *Nine Abstract Artists*, London 1954, p.3). The critic Lawrence Alloway, whose important book gave form and expression to the diverse tenets of this movement, characterised its inception as 'a pattern of conversions . . . with Victor Pasmore as culture-hero' (op. cit., p.3). The conversions in question were those of Pasmore himself between 1947 and 1951, Kenneth Martin in 1949–51, Adrian Heath in 1950, Mary Martin in 1950–51, Roger Hilton in the late forties, Anthony Hill in 1950, Robert Adams in 1950–51 and William Scott in 1951–3. These artists, together with Terry Frost, were the subject of Alloway's text of 1954 and an exhibition based on the book held at the Redfern Gallery in the following year, although they were by no means consistent in their approach to abstraction. Scott, Hilton, Frost and, by association, Alan Davie (who was not included in the book) were seen by Alloway as representative of 'irrational expression by "malerisch" means' (op. cit., p.3), Frost, in particular, embodying the taste of St Ives, 'where they combine non-figurative theory with the practice of abstraction because the landscape is so nice nobody can quite bring themselves to leave it out of their art' (op. cit., p.12). It is, however, with the artists identified by Alloway as members of the Pasmore circle that the following entries are concerned: Kenneth Martin, Adrian Heath, Robert Adams and Pasmore himself. Throughout the fifties they were striving to create work in a variety of different media, composed of concrete elements, free of all descriptive or allusive content, which would challenge conventional spatial concepts.

The artists concerned were drawn together by a number of exhibitions prior to 1955, the London Group exhibition of February–March 1951, one at the Artists International Association in June 1951, accompanied by the group's first publication, *Broadsheet No. 1: Devoted to Abstract Art*, and *The Mirror and the Square*, also held at the AIA, in 1952. However, as Alastair Grieve points out in a forthcoming article, 'the most stimulating displays of their work in this year and the next (1952–3), were three weekend exhibitions which Adrian Heath organised in his studio at 22 Fitzroy Street'. (This article, which is due to be published in the November 1990 issue of the *Burlington Magazine*, is called 'Towards an Art of the Environment. Exhibitions and Publications by a Group of Avant-Garde Abstract Artists in London 1951–55'. We should like to record our gratitude to Dr Grieve for permission to consult the text prior to publication.) The exhibitions consisted of sculpture, mobiles, paintings, constructions and prints, not just by members of the immediate group but also by other artists such as Nicholson, Hepworth, Paolozzi and Nigel Henderson (1917–85) who were considered sympathetic in spirit. Despite the informality of the setting, there was nothing casual or unconscious about the arrangement of the work, which was displayed as part of a proper installation designed by qualified architects. By integrating architectural, pictorial and sculptural elements, the Fitzroy Street exhibitions exemplified 'an art of the environment', the subject of Kenneth Martin's essay in the second manifesto, *Broadsheet No. 2*, 1952. Later, in an unpublished paper of 1955, 'Architecture, Machine and Mobile', Martin expanded further the rationale behind this all-embracing vision:

Mondrian, who sought and achieved equivalence in his paintings, placed round his walls rectangles and squares cut in different primary colours. The walls of his rooms both in Paris and New York were pitted with pin holes where he had changed the position of the cards or added another to their number as he sought for the satisfactory dynamic equilibrium. From his researches and achievements and from this movement out from the picture space into the space of architecture springs the notion of synthesis, whose pure form is an architecture created jointly by painter, sculptor and architect. In this there are no objects of art as such, no paintings on the wall, no sculpture on mantelpiece or pedestal which exist in their own right. But it is an architecture in which all three have pooled their resources to create – only architecture. (Quoted on page 14 of the Kenneth Martin exhibition catalogue, Yale Center for British Art, 1979.)

Linocut was the medium chosen by Martin, Pasmore, Heath and Adams for the prints they included in the Fitzroy Street exhibitions (with the exception of one lithograph by Martin), although it was by no means popular among printmakers in general at this time. However, apart from the low cost of the materials involved, it was well suited to a Constructivist aesthetic. Furthermore, like collage, it was often associated with the teaching methods for basic design, derived from Bauhaus practice in Germany in the twenties, for which abstract artists like Pasmore proselytised throughout the fifties as an essential foundation for fine as well as applied art students (see *The Developing Process*, published by King's College in the University of Durham on the occasion of an exhibition at the Institute of Contemporary Arts, London 1959).

Kenneth Martin

1905–1984

Born in Sheffield, he studied at the School of Art there in 1921–3 and 1927–9, working as a designer in Sheffield after completing his first course of study. In 1929 he won a scholarship to the Royal College of Art, where he met his wife, Mary Bamford, with whom he worked closely until her death in 1969. Martin's career as an artist did not really begin to flower until the late 1940s when he met William Coldstream and Victor Pasmore on the staff of Camberwell School of Art. By the end of the decade he had become dedicated to a constructive form of abstraction as opposed to a reductivist process of simplification.

His first abstract painting of 1948 was followed by work in three dimensions in wire, wood and cut metal, which resulted in his first mobile of 1951. By this stage he was closely involved with the radical group of artists described in the introduction to this section, who were committed to non-figurative art. Martin explained the purpose of his own work in 'An Art of the Environment' in 1952: 'The mobile creates space by proportions which reach out into space. The painting becomes the relief and the forms of the relief escape from the bounding rectangle' (*Broadsheet No. 2*, p.3). The screw mobile followed in 1953, influenced by the same fascination with spiral forms which Pasmore had also evinced. Mobiles, paintings, drawings and prints were seen by Martin as integral parts of a working process which was important in its own right, not just as a stepping stone to a final resolution. The best-known expression of this concept was his *Chance and Order* series of paintings, drawings and prints of 1969–75, which then became *Chance, Order and Change* in the late 1970s. This was the period of his greatest success, with the award of the OBE in 1971 and large retrospectives at the Tate Gallery in 1975 and at the Yale Center for British Art in 1979.

Apart from the early lithographs and linocuts described in the entries below, Martin's excursions into printmaking largely date from the 1970s when his dealer, the Waddington Galleries, published a series of screenprints parallel to his paintings and drawings.

Bibliography

Martin published an extensive number of articles and statements from 1951 onwards: a bibliography of these is provided in volume 1 of the catalogue for the 1975 exhibition at the Tate Gallery, together with a selection of thirteen texts from 1955–73. The second volume of this catalogue consists of essays written especially for the exhibition by Andrew Forge, Joost Baljeu, Anthony Hill, William Tucker, François Morellet, Gerhard von Gravenitz, Michael Morris, David Bohm and Michael Compton. The 1979 catalogue by Andrew Forge for the Yale Center for British Art, New Haven, also contains a selection of the artist's writings. The most recent exhibition of the work of Kenneth and Mary Martin was at the Annely Juda Gallery, London, in 1987. The only publication devoted exclusively to Martin's drawings and prints was a catalogue of the work of the 1970s issued in 1977 by the Arts Council as part of a series of 'Working Methods' exhibitions. We should like to thank Ken Powell and Paul Martin for their assistance with the entries which follow.

180 Composition, 1950

Lithograph printed in black, light grey, dark grey, slate blue, pale yellow, orange and brownish-beige. 322 × 256mm

1986–6–21–32

See colour illustration

The artist was working on this lithograph in 1949–50, at the same time as a painting, *Composition 1949* (now in the Tate Gallery), which was almost identical in composition but used a different range of colours. The print was exhibited under the title 'Abstract' at the Redfern Gallery in December 1950 (no. 29, priced at 3 guineas), and again in November the following year as no. 316, 'Abstract, Grey and Yellow'. It was also shown at the first Biennale in São Paolo in 1951 and in the first of Adrian Heath's studio exhibitions in March 1952.

The painting to which the print is related was first shown in a London Group exhibition in February 1951 and reproduced in May 1951 in Martin's essay on 'Abstract Art' which was published by the AIA as *Broadsheet No. 1*. According to the information given to the Tate Gallery by the artist, he spent a long time on this painting in order to achieve the greatest degree of flatness possible, by eliminating all traces of brushstrokes. 'At the time of its exhibition in 1951, *Composition* was the purest expression of abstract art [he] had arrived at' and he continued to develop this theme of coloured areas, rectangles, circles and their derivatives until the second half of the decade, at which point he became more involved with lines and their directions (Tate Gallery, *Illustrated Catalogue of Acquisitions 1972–4*, pp.195–6). In *Nine Abstract Artists* Lawrence Alloway characterised this type of composition as possessing 'a slightly disordered geometry, reminiscent of collages assembled by dirty hands. They were smudged and atmospheric and the rectangles were set in lively relationships by small departures from horizontal and vertical axes.'

Apart from *Chalk Farm*, which was exhibited at the Redfern Gallery in 1949, *Composition 1950* was the only lithograph made by Martin at this period. His other prints of the 1950s were all linocuts.

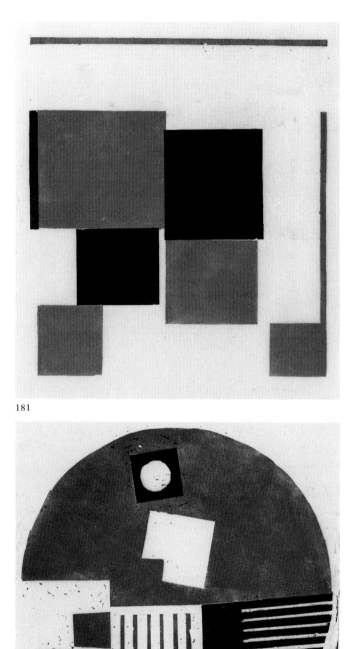

181

182

181 Abstract, Yellow and Brown(?), 1951

Linocut printed in black and brown on thin paper. Signed in
pencil. 347 × 313 mm

1986–6–21–34

The title given above was supplied by the artist's son Paul
Martin in a letter dated 12 March 1986, in the files of
the Department of Prints and Drawings at the British
Museum. The same image was called 'Linoprint (Black
and Grey)' in the 1975 Tate Gallery exhibition catalogue
(no. 31), where it is reproduced so that the right-hand
side of the British Museum's impression appears as the
upper edge of the composition; quite possibly Martin
varied both the colouring of different impressions and the
position of his signature. Linocuts by Martin were
exhibited by the Redfern Gallery in 1952, 1954, 1955,
1957, 1958 and 1959. The Lords Gallery in 1962 showed
three 'abstract' prints dated 1958 and 1956–62; the Tate
Gallery in 1975 exhibited six 'linoprints' dating from
1951–5 (nos 28–33). This print cannot be securely identified with any of the linocuts that Martin exhibited at the
Redfern Gallery during the 1950s, but it undoubtedly
belongs to that period.

One of the essays in the 1975 Tate catalogue describes
how the author, Michael Morris, used another of Martin's
early linocuts, *Linoprint (Red and Black)* of 1953 as the
basis for an experiment in 'psychological aesthetics' in
1955. He chose this print because it had 'a limited number
of well-defined elements (four black and two red rectangles) not arranged in an immediately obvious pattern'.
With the purpose of investigating the assumption that 'the
most pleasing is the most artistic or aesthetically valuable', a replica of Martin's original was assembled on a
wall and the seventy-seven participants were at liberty
to determine the position of the constituent elements
according to their predilections. The conclusion drawn
from the exercise was, perhaps unsurprisingly, that 'the
most pleasing positions and arrangements [to the partici-
pants] are not necessarily the most aesthetically valuable'
(vol. II, pp. 33–4).

182 Circular Abstract, 1952

Linocut, printed in black and grey-blue on thin paper. Signed
and numbered 4/20 in pencil. Diameter 294 mm

1986–6–21–33

This print was first shown in the second of Adrian Heath's
studio exhibitions in July 1952; at the end of that year
it appeared as no. 163 in the Redfern Gallery's print
exhibition, priced at 4 guineas. The nominal edition size
of 20 was unusually large for Martin's linocuts, but may
never have been fully printed. On one occasion in the winter of 1952 Martin printed an exceptionally large linocut
in a unique impression for an acquaintance, as a means
of earning money to pay for Christmas presents.

183

183 Endless Theme, 1952

Linocut, printed in black, yellow and grey on thin paper. Signed
in pencil in bottom left corner. 405 × 396 mm

1988-1-30-5

This was also included in the July 1952 exhibition at
Adrian Heath's studio and in the exhibition of the same
year at the Redfern Gallery, where it was no. 164, priced
at 5 guineas. The British Museum's impression is not
numbered, but another one shown in the Annely Juda
Gallery exhibition of 1987 (no. 107) indicated that the
edition was of 10.

Robert Adams

1917–1984

Born in Northampton, he began studying sculpture at the
Northampton School of Art at the age of 16, attending
evening classes for nine years while supporting himself
in a variety of jobs, including one in a printer's workshop.
His first one-man show was in 1947 at Gimpel Fils, where
he exhibited on numerous occasions throughout the
1950s. From 1949 to 1959 he taught at the Central
School, maintaining his own studio in Pilgrim's Lane,
Hampstead. By 1951, when the abstract artists discussed
in this section really coalesced as a group, Adams, like
Pasmore, already had an established reputation. His

approach differed from that of the others in so far as he
'did not use mathematical calculations and he confined
himself, with a few exceptions, to traditional materials
worked with careful craftsmanship. His sculptures of this
period, in wood, stone or brass, are mostly small in scale,
concentrated, built up from basic forms . . . They were
probably the most abstract sculptures being produced in
Britain at this time, with a quiet but immediately appeal-
ing organic life of their own' (Alastair Grieve, 'Construc-
tivism after the Second World War', in *British Sculpture
in the Twentieth Century*, Whitechapel Art Gallery, 1981,
p.159). In 1952 and 1962 Adams was among the artists
chosen to represent Britain at the Venice Biennale.

Printmaking played a more important part within
Adams's work as a whole than in that of any of his
immediate colleagues among the Constructivists. He
experimented with a wide variety of imagery in several
different media from the late forties onwards, when he had
access to the Central School's printmaking facilities:
monotype, linocut, lithography, engraving and aquatint.
The first of his prints to be exhibited were included in the
December 1949 show at the Redfern Gallery: these were
two lithographs and five monotypes. After 1949 he does
not appear to have sent in any more monotypes, confining
himself to lithographs and linocuts in exhibitions held by
the Redfern in 1950, 1951, 1952 and 1957. In February
1956 Gimpel Fils put on a joint exhibition of his work
and that of William Gear; this included a group of five
prints (nos 50–54) comprising an engraving and an

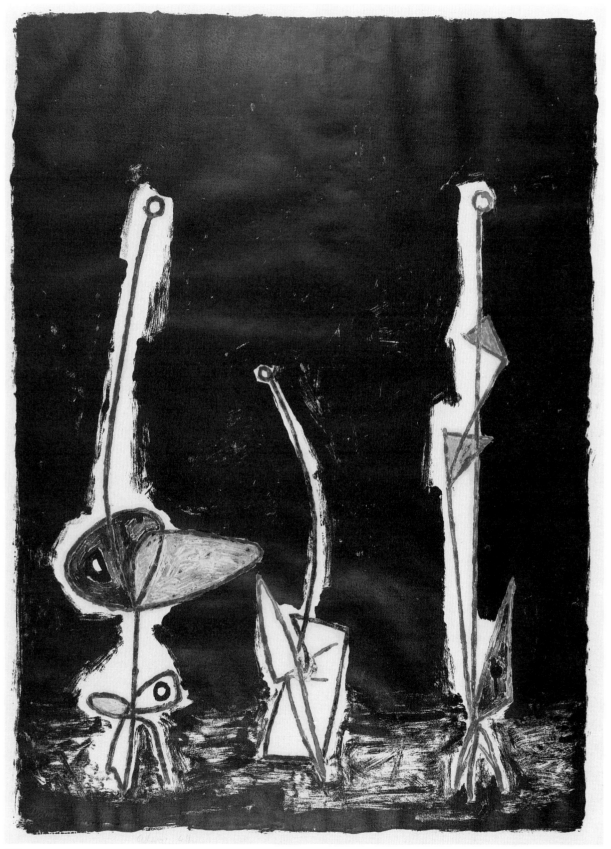

184

aquatint called *Descending Forms* and another untitled engraving, all printed in editions of 25, and two monotypes called *Rectangular Forms*. During the 1960s Adams continued to make prints, not only lithographs but also an embossed image in three versions known as *White-print*, dated 1968. Impressions of a considerable number of the prints were in the artist's estate at the time of his death, from which the British Museum purchased the three items catalogued here with 1985 registration numbers; the Tate Gallery also acquired some examples.

Bibliography

The literature on Robert Adams is very sparse indeed and mainly confined to general surveys on sculpture of the period such as the Whitechapel exhibition of 1981, mentioned above. Retrospectives of his work (sculpture, paintings and drawings) were held at the Ferens Art Gallery, Hull, in 1961 and the Camden Arts Centre, London, in 1971. Gimpel Fils owns Adams's 'Opus Book', a complete catalogue of all his early sculpture, and the Tate Gallery Archive possesses a number of his sketchbooks. Dr Alastair Grieve of the University of East Anglia is currently preparing a volume on Adams's sculpture to be published by Lund Humphries in 1991, together with a companion volume on his sketchbooks which will be brought out by Tate Gallery Publications.

185

184 Composition with Three Sculptural Forms, 1949

Monotype printed in black, red, grey, blue and green. Signed and dated in pencil. 672 × 490 mm

1987–11–7–18

185 Figure and Trees, 1949

Lithograph. Signed, dated and numbered 1/20 in pencil. 500 × 340 mm (maximum dimensions)

1985–12–14–22

Figure and Trees was one of the lithographs exhibited at the Redfern Gallery in December 1950 (no. 122, priced at 4 guineas). Adams submitted a set of three of these Klee-like compositions to the São Paolo Biennale in 1954, where they were awarded third prize in the lithography section.

186 Composition with Drawn Forms, 1949

Lithograph, printed in bluish-black. Signed, dated and numbered 9/25 in pencil. 475 × 315 mm

1985–12–14–21

This image can possibly be identified with no. 123 in the 1950–51 Redfern exhibition, 'Two Figures, Blue Background', priced at 3 guineas.

186

187

187 Tambourinist, 1950

Lithograph printed in black and red. Signed and dated in pencil;
titled on verso (possibly in the artist's hand). 415 × 294 mm

1985-12-14-20

188 White Rectangle, 1952

Linocut in blue and black. Signed and dated in pencil; the title
is in the bottom right corner (possibly in the artist's hand).
301 × 255 mm

1986-6-21-20

See colour illustration

White Rectangle, which had a companion linocut, *Black
Diamonds*, when it was exhibited at the Redfern in November 1952, was one of Adams's most overtly Constructivist
compositions. It was shown alongside Adrian Heath's
linocut *Composition in Black and Red* (cat. no. 189 below)
in the second Fitzroy Street studio exhibition in July 1952.
The linocuts made in 1952 relate closely to the paintings
that Adams exhibited at Gimpel Fils in July 1951.

Adrian Heath

born 1920

Born in Burma but brought up in England. After studying
for six months under Stanhope Forbes in Newlyn, Cornwall, in 1938, he attended the Slade in 1939-40 before
joining the RAF. He was a prisoner-of-war in Germany
from 1941 to 1945, and it was there that he met Terry
Frost, whose friendship after the war helped to forge
Heath's own links with the St Ives school of artists. He
returned to the Slade from 1945 to 1947. In 1948, after
a painting trip to the South of France, his interest in
abstract composition began to crystallise in the drawings
he decided to make in Paddington Station: 'I became
involved in plotting the distances between the iron sup-
ports, in carefully relating the horizontal girders to each
other and to the curves of the vast domed roof. I was obsessed with a sense of accuracy and precision' (Bristol
City Art Gallery exhibition catalogue, 1971).

By 1951 Heath was thoroughly committed to non-
figurative art and played a leading role in the Constructivist group through the weekend exhibitions held at his
studio in Fitzroy Street in 1952-3. In 1953, the same year
as his first one-man show at the Redfern Gallery, he published an historical essay on 'Abstract Art'. His work
nevertheless remained very painterly, influenced by the
handling and composition of Parisian artists such as Serge
Poliakoff and Alfred Manessier. In the latter part of the
1950s and early 1960s he began to make greater use of
organic shapes derived from studies of nudes or landscape.
From 1955 to 1976 Heath taught at Corsham, and more
recently, since 1980, on the Fine Art course at Reading
University.

Heath's printmaking was confined in the 1950s to
the three linocuts of 1952 discussed below and three
lithographs called *Composition 1956 I, II* and *III*, which
were exhibited at the Redfern Gallery in November 1956
at 7 guineas each (nos 472-4).

Bibliography

The Tate Gallery's 1985 *St Ives* exhibition catalogue
contains a biography and short bibliography for Adrian
Heath. Otherwise, the most informative sources are the
catalogues of a retrospective of his work held at Bristol
City Art Gallery in 1971, with an introduction by Norbert
Lynton, and of an exhibition titled *Adrian Heath 1951-
1959 and Recent Works*, Pallant House, Chichester, 1981,
which contains a statement by the artist.

189

190

189 Composition in Black and Red, 1952

Linocut printed in two colours on thin paper. Initialled in pencil.
294 × 202 mm

1986–6–21–30

An impression of this print was shown in the second of
Heath's studio exhibitions in July 1952, alongside Robert
Adams's *White Rectangle* (cat. no. 188 above). No more
than three or four proofs of any of Heath's linocuts were
printed. In this impression the oil in the black ink has
spread into the thin paper, and thus created the penumbra
of discoloration around the black.

190 Composition in Black and Yellow, 1952

Linocut in two colours. 302 × 196 mm (maximum dimensions)
1986–6–21–30*

Heath executed one other linocut similar in composition
to this print. He relates the vertical arrangement of curved
shapes to boats he had recently seen on a beach in Spain.
They also share an affinity with Terry Frost's arrangements of elliptical forms inspired by the boats in the harbour at St Ives (see cat. no. 171).

Victor Pasmore

born 1908

The son of a doctor, he was educated at Harrow until 1926 when his father's death meant he had to find employment. From 1927 to 1937 he worked as a clerk in the Public Health Department of the London County Council, but pursued his artistic interests through evening classes under A.S.Hartrick at the Central School until 1930. In 1934 he showed in the exhibition of *Objective Abstractions* at the Zwemmer Gallery; then in 1937, together with Claude Rogers and William Coldstream, he founded the Euston Road School (1937–40) to teach an 'objective realism' which owed much to the inspiration of Sickert. His style underwent a further change in the early forties when he moved to live on Chiswick Mall, then Hammersmith Terrace, where he painted a group of Whistlerian landscapes. By 1947, however, the elements of his landscape compositions had been resolved into distinctive groups of patterns and shapes which presaged his move towards complete abstraction over the next two years; Lawrence Alloway described how 'his art developed from being a window onto "nature" through an elliptical sign language to the picture as an object' (*Nine Abstract Artists*, p.5). During this period Pasmore was teaching at Camberwell, exploring geometric theories in paper collages as well as paintings, and drawing analogies between abstract art and music. In 1948 his first entirely abstract show was held at the Redfern Gallery; shortly afterwards he published a compilation of statements on *Abstract Art* through Camberwell and then moved to the Central School to teach in the Basic Form Course established in the Department of Industrial Design by the new director, William Johnstone.

After a series of 'spiral motif' paintings in 1949–51, Pasmore abandoned painting for a while to concentrate on relief and architectural constructions. These strongly influenced the work he did for Peterlee New Town from 1954 onwards as Consulting Director of Urban Design, and the courses in basic abstract studies which he introduced at Newcastle when he was Head of Fine Art from 1954 to 1961.

Pasmore had received recognition before the war from Kenneth Clark, who became one of his earliest patrons; in 1959 he was awarded the CBE and in 1960 he represented Britain at the Venice Biennale (with Paolozzi). The following year he left Newcastle, and the Marlborough Gallery became his dealer. He now worked full-time in his studio, first in London (where he served as a trustee of the Tate Gallery, 1963–6), then in Malta, where he bought a house in 1966. Since then the emphasis in his work has fallen very much upon painting, which has become increasingly saturated with colour although it often makes use of forms well established in his previous vocabulary. To quote, once more, Lawrence Alloway's assessment of 1954: 'One of the admirable things about Pasmore is that he constantly remakes his career. Each

phase of his activity alters the significance of what went before. This is expressed by the lingering revisions to which he subjects his work, which seem to be revaluations rather than a fulfilment of the original intention' (p.7). He was made a Companion of Honour in 1981 and a Royal Academician in 1982.

Pasmore's first published print appears to have been an abstract lithograph he exhibited at the Redfern Gallery in 1948 for 8 guineas, which was used as the poster for a London Group exhibition in the same year (see Redfern Gallery, *British Prints, the Post-War Years 1945–60*, 1986, no. 81). In 1949 he showed two abstract lithographs, again at the Redfern, one of which was undoubtedly the same as the print previously exhibited. In the early fifties Pasmore began the series of lithographs and linocuts of linear or spiral motifs discussed below, which he made as an adjunct to his drawings and exhibited at the Redfern Gallery until the end of the decade. His printmaking gathered momentum from the mid-sixties when Kelpra printed an extended series of screenprints called *Points of Contact* (1965–74). In 1970 he embarked upon a long relationship with the 2RC workshop in Rome; together with White Ink Ltd in London they continue to print the etchings and aquatints on which Pasmore has concentrated as a graphic artist for the past fifteen years.

Bibliography

The first book to be published on Pasmore was written by Clive Bell for the Penguin Modern Painters series in 1945. Alan Bowness and Luigi Lambertini edited the *Catalogue Raisonné of Paintings, Constructions and Graphics, 1926–1979*, London 1980, which contains a full chronology and select bibliography (this is currently being updated by Marlborough Fine Art). Since Pasmore is one of the most widely exhibited of all twentieth-century British artists, there has been a stream of exhibition catalogues from the early forties onwards. The present authors are particularly indebted to those of a Tate Gallery retrospective in 1965 (with an introduction by Ronald Alley), an Arts Council travelling exhibition in 1980 (with an introduction by Alastair Grieve), and a retrospective at the Yale Center for British Art, New Haven, in 1985 (by Malcolm Cormack with essays by Lawrence Gowing and Leif Sjoberg). The last of these has a full chronology up to 1985 and a bibliography to 1987 including references to Pasmore's own published statements.

191 Spiral Motif, 1951

Linocut. 177 × 255 mm (to margin drawn in pencil)
1988–3–5–18

Pasmore's early linocuts and lithographs were all a product of the fascination with spiralling forms which dominated his painting in 1950–51. Although these had begun to appear in his work in 1948–9, the motif received

191

further impetus from Pasmore's visit to St Ives in the summer of 1950, when he made a series of diagrammatic drawings of the waves on Porthmeor Beach. These provided the basis for several of the paintings he exhibited at the Redfern Gallery at the end of the year. William Townsend recorded his first glimpse of this work on a visit to Pasmore's studio on 26 October 1950:

Victor now has, hanging and standing by the bookshelves in the long room, enough new 'abstracts' to make a show; the shapes are no longer limited to rectangles and triangles but, as he said, he has tried to invent more complex shapes 'and it isn't easy'. There are several very beautiful ones composed with spirals. Also saw the drawings and a model showing the design *in situ* for the tiled decoration V. is doing for a restaurant in the 1951 exhibition; a vastly enlarged drawing, in black, white and grey lines of a waterfall. The design is derived from drawings (of the sea) done by Victor during the summer at St. Ives. A good many of the drawings he did there have been turned into lithographs too, extremely simple designs of houses, rocks, cliffs and spiralling shapes of water, redrawn on transfer paper from sketches made on the spot (*The Townsend Journals*, ed. Andrew Forge, Tate Gallery, 1976, p.90).

The major compositions of this period were *The Coast of the Inland Sea* I and II, 1950 (Tate Gallery and Private Collection: Bowness and Lambertini 154 and 157), *The Snowstorm*, 1950–51 (Arts Council, commissioned for the Festival of Britain; B and L 158) and the ceramic mural for the Regatta Restaurant on the South Bank, which no longer exists. Pasmore was certainly indebted to Leonardo da Vinci's drawings of rocks and whirlpools, but he explained, as a prelude to a discussion of his 1950 Redfern Gallery exhibition at the ICA in January 1951, that what he had done was

not the result of a process of abstraction in front of nature, but a method of construction emanating from within. I have tried to compose as music is composed, with formal elements which, in themselves, have no descriptive qualities at all. The spiral movement which can be discerned throughout nature, in many different forms, is reduced to its single common denomination – the simple spiral ('The Artist Speaks', *Art News and Review*, vol. III, no 1 (February 1951), p.3).

None of the prints of spiral or linear motifs from the early fifties was ever published in proper editions at the time, although the one catalogued here was reprinted in the 1960s in an edition of 20 by White Ink Ltd on thin greenish coloured paper, signed with the artist's monogram and dated '51. Since it is the only one of the group to be included in the graphics section of the catalogue raisonné (B and L 1), the only source of information about the others is in the Redfern Gallery exhibition catalogues of the 1950s. This print may have been one of the three linocuts shown there in November 1972 (nos 225–7) under the title 'Linear Motif I, II and III', priced at 6, 4 and 6 guineas respectively; the artist now refers to them as 'Spiral Motifs'. The Arts Council retrospective of Pasmore's work in 1955 included one of the linocuts of 1951 which was closely related to the painting *Spiral Motif in Black and White* (B and L 164) and a lithograph, together with a number of the St Ives pen and ink drawings (nos 43–8). None of the prints of this period has featured in more recent exhibitions.

10 Post-War Etching

Whereas in the 1920s and 1930s etching had been the pre-eminent medium of printmaking, the situation after the Second World War was completely reversed. The dominant position was now held by lithography, with etching and the other intaglio processes coming far behind. As a result, the artists of the late 1940s and 1950s grouped together in this section are a varied miscellany with little in common beside their technique. Three of the artists included – Nicholson, Evans and Hamilton – had made prints before the war. On the other hand Graham Sutherland, one of the best-known pre-war etchers, rejected his past completely and in the 1940s and 1950s made only lithographs. Indeed, he passed some of his etching equipment on to Lucian Freud in the 1940s as something he would never need again.

After the collapse of the market in conventional etching in the late twenties, there was no obvious vehicle for selling intaglio prints. The post-war Redfern Gallery exhibitions, which were almost the only regular shows of prints in London, were until the latter part of the fifties largely presented as exhibitions of colour prints, containing almost entirely lithographs and monotypes. Etchings suffered from the disadvantages of being traditionally small in size and rarely coloured. As a result, those etchings that were shown after the war normally appeared tacked onto one-man exhibitions of paintings or sculpture, at galleries such as the Lefèvre or Gimpel Fils that had no particular interest in printmaking.

The lack of outlets for etchings in turn discouraged artists from making them. Thus Lucian Freud, whose style of drawing lent itself perfectly to the medium, made only a handful of plates at the time, as did Ben Nicholson, whom, moreover, Denis Mitchell remembers as saying that every sale of a print was the loss of a sale of a painting. In this climate commercial facilities for making and printing plates withered away; etching became something of a home-grown product dependent on art schools and a handful of artists who maintained their belief in the virtues of intaglio. Most of these, with the exception of Merlyn Evans, were former associates of Hayter: Buckland Wright, Gross and Trevelyan were teaching at the Slade and the Royal College of Art and Evans was at the Central, while Hayter himself was living in New York, then Paris again after 1950.

It was not until the establishment of the St George's Gallery in 1955 that a publisher and dealer appeared who was as interested in intaglio as in the other media. It is to Robert Erskine's patronage that we owe, for example, Merlyn Evans's *Vertical Suite in Black*, Anthony Gross's *Le Boulvé Suite* and plates by Dos Santos and Michael Sandle. In the 1959 exhibition *The Graven Image*, at the Whitechapel Art Gallery, sixty-nine intaglio prints were shown as against fifty-seven lithographs, eighteen relief prints and seven screenprints. In the introduction to the catalogue Erskine remarked that 'The first striking feature in the exhibition is the lack of little black etchings in large white mounts. As a source of expression among artists today the little black etching has died . . .'. Indeed, almost all his publications were notable for their substantial size; large etched plates were tackled by a variety of different artists, with those who also worked in sculptural media, like Evans and Geoffrey Clarke, being particularly drawn to them.

Their work demonstrated that intaglio prints could serve the same decorative needs as lithographs, but as Hayter pointed out in his book of 1962, *About Prints*, there were few places in England with the necessary facilities for their execution. Thomas Ross and Co. continued to print commercial plates but the sole representative of the tradition of the master-printer who collaborated with artists was C. H. Welch, whom Erskine used extensively for his publications. Welch was eventually forced by rent rises to move to a smaller workshop; then, when he retired, the business ended with him and his presses were bought by Merlyn Evans and Anthony Gross. A professional printmaker who also printed plates for other artists in the second half of the fifties was John Brunsdon (b. 1933), who studied at the Royal College under Julian Trevelyan. His own work was mainly done on steel using unorthodox implements such as wire brushes for removing rust from railings, and he had the equipment to print on a very large scale. Denis Bowen, one of the artists for whom Brunsdon printed, drew through a hard ground onto a steel plate by means of a stone (see J. Brunsdon, *The Technique of Etching and Engraving*, London 1965, pl. 23).

Geoffrey Clarke resorted to expertise in Paris for his plates of 1956, working with Jean Frélaut who had been the chief printer at the Atelier Lacourière and then ran the firm with Roger Lacourière's wife after the latter's gradual retirement. He had a legendary reputation for his work with Picasso in the 1940s and 1950s: when Henry Moore became seriously interested in intaglio methods in the sixties, Frélaut came over to England to assist with the printing. The plates were proofed at the Royal College, then taken to Paris for the printing of the actual editions.

Erskine's efforts undoubtedly helped to educate a new taste for intaglio prints and some of his own publications enjoyed considerable success, among them Michael Sandle's *Japanese Armour* of 1958, of which the entire edition of 50 was sold. This renewed interest blossomed most notably in the early work of David Hockney, which lies just outside the scope of this exhibition.

Ben Nicholson

For biography and bibliography, see pp.90–92

192 ICI Shed, 1948

Drypoint. Signed and numbered 7/10. 200 × 250mm
Victoria and Albert Museum, Circ. 494–1948

ICI Shed and *Trendrine* (cat. no. 193) belong to a group of six drypoints printed by Nicholson in 1948 when he was living in St Ives. The remaining four subjects were *Halse Town*, *Newlyn*, *Two Pears* and *Mug and Goblet Forms*. Four of these drypoints, including *ICI Shed*, were on sale for £1 10s. each at the Lefèvre Gallery in London in November 1948 as part of an exhibition of *Recent Paintings 1947–48 by Ben Nicholson*, and the group as a whole may well have been made with this exhibition in mind. Between 1948 and 1965, when Nicholson encountered François Lafranca in Switzerland, he made only three isolated prints, two drypoints of Pisa and San Gimignano in 1951 and 1953, and a further one in 1957 known as *Goblet Forms*.

192

193

The quality of line produced by drypoint had a particular appeal for Nicholson, who in 1968 dismissed the notion that he was an etcher in the true sense '. . . I suppose mine are really drawings on prepared copper (and I like very much the clear line and resistancy of the material and the smooth run of the implement)' (extract from a letter quoted from *Ben Nicholson*, ed. Maurice de Sausmarez, Studio International Special, London 1969, p.66).

193 Trendrine, 1948

Drypoint. Signed in the plate. 175 × 247mm
Victoria and Albert Museum, Circ. 448–1965

Trendrine was one of the farms on the Land's End road out of St Ives. Nicholson made the same view the subject of a drawing and a painting executed in the summer of 1947 (LH 1.177) and on 13 December 1947 (LH 1.201), before making the drypoint in the following year.

Richard Hamilton

born 1922

Born in London, he left school in 1936, at the age of 14. He then worked in advertising during the day, while studying art at evening classes. In 1938 he became a full-time student at the Royal Academy Schools, but when the Schools closed in 1940 he went to work as an engineering draughtsman. After the war he resumed art school, first returning to the Royal Academy Schools until he was expelled for 'not profiting from the instruction given', and then from 1948 to 1951 at the Slade. In 1951 he organised an exhibition, *Growth and Form*, at the Institute of Contemporary Arts as its contribution to the Festival of Britain, and the following year was one of the founder-members of the Independent Group there, together with Nigel Henderson, whom he knew from the Slade, and Eduardo Paolozzi. He played a major role in the exhibition *This is Tomorrow* at the Whitechapel Art Gallery in 1956.

Hamilton's first prints were fifteen etchings made while a student at the Central School before the war. He made a few more in 1946, but his first significant sequence was the *Reapers* in 1949 (see below). Hamilton continued to etch occasional plates through the 1950s, including a group of three Cubo-Futurist compositions made in Newcastle, where he ran an evening class in etching while he was attached to the University of Durham's Fine Art Department there. It was not, however, until his first collaboration with Chris Prater of Kelpra in screenprinting in 1963 that his prints began to attract the wide international acclaim that they now enjoy. He resumed etching in the late sixties; since 1973 his work in intaglio printmaking has been almost entirely conducted in conjunction with the studio of Aldo Crommelynck in Paris.

Bibliography

A large retrospective exhibition was held at the Tate Gallery in 1970, and another at the Guggenheim Museum in New York in 1973. Hamilton has compiled his own catalogue of 134 plates of his graphic works, *Prints 1939–1983*, London 1984, to which *Richard Hamilton, Image and Process: Studies, Stage and Final Proofs from the Graphic Works 1952–82* by Richard S. Field, London 1983, is a companion volume. An earlier catalogue, *The Prints of Richard Hamilton*, also prepared by Richard S. Field for an exhibition in 1973 at the Davison Art Center at the Wesleyan University, Middletown, Connecticut, is still valuable. For Hamilton's most recent work, see Stephen Coppel, 'Richard Hamilton's *Ulysses* Etchings, an Examination of Work in Progress', *Print Quarterly* VI (1989), pp.10–42. His role in the Independent Group is described in the catalogue of the ICA exhibition *The Independent Group: Post-War Britain and the Aesthetics of Plenty*, London 1990.

194 Reaper (d), 1949

Drypoint and roulette. Inscribed 4/20 in pencil. 173 × 270 mm
Hamilton 1984, no. 23
Tate Gallery (P.07648)

195 Reaper (g), 1949

Etching. Signed and numbered 8/20 in pencil. 171 × 247 mm
Hamilton 1984, no. 26
Tate Gallery (P.07651)

The *Reaper* series consists of seventeen prints (of which two were variant states of a single plate), all of which show different views of a reaping machine. The series was made in 1949 when Hamilton was at the Slade School, where John Buckland Wright was then teaching etching, and was exhibited complete at Gimpel Fils in February 1950 under the title 'Variations on a Theme of a Reaper'. The 'variations' of the title refer not only to the variety of views of the machine but also to the range of printmaking methods used in these plates, which include etching, drypoint, engraving, roulette and aquatint; two were printed in colour.

In 1982 Hamilton wrote of these prints that 'their style and treatment slots them perfectly into the pre-Festival of Britain provincial art scene' (Richard Hamilton, *Collected Words*, London 1982, p.84), and for many years he excluded them from surveys of his graphic work 'largely because he felt a danger that the output of prolific early years might dilute that of more mature deliberation' (*Prints 1939–83*, p.7). They remain, however, his first exhibited prints, and connect closely with the interests that dominate his later work. In a note in the 1984 catalogue, Hamilton records that the series 'was inspired by Giedeon's *Mechanization takes command* [London 1948]. Repetition of the simple contrasting forms of the agri-

cultural machine provided material for investigating the technical resources of the Slade School' (p.23). Dawn Leach-Ruhl ('The Chronology of Hamilton's *Reaper* Series', *Print Quarterly* V (1988), pp.66–71), has argued, however, that a stronger influence was d'Arcy Thompson's *On Growth and Form*, Cambridge 1917. There is also a clear link with some of Paul Klee's drawings of the 1930s, such as the *Landschaftswagen* series of 1930 (reproduced in the exhibition catalogue *Paul Klee, das Werk der Jahre 1919–1933*, Kunsthalle Cologne, 1979).

Field (1983, p.17) observes that each of these prints

probes the mechanism with differing technical means, so that the entire series metamorphoses the machine not so much in a mechanical-cubist manner, as in a thoroughly humanist one. The machine comes alive through the serialisation and variation of its image. Nothing anthropocentric is suggested; vitality of expression resides in the changes of technique and not at all in the artist's 'expressive' intervention. Hamilton's habit of allowing process to replace intention is evident here.

The fifteen black and white prints in the series were offered for sale at Gimpel's in 1950 at 3 guineas each, and the two coloured ones at 5 guineas. Very few impressions were actually printed or sold at the time, and the edition numbers found on these impressions merely reveal an intended maximum.

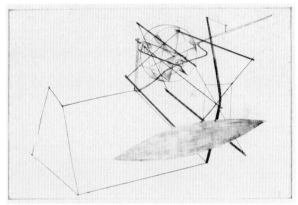

194

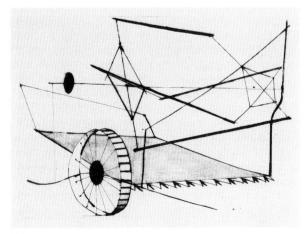

195

196

196 Self-Portrait, 1951

Etching, soft-ground etching, engraving, drypoint, aquatint and punch. Signed and titled in pencil. 300 × 196 mm

Hamilton 1984, no. 42

Tate Gallery (P.07657)

In a comment in his 1984 catalogue, Hamilton records that this was one of the plates 'produced during the period that most of my energy was engaged on the *Growth and Form* exhibition based on d'Arcy Thompson's book of that name. All are influenced by Thompson's morphological subject matter' (p.35). Field comments: 'This self-portrait is a humorous reflection on the Darwinian idea of very complex (both structurally and psychologically) entities evolving from the simplest life forms. A head is compounded from features representing primitive organisms (bull sperm, sea urchin, flat-worm, etc) ...' As in *Heteromorphism*, another of Hamilton's etchings of 1951, 'a multiplicity of technical means is used to keep the elements separate and to retain their individual character' (1973, p.20). The pendulum-like object symbolises the artist's interest in movement (see Richard Morphet in the 1970 Tate catalogue, p.23).

The plate was never editioned, and the few proofs were printed by the artist at the Slade School. A closely related drawing is in the Victoria and Albert Museum (reproduced on page 70 of the 1990 ICA exhibition catalogue).

Lucian Freud

born 1922

Born in Berlin, son of Ernst Freud, an architect, and grandson of Sigmund Freud. He emigrated to England with his parents in 1933, and was educated at Dartington Hall. In 1938 he enrolled for a general course at the Central School of Art, and in the summer of 1939 joined Cedric Morris's East Anglian School of Drawing and Painting. The first publication of his work – a pen and ink self-portrait – was by Peter Watson in *Horizon* in April 1940. From 1942 until 1945 Freud shared a studio, provided by Watson, with John Craxton. In 1943 Craxton introduced Freud to Graham Sutherland, who in turn introduced him to Francis Bacon, later to become one of the major influences upon his painting. Although Freud executed a number of drawings of animals, plants and landscape at this period, portraiture was and has remained his principal interest. He has professed a particular liking for Cedric Morris's portraits with their 'alarming candour' (see Nicholas Penny in the 1988 Hayward Gallery catalogue, p.8), and his own portraits of the 1940s are characterised by the extreme intensity of the artist's scrutiny, which is often projected back onto the spectator by the unwavering stare of the sitter's eyes. One sitter of 1947, Waldemar Hansen, a friend of Peter Watson, described Freud's surroundings with 'a zebra head on the wall, an old fashioned phonograph with a huge horn, and a live falcon which swoops around the room and alights on the master's wrist. I think he is going to do a drawing of me, and I'm rather intrigued to see what I'll look like after going through that strange personal prism' (Michael Shelden, *Friends of Promise*, p.184).

In 1951 Freud's commission from the Arts Council for the Festival of Britain, the painting *Interior near Paddington*, elicited this accolade from Sir Colin Anderson: 'Very good indeed – vision, design and craftsmanship' (Tate Gallery Archive). Yet the 1950s were to be a difficult phase in Freud's career. Drawing as an independent activity ceased between 1954 and 1961; by the end of the decade he had developed a broader manner of painting which appeared to free him from his earlier impasse.

Freud has made a small number of prints at intervals through his career. Apart from two very early linocuts and one lithograph, all have been etchings. Of these, five were made between 1946 and 1948 (see below); after a long break, another fifteen followed in 1982. A further six plates made in 1984–6 were published in 1986.

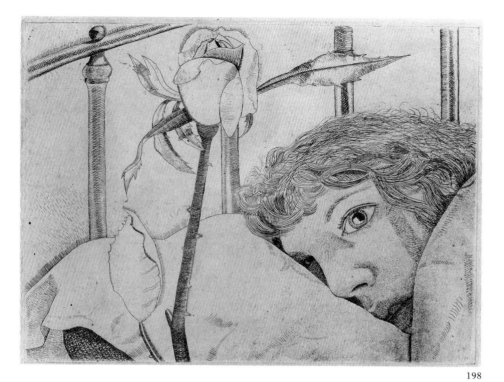

198

6/10

Lucian Freud

197

Bibliography

A first retrospective exhibition by the Arts Council was held in 1974, and another larger one at the Hayward Gallery in 1988. A monograph, *Lucian Freud*, by Lawrence Gowing was published in London in 1982. Freud's prints have been catalogued in two complementary articles in *Print Quarterly* III (December 1986): Matthew Marks, 'The Graphic Work of Lucian Freud', pp.321–34, and Roger Bevan, 'Freud's Latest Etchings', pp.334–43. Most of his prints were also included in the catalogue of the South Bank Centre touring exhibition *Lucian Freud, Works on Paper*, 1988, by Nicholas Penny and Robert F. Johnson.

197 Girl with a Fig Leaf, 1947

Etching. Signed and numbered 6/10 in pencil. 298 × 238 mm

Marks 6

Collection of James Kirkman

According to information given by the artist to Matthew Marks, it was Graham Sutherland who taught Freud to etch during the 1940s, and indeed later gave him his own etching equipment. Freud's first etchings were made in Paris in 1946, using the basin of his hotel room to hold his acid bath, although Paolozzi, who saw Freud during his own sojourn in Paris in 1947–9, recalls that he did have some recourse to professional assistance: 'the first etching I ever saw Lucian Freud make, he just painted a copper plate with Brunswick black and tied a needle onto a pencil; then there were so many facilities in Paris, he just took it somewhere and had it bitten and then he took the bitten plate somewhere else . . .' (in conversation with the authors, February 1990). This portrait of the artist's first wife, Kitty, the daughter of the sculptor Jacob Epstein, was made in the summer of 1947 while they were in Aix-en-Provence with the Sutherlands.

198 Ill in Paris, 1948

Etching. Not signed or annotated. 127 × 178 mm

Marks 8

Collection of James Kirkman

Another portrait of the artist's wife, made in Paris at the same time as another smaller plate showing just her forehead and eyes. Ten impressions were printed, but, like the previous print, this etching does not ever seem to have been formally published. The remaining two etchings made at this time were *The Bird* and *Chelsea Bun*, both small plates measuring 60 × 89 mm and printed in tiny numbers.

Merlyn Evans

1910–1973

Born in Cardiff of Welsh parentage, he moved with his family to Glasgow at the age of three. He attended the Glasgow School of Art from 1927 to 1930, where he was taught etching by Charles Murray, and from 1931 to 1933 held a scholarship at the Royal College of Art in London. In the mid-1930s he visited the Continent, and became briefly interested in Surrealism, participating in the 1936 Surrealist exhibition in London. In 1938 he went to take up a teaching post in Durban, from where he entered the Army in 1942. On discharge he settled again in London, which remained his home for the rest of his career. In 1950 he married the pianist Margerie Few, and later taught drawing and engraving at the Central School and at the Royal College of Art. He also made sculpture throughout his career.

Evans's first few prints were made in the 1930s, and show either abstract or biomorphic forms; these are very rare, and seem never to have been sold. After the war, in 1946, he in effect started again, and henceforth practised intaglio printmaking as seriously as his painting. During the later 1940s and 1950s he was undoubtedly the most highly regarded etcher in Britain, on account of both the size and the ambition of his plates.

Bibliography

The catalogue of a retrospective at the Whitechapel Art Gallery in 1956 includes notes by the artist, while an autobiographical 'Background' prepared for that same exhibition was first published in 1985, in *The Political Paintings of Merlyn Evans*, the catalogue of an exhibition at the Tate Gallery. A memorial exhibition was held at the National Museum of Wales and in Glasgow in 1974, and another retrospective at the Mayor and Redfern Galleries in 1988; this reprints an essay by Evans on 'The Printmaker and the Peintre Graveur'. The main publication on the prints is *The Graphic Art of Merlyn Evans*, with essays by Robert Erskine and Bryan Robertson, published by the Victoria and Albert Museum in 1972. However, no complete catalogue of them has yet been published.

199 The Chess Players, 1949

Etching with surface tone. 410 × 409 mm

1988–3–5–17

The composition of this print closely follows that of a painting of 1940 with the same title and same proportions. Two preparatory drawings for it – which, like the painting, show the marked influence of Wyndham Lewis – are reproduced as figs 10 and 11 of the 1972 V & A booklet. One of these makes it clear that the object below the left picture in the background is an alarm clock; the book in the lower right corner is labelled 'Hegel'. The subject commemorates the Ribbentrop-Molotov pact of August 1939, when Stalin and Hitler signed a non-aggression treaty and shared out their neighbours' territories between themselves. The two figures are seen exchanging pieces with a view to gaining a mutual advantage; this was the effect of a second secret accord in September, when Germany transferred Lithuania to the Soviet sphere in return for an extension of the German area in Poland.

This print was published in two different editions, one in 1949 and the other in 1951. The first edition, exhibited at the Redfern Gallery in 1949 at the price of 6 guineas,

199

30/3/57

Evans.

200

was printed in colours and the stated edition size was 25 (though there is every reason to suppose that only a few impressions of this edition were ever printed). An impression of this, annotated '2nd state', was illustrated in black and white in the 1988 Mayor/Redfern catalogue, p.33. Comparison with the British Museum impression (for which we are most grateful to its current owner) shows that the BM impression is identical in its state to the main plate which carried the design; the second plate carried the colour, which was brushed onto an unworked plate in monotype fashion in red and grey inks. In 1951 Evans reworked the plate (the new date is added in the plate) and added a layer of aquatint; this state was published in monochrome only in an edition of 25. The British Museum also possesses an impression of the 1951 edition (1971-2-15-17).

200 Helmet Mask, 1957

Lift-ground aquatint, signed and dated '30/3/57' in the plate.
Signed, dated, titled and numbered 41/50 in pencil.
740 × 503 mm
1971-2-15-10

This is the first of the six plates in the series *Vertical Suite in Black*, commissioned and made in 1957 and published in February the following year by St George's Gallery Prints, with a booklet containing notes on the prints by Evans himself:

This series or suite of etchings may, in part, find their source or origin in my friendship with two great authorities on African sculpture, Margaret Webster Plass and William Fagg [then Keeper of the Department of Ethnography at the British Museum]. My enthusiasm for African sculpture was not a new one; I had studied it in many parts of the world and in Africa, where I spent some years ... About this time I began *Vertical Suite in Black*, in homage to African carving, from which these designs derive. Thus *Helmet Mask* bears a strong resemblance to the great Baga dance mask representing a maternity goddess, recently acquired by the British Museum.

This famous helmet mask (1957.Af7.1) is reproduced (for example) on pages 106–7 of *Henry Moore at the British Museum*, London 1981, where it is accompanied by an enthusiastic appreciation by Moore. The other prints in the set (reproduced as figs 60–64 in the V & A booklet) also echo African sculpture; Evans gives his source for each image in the St George's Gallery booklet quoted above.

In these prints Evans used sugar-lift aquatint for the first time, having learnt the technique shortly before on a visit to Paris (according to Anthony Gross in the catalogue of the exhibition *Tribute to Merlyn Evans* held at the Cartwright Hall, Bradford, in 1974; for the process see Geoffrey Clarke, cat. no. 203 below). This allowed him to obtain the effect of broad sweeps of the brush.

The plates were printed on a giant 44-inch rotary press belonging to the professional printer C.H. Welch. This

press has its own history: it was specially constructed for Welch in 1901–2 at a cost of £400 in order to print the huge etchings of Frank Brangwyn. The documents on the publication of the *Vertical Suite in Black* in 1957 show that it was Welch who printed these plates for Evans (who usually did his own printing); at some point after this, Evans bought the press himself, and a photograph of Evans printing from it in his Hampstead studio was published in *Private View* by Bryan Robertson, John Russell and Lord Snowdon, London 1965. After his death, it was acquired by the etcher Norman Ackroyd, who still uses it for printing his own plates (and to whom we are indebted for this information).

Robert Erskine was particularly proud of his revival of what he described as 'the Vollard concept of the "Suite" of prints', which he regarded as the most viable form of print publishing as well as providing the artist with scope for the development of a theme.

Geoffrey Clarke

born 1924

Born in Derbyshire. After service in the RAF during the war, he studied sculpture at the Royal College of Art from 1948 to 1952 and later taught there. He achieved success early, winning the silver medal for sculpture at the Milan Triennale in 1951. Since the mid-1950s he has made a large number of pieces of public sculpture on commission for specific sites, including various items for Coventry Cathedral; these he casts himself in his Suffolk studio. He became a member of the Royal Academy in 1976.

Clarke has always been best known for his iron sculpture – cast aluminium since 1959 – in which the human figure or parts of the figure are reconstructed out of metal parts. But in the first three years of his career, from 1949 to 1951, he made a remarkable group of etchings or sugar aquatints on steel plates – thirty-three, according to a list supplied by the artist. Thirty-one of these were shown at his first one-man exhibition at Gimpel Fils in April 1952, the same year that his sculptures and etchings were shown in the British pavilion at the Venice Biennale. A few further plates followed in 1953–4, and a more numerous group (about a dozen), mostly on a much larger scale, in 1956. In 1957 he was awarded a major prize at the First International Exhibition of Prints held in Toyko. He seems to have made no etchings after 1958, but did make a large number of transfer monotypes in the 1960s and 1970s. The five items shown here have been selected from a group of eight purchased by the British Museum from the artist in 1990.

Bibliography

The manuscript list of the artist's prints referred to above was passed to us through the courtesy of Peter Black. The fullest published list of etchings is that of twenty-four

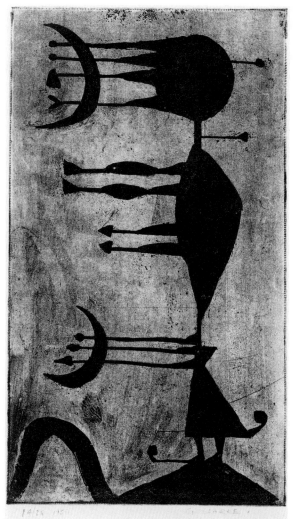

201

items contained in the catalogue of an exhibition, *Geoffrey Clarke, Early Engraved Work and Iron Sculpture*, held at the Taranman Gallery in London in 1976. This contains an essay on Clarke's work by W.J.Strachan, who has also commented on it in his book *Towards Sculpture, Maquettes and Sketches from Rodin to Oldenburg*, London 1976.

201 Man, 1950

Etching. Signed, dated and numbered 14/25; in the margin the title 'Man 3G' in pencil. 354 × 203mm

1990-3-3-31

202 Men Isolated, 1950

Etching. Signed and annotated A/P in pencil. 239 × 430mm

1990-3-3-33

203 Man (Complexities of Man I), 1950

Etching. Signed and annotated A/P in pencil. 176 × 250mm

1990-3-3-32

According to the artist's notes, all three of these plates were made in February 1950, a month in which no less than eight plates were completed. Almost all his prints of this period have stated intended edition sizes of 25, but no more than three to six impressions of each were sold. They were printed at the Royal College either by the artist himself or by Richard Fozard. These three prints were respectively nos 2, 4 and 9 in the 1952 Gimpel Fils exhibition (of which the list of exhibits has been kindly made available to us by that gallery). All three were priced there at 3 guineas; *Blue Head* (cat. no. 204 below) was priced at 5 guineas, as were the three other colour prints. The

202

203

second alternative title for the third print was used after 1952, presumably in order to distinguish it from other plates of the same title.

All Clarke's etchings were made using rolled steel plates, of 'bright finish' as supplied to car makers, and this gives them much of their individual character. The broadly bitten areas were defined using a gouache containing a sugar solution brushed onto the plate. The sugar swells and lifts off the plate in a bath of water, thus exposing the drawn area for biting. It is usual then to cover the exposed areas with an aquatint ground in order to control the action of the acid and prevent foul biting, but in this case this was not necessary because steel or iron (unlike copper or zinc) has the property of producing a natural aquatint-like grain when openly bitten by acid.

The ideas which Clarke had begun to explore in his prints were simultaneously interpreted through his sculpture from 1950 onwards. 'The work of that time began with the black and white aquatints in 1949. These generally comprised man, his influences, surroundings and belief in an external force. The first sculptures were virtually iron versions' (Tate Gallery, *Illustrated Catalogue of Acquisitions 1976–8*, p.37). Symbols for man, woman and child were a constant feature of Clarke's work at this time. Monotype illustrations of some of the symbols he used to denote these figures were included in his thesis of 1951 for the Royal College of Art, 'Exposition of a Belief' (see Tate Gallery, *Illustrated Catalogue of Acquisitions 1972–4*, p.101).

204 Blue Head, 1951

Etching printed in colours *à la poupée*. Signed, numbered 8/50 and dated 'Jan. 51' in pencil. 448 × 215 mm

1990-3-3-35

Clarke made five plates for printing in colour in January 1951. Most, like this one, were printed from a single plate using cloth dabbers (*poupées* in French) to lay the different colours. According to Strachan, only one was made using

the alternative method of multiple plates. Clarke made two further colour prints in November 1953, all the impressions of which were varnished before sale. Other colour plates followed in 1956–8.

205 Warrior 2, 1956

Etching. Signed, titled and annotated 'Proof 8 '56' in pencil within the image. 974 × 600 mm

1990-3-3-37

When shown at the Venice Biennale in 1960, the stated edition size was 25. But a typed note initialled by the artist on the back of the frame states: 'An edition has never been

204

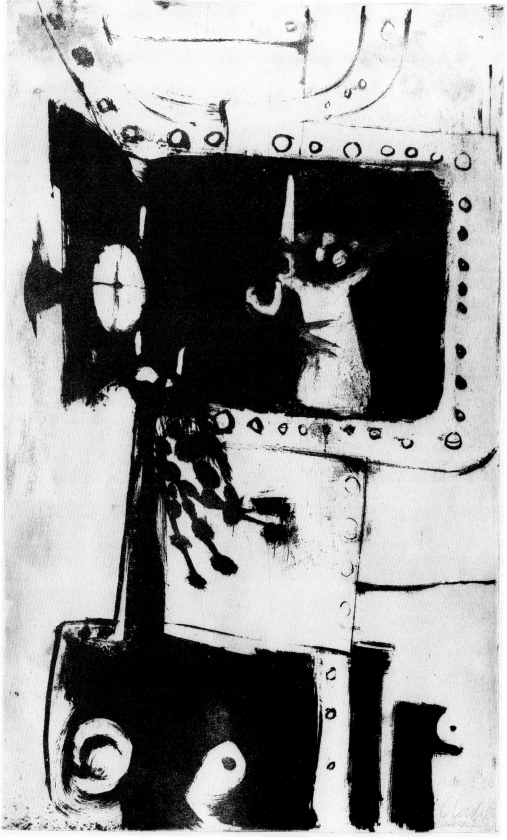

205

printed. The plate was mislaid soon after proofing by Frélaut in Paris in 1956.'

The image on this, and on three other very large plates also made in Paris in August 1956, is of a human head seen through a tank observation hatch. The contrast of the vulnerable organic head and the plate armour links the ideas of insecurity and aggression, and is not dissimilar in concept to Henry Moore's *Helmet Head* sculptures of 1950.

Michael Sandle

born 1936

Born and brought up in the west of England and then the Isle of Man. After National Service, he studied part-time at various art schools before entering the print-making school at the Slade full-time from 1956 to 1959. Here he was taught etching by Anthony Gross and lithography by Lynton Lamb and Ceri Richards. The catalogue of his first one-man exhibition at the Drian Galleries in Porchester Place, London, in 1963 recorded: 'Whilst at the Slade School of Art he developed a serious interest in printmaking, and after a short stay in Italy went to Paris in order to further his knowledge of printing techniques. In January 1960 he became employed as a lithographer at the Atelier Patris, a professional studio which specialised in collaborating with artists to produce editions of fine art lithographs [and where Stanley Jones had previously trained]. During his stay there he printed editions and assisted at the production of artists' proofs for Soulages, Sugai among others.' He returned in 1961

to various teaching jobs in England. Sandle began to introduce sculptural elements into reliefs at the beginning of the 1960s; his first fully three-dimensional work followed in 1966, since when he has worked almost entirely in sculpture and drawing. He left Britain in 1970, teaching first in Canada from 1970 to 1973 and since then in Germany, at Pforzheim and Karlsruhe, where he is Professor at the Akademie der Bildenden Künste.

Since he turned to sculpture, Sandle has made few prints. But between 1956 and the early 1960s he produced a considerable body of work in etching and lithography. Little of this was ever exhibited in Britain, apart from two etchings shown at the *Graven Image* exhibition at the Whitechapel Art Gallery in 1959 (see below) and the (unlisted) items in the 1963 Drian Gallery exhibition. Some prints were also shown in exhibitions abroad (listed on page 84 of the 1988 catalogue). In 1988 the British Museum acquired directly from the artist a group of twenty of his early prints, mostly lithographs, which show a remarkable experimental inventiveness in both technique and imagery (1988–12–10–10 to 29).

Bibliography

Michael Sandle, Sculpture and Drawings 1957–88 was published as the catalogue of a large retrospective held at the Whitechapel Art Gallery and the Stuttgart Kunstverein in 1988–9. It includes an essay by Marco Livingstone; on page 86 are two photographs of Sandle inking a stone and printing a lithograph at the Slade School in 1957. Other catalogues of recent exhibitions of Sandle's work have nothing to say about the prints that he made in his early years.

206

207

206 Warriors, 1958

Etching. Annotated in lower margin 'Variation 10'.
440 × 600 mm
1988–12–10–24

Whereas none of Sandle's lithographs of the 1950s seem to have been published, two etchings were commissioned and published by the St George's Gallery but were both printed by Sandle himself at the Slade. These were *Blue Lozenge and White Rosette* and *Japanese Armour*, both of which were shown, as nos 126–7, in the 1959 *Graven Image* exhibition. The latter was printed in black, gold and red, and created such a sensation that the edition of 50 was quickly sold out.

Livingstone (p.11) records that Sandle cites the work of the German Expressionist Karl Schmidt-Rottluff as a major influence on his early etchings. Other etchings of the period show his familiarity with George Grosz and Otto Dix.

207 Head, 1957 or 1958

Lithograph, printed in black and red from a single stone. Torn around the incisions for registration in the centre of both sides.
635 × 480 mm
1988–12–10–19

Two other lithographs, *Horse and Rider* and *Childbirth*, reproduced on page 41 of the catalogue of the 1988 retrospective, are dated 1958, while the photographs dated 1957 on page 86 show further lithographs in the same style; hence the date assigned to this print here. The pock-marks on the image were caused by throwing acid directly at the stone (as the artist informs us), a method somewhat reminiscent of Ceri Richards's improvisations with etches and abrasives applied to lithographic plates (see cat. no. 210 below). The unusual technique of using the same stone twice to print both colours in the same lithograph had previously been employed by Kirchner and other members of Die Brücke. This – and the deliberately imprecise registration – means that each impression is a monoprint, for no two printings will be the same.

Bartolomeu Dos Santos

born 1931

Born in Lisbon, he trained at the Escola Superior de Belas Artes there from 1950 to 1956. He came to London to study printmaking under Anthony Gross at the Slade School, where he remained until 1958. He then returned to Portugal for three years, while maintaining his connection with Britain by exhibiting with London dealers. In 1961, following the retirement of Gross, he was invited to succeed him as professor of printmaking at the Slade, which post he still occupies. He has continued to exhibit frequently in Portugal as well as in many other countries.

Dos Santos has always specialised in intaglio printmaking, and specifically in etching. In his early years, in the 1950s and 1960s, he worked most frequently in aquatint. Since the 1970s he has also incorporated photographic imagery into his plates.

Bibliography

A retrospective exhibition was held at the Centro de Arte Moderna of the Gulbenkian Foundation in Lisbon in 1989. The substantial catalogue contains a biographical chronology, together with a large number of reproductions of his work.

208 The Feast, 1958

Aquatint. Signed, dated and numbered 19/30 in pencil.
528 × 600 mm
Collection of the artist

This large plate was made in London in 1958 shortly before Dos Santos's return to Portugal. It was commissioned (together with another plate, *Still Life in Silence*) by Robert Erskine and published by the St George's Gallery. Both were included, as nos 128–9, in the 1959 *Graven Image* exhibition at the Whitechapel Art Gallery.

Dos Santos has informed us that there are three states of the plate, all of which (most unusually) are in pure aquatint without the addition of any etched line; the edition was printed from the last of these states. Because of its size it was printed by Frank Welch on the giant press then at the premises of C.H. Welch in Shepherd's Bush (see cat. no. 200 above). The artist describes the print as containing echoes of Pompeii, as well as of the work of Morandi and de Chirico. It is one of a number of similarly mysterious images of figures, sometimes wearing bishops' mitres, presiding over the apparent debris of a long-finished banquet.

208

11 1950s Lithographs and Screenprinting

The most significant development in the practice of commercial lithography during the 1950s was the rapid spread of photo-mechanisation; this rendered the old hand-operatives redundant and destroyed the basis of the type of working relationship between artists and printers fostered by the Curwen Press before the war and so vigorously championed by Barnett Freedman (see, for example, 'Autolithography or Substitute Works of Art', *The Penrose Annual*, 1950, pp.62–3). For single-sheet prints as opposed to book illustration, there had always been certain limitations, from an artistic point of view, to collaborations of this nature. Union regulations restricted the extent of the artists' intervention and the printers stamped their own orthodoxy on the finished product according to the accepted procedures of the trade. It was these factors which prompted Peter Floud's contention in 1950 that the reproductive lithographs among the series published for mass distribution like School Prints were either indistinguishable from the autographic ones or even distinctly superior ('Some Doubts Concerning Auto-Lithography' in *Image* no. 3, pp.61–8).

The opportunities for original lithography thus became severely restricted in Britain where, as Philip James had pointed out in 1949 (see the introduction to section 8 above), there was no equivalent to the multitude of lithographic ateliers in Paris, ranging from tiny outfits like that of Jean Pons used by William Gear to the substantial house of Mourlot Frères used by Graham Sutherland and John Piper. Some artists, like Reg Butler, were sufficiently interested to construct equipment of their own, but by and large the main option available to British artists lay in art school facilities, which were frequently operated by the very technicians for whom the commercial firms no longer had a role. The most accomplished of these art school lithographic printers were the Devenish brothers, George and Ernest, at the Central School; their father had been a specialist in the same trade and they had also had the benefit of a Parisian training. When Edwin LaDell was invited from the Central to teach lithography at the Royal College of Art in the late forties, he brought with him George Devenish, to the fury of William Johnstone, Principal of the Central. LaDell transformed the teaching of lithography at the Royal College, which had hitherto been a very minor aspect of its printmaking. He invited established artists such as Ceri Richards, John Piper and William Scott to make use of the facilities, a practice which continues to this day, giving students the benefit of contact with a wide variety of practising artists. Furthermore, he initiated the publication of series of lithographs by the students, staff and visiting artists at the college, starting with the *Coronation* set of 1953, followed by *From Wapping*

to Windsor of 1957–60 and the *Shakespeare Anniversary* portfolio in 1964 (see Alistair Grant's introduction to the 150th anniversary exhibition, *Printmaking from the Royal College of Art*, at the Barbican in 1987).

Nevertheless, when Robert Erskine started the St George's Gallery in the mid-fifties, he complained that the lithographs artists produced for him were 'crooked on their paper, punched through with ugly registration slots, and seldom matching the colours of the accepted proof . . . So I looked for printers to professionalise the artists' output' ('St. George's Gallery' in *A Decade of Printmaking*, ed. Charles Spencer, London 1973, pp.20–21). Initially this took him to commercial firms like Harley Bros in Edinburgh; but then in 1957 he sought out Stanley Jones, who had gone to Paris from the Slade in 1956 at Ceri Richards's suggestion because there was no proper system for learning stone lithography in England. Jones returned early in 1958, at the prompting of Erskine and Timothy Simon of Curwen, to run a pilot scheme in St Ives while awaiting the completion of a specialist lithography studio for artists on a site adjacent to the Curwen Press.

The relationship common in France between master-printer and artist was one of gradual evolution, as the artist acquired greater knowledge of the medium and the printer came to understand the artist's imaginative requirements. In the early days of the Curwen Studio, Stanley Jones had to grapple with the idiosyncrasies of some of the artists from whom Erskine commissioned work, like Colquhoun and MacBryde who were both inexperienced and inebriated, or one like Reg Butler who was an auto-didact in the field, with no reverence for time-honoured practices. Ceri Richards was the first artist to profit from Jones's expertise and the acclaim with which his *Hammerklavier Suite* was received in 1959 helped to establish the studio's reputation. (We are indebted to Stanley Jones for his recollections of this period.)

Silkscreen printing was practised within a purely commercial context in Britain during the forties and much of the fifties, the only official instruction available consisting of courses for technicians run as part of government training schemes or taught at vocational institutions for the trade like the London Schools of Photo-Engraving and Printing. Those who were interested in screenprinting as a vehicle for creative expression had to rely almost entirely upon American manuals (e.g. Harry Shokler, *An Artist's Manual for Silk Screen Print Making*, New York 1946), with occasionally the benefit of direct assistance from American-trained artists, as was the case with Peter Lanyon and William Gear. Yet despite the American domination of the subject at the outset, by the end of the fifties a specialist studio had been established in London which seized the initiative in screenprinting for artists to such an extent that its founder, Chris Prater, was later to be credited with having 'singlehandedly moved screenprinting from a commercial medium to a fine art form' (see Pat Gilmour, *Ken Tyler: Master Printer and the American Print Renaissance*, New York 1986, p.36).

Prior to Prater's success in the early sixties, the story was largely one of isolated experimentation by a small body of curious artists, which from the mid-fifties onwards became more concerted, spurred on by the impetus given to printmaking in general by the publishing activities of Robert Erskine. One of the medium's earliest and most eloquent advocates was Francis Carr (b.1919), whose points of departure were F.W.Mackenzie's course at the School of Photo-Engraving, the texts written by American pioneers and his own interest in Japanese hair stencils, which he used to buy from a shop in Sicilian Avenue near the British Museum. Carr, who ran the screen process printing department at the London School of Printing from 1954 to 1963, published numerous articles on the subject with his wife, Dorothy (for example 'Silk Screen as a Creative Medium', *The Artist*, September and October 1952), culminating in *A Guide to Screen Process Printing*, London 1961. His activities brought him into contact with Chris Prater, whose own experience derived from an evening class at the Working Men's College run by John Vince (later to teach screenprinting at Corsham), followed by a three-month Government training course in 1951 and a succession of jobs with commercial screenprinters in London. Carr recalls that Prater and Vince proposed setting up a studio purely to reproduce artists' work, but that he himself withdrew because he had no wish to be a technician and the scheme went no further. Subsequently, in 1957, Prater did go into business on his own as a commercial screenprinter in Kentish Town, North London, under the trade name of Kelpra; it was from a base in advertising work, including posters for the Arts Council and the Institute of Contemporary Arts, that his 'original' printmaking with artists received its initial impetus.

A non-commercial attempt to provide screenprinting facilities for artists was undertaken by John Coplans (b.1920; later editor of *Art Forum* in New York) in his studio in Hampstead in the mid-fifties because 'there was nowhere for the contemporary painter to just walk in and make prints. I'd read about American screenprinting in the 30's, so I just tried it out . . .' (quoted by Dave and Reba Williams from an interview with Coplans in 1987 in 'The Later History of Screenprinting', *Print Quarterly*, vol. IV, no. 4 (December 1987), p.393). Alan Davie and William Turnbull were among those invited in 1956 to use Coplans's facilities, together with Denis Bowen (b.1921) who from 1956 to 1966 directed one of the most adventurous galleries in London committed to abstract work, the New Vision Gallery (see Margaret Garlake, *New Vision 56–66*, The Warwick Arts Trust, London 1984). At the end of the year a small display of 'British artists' screenprints' was mounted in the library of the ICA representing the work of Davie, Turnbull, Bowen and Frank Avray Wilson (b.1914), another founder member of the New Vision Gallery.

Robert Erskine included a demonstration of screenprinting by Coplans in the film *Artist's Proof*, released in 1957, and in July of that year silkscreens by Coplans (*Cinema Screen*) and Avray Wilson (*Triple Form Red*), were among the items selected for exhibition at the St George's Gallery as the best examples of recent printmaking. The Redfern Gallery adhered to the French term for stencil, 'pochoir', to refer to screenprints, which they began to specify in their colour print exhibitions from 1957 onwards, although a few examples by Lanyon and Gear had appeared earlier.

As a medium in its infancy, 'artistic' screenprinting was particularly vulnerable to any confusion between reproductive and original work, hence the definition laid down in 1940 by Carl Zigrosser, curator of the Philadelphia Museum's print collection, that a serigraph or an original silkscreen print was one 'which the artist made after his own design and for which he himself executed the component parts'. His definition became untenable by the early sixties when screenprinting captured the imagination of Eduardo Paolozzi and Richard Hamilton by virtue of its capacity to assimilate a wide variety of photographic processes. Throughout the following decade, screenprinting was to be the principal focus of the debate as to whether any medium involving photographic elements could be admitted to the accepted canon of original printmaking techniques. (For a good account of this, see Pat Gilmour, *Kelpra Studio*, Tate Gallery, 1980, pp.16–18. We should also like to thank Francis Carr and Dave and Reba Williams for placing their material on the history of screenprinting at our disposal.)

Ceri Richards

For biography and bibliography, see pp.103–4

209 Two Females, 1949

Lithograph printed in red. Signed and dated in pencil.
504 × 401 mm
Sanesi 17
1990-6-23-43

Two Females was printed in green in an edition of 25 by the Curwen Press for the Redfern Gallery, with a few proofs in red on cream paper like the impression catalogued here. Another of these proofs is inscribed on the verso 'The Lamp (Yellow and Red) 1949' (Redfern Catalogue IV, *British Prints: The Post-War Years 1945–60*, no. 85). The title *Two Females* is taken from the composition on which the lithograph is based, a painted wooden relief of 1937/8, now in the Tate Gallery, which is related to another composition of 1937, a painting entitled *The Female Contains All Qualities*.

The painting's title was taken from the line 'The female contains all qualities and tempers them' in Walt Whitman's poem 'I Sing the Body Electric', which appeared in *Leaves of Grass* published in 1855. When the Tate Gallery acquired the painting in 1966, Richards provided the following explanation of its subject:

This painting commenced by way of two themes which I was using in constructions and paintings just then, the 'Sculptor in his Studio' and the 'Artist and his Family' . . . Anyway the 'Artist and his Family' theme in the *Female contains* . . . painting gradually gave way to 'Sculptor in his Studio' and both themes developed into the painting you now have and which then (to me) didn't seem to be bound by these motives when completed – it was then I thought of finding a title by very easy but very exciting means – opening a book at random and taking whatever line my finger fell on as right and sufficient. Of course opening *Leaves of Grass* at random would be a 'safe bet' (begging WW's pardon) and my finger miraculously fell on 'The female contains . . .'. I felt it was beautifully apt . . . it affirmed the mood and meaning of the painting in a marvellous way to me (Tate Gallery Report, 1965–6, p.41).

The symbolic function of the figures juxtaposed in the two earlier compositions becomes more explicit still in the lithograph of 1949. The hieratic construction surmounting a pedestal is a witty metaphor for the idealised concept of womanhood, as contrasted with the overtly sexual hybrid kneeling on the apple to the left. This anthropomorphised vegetal form underwent a considerable change between the relief of 1937/8 and the lithograph; it

209

210

222

acquired a fluidity and energy which cannot simply be explained by the difference in medium. The source of the transformation lies in the imagery of Dylan Thomas's poem 'The force that through the green fuse drives the flower/drives my green age', which Richards began to explore in his paintings in 1943–4 and later in the three lithographs he drew to accompany the poem in *Poetry London* vol. 3 (1945). In one of these (Sanesi 4b), the essential characteristics of the subsequent figure emerged, surfacing again in the lithograph Richards printed at the Curwen Studio in 1965 using the same Dylan Thomas poem as his inspiration.

210 Costers Dancing, 1952

Lithograph printed in black. Signed and dated in reverse in the image; also signed and dated below in blue pencil and inscribed 'Artist's Proof'. 435 × 587mm

Sanesi 22

1987-3-7-3

Costers Dancing was the theme of four lithographs (Sanesi 21–4) executed by Richards in 1951–2, all printed by him at the Royal College of Art in a handful of proofs, with the exception of the first which was printed in six colours and issued in an unlimited edition by the Royal College for the Festival of Britain. The version described here is an unrecorded black and white proof for a lithograph ultimately printed by Richards in three colours, of which no more than three copies are known to have been pulled; another of the proof impressions from the artist's estate has the background printed in orange. A preparatory drawing for yet another version of *Costers Dancing*, which was never turned into a lithograph, is in the British Museum (1987-12-12-123).

Richards's lithographs for the Redfern Gallery in the late forties and early fifties were all printed professionally. At the end of the decade, in 1959, he began a long collaboration with the master-printer Stanley Jones, a former pupil of his from the Slade, at the Curwen Studio, starting with the *Hammerklavier Suite* of six lithographs. But in many respects, some of Richards's most remarkable prints were those he printed himself between 1951 and 1955, either at the Royal College or at the Slade.

Stanley Jones has provided a critical account of Richards's auto-didactic approach to lithography in the mid-fifties:

At this time he preferred to use zinc plate rather than stone. I think the time element spent in its preparation somewhat deterred him, rather than indicating a preference for the metallic surface. We watched, with a mixture of curiosity and trepidation, as each week he would bring into school freshly drawn plates to print on the offset machine. The sequence of events was fairly predictable. After several pulls had been achieved, the image would take on a distinctly blighted look as the chemistry he had employed began to deteriorate. Usually this meant two things: either he gave up the idea completely or, with varying degrees of exasperation the situation would be a signal for renewed alteration or improvisation

of his original idea through the use of etches and abrasives. The results were sometimes surprising both to him and us; the frustration was the destruction of his printing surfaces under this kind of graphic punishment (Pat Gilmour, 'Ceri Richards, his Australian Printer and Stanley Jones', *Tamarind Papers*, vol. 10, no. 1 (Spring 1987), p. 32).

The technical imperfections described by Jones were quite inimical to any proper editioning, yet the element of chance in the whole operation gave a sense of immediacy to the surface texture of the compositions which is not always to be found in the more competently printed lithographs made later.

Richards clearly profited from the example of Picasso's astonishing virtuosity with lithography, which he could have observed at first hand in the exhibition of fifty-five lithographs of 1945–7 shown in London in 1948 by the Arts Council. Nonetheless, the *Costers Dancing* of 1951–2 were the culmination of a theme which Richards had made entirely his own, progressing from the static representation of *Costers in a Pub* of 1940, his very first attempt at lithography (Sanesi 4), to these extravagant evocations of a 'cockney saturnalia' (the phrase of Mel Gooding in *Ceri Richards Graphics*, 1979).

Alan Davie

born 1920

Born in Scotland; his father was a painter and topographical etcher. He studied at the Edinburgh College of Art from 1937 until 1940, when he entered the Army. On his discharge in 1946 and marriage the following year, he earned a living for a time as a jazz musician and maker of jewellery. He became interested in primitive art after seeing an exhibition of African sculpture at the Berkeley Galleries in 1946. In 1948 he took up a travelling scholarship for a year, with which he went through France to Italy. He held his first exhibition in 1950 at Gimpel Fils, with whom he continues to exhibit, and from about 1955 achieved a high reputation for his large abstract paintings with their expressionist handling of paint and bold colour. In these he used a large range of symbols and ideographs derived from non-Western cultures. In 1956–9 he was the Gregory Fellow in Painting at the University of Leeds.

Davie's first prints, a few linocuts and the monotypes described below, were made in 1948 at the very beginning of his career. He made a few more monotypes in 1949 and 1950, but apparently returned only once to the medium: two monotypes described as *Dream of Sculpture 3* and *Mechanism for Emotion 2*, both dated 1952, were shown in an exhibition of his work at Nottingham University in 1958. In the latter half of the fifties he tried screenprinting in John Coplans's studio; then in the 1960s he also made some lithographs for the Curwen Press, and in 1965 at the Matthieu Press the *Zurich Improvisations* published by Editions Alecto, for which he was awarded the first prize in the 1966 Cracow print exhibition.

212

Bibliography

A monograph, *Alan Davie*, edited by Alan Bowness and published by Lund Humphries, London, in 1967, contains a catalogue of the paintings executed to that date with numerous reproductions. An article with a list of the 1948 monotypes has been published by Charles Booth-Clibborn of the Paragon Press, in *Print Quarterly* VI (1989), pp.318–20.

211 Portrait of an Anonymous Spirit, November 1948

Monotype. 311 × 237 mm

1989-9-30-253

This is one of the two earliest monotypes of the 1948 group, discussed more fully below.

212 Ghost Wall, December 1948

Monotype. Signed lower right. 247 × 399 mm

1989-9-30-252

A full account of these monotypes has been given by Booth-Clibborn in the article referred to above, which reproduces two examples now in the collection of the Tate Gallery, bearing the titles *Obscure Biological Function Surrounded by Nerve Impulses* and *Spirit over an Empty Landscape*. Davie arrived in Venice in June 1948, in time to see the Biennale which included recent works by Picasso, Klee and Chagall; he also visited the Guggenheim collection, where he saw the work of Jackson Pollock among others. He then moved to Florence in September to prepare for a one-man exhibition which he had been

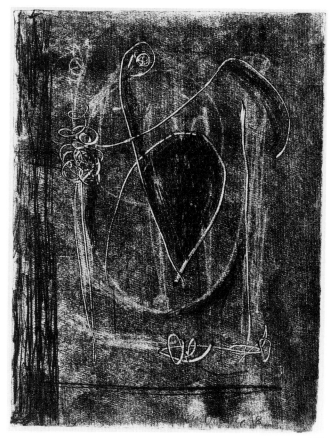

211

offered. In a letter to his father dated 18 November he wrote: 'I have perfected the technique of monotype . . . the secret is to use printer's ink on glass and to print on a fine Ingres paper (French). I am really finding something in the black and white mediums – discovered a lot of Paul Klee's tricks too.'

In another letter of 20 December he added that he had now done about a hundred monotypes. Of these only thirty-one now survive; they are listed by Booth-Clibborn. They were shown at Edinburgh College of Art, where he was then teaching, in 1949, but not seen again until 1988. The excitement Davie felt in making these prints is expressed in another letter: 'Through this wonderful medium I have discovered so much and developed so much so rapidly . . . I am amazed . . . my work is becoming something very strange.' Davie gave titles to the prints after making them, and these were written on the backing sheets on which they were mounted for the 1949 exhibition. He followed the same practice with his paintings, explaining that 'my titles are really poetic interpretations of the visual image and not meant to be taken literally' (Tate Gallery, *Illustrated Catalogue of Acquisitions 1972–4*, p.98).

Davie's continental journey in 1948–9 had a profound effect upon his work and he returned with a new interest in automatic techiques; however, he attributed this more to the influence of Klee and Arp than to the Pollocks he saw in Peggy Guggenheim's collection: 'they had a poetic feeling and a childlike magic that was closest to my own feelings' (Tate Gallery, op. cit., p.98). The abstract compositions of this period were to be approached in the same spirit as pieces of music, representing 'an attempt to get behind the calm outward appearance of things to the rush and movement, the relationship of form between atoms and universe, of cosmology' (quoted in a review of Davie's exhibition at Gimpel Fils in November 1950, in the *Scottish Field*).

William Gear

born 1915

Born into a Scottish mining family in Fife, he studied at the Edinburgh College of Art from 1932 to 1936. A travelling scholarship enabled him to spend a year on the Continent in 1937–8, during which time he studied at Léger's school in Paris. In 1940 he joined the Royal Signal Corps, and served in the Middle East, Italy and Germany; in 1946–7 he was attached to the Monuments, Fine Art and Archives section of the Control Commission for Germany. At Schloss Celle he staged several exhibitions of material which was in custody there from the Berlin Print Room and other museums, as well as showing his own work in Celle and Hamburg. His first one-man exhibition in London was held in 1948 at Gimpel Fils, where he showed regularly throughout the following decade. Gear lived in Paris from 1947 to 1950, a period which proved particularly valuable for his own development: he came into contact with many of the leading post-war generation of Parisian artists, including Atlan, Hartung and Soulages. He identified closely with the COBRA group, with whom he exhibited in Amsterdam and Copenhagen in 1949, the same year in which he shared an exhibition at the Betty Parsons Gallery in New York with Jackson Pollock. He returned to settle in England, in Buckinghamshire, in 1950; the following year the award of a £500 purchase prize to Gear for his painting *Autumn Landscape*, commissioned by the Arts Council for the Festival of Britain, provoked a public furore in the newspaper correspondence columns which continued with renewed invective when the exhibition *60 Paintings for '51* was shown at Manchester City Art Gallery. In 1954 a retrospective of his work was held at the South London Art Gallery. From 1958 to 1964 he was curator of the Towner Art Gallery in Eastbourne, where he earned the praise of the *Times* art critic, Neville Wallis, for his efforts in building up a collection of contemporary avant-garde British painting. In 1964 he was appointed Head of Fine Art at Birmingham College of Art (later Polytechnic), where he remained until his retirement in 1975.

Printmaking has always been closely allied to Gear's painting in oil and gouache. He has made a particularly inventive use of the various monotype techniques throughout his career and was one of the first artists in Britain to experiment with silkscreen techniques, producing a succession of images during the 1950s and 1960s, all of which he printed and editioned himself. His lithographs and screenprints were exhibited at the Redfern throughout the fifties.

Bibliography

A touring exhibition of paintings from 1948–68 was organised by the Arts Council of Northern Ireland in 1968. More recently there has been a spate of exhibitions, several of which have concentrated on the early work of the COBRA years: *William Gear. The Cobra Years 1948–51*, Redfern Gallery, London 1987; *William Gear: Cobrabstractions 1946–49*, Galerie 1900–2000, Marcel Fleiss, Paris 1988; *William Gear. Cobra Years*, England and Co., London 1989; *William Gear, Arbeiten aus dem Atelier 1946–86*, Karl & Faber, Munich 1988–9 (this includes twenty-nine of his prints from 1949–69); and *William Gear* at the Galerie Gabriele van Loeper, Hamburg 1989, and at the Kunsthandel Leeman, Amsterdam 1990. He was also included in *Scottish Art since 1900*, Scottish National Gallery of Modern Art, 1989. We should like to thank the artist for his assistance with these entries.

213 Untitled (Head Shape), 1948

Traced monotype in green with overdrawing in black and red
gouache. Signed and dated 'Jan. 48' in pen. 299 × 242 mm

1989-12-9-7

Gear's earliest monotype was made in 1945 when he was
stationed in Norwich, awaiting a posting to Germany.
However, the real impetus for his interest in the medium
came in 1946-7 when he befriended the German artist
Karl Otto Götz. When Gear met him in Saxony, Götz had
just been experimenting with what he described as 'Lack-
drucktechnik' (lacquer printing technique); this involved
dribbling a quick-drying varnish on to hardboard to create
a design in relief, then inking both the relief and the areas
in between and finally taking an impression by rubbing
the back of a sheet of paper placed face down on the board
(for an account of this see K. O. Götz, *Erinnerungen und
Werk*, Concept Verlag, Düsseldorf 1983, vol. 1a, pp.327-
8). Gear was able to assist Götz with basic materials and
together they experimented with a variety of monotype
techniques at Schloss Celle. The traced method for
transferring a monotype image, associated with Klee, was
already known to Götz, while Gear recalls having it
demonstrated to him by Jankel Alder in London when he
was on leave. From the late forties Gear's monotypes often
served as the basis for more elaborately worked gouache
compositions, a practice which he continues to this day.
The example catalogued here, together with the following
item, was one of several executed in Paris. It was purchased directly from the artist, in common with the other
entries bearing 1990 registration numbers.

214 Monotype, 1949

Monotype in black. Signed and dated in pencil. 166 × 242 mm

1989-9-30-254

This example shows a completely different handling of the
medium from cat. no. 213. Its gestural sweep, albeit on
a small scale, is particularly reminiscent of some of the
effects also achieved by Götz.

215 Trees, 1949

Lithograph printed in black and green. Signed and dated in
pencil. 445 × 333 mm

1990-3-3-3

On the back of this print are various notes by the artist,
which state that it was made in Paris in February 1949,
and printed at the Atelier Jean Pons. According to the
numbering on other impressions, there was an edition of
25. All Gear's early lithographs were printed at the same
workshop in Paris, even after he returned to live in England in 1950; he describes the premises of Pons as being
located in a former Resistance hideout in the basement
of a dress shop which could only be entered via a trapdoor
in the floor above. Pons executed prints for de Staël, Soula-

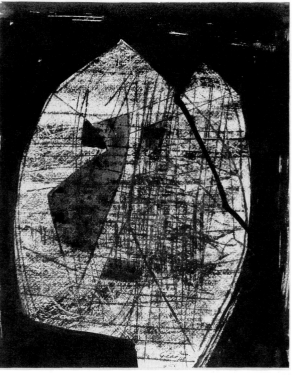

213

ges, Manessier and Stephen Gilbert, the other British
member of COBRA, among others.

Trees displays the type of armature characteristic of
Gear's work at this date, in which the colour is locked
into a trellis of pronounced black lines. During the fifties
the underlying structure in Gear's works gradually dis-
solved to permit a more dappled use of colour. A
lithograph he made at the end of the fifties was commissioned by Robert Erskine and printed by John Watson.

216 Black and Orange, 1952

Screenprint in two colours. Signed, dated and numbered 19/20
in pencil. 395 × 255 mm (maximum dimensions). On the verso
are various notes, including a statement of the title of the print.

1990-3-3-4

Gear was first introduced to screenprinting in Paris in the
late forties by an American artist, Dorr Bothwell (b.
1902), who from 1949 to 1951 tried, unsuccessfully, to
persuade the French to accept it as a serious medium for
original printmaking: 'My earliest experience of screenprints being treated as a proper medium by an artist . . .
was when I knew an American printmaker in Paris called
Dorr Bothwell, and she showed me screenprints. This
must have been in 1948 or 1949 . . . I wasn't aware of
any other artists in Europe doing screenprints.' (See Dave
and Reba Williams, 'The Later History of the Screenprint',
Print Quarterly vol. IV, no. 4 (December 1987), p.390.)

On his return to England, Gear maintained his interest
in the medium and sought further advice from Sam Wells,

214

216

215

a commercial artist who produced screenprinted material for grocery stores. *Black and Orange* and cat. no. 217, *Forms in Four Colours*, were thus printed with the artist's own equipment on the kitchen table in the farmhouse he was renting in Buckinghamshire. He had trouble obtaining the right inks and stretching the material, so he sought the advice of a local tradesman in October 1952.

217 Forms in Four Colours, 1952

Screenprint in colours. Signed, dated and numbered 23/25 in pencil. 427 × 274 mm (maximum dimensions)

1990−3−3−5
See colour illustration

The first screenprint exhibited by Gear appears to have been one included in his April 1953 exhibition at Gimpel Fils, for which no title was given. At the Redfern two items by Gear were identified as 'silk-screens' in December 1954, at 5 guineas each: nos 410 and 411, *November 5th* and *November 11th*. *Forms in Four Colours* was not exhibited at the Redfern until November 1956 (no. 454 at 8 guineas).

218

When Gear moved to Eastbourne he set up a print room at the Towner Art Gallery, where he continued to do his own screenprinting, also producing posters for the gallery's exhibitions.

218 Monoprint – Blue/Green, 1953

Monotype in colours. Signed and dated in pencil on the recto; on the verso also signed, titled and dated October 1953.
392 × 548 mm (sheet size)

1990–3–3–7

Gillian Ayres

born 1930

Born in London, she studied at Camberwell School of Art in 1946–50. She then got a job working at the AIA gallery, with Henry Mundy whom she later married. She held her first one-man exhibition in 1956, then in the following year was one of the artists included in the Redfern Gallery's exhibition *Metavisual, Tachiste, Abstract*. From 1959 to 1966 she taught part-time at Corsham; from 1966 to 1978 at St Martin's, and finally from 1978 to 1981 at Winchester, since when she has worked full-time on her painting in Wales. Throughout her mature work she has remained a consistent abstractionist, influenced by the work of the Parisian 'Tachistes' and the American Abstract Expressionists as well as by that of Roger Hilton.

In the 1950s Ayres made a few lithographs and screenprints. The latter were made with John Coplans at his studio in Hampstead.

Bibliography

The most recent survey of Ayres's work is the catalogue of an exhibition held by the Arts Council in 1983, with an introduction by Tim Hilton.

219 Green, Orange, Black and White, 1956

Lithograph printed in three colours. Signed and dated in pen.
558 × 405 mm
Collection of Ken Powell
See colour illustration

The artist has informed us that this print was made at an evening class in lithography that she attended in Hammersmith. The tutor there was Alistair Grant, who was asked to demonstrate lithographic techniques in the film *Artist's Proof*. Grant, who was also an etcher, became head of printmaking at the Royal College of Art in 1970. Among Ayres's fellow pupils on the Hammersmith course was Howard Hodgkin.

The fourth colour mentioned in the title of the print is of course the white of the paper itself. As with Ayres's other lithographs of this period, the impressions were only printed in small numbers, and sold by the artist herself without the involvement of any publisher. This particular image was exhibited at the Redfern Gallery in November 1956 – January 1957, together with another lithograph, *Orange, Black and White* (nos 401–2, at 6 and 5 guineas respectively). Two further compositions were shown at the end of 1958: *Abstract, Reds and Black* and *Tachiste, Red and Orange* (nos 843–4, at 5 and 8 guineas); in December 1959 these were joined by three more described as *Tachiste I, II* and *III* (nos 853–7, at 10 guineas each).

Reginald Butler

1913–1981

Born in Hertfordshire, he initially trained and worked as an architect throughout the 1930s. During the war, as a conscientious objector, he worked as a blacksmith. He then returned to architectural journalism, while working a couple of days a week at sculpture. His first exhibition in 1949 was followed by the award of a Gregory Fellowship to the University of Leeds in 1950–53, during which period his work matured. In 1953 he leapt to national and international fame when he won a prize for his model for the monument to 'the unknown political prisoner' (the monument itself was never built). With the prize money he bought a new house near Berkhamsted, where he remained for the rest of his life, travelling regularly to London to teach sculpture at the Slade. After 1963 he dropped out of public sight, exhibiting again only once, in New York in 1973. In these final years his work changed completely, and the bronze casts of the 1950s were replaced by large painted bronze figures of female nudes.

Butler made a few wood-engravings between 1936 and 1945, but his major group of prints was the lithographs he made between about 1951 and 1957 on a lithographic press he had constructed himself at home. These prints were scarcely ever exhibited (with the exception of cat. no. 220 below), and have remained virtually unknown despite their remarkable quality. According to his widow, Rosemary, Butler used lithography as a means of escape when he met with intractable problems in his sculpture; he would then close his studio door and cut himself off from the world. In 1962–3, and again in 1968–9, he made a few lithographs, which were too large to be printed on his own press, on zinc plates at the Curwen Press, using his own home-made transfer paper, but was

220

never satisfied with them. He was working on several more colour lithographs at the time of his death (Tate Gallery catalogue, 1983, p.79).

Bibliography

The main publication on Butler is the catalogue for a memorial exhibition held at the Tate Gallery in 1983, carefully researched and with an introduction by Richard Calvocoressi. Nothing has been published about his prints. The items catalogued here have been selected from a group of seventeen lithographs purchased from Rosemary Butler in 1985 (1985-7-13-19 to 35); we are most grateful to her for much of the information.

220 Study of a Head Looking Up, 1952

Lithograph in pink and black. 367 × 264 mm
1985-7-13-26

This print was shown in the British Pavilion at the 1954 Venice Biennale, among a group of sculptures and drawings by Butler, and is titled and dated in the catalogue. The composition is related to the heads of the three 'watchers' which were to be placed at the foot of the monument to the unknown political prisoner; intended to be at least eight feet high, they were to represent the

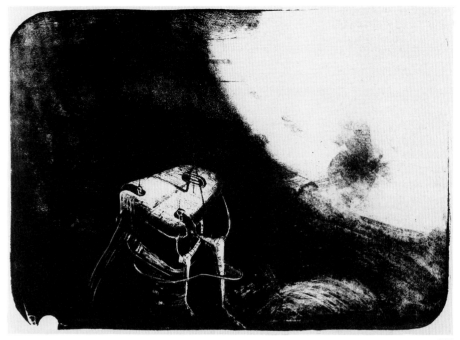

221

three women in whose minds the unknown prisoner is remembered, and were modelled as portraits of Butler's mother and his first and second wives (see Robert Borstow, 'Butler's Competition Project for a Monument to *The Unknown Political Prisoner*: Abstraction and Cold-War Politics', *Art History* XII (1989), pp.472–96). Butler made a number of small bronze studies for these heads, as well as various drawings (e.g. Tate Gallery catalogue nos 49 and 98).

Another related impression of this print in the British Museum has the composition reversed, apparently after a transfer to another stone (1985–7–13–27).

221 Composition Related to Upturned Head, 1952

Lithograph printed in dark purple. 261 × 367 mm

1985–7–13–25

This composition derives from the same type of upturned head as in the previous print. A drawing of 1951 entitled *Ophelia* (Tate Gallery catalogue no. 93) shows the head in the process of becoming a platform. In this print the transformation is complete, with a small subsidiary structure arising from the platform itself.

222 Figure in Space, 1952

Lithograph in pink, purple and black. Signed, dated and numbered 3/3 in pen. 370 × 264 mm

1985–7–13–34

This takes to an extreme of abstraction the standing female figure which Butler had used in a number of sculp-

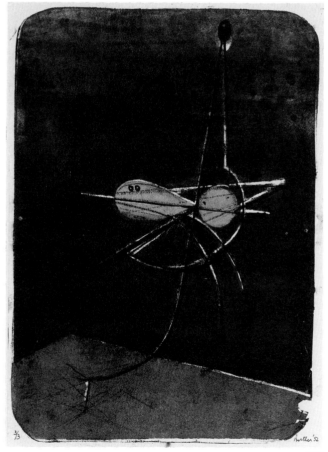

222

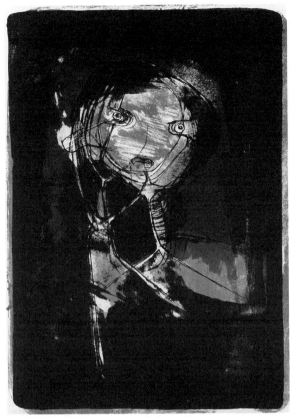

223a

tures of the late 1940s and early 1950s. A clue to the identity of the figure can be found in the small head at the top. From this extreme, Butler retreated in the following years. His sculpture became more solid, and less based on wire.

All these first three lithographs were printed from the same stone: the same chip and crack can be seen in the corner. The colours were added by overprinting again with the same stone, but this time differently inked. Many variant colours are known: the British Museum possesses another impression of this print in greys and black (1983–6–25–22).

223 Head, *c.*1953/4

Lithograph. Main stone 360 × 250 mm

(a) Printed in two shades of pink and black. Annotated 'Proof' in pencil
1985–7–13–19

(b) Printed in pink, grey, green and black
1985–7–13–21
See colour illustration

(c) Printed in pink and dark purple
1985–7–13–22

(d) Printed in buff and pink. Annotated 'Proof' in pencil
1985–7–13–24

The above impressions have been selected from a group of six variants in the British Museum's collection. The

223c

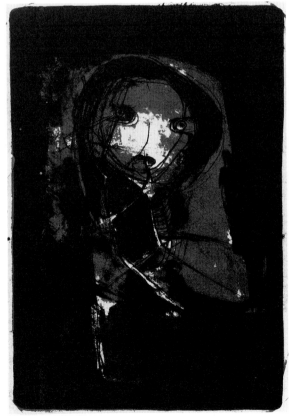

223d

224

same basic stone gave the composition of the head, but other stones allowed a remarkable range of colour variations to be tried. There was apparently no definitive state; all impressions were simply variant proofs. The date is not certain, but on stylistic grounds this subject seems to come between the other prints catalogued here.

224 Figure and Italian Newspaper, 1955

Lithograph in black and mauve. Signed, dated and numbered 3/15 in pencil. 300 × 333 mm
1985-7-13-28

The composition drawn on the stone shows a female pulling her clothes over her head. Similar types are found in Butler's drawings of the mid-1950s. Onto this stone was then transferred part of a page from an issue of the *Corriere della Sera*; this would have been done by soaking the paper with lighter fuel or a similar substance, so that the ink was loosened and susceptible to being pressed down onto the stone. The mauve was finally printed from a separate stone.

The use of transferred newsprint is a remarkable surprise, for it is often assumed that Robert Rauschenberg invented this technique in his drawings and lithographs of the early 1960s. The British Museum's collection contains two other Butler lithographs of 1955 with newsprint added in this way.

Rosemary Butler remembers being sent to buy reams of newspapers for this purpose. Butler's favoured texts were Italian, although he did not in fact know the language. The choice of page was dictated not by its content, but simply by its visual appearance. The *Corriere della Sera* was frequently employed, as its ink offset more satisfactorily than that of the other newspapers he tried.

Eduardo Paolozzi

born 1924

Born in Edinburgh; his parents were Italian immigrants who ran an ice-cream parlour. He studied at the Edinburgh College of Art and then, after a spell in the Army, at the Slade School in Oxford and London from 1944 to 1947. In 1947 he went to live in Paris for two years on the proceeds of his first one-man exhibition at the Mayor Gallery, where he met Dubuffet and Giacometti. After his return to London he taught textile design at the Central School, and later sculpture at St Martin's. In 1952 he was one of the young British sculptors shown at the Venice Biennale. In the same year, with his friends Nigel Henderson and William Turnbull, he was a founder of the Independent Group at the Institute of Contemporary Arts, which stimulated a series of radical discussions, lectures and exhibitions culminating in 1956 in the *This is Tomorrow* exhibition at the Whitechapel Art Gallery. Since 1968 he has taught in the Ceramics Department at the Royal College of Art as well as in Salzburg, Cologne and Munich, where he was appointed to the chair in sculpture at the

Akademie der Bildende Kunst in 1981; he became a full member of the Royal Academy in 1979, and was knighted at the beginning of 1989.

Paolozzi has always been primarily a sculptor, but also a prolific draughtsman and printmaker throughout much of his career. In the late 1940s and early 1950s his most characteristic works were collages, made of elements taken from American comic magazines; at the same time he compiled scrapbooks of ephemera which provided the visual material for his famous 'Bunk' lecture to the Independent Group at the ICA in 1952. The 'Krazy Kat' archive, as he later called it, is now in the care of the Victoria and Albert Museum, at Blythe Road, London W14, where it continues to grow as Paolozzi's interest in 'the iconography of the present' – in the magic or sublime of everyday life – remains a constant feature of his work. In the late 1960s he achieved international renown for the screenprints he made at Kelpra, in particular the *As Is When* series of 1965, based on material from his scrapbooks. The catalogue raisonné by Rosemary Miles (based on one compiled by Lucius Grisebach for an exhibition at the Kupferstich Kabinett in Berlin in 1975) lists 199 prints produced up to 1975. In the early seventies he branched out into etching with the *Ravel Suite*, and more recently has worked variations on some of his early images in both etching (e.g. the *Beetle Heads* of 1984) and woodcut.

Bibliography

The first monograph on Paolozzi was published by Diane Kirkpatrick in 1970; a second was published in German in 1984 by Winfried Konnertz (Dumont Verlag, Cologne). His first retrospective was held at the Tate Gallery in 1971, followed in 1975 by another retrospective in Berlin at the Nationalgalerie and the Kupferstich Kabinett and a comprehensive exhibition arranged by the Arts Council in 1976. A catalogue of the *Complete Prints of Eduardo Paolozzi: Prints, Drawings, Collages 1944–77*, by Rosemary Miles, was published by the Victoria and Albert Museum in 1977. The major themes running through Paolozzi's work in all media were analysed in an exhibition chosen by Robin Spencer for the Lenbachhaus in Munich in 1984, while his preoccupation with the human head is documented in two more recent exhibition catalogues: *Köpfe* at the Skulpturenmuseum, Marl, in 1987 and *Paolozzi Portraits* at the National Portrait Gallery, London, in 1988. Paolozzi's very particular fusion of popular culture, technology and tribal art was presented in an exhibition at the Museum of Mankind, London, in 1985, *Lost Magic Kingdoms*, a homage, in part, to the influence of the British Museum's ethnographic collections on the artist. Most recently of all, a monograph entitled *The Independent Group, Post-War Britain and the Aesthetics of Plenty*, edited by David Robbins, was published in conjunction with an exhibition that began at the ICA in 1990 and toured to four other venues in Spain and America. We wish to thank the artist for his assistance in compiling these entries.

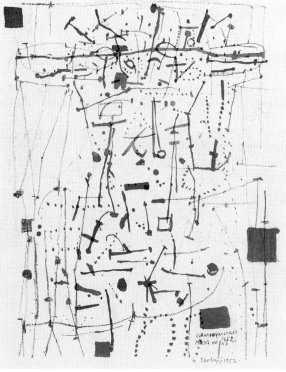

225

225 Man's Head, 1952

Lithograph in blue and green. Titled and dated both in the image and in pencil. 510 × 390 mm

1985-10-5-16

Paolozzi's first prints were two lithographs, *Marine Composition* and *Design* (or *Composition*) commissioned by Miller's and published in 1950 and 1951 respectively. This print, *Man's Head*, followed in 1952, but was published directly by the Redfern Gallery, which included it in their exhibition of English lithographs in November (no. 162). All three lithographs were done on transfer paper, which Paolozzi recalls finding rather difficult to use (in conversation with the authors, 19 February 1990). Robert MacBryde apparently acted as an intermediary between the Redfern and the artist in the case of *Man's Head* and brought the transfer paper round to Paolozzi with a view to instructing him in the technique. Paolozzi received 12 guineas for the commission and the print itself was initially advertised at 4 guineas in 1952, rising to 10 guineas by 1957 in the Redfern catalogues.

Paolozzi had produced a number of plaster heads in 1950 with 'drawn' surfaces covered in the same calligraphic elements of which the head in the lithograph is composed. The pictographic quality of the image also reflects the teaching and practice of Paul Klee, whose work exerted such a pervasive influence on the British avant-garde of all stylistic persuasions during the postwar period (a good account of this is given in David Thistlewood's essay 'The Independent Group and Art Education in Britain, 1950–1965' in the ICA Independent Group catalogue, 1990, pp.213–20). It was Klee's eclecticism which particularly appealed to Paolozzi: 'Consider for example the kind of world tapped by Paul Klee, which among other things, was the world of the ethnographic. He also drew on microbiology and memory traces, psychological matter and folk art' (Paolozzi, 'The Iconography of the Present', in the Arts Council catalogue, 1976, p.27).

Man's Head is similar in composition to the coelacanth portrayed in *Marine Composition*, 1950. The second of these early lithographs, however, *Composition* of 1951, made use of more diverse elements, incorporating rubbings on transfer paper to create a variety of different textures.

226 Head, 1953

Monotype, worked over with white gouache. Signed and dated.
520 × 435 mm
British Council (P3040)

In March 1953 the exhibition *Wonder and Horror of the Human Head* at the ICA presented the broadest possible anthology of the subject, in which the work of twentieth-century artists was juxtaposed with objects from a vast range of cultural sources: Francis Bacon, Reg Butler, F.E.McWiliam and Henry Moore were the British artists chosen for inclusion. One of the premises on which the exhibition was based was the universal inclination of mankind to discern human facial characteristics within every conceivable form, often deducing these from the most minimal information available. 'Leonardo had "seen" facial expressions in stains on walls; Max Ernst had found them in rubbings of floorboards, leaves and stones; for Tanguy, strange oneiric faces had appeared unbidden in the midst of his Surrealist images; and both Masson and Sutherland had discovered faces in their depictions of landscapes and natural forms' (David Thistlewood, op. cit., p.216). Against this background of ideas, 'the head crudely drawn, simply modelled, or assembled from collected junk, became an important motif for Hamilton, Turnbull and Paolozzi as well as for their students. It was question of perceiving the difference between creating a resemblance and a presence' (Thistlewood, ibid.).

A second exhibition of 1953 which is important for the illumination of Paolozzi's intentions was *Parallel of Art and Life*, held in September, also at the ICA: Paolozzi was one of its principal organisers. It was a largely photographic display invoking the images created by new techniques of aerial and microscopic photography, an exemplification of the morphological approach to art for which d'Arcy Thompson's widely read text *On Growth and Form* (Cambridge 1917) had provided a point of departure in the late forties. Among the many exhibits was a reproduction of an Alaskan Eskimo whalebone carving of a human head; it was chosen as the cover for the October issue of *Architec-*

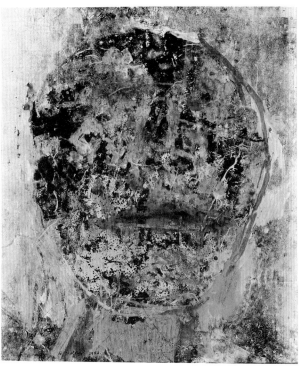

226

tural Review and was very much the type of object with which Paolozzi's monotypes of that year shared an affinity.

The *Head* monotypes of 1953 (the British Council owns one other example which was shown in the Independent Group exhibition at the ICA, no. 64) are simple offsets of an ink wash, reworked with gouache, creating a mottled, coruscated surface reminiscent of Max Ernst's frottage techniques and the brutalist imagery of Dubuffet. Paolozzi achieved similar effects with varying combinations of collage, oil, gouache and ink (see Independent Group catalogue, no. 63, and Anthony d'Offay Gallery, *Paolozzi Collages and Drawings*, 1977, no. 18). Both the collages and the monotypes had a degree of physicality conducive to the suggestion of a 'presence' which Paolozzi clearly sought to convey in these works. Another of the Independent Group, Magda Cordell (b. 1921), used a method of monotype printing in oil from a marble slab for her images of female torsos (Independent Group catalogue, p.65).

227 Automobile Head, 1954

Screenprint. Signed and dated 1954 in the design; also signed and dated 1958 in pen. 440 × 242 mm
1980–1–26–4

According to Rosemary Miles's catalogue, Paolozzi's first screenprint was made in 1951 and was titled *London Zoo Aquarium* (reproduced as fig. 111, p. 62, of W.Konnertz, op. cit.). This is his second screenprint, and is dated 1954 in the screen. The publication history of this print is, however, extremely complicated. The impression owned by the British Council (reproduced on page 108 of the Independent Group catalogue) has a pen date of 1948 added; this must be a mistake for 1958. Kirkpatrick (p.26) records impressions printed in 1954, 1957, 1958 and 1963. The British Museum example has 1958 added; and the final edition of 10 numbered impressions was printed by Kelpra and published by Paolozzi himself in 1962, according to Miles. The screen used in 1954 was employed again for the impressions printed in 1957 and 1958; however, for the proper edition of 1962 Chris Prater at Kelpra made a new screen based on the original collage.

The 'head' is photographically produced from a collage of different machine parts cut out of a motor catalogue, with a crankshaft serving as the spine and engines standing for the brain. As early as 1946 Paolozzi had begun to create composite masks and heads using a surrealist collage technique to incorporate mechanical elements culled from secondhand books he found in Oxford. *Automobile Head* was the symbol *par excellence* of the 'new brutalism' which lauded the aesthetic superiority of man-made icons of contemporary life. The subject has been

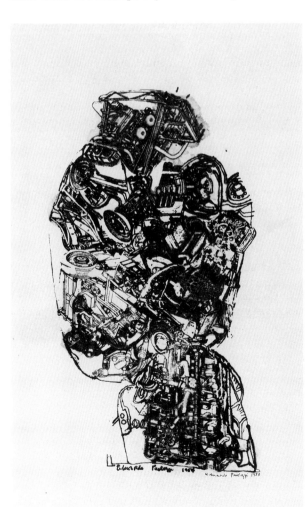

explored by Paolozzi in several different print media throughout his career: silkscreen, photogravure, etching and woodcut. Part of the importance of *Automobile Head* and the collages he produced on the same theme in 1954–8 was their role as graphic equivalents to his sculptural experiments of 1955–8 whereby he developed a technique for embedding real objects in the surface of his bronzes:

Taking random objects, he presses them into slabs of clay, forming a negative impression into which he then pours liquid wax. When the wax solidifies with all the impressions on it, he has a storehouse of designs from which he can draw at will assembling them into wax figures. These he sends off to the bronze foundry for unique castings (Peter Selz, *New Images of Man*, Museum of Modern Art, New York, 1959, p.118).

Paolozzi's introduction to screenprinting was made through the textile department at the Central School, where the technique was demonstrated to him by one of the technicians, Anton Ehrenzweig, a Viennese émigré and the author of *The Psycho-Analysis of Artistic Vision and Hearing*, London 1953. Paolozzi made a multitude of small screenprints based on collages which were then stored in scrapbooks for future use in some of his compositions. The earliest impressions of *Automobile Head* were almost certainly printed in the same way at the Central School in 1954. Those printed in 1957 and 1958 were done by the artist on his own, together with his third screenprint of 1958, a standing automobile figure based on a collage of 1956 (see Tate Gallery catalogue, 1971, fig. 20b). Paolozzi professes a particular fondness for the image, with its endearing traces of amateurism in the clogged screen, which flew in the face of the preciosity still evident at the Central School towards 'craft' skills. Screenprinting was ideally suited to Paolozzi's 'collagiste' method of working; without its development 'the realisation of Paolozzi's complex concepts would never have been possible. It was not until screenprinting that the seemingly conflicting component parts of a collage, a screen cliché and a flat coloured surface, photo and design structure, Frank Stella reproduction and banana girls could meet together on one and the same plane' (Wieland Schmied, 'Bunk, Bash, Pop', Arts Council catalogue 1976, p. 24).

227

William Turnbull

born 1922

Born in Dundee, where his father was an engineer working in the shipyards. He left school at the age of 15, and, after studying drawing in evening classes, obtained a job as a house illustrator for a magazine publisher. He enlisted in the Royal Air Force in 1941, and served in the Far East. After demobilisation, he studied fine art at the Slade School from 1946 to 1948; a fellow student and friend was Paolozzi. Turnbull then lived for two years in Paris, where he became familiar with contemporary Continental art and met Hélion, Giacometti and Brancusi. His sculpture was shown at the Venice Biennale in 1952, the same year that he joined the Independent Group at the ICA, and in 1956 he participated in the *This is Tomorrow* exhibition at the Whitechapel Art Gallery. Since 1950 he has remained based in London, teaching experimental design at the Central School from 1952 to 1961 and later sculpture at the same school from 1964 to 1972.

Turnbull is both painter and sculptor, though it was in the latter field that he first achieved a reputation in an exhibition he shared with Paolozzi at the Hanover Gallery in 1950. At this point his work consisted of compositions constructed out of sticks of uniform thickness but varying shapes. In the early 1950s he abandoned these linear constructions in favour of solid forms, especially heads or masks, of regular shapes crudely scored or marked on the surface. From 1957, when he first visited the United States, his interest turned to large standing figures of a totemic kind, latterly with two or more elements standing above each other. In the 1960s his work became progressively more abstract and indeed minimalist in nature.

Turnbull's most familiar prints are the lithographs he made in the late 1960s. In the 1950s, however, he made a remarkable body of experimental prints, starting with a group of monotypes of 1953 (twelve examples of these are in the British Museum's collection) and then the sequence of screenprints in 1956 which is described below. He has made no further prints since the first half of the 1970s, when he was working with drypoint and aquatint.

Bibliography

The main publication on Turnbull is the catalogue by Richard Morphet of a large retrospective exhibition held at the Tate Gallery in 1973. His contribution to the Independent Group is discussed in the catalogue to the 1990 ICA exhibition of that title. The sculpture of his earliest period, 1946–62, together with recent work from 1985–7 was the subject of a Waddington Galleries exhibition in 1987, with an introduction by Roger Bevan. The only catalogues specifically concerned with his prints have been those produced by the Waddington Galleries dealing with work since 1961.

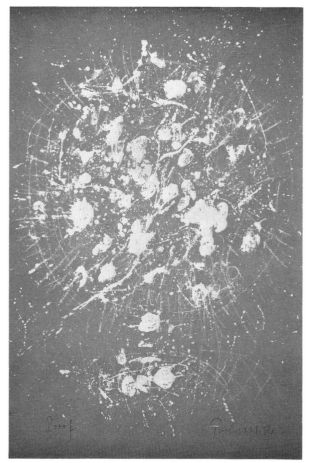

228

228 Head, 1956

Screenprint printed in white on blue paper, signed and dated in pencil and inscribed 'Proof', 777 × 521 mm (sheet size)
Collection of the artist

229 Head, 1956

Screenprint printed in red on white paper, signed and dated in pencil and inscribed 'Proof', 765 × 559 mm
Collection of the artist

230 Head, 1956

Screenprint, printed in black on white paper, signed and dated in pencil. 765 × 559 mm
Collection of the artist

In 1956, when Turnbull was living in Fellows Road, Hampstead, he recalls dropping in to play chess with John Coplans whose studio was around the corner. He was attracted to the idea of experimenting with silkscreen but disliked the heavy deposits of ink and sharply defined images produced with cut stencils which he had observed among the other artists working with Coplans at the time.

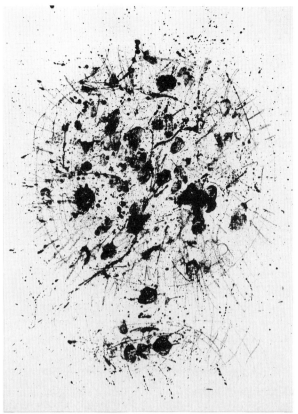

229

230

Turnbull preferred the more painterly method of drawing on silk with lithographic chalk, covering the surface with a water-soluble glue then washing it out with white spirit; this enabled him to print with relatively thin inks, the results being 'reminiscent of an haboku "flung ink" drawing', according to one commentator (Pat Gilmour, *The Mechanised Image*, Arts Council, 1978, p.92).

In the course of these experiments in 1956, Turnbull produced an extended sequence of variations on images which arose from his paintings of 1955–6 (see Morphet, op. cit., pp.32–3), whose surfaces resembled some of the photographic enlargements of living organisms shown in the *Parallel of Art and Life* exhibition of 1953, as well as the work of Dubuffet.

From about 50–56 I titled a number of paintings and sculptures 'HEAD'. The word meant for me what I imagined the word 'Landscape' had meant for some painters – a format that could carry different loadings. Almost anything could be a head – and a head almost anything – given the slightest clue to the decoding . . .
The sort of thing that interested me was –
   how little will suggest a head
   how much load will the shape take
     and still read head
   head as colony
   head as landscape
   head as a mask
   head as ideogram
   head as sign, etc. . . .
(Quoted from notes made by Turnbull in 1960 in Morphet, op. cit., p.33.)

Using up to four separate screens, he ran through over twenty trial proofs printed in monochrome, single or several colours, on a variety of shades of paper. Four slightly different images emerged, which were finally printed in editions of 25, all on plain white paper; one of these was printed only in black, the other three in combinations of colour. Proofs of two of the variant images are catalogued above; nos 228–9 share the same halo of concentric circles with dynamic lines radiating from the 'head', while the third example, in black, has a kind of penumbra instead. Yet another screen printed in black, for which the artist also has proofs, was used to create a rather different type of 'head' based on the notion of a Chinese ideogram.

Apart from the unspecified examples shown in the ICA's *Serigraph* exhibition in December 1956, one of the editioned versions was exhibited at the Redfern Gallery at the end of 1956 (no. 583, at 7 guineas) and further impressions described as 'Face' were shown in 1958 and 1959.

General Bibliography

This bibliography makes no attempt at completeness, and includes only some of the general sources that we have found helpful in compiling this catalogue. Literature about individual artists is given in the bibliographies in the main catalogue, and other more specific references will be found in the introductory text to each section of the catalogue. A convenient general bibliography on British painting and sculpture of this period appears in the catalogue of the 1987 Royal Academy exhibition *British Art in the Twentieth Century*, pp. 449–52.

Unless otherwise stated, all books were published in London.

1 Books on British printmaking published c. 1914–1960

1913 Charles Holme (ed.), *Modern Etchings, Mezzotints and Drypoints*, The Studio

1917 Malcolm C. Salaman, *The Graphic Arts of Great Britain*, The Studio

1919 Malcolm C. Salaman, *Modern Woodcuts and Lithographs by British and French Artists*, The Studio

1919 Thomas Simpson, *Modern Etchings and their Collectors*, Bodley Head (with extensive price tables)

1920 Malcolm C. Salaman (ed.), *The Charm of the Etcher's Art*, The Studio (3 parts, each with 12 facsimile plates)

1920 E. Hesketh Hubbard, *On Making and Collecting Etchings*, Print Society

1920 Joseph Pennell, *Etchers and Etching*, T. Fisher Unwin

1921 R. J. Beedham, *Wood-Engraving*, St Dominic's Press, Ditchling

1922 W. P. Robins, *Etching Craft, a Guide for Collectors and Students* (with an introduction by M. Hardie), Bookman's Journal

1922 Campbell Dodgson, *Contemporary English Woodcuts*, Duckworth (introduction with plates)

1924 Herbert Furst, *The Modern Woodcut, a Study of the Evolution of the Craft*, John Lane

1925 E. S. Lumsden, *The Art of Etching*, Seeley, Service & Co.

1926 E. Hesketh Hubbard, *How to Distinguish Prints*, Print Society

1927 Malcolm C. Salaman, *The Woodcut of Today at Home and Abroad*, The Studio

1928 D. P. Bliss, *A History of Wood-Engraving*, Dent

1929 James Laver, *A History of British and American Etching*, Ernest Benn

1929 William Gaunt, *Etchings of Today*, The Studio (introduction plus 120 plates; with directory of artists, their addresses and the galleries handling their work)

1930 Malcolm C. Salaman, *The New Woodcut*, Spring number of *The Studio*

1930 Frank L. Emanuel, *Etching and Etchings, a Guide to Technique and Print Collecting*, Pitman

1930 Muriel Clayton, *Print Collector*, Jenkins (for the amateur collector)

1931 Herbert Furst, *Original Engraving and Etching, an Appreciation*, Nelson & Jack (a general history presented as a series of plates with commentary)

1931 F. J. Harvey Darton, *Modern Book-Illustration in Great Britain and America*, Winter number of *The Studio*

1932 Clare Leighton, *Wood-Engraving and Woodcuts*, The Studio

1932 Bernard Sleigh, *Wood-Engraving since Eighteen-Ninety*, Pitman

1932 A. S. Hartrick, *Lithography as a Fine Art*, Oxford

1936 Clare Leighton, *Wood Engraving of the 1930s*, Winter number of *The Studio*

1937 Basil Gray, *The English Print*, A. & C. Black

1940 T. E. Griffits, *The Technique of Colour Printing by Lithography*, Faber

1949 S. W. Hayter, *New Ways of Gravure*, Routledge and Kegan Paul

1951 Thomas Balston, *English Wood-Engraving 1900–1950*, Art & Technics (reprinted from *Image* v, 1950)

1953 John Buckland Wright, *Etching and Engraving: Techniques and the Modern Trend*, The Studio

1958 J. R. Biggs, *Woodcuts, Wood-Engravings, Linocuts...*, Blandford Press

1960 Henry H. Trivick, *Autolithography, the Technique*, Faber

2 Some significant periodicals and part publications c. 1914–1960

The Studio (published throughout this period

1911–1942 *Print Collector's Quarterly*

1919–1939 *Print Prices Current*, with exhaustive notes on the quality and condition of the items, by F. L. Wilder and E. H. Courville

1919–1926 *The Bookman's Journal and Print Collector*

1922–1938 *Fine Prints of the Year*, an annual review of contemporary etching and engraving, edited by

M. Salaman (to 1935), then by Campbell Dodgson. Halton & Truscott Smith

1924–1931 *Artwork*, an illustrated quarterly of arts and crafts

1925–1932 *Modern Masters of Etching*, The Studio (33 parts, one per etcher, each with 12-pp. introduction by M. Salaman and 12 plates)

1927–1933 *Masters of the Colour Print*, The Studio (9 parts, each with 6 pp. of text and 8 plates)

1927–1930 *The Woodcut*, an annual, edited by Herbert Furst (4 vols)

3 Exhibitions of prints held between 1914 and 1960

An important source are the catalogues of the annual exhibitions of such organisations as the Society of Graphic Art (1921–40), the Royal Society of Painter-Etchers and Engravers (throughout the period), the Society of Printmakers (1924), the Society of Wood-Engravers (1920–39, 1949 onwards), the English Wood-Engraving Society (1925–31), and the Senefelder Club (annual exhibitions 1910–38; occasional thereafter). Also important are general exhibitions held by dealers: the most significant are those of the Redfern Gallery throughout this period, including those of the linocut artists in the early 1930s and the post-war Christmas exhibitions of colour prints.

4 Literature on British printmaking published since 1960

a. *General*

1962 S. W. Hayter, *About Prints*, Oxford University Press

1970 Pat Gilmour, *Modern Prints*, Studio Vista

1973 Charles Spencer (ed.), *A Decade of Printmaking*, Academy Editions

1978 Pat Gilmour, *The Mechanised Image, an Historical Perspective on Twentieth-Century Prints*, Arts Council

1978 Richard T. Godfrey, *Printmaking in Britain, a General History from its Beginnings to the Present Day*, Phaidon, Oxford

1985 Fitzwilliam Museum, Cambridge, *The Print in England 1790–1930, a Private Collection*

1988 Bolton Museum and Art Gallery, *The Sycamore Collection. Twentieth-Century Prints from a Private Collection*

Important information has also been published in recent years in catalogues produced by a number of dealers, notably the Redfern Gallery, Michael Parkin, Robin Garton, Gordon Cooke and William Weston. The magazine *Arts Review* has also given extensive coverage to contemporary printmaking.

b. *Intaglio*

1963 Julian Trevelyan, *Etching, Modern Methods of Intaglio Printmaking*, Studio Books

1965 John Brunsdon, *The Technique of Etching and Engraving*, Batsford

1977 Kenneth Guichard, *British Etchers 1850–1940*, Robin Garton

c. *Linocut*

1962 Michael Rothenstein, *Linocuts and Woodcuts*, Studio Books

d. *Lithography*

1961 Arts Council, *The Senefelder Group 1910–1960, an Exhibition of Lithographs*

1967 Stanley Jones, *Lithography for Artists*, Oxford University Press

1977 Pat Gilmour, *Artists at Curwen*, Tate Gallery

e. *Wood-engraving*

1962 A. C. Sewter, *Modern British Woodcuts and Wood-Engravings in the Collection of the Whitworth Art Gallery, University of Manchester*

1978 Albert Garrett, *A History of British Wood-Engraving*, Midas Books, Tunbridge Wells

1979 Francesca Calvocoressi, *Graven Images, the Art of British Wood-Engraving*, Scottish Arts Council

1979 Betty Clark *et al.*, *'Shall we Join the Ladies?': Wood-Engravings by Women Artists of the Twentieth Century*, Studio One Gallery

1983 Portsmouth City Museum, *British Wood-Engraving of the 1920s and 1930s*

1988 Patricia Jaffé, *Women Engravers*, Virago Press

f. *Screenprinting*

1961 Francis Carr, *A Guide to Screen Process Printing*, Studio Vista

1980 Pat Gilmour, *Kelpra Studio, Artists' Prints 1961–80*, Tate Gallery

1987 Reba and Dave Williams, 'The Later History of the Screenprint', *Print Quarterly* IV, pp. 379–403

Index of Artists

References are to catalogue numbers